✠ ✠ ✠

PHILOSOPHY OF ST. AUGUSTINE

✠ ✠ ✠

✛ ✛

INTRODUCTION TO THE
PHILOSOPHY OF
SAINT AUGUSTINE

AUGUSTINUS

Selected Readings and Commentaries

John A. Mourant

✛ ✛

THE PENNSYLVANIA STATE UNIVERSITY PRESS
University Park, Pennsylvania

Library of Congress Catalog Card Number: 64-15064
Copyright © 1964 by The Pennsylvania State University.
All rights reserved.
Printed in the United States of America by Kingsport Press, Inc.
Designed by Maxine Schein.

✠ ✠ ✠

ACKNOWLEDGMENTS

✠ ✠ ✠

To the Reverend Robert P. Russell, O. S. A., Chairman of the Department of Philosophy at Villanova University for reading the entire manuscript and contributing many valuable suggestions in the preparation of the textual material. Father Russell also contributed the translation of *The Ideas,* question forty-six of St. Augustine's work entitled *Eighty-three Different Questions.*

To the Reverend John H. Taylor, S. J., for his kind permission to use his translation of the material from Book 12 of St. Augustine's *The Literal Meaning of Genesis.*

To the Augustinian Fathers of Villanova University for their permission to use Father Tourscher's translation of St Augustine's *The Teacher* which we have adapted with certain revisions.

To the University of Virginia Press for their kind permission to reprint the material translated by Carrol Mason Sparrow from St. Augustine's *Freedom of the Will.*

To the Westminster Press we are grateful for their permission to use the selection from *The True Religion* which was translated by John H. S. Burleigh and appears in Volume VI of the Library of Christian Classics entitled *Augustine: Earlier Writings.*

To the Newman Press of Westminster, Maryland for their kind permission to use the material from *The Greatness of the Soul,* translated by Joseph M. Colleran, and *Against the Academics* translated by J. J. O'Meara. These works appear as volumes 9 and 12 in the Ancient Christian Writers.

We also appreciate the kindness of the Catholic University of America Press for their permission to use the material from *Letter 120* and the *Soliloquies* of St. Augustine. The former was translated by Sister Wilfred Parsons, S. N. D., and the latter by the Rev. Thomas F. Gilligan, O. S. A., M. A.

To the College of the Liberal Arts of The Pennsylvania State University we are indebted for an award of Liberal Arts

Research Scholar—an award which made possible much of the work involved in this volume.

Sermon 126 has been taken from the Oxford translation of the Library of the Fathers of the Holy Catholic Church, ed. by John Henry Parker and published in 1845.

The selections from *The Confessions* are from the translation of Edward B. Pusey in the Crowell-Collier edition.

The selections from *The Morals of the Catholic Church, The Enchiridion, The Predestination of the Saints,* have been taken from the Library of the Nicene and Anti-Nicene Fathers, edited by Philip Schaff, 1887.

The selections from *Letters 137, 143, 167, The Advantage of Believing, The Trinity,* the *City of God, Christian Doctrine, The Gift of Perseverance, The Spirit and the Letter,* and *Grace and Free Will,* are all taken from the T. and T. Clark edition of the *Works of Aurelius Augustine,* ed. by Marcus Dods, 1887.

✝ ✝ ✝

CONTENTS

✝ ✝ ✝

vii

Truth   99-10.2 (look index).

✠ ✠ ✠

PHILOSOPHY OF ST. AUGUSTINE

✠ ✠ ✠

✛ ✛ ✛

INTRODUCTION

✛ ✛ ✛

Foreword In the history of western thought few men have attained the profundity, the originality, and the intellectual stature of Augustine. He has been aptly characterized as one of the great seminal thinkers of all time. In western civilization he created a whole climate of philosophical and theological opinion which not only determined the course of western thought in its formative period but virtually affected the whole of its historical development even down to the present. In a word, Christian thinking and ways of believing have always had and always will have the impact of his genius.

The story of the life and the conversion of Augustine is well known to all who have admired his famous *Confessions*. In a limited introduction of this type it would be impossible to capture both the spirit and the content of the Augustinian experience. For this reason we have presented in our appendix a brief outline of the more significant events in the life of the great African saint. This should provide a limited but satisfactory orientation for the reader.

Our introduction will be limited to the following objectives: (1) the sources of the Augustinian philosophy, (2) the principal features of the Augustinian philosophy, (3) a brief and summary outline of the more important works of Augustine. The introduction will be supplemented by brief commentaries on each of the individual selections taken from the writings of Augustine. The ordering of the divisions of the selections has been somewhat arbitrary, for Augustine himself did not impose any strict logical order upon his writings. Consequently, there may frequently be an overlapping of material from one set of selections to another and even from one selection to another. For example, the reader should be prepared to supplement the selections on the theory of knowledge with the pertinent material for this problem which will also appear in the selections from *Freedom of the Will* on the existence of God.

3

Augustine may have known little of the Greek language. His acquaintance with the Greek philosophers was based on Latin translations and commentaries. The extent of his indebtedness to the Greek philosophers and the form that this indebtedness took is still a matter of dispute among Augustinian scholars. But certain facts in the philosophical background of Augustine seem to stand out with some certainty.

From his own testimony we know that he was first introduced to philosophy through the *Hortensius* of Cicero, a not too significant work, and one no longer extant, but a work which made a profound impression on the youthful Augustine in his nineteenth year. It marked his conversion to philosophy and gave him his first knowledge of Greek philosophical thought.

Pythagoras is mentioned with favor, particularly because of his contribution to mathematics and his account of philosophy as the life of contemplation. Augustine's interest in the science of numbers is revealed in many of his writings, e.g., *Music* VI, the *Confessions* V, X, XI, *Freedom of the Will* II, 8 (where numbers have a role in the argument for the existence of God), and *The Trinity* IV, 4 (in which numbers are given a rather extended mystical and allegorical role in the exegesis of Scripture— a kind of Christian Pythagoreanism). This influence is clearly Pythagorean, but it seems most probable that the Pythagorean element in Augustine may have been derived indirectly and largely through his reading of Nicomachus of Gerasa, a Pythagorean Platonist whose works were translated into Latin by Apuleius at the close of the first century. On the other hand, there can be no doubt of Augustine's adulation of Pythagoras, such as occurs toward the close of *Divine Providence*. This praise is later withdrawn by Augustine in the *Retractions I, 3, 3*. This rejection of Pythagoras may probably be primarily attributed to the replacement by Augustine of the ideal of Christian wisdom for the Pythagorean ideal of philosophical contemplation and even more because of his rejection of the Pythagorean doctrine of the transmigration of souls.

Socrates, of course, is commended for his concern with the moral problem, his disdain of the life of pleasure, his belief in a future life, and his recognition of the existence of one God. In all likelihood, Augustine probably learned of the Socratic philosophy from his reading of Cicero and the classical Latin literature of the time.

The extent of the influence of Plato on Augustine is de-

4

batable. It has been said that he may have read directly or in-directly portions of such dialogues as the *Meno,* the *Timaeus,* and the *Phaedo.* He certainly speaks more highly of Plato than of any other philosopher. In the *City of God* he writes of the Platonic philosophers that "none come closer to us than they do" (VIII, 5), and "They are nearer the truth than any others." (XI, 5) Much earlier, in *Against the Academics* (III, 20, 43), he declares: "I am so minded that I impatiently desire to grasp the truth not only by believing but also by understanding, and I have confidence that I shall find in the Platonic philosophers that which is not contrary to our mysteries." However, Augustine is clearly aware, as the *Retractions* reveal, that there are basic and important differences between Plato and Christianity. Thus the Platonic cosmology, the Platonic conception of the eternity of the world, the doctrine of recollection in the Platonic episte-mology, and the Platonic notion of the pre-existence of the soul are all opposed to Christian doctrine. And Augustine never com-promises his Christianity with Platonism. Grandgeorge notes that Plato was cited 52 times by Augustine. Commenting on the in-fluence of Plato in this period he states:

"The renown which Plato enjoyed was still great at the time of Augustine. It was to him above all that the pagans turned to defend their ideas or to pretend that the Christians had based their doctrines on Hellenism. It was above all to him for their part, that the Christians turned to attempt a conversion of the pagans to show that their doctrine was already contained in germ in their greatest philosophers." [1]

The influence of Aristotle on Augustine appears to have been negligible. Grandgeorge notes that Aristotle is cited three times and generally was held to be inferior to Plato, although in the *City of God* (VIII, 12) Augustine mentions him as being a man of extraordinary genius and wide reputation. Certainly at least, Aristotle was one of the first philosophers with whom Augustine was to become acquainted for he mentions him in the *Confessions* (IV, 23) and observes that he learned of the ten categories of Aristotle while he was still a youth of twenty.

The attraction of the Romans for the Stoics and Epicureans led Augustine to a knowledge of their philosophies. They are cited fairly frequently and often singled out for criticism. The Epicureans seem to come in for the more severe and satirical remarks, primarily because they represented materialistic philos-ophy with its rejection of religion and an acceptance of the life of pleasure as man's highest end. Stoic morality is criticized by

Augustine for its teaching of apathy and the doctrine of the equality of sins. More frequently, however, the doctrine of the Stoics is criticized because of its conception of God as fire and the soul as possessing a corporeal nature. Stoicism is also rejected for its contention that man's highest good is to be sought in the activity of reason rather than in God. Portalié notes that the Stoics are cited 23 times and the Epicureans 22 times.[2]

The Academics (or Academicians) exercised a brief and early influence on the development of Augustine's thought. By the Academics he understood the New Academy as exemplified by Arcesilaus (315-240 B. C.)[3] and Carneades (219-129 B. C.). Very briefly, Arcesilaus held that nothing could be known, even the proposition that one knows nothing. And since equally strong reasons could be given for supporting either side of any question, all assent should be withheld. He is said to have been the first to practise the *epoche* or suspension of judgment. Carneades attacked what he considered to be Stoic dogmatism. He denied the possibility of certainty and of any criterion of truth. He argued that neither sense nor reason can establish any criterion of truth. The extent to which Augustine at one time accepted the scepticism of the Academics is debatable. In any event it was not a position that could hold for long the restless and inquiring mind of Augustine. In all likelihood his brief acceptance of scepticism was probably the immediate result of his disavowal of Manicheism.

The influence of Neo-Platonism upon Augustine is not only indisputable but also considerably greater than that of any other philosophical school. The importance of its influence upon Augustine has occasionally led some to overestimate this influence. Alfaric[4] developed the thesis that Augustine was converted both morally and intellectually to Neo-Platonism before his conversion to Christianity. This thesis is now rejected by the majority of Augustinian scholars. It would tend to render meaningless Augustine's baptism in 387 A. D.

By the Neo-Platonic influence most writers would mean the impact of Plotinus upon Augustinian thought, although O'Meara maintains that Porphyry exerted at least an equal influence on Augustine.[5] Augustine himself refers to the *Platonici* in the *City of God (VIII,* 12) and mentions specifically Jambilichus, Porphyry, Plotinus, and Apuleius. The *Enneads* of Plotinus are highly praised by Augustine in some of his earlier dialogues and in general many of the basic metaphysical theses of Plotinus, e.g., the nature of evil, the three hypostases, the idea of beauty,

6

and the divine illumination, all had a marked effect upon the thought of Augustine. It should be observed, however, that such metaphysical theses are always modified within the context of Christian belief. In addition, Augustine opposes some aspects of the Neo-Platonic metaphysics in his own doctrines on creation, providence, the nature of the soul, and the freedom of man.

Once all the assessments of the relative influence of the various schools of Greek philosophy upon Augustine are completed, there remains one overriding consideration which cannot be overlooked. Augustine was wholly and essentially a Christian philosopher or a Christian who used philosophy to explicate his faith. Scripture and doctrine are predominant considerations for any attempt to evaluate the direction of his philosophical thought. Whether he is designated as a Platonist or Neo-Platonist, any such labelling must always have the qualification that he was a Christian Platonist or a Christian Neo-Platonist, as the case may be. For his primary concern was not the development of a philosophy *per se* but the development and the defense of a Christian way of life and a Christian doctrine.

Principal Features of the Augustinian Philosophy

Bearing in mind that Augustine was primarily a Christian philosopher, that his works always exhibit an overlapping of philosophy and theology, and that his conversion was the central fact in his career, it should be expected that his philosophy will appear at all times within a religious context. This is true whether the problem he is dealing with is one of epistemology, cosmology, metaphysics, or psychology. Even in those instances in which the philosophical writings can be extracted in good part from their theological context, the direction of the philosophy is always religiously orientated.

The specific pattern or order that the Augustinian philosophy takes depends largely upon the individual interpretation. Certainly Augustine himself gives no systematic account. If, as in Book VIII of the *City of God,* he indicates the divisions as consisting of Natural Theology, Logic, and Ethics, no attempt is made to develop systematically such a division. The ordering of the topics that follow, therefore, is more or less arbitrary, but in a philosophy that depends so much upon its Christian orientation it may be well to begin with the subject of faith and its relation to reason or understanding.

7

The basic principle which Augustine contributed to the development of medieval philosophy was that of *Fides quaerens intellectum*—faith seeking understanding. Every Augustinian of the Middle Ages bases his philosophy upon this principle and no Christian philosopher will deny it.

The significance of Augustine's conception of the relation between faith and reason lies in his insistence upon the primacy of faith over reason and the need for faith if we are to have understanding. Reason alone in its pursuit of mere philosophical truth does not yield wisdom and the highest truth. The very depth of Augustine's own religious experience convinced him that true wisdom is religious wisdom and that only through faith can man attain truth and the Truth itself. Once we possess such a faith, then truth will be made evident to us and we can order our lives accordingly.

However, it must not be forgotten that the relationship between faith and reason is a reciprocal one. Augustine does not fall into the error of those religious enthusiasts who would deny the value of reason. "God forbid that He should hate in us that faculty by which He made us superior to all other living beings." (*Letter 120*) There is no *credo quia est absurdum* for Augustine, no derogation of reason. For in the hereafter reason and the light of glory will be our only means for the knowledge of God. In such an existence faith is unnecessary and reason with the light of glory will be the sole source for the perfection of our knowledge. Furthermore, we could not believe unless we had rational souls.

But what exactly does Augustine mean by faith and what is the precise nature of its relationship with reason?[6] Few points in the Augustinian doctrine show greater complexity and more subtle ramifications. To clarify this difficult issue it is necessary to consider the meaning of faith in both its philosophical sense and its religious sense. Philosophically his notion of faith may be said to have its origins in Aristotle and in the Stoic conception of assent. Faith is an aspect of knowledge. "Our knowledge, therefore, consists of things seen and believed." (*Letter 147*) Drawing upon this distinction between seeing and believing, he observes that to believe is to assent to something upon the testimony of others. To *see* that something is true may mean either to see it intellectually as a demonstrated conclusion or to perceive it directly and as visibly present. To believe is to have a knowledge of that which is absent and which depends for what certitude

8

it has upon the witness of others. Belief on this level may be equated with opinion; to believe solely upon the testimony or witness of others constitutes a kind of faith but not in the religious sense. Faith in the religious sense is a form of religious knowledge. It is constituted by our assent to the word of God. It is much more than mere belief or opinion in any philosophical sense. For the individual is moved toward religious faith by the authority of God rather than the authority or testimony of man. "We are impelled toward knowledge by a twofold force: the force of authority and the force of reason." (*Against the Academics* III, 43) "Authority demands belief and prepares man for reason." (*The True Religion* XXIV, 45)

To accept the authority of Scripture is to accept the revealed word of God, the eternal truths that God makes known to man. Faith here has the highest possible certitude because it is based on the authority of God. To assent to such God-given truths requires something more than the mere will to believe. The will must be moved to assent by a power bestowed upon it by God himself. This is the origin of faith in the religious sense, for faith is the grace of God acting upon our wills and moving us to give assent to the truths revealed by God. In this manner faith becomes a theological virtue and a means whereby the individual attains his eternal salvation.

The relationship between faith and reason is best exemplified in Augustine's frequent commentaries upon his reading of the Septuagint text of Isaiah 7:9 "Unless you believe you shall not understand." This is expanded in *Sermon 43* into the formulae "understand that you may believe; believe that you may understand." Augustine wishes to show by such a formula, and others, that the polarity between faith and understanding is overcome in a reciprocal relationship, for man is a rational creature and the assent to faith cannot avoid an intellectual act.

His explanation of the relationship seems to be that we must have some kind of knowledge or understanding of that which is offered to our belief. No reasonable person believes blindly; he is at least aware of the possibility of the truth of that which is offered as an object of belief. Thought is present in belief, not in the sense of a demonstrative requirement but at least as involving the meaningfulness of that which is to be believed. Some understanding of Scripture and the words of faith are necessary if one is to believe.

From this analysis the meaning of the statement "to believe is to think with assent" may be clarified. To assent is first of all

9

an intellectual act; we cannot believe without some mental activity, we must have some understanding of that which is proposed to our belief. To assent is also an act of will; it involves the exercise of a freedom, the freedom to choose to believe or not to believe. And for Augustine faith in the religious sense, requires the grace of God so that such freedom may be given the power to believe, to give assent, to what formerly appeared obscure. Such grace gives certitude and establishes the true priority of faith.

Belief, in this analysis, involves the preparation of the understanding by faith. We believe because "we shall come to a great understanding of incorporeal and unchanging things." Belief anticipates knowledge; it gives a certitude to what is now held by the understanding as probable or obscure. It renders understanding itself possible by giving it an initial certitude rather than the absolute doubts of the sceptics. Finally, as Augustine would say, faith has its own eyes and sees as true what it does not yet see—hence faith directs reasoning to the true and away from the false.

Understanding, in this analysis, may mean merely a knowledge of what the words of a statement mean, or it may signify that once one has accepted on faith the truth of a statement, the understanding of it involves a further explication of its meaning, particularly in its relation to other statements. Understanding in this sense is what will later be termed theology.

In this reciprocal relationship of faith and reason the religious and moral experience of the individual must not be overlooked. Faith is not a demonstration of religious truths but their acceptance through the grace of God. Reason and faith can never be absolutely separated, for we are rational beings, we do have a knowledge of what we believe, and we give reasons for our belief. Yet in the final analysis the assent of the individual to religious truth depends upon the grace of God. We must not only believe God, but we must believe on Him. And to believe on Him enables us to believe in Him. "What then is 'to believe on Him?' By believing to love Him, by believing to esteem highly, by believing to go unto Him and to be incorporated in His members. It is faith itself then that God exacts from us: and He finds not that which He exacts, unless He has bestowed what He may find."[7]

The Existence of God

Within the Augustinian writings there is a lack of any extended or formal arguments for the existence of God. The best approximation to a formal argument is that which occurs in the *Freedom of the Will*. This is an argument based upon the existence of eternal, immutable and necessary truths present to but transcendent to the human mind. The existence of such truths then leads to the affirmation that God exists as Truth itself. Boyer observes that the formal character of the argument runs: "Ainsi le raisonnement fondamental de saint Augustin revient à ce syllogisme: S'il est quelque chose au-dessus de notre raison, Dieu existe. Or, il est quelque chose au-dessus de notre raison. Donc Dieu existe." [8]

It may be objected (cf. Aquinas) that the argument contains an unwarranted inference from the existence of truth to Truth itself as God. However, I think that the formal deficiencies of the argument were not of great concern to Augustine. For him the argument was a clear explication of what he accepted on faith. He apparently felt that the identification of truth with Truth itself as God was so self-evident that it needed no further justification or argument.

The Thomistic emphasis on arguments for God's existence from the world about us, has led some commentators, notably Boyer and Gilson, to look for such an empirical approach in the writings of Augustine. There are many statements in which it might be said that Augustine argues from creation to God as the cause of creation, but there is no explicit formulation by Augustine of any argument based upon such an approach.[9] We do not agree with Gilson that the Augustinian proof proceeds from the world to the soul and from the soul to God. Rather the Augustinian approach appears to be more directly from the soul and its knowledge to God Himself. For Augustine, we must first recognize or discover God within us—as in the eternal truths present to our mind—and then proceed to the discovery of God in nature. God must first reveal himself to me before I can recognize him in nature. To say as Augustine does that the universe proclaims the existence of God as its creator is not a formal argument but rather an explication of what has already been achieved through faith. It must not be overlooked that the *crede ut intellegas* pervaded the whole ontology and epistemology of Augustine. Hence rather than a belief in God following inferentially from the evidence of nature, the evidence of God in nature becomes apparent and a source of wonder and conviction to the individual who first possesses faith.

What is more significant and certainly true in the commentaries of Gilson on Augustine is that the quest for God as ultimate wisdom is not merely an intellectual quest but a moral quest. In such a quest the will of the individual must be purified and directed toward God. To attain God and the good life, it is not sufficient to have a knowledge of the truth or to know the moral laws. For without the grace of God, the will is powerless to obey the laws of God or to direct its love toward God. God must first love us if we are to love Him. The attainment of God is brought about by God Himself, revealing Himself to the individual, and bestowing His grace upon the individual so that His presence is known. The conversion of Augustine, the testimony of the *Confessions* best exemplifies this approach to God.

Thus the Augustinian approach to God is existential rather than dialectical. It is an approach that moved from the troubled existence and moral turbulence of Augustine to the moral demand for a God who would give meaning to his existence. As I have stated elsewhere: "The philosophical explication of the conversion of Augustine is the achievement of God as that transcendent being who makes Himself known to us by what He does to us. It can never be overlooked in any interpretation of Augustine that God exists as a moral necessity for man—that to attain God we must first become moral."[10] As Augustine put it: "it is certainly perverse and preposterous to see the truth so that you may purify your soul, which should rather be purified that you may see." [11]

God, then, is not a problem to be solved by logical argument. He is a mystery to be apprehended through faith. "He is more truly thought than expressed; and He exists more truly than He is thought." [12]

The Augustinian Psychology

The Augustinian psychology is not a psychology in any modern sense of the term. In content it is closer to what later scholastics will call rational psychology; it is highly metaphysical in its account of the structure of the soul and it is mystical in its God orientation. In method it is both analytical and introspective.

The Augustinian psychology centers around the nature of man, his origin, and his end. This conception of man is developed within the context of the Christian faith and Augustine's own personal religious and moral experience. To the religious context must be added a philosophical and theoretical explanation borrowed largely from Plato and Plotinus. Out of these divergent sources there emerges a conception of man as identified with the soul,[13] of man defined as a soul using the body, of the spiritual nature of the soul and its manner of union with the body, and

12

finally the problems of its origin and its end. As will be seen this conception of man was to have considerable significance for the Augustinian theory of knowledge.

It is important at the outset to distinguish the Platonic and the Neo-Platonic elements in the Augustinian psychology from the demands of a Christian faith. Because of the latter Augustine always stops short of a completely Platonic or Neo-Platonic conception of man. The spirituality of the soul and its distinct superiority to the body is acknowledged. The body is regarded as an instrument of the soul, but the consequent is never drawn (as it is in Platonism) that the body is somehow evil, that it has no value in itself and is something which the soul would be better rid of. Augustine's faith, his Christian anthropology so to speak, demanded that as a created being the body possesses the goodness that characterizes all created being. The body is never described as the prison house of the soul. Christian teaching would not permit any derogation of the body, for the dogma of the resurrection of the body conferred at once a dignity upon the body, glorifying it and making it a spiritualized body. Since the body will be eventually reunited with the soul it has an importance that it could never obtain in Platonism.

The Platonic teaching that the soul is just one form among many, that it enjoys an eternal existence varied by its habitation in different bodies and restricted by the constant interruptions of a cyclical existence, aroused the particular displeasure of Augustine. For Augustine the soul has no previous existence; both Platonic and Origenistic theories of such forms of previous existence for the soul are explicitly rejected in his later writings.[14] On the origin of the soul, Augustine accepted the teaching of faith that the soul of man—that in which he is the image of God—is the direct and unique creation of God. Exactly how the soul of man was created and introduced into a body gave rise to serious problems for Augustine. The selections will show that he did not arrive at any definitive solution to these problems.

On the question of the union of the soul with the body, the nature of such a union always remained essentially a mystery for Augustine. The problem of such a union arises because of the disparate nature of the two entities. Body is obviously material in nature. But that the soul is just as evidently of a spiritual nature is a matter of direct and intuitive knowledge for Augustine. Thought reveals the essence of the soul as utterly distinct from the essence of body. It is only our imagination, he contends, that leads us to conceive of the soul as a body and as extended. In

13

contrast with Aquinas—and this will become a cardinal principle of Augustinianism—Augustine insists that we have a direct knowledge of our soul. In fact, nothing except God is more self-evident to the soul than its own nature.

Although the soul is wholly spiritual and completely unlike the body, it does nevertheless exist in union with the body. In contrast with the teaching of Plato and Aristotle, Augustine held that the soul has no special locus within the body. Rather, as Plotinus taught, it exists in all parts of the body. As Augustine expressed it: "The soul, however, is present at the same time and entire, not only in the entire mass of its body, but also in each of its individual parts."[15]

Granting, then, that there is a union between the soul and the body, precisely how is such a union to be explained? Several theories based on the texts of Augustine have been suggested: (1) The Platonic view that the union between body and soul is purely accidental and based upon the conception that the body is an instrument of the soul. (2) The Aristotelian view that there is a substantial union of body and soul. (3) The doctrine of Plotinus that there is a union of two substances, body and soul. Such a union is more than a mere juxtaposition, and it excludes any notion of the mixture of the two substances. The union is a kind of hypostatic one.

Most Augustinian scholars reject outright the first two theories: the Aristotelian theory simply because there is insufficient evidence for it; the Platonic view because of its points of conflict with a Christian theology. This leaves the Neo-Platonic or Plotinian view, which, centering wholly upon the problem of the union of soul and body, seems to be the solution more clearly marked in Augustine's later writings. Such a view maintains the necessity of a union between two created substances, body and soul, and it had the further attraction for Augustine of lending itself to suggested solutions for the problem of the union of the divine nature and the human nature. As a philosophical explanation of the relationship between body and soul it still leaves much to be desired, but Augustine provides no further solution.[16]

The Problem of Knowledge

The intellectual development of the youthful Augustine was marked by his attraction to the Manichean sect. Convinced at first that they possessed the true philosophy, Augustine's final disillusionment with the Manichean pretentions to knowledge came after his interview with Faustus the Manichean leader. For Faustus offered little more than evasive answers to the more searching questions of Augustine. From the Manicheans Augustine turned to the philosophies of antiquity. For a brief time he seems to have been attracted to the scepticism of the Academics. However, his religious leanings, the needs of his moral nature, and finally his conversion made any form of scepticism intolerable. The rejection of philosophical scepticism appears most directly and explicitly in the dialogue *Against the Academics* written shortly after his conversion. In this dialogue and elsewhere [17] he developed what might be termed the Augustinian *cogito*. This was an analysis of scepticism that clearly anticipated the Cartesian method of doubt but differed from it in certain significant respects.

First, Augustine made no attempt, as did Descartes, to erect a system of philosophy upon the sole certitude of a thinking mind. Augustine's analysis and rejection of scepticism yields many certitudes.[18]

Second, with Augustine scepticism is an obstacle to knowledge and faith and not a method of arriving at truth. His real concern in his analysis of scepticism is to reject it for its folly in denying the possibility of all knowledge or in reducing knowledge to mere probabilism.

Augustine's own theory of knowledge is far from systematic and for the most part is developed within a context of religious ideas. Its principal features are an activist theory of sensation, the function of imagination and memory, the nature of learning, the celebrated theory of the divine illumination, and the distinction between science and wisdom.

Sensation. Philosophically Augustine's theory of sensation is perhaps the weakest and least defensible aspect of his theory of knowledge. Sensation is explained wholly in terms of conscious activity and to the apparent exclusion of any causal activity on the part of the body. It may be termed the "active" or "activist" theory of sensation.[19] Basically the position of Augustine is realistic, involving the physical object, the sense impression, and sensation itself as "a bodily experience of which the soul is not unaware." What hinders Augustine's analysis from becoming a fairly simple realistic explanation of sensation is his inability and unwillingness to admit that that which is inferior to the soul can act upon the soul. Hence the soul alone can produce a sensation. Sensation is neither the function of the sense organ nor the physical body but rather the result of the attention which the soul gives to the action of a physical object upon the body. "In short," Augustine says, "it seems to me the soul, when it has sensations in the body is not affected in any way by it, but it pays more attention to the passions of the body." (*Music* VI, 5, 1)

Actually, Augustine offers no positive explanation of sensation, and the theory is open to the particular difficulty that no adequate reason is given for the soul's awareness of a bodily passion, if the body cannot act upon the soul. Also the veracity of sense knowledge may be questioned, for how do we know that a sensation that the soul produces corresponds to the actual physical object? The existence of physical objects was never questioned by Augustine, but his theory certainly fails to account for our knowledge of them. The soul, then, with its activity of sensing remains excluded from the physical world. It might be suggested that the passions of the body are simply the *occasions* for the activity of the soul, but there is little evidence for any theory of *occasionalism* in Augustine. Furthermore, the inadequacy of his attempt to account for sense knowledge is reflected in his account of the relationship between body and soul. He appears to be content with what Bourke calls a kind of "unilateral interactionism" without being aware of the logical difficulty this poses. The body serves the soul as an instrument, it exists in union with the soul, it communicates with the soul and is acted upon by the soul, but in turn it cannot act upon the soul because it is of an inferior material nature.[20]

In his account of the senses, Augustine follows tradition for the most part. He notes the existence of the five senses but concentrates his attention upon the activities of sight and hearing because of the part they play in communication. Of particular interest here is his attempt to establish the objectivity of vision by an analogy with the sense of touch. Just as I may reach out and touch an external object with a stick (the stick becoming in a sense a part of me), so a visual ray emitted from the eye may be regarded as analogous to the stick, for it touches the external object and gives rise to the sensation we have of that object. Again, however, the object does not cause the sensation. The actual sensation occurs, and we repeat, only because the soul produces an image of the object. And the soul knows only the image it has created and not the external object.[21]

In addition to the five senses there is an interior sense "which presides over all of them in common." It perceives, judges, and distinguishes between the other senses. It is not identified in any way with reason, for animals also possess it. It enables the creature to seek that which is good and to avoid evil; it is a kind of "estimative" faculty.

16

Imagination and Memory. Closely related to the senses are the imagination and the memory. Imagination is the peculiar function of *Spirit.*[22] Spirit (*spiritus*) is more than a sensible faculty; it is that faculty by which the soul knows and forms images.[23] It resembles what might be termed the reproductive or creative imagination. In sensation it is that activity by which the soul immediately produces within itself an image of a sense impression.[24]

Memory is distinguished between sensible memory and intellectual memory. The function of sensible memory is to conserve the images of corporeal things. This function, too, is identified with spirit. Sensible memory is necessary for sense perception. In fact sense experience is so fleeting that it would be unknown without memory.[25]

Intellectual memory is concerned with the remembrance of the incorporeal and the intangible; with the remembrance of ideas, of numbers, of feelings (not the experience), of memory itself, and of forgetfulness.[26] Even the idea of God exists in our memory, for all men have the idea of perfect happiness and desire such happiness. The analysis of intellectual memory enables Augustine to show how God is present to man in the process of knowledge, for God is revealed as ever present to the soul. Actually God is not a being that is recalled by memory or that lives within the recollection of man. Rather the whole conception of memory is enlarged to that of a memory of the present and of the presence of God. What Augustine seems to be saying is that God is with all of his creatures, but that only man has that kind of memory which enables him to know God in this manner.[27] Observe that in this analysis intellectual memory becomes equated with consciousness in the broadest sense of that term. It may be said to include the subconscious and the unconscious. Certainly it means more than a remembrance of the past.

Learning and the Origin of Ideas. A serious difficulty in the development of Augustine's theory of knowledge is his need to provide for an explanation of the origin of our ideas. Thus far his theory rules out sense knowledge as the source of ideas as intelligible realities, but it has indicated that ideas are present to the intellectual memory. Apparently, then, ideas must come from within or possibly they may be communicated to us by others in the process of learning. On the supposition that ideas must come from within there seem to be three alternatives: (1) ideas are innate, (2) ideas are created in some manner by the soul, (3) ideas are discovered within the expanse of intellectual memory. The first alternative is rejected because it would lead to the Platonic doctrine of recollection and the implication of the pre-existence of the soul. The second alternative is rejected because the ideas possess the qualities of immutability, necessity, and eternality and thus transcend a mind that lacks these qualities. This leaves us with the third alternative.

But what of the possibility that ideas may in some sense be communicated by others. This would not solve the problem, since it would lead to an infinite regress, but it does lead Augustine to an interesting analysis of teaching and learning in his dialogue *The Teacher*. The conclusion of his analysis is that a parallel exists between the acquisition of ideas and of sensations. Both are essentially the result in one way or another of the activity of the soul. The soul through spirit creates corporeal images. The soul through memory discovers incorporeal ideas. In neither case do the images or the ideas come from without. That ideas do not come from without means that nothing can be learned—*nusquam discere*. In the relation between master and pupil, the master does not teach in the sense of transferring his knowledge to that of his pupil. Rather he is the occasion whereby the pupil acquires a knowledge of ideas that already exist within him; and since these ideas possess those qualities that transcend the nature of the mind itself, there can be but one source for them and that is God. The conclusion of the dialogue leads to the notion of God as the Interior Master who alone communicates such knowledge to us. Consequently both in memory and in learning the soul must turn to God for its illumination. The analysis of knowledge culminates in the theory of the Divine Illumination.

Divine Illumination. We shall touch upon only three aspects or problems of the theory. First, the theory establishes the dependence of man upon God for knowledge. This does not mean necessarily that the individual intellect is purely passive in its relation to deity. God is the ultimate source of all knowledge and truth but the Augustinian intellect does act by judging in the light of the eternal rules and thus participates in the divine knowledge. The basic difference between the Augustinian and Thomistic epistemology is that for Aquinas no special illumination by God is required for the attainment of knowledge. The Thomistic intellect has a degree of independence which the Augustinian does not have. The Thomistic intellect has the capacity for producing truth by itself and not merely receiving it. It can both abstract and judge; the Augustinian intellect can judge, if it is illuminated, but it cannot abstract.

Second, the theory raises the question of how the illumination takes place. The facts are that we have a knowledge of such intelligible realities as the Ideas. These are variously described as *formae, rationes, regulae,* species, archetypes, and exemplars. They subsist in God and they possess the qualities of eternality, immutability, and necessity. Since we know them, and they are neither innate nor abstracted from sense, the problem is to explain just how they are made known to us by means of a divine illumination. Several theories have been proposed but no one theory adequately accounts for all the Augustinian texts.

An explanation favored by the mystics, and accepted by Malebranche and Gioberti, is that by the divine illumination the mind sees the Ideas in God. There are texts in Augustine to support such a view, but in effect it would imply that a direct knowledge of the Ideas in the Mind of God would be equivalent to seeing God Himself and other texts of Augustine belie any such claim. Some philosophers [28] have endeavored to modify this view by distinguishing between the eternal Ideas and the essence of God, thus claiming that to have a knowledge of the Ideas does not mean that we have a similar direct knowledge of God Himself. But as Gilson well points out the Ideas of God are identical with God Himself; they are not creatures to be discerned apart from His nature.[29]

Gilson's theory is that the Ideas are the eternal rules in the mind of God and that the illumination is essentially an action of God on our mind which enables us to judge in accordance with such rules. Gilson grants that his interpretation is at best probable. However, such a view does have the merit of avoiding the tendency to relate the Ideas to concepts and the illumination to some form of abstraction by an active intellect. In addition, it emphasizes the importance and the nature of judgment on the part of the human intellect. On the other hand, it may be questioned whether such a theory actually surmounts the problem of seeing all things in God. In any event the theory does not cover all the Augustinian texts as Gilson himself admits.

Cayré offers a theory of indirect intuition or mediate vision of basic truths.[30] Such an intellectual perception or intuition of truth is made possible and sustained by God. The intuition may be limited to natural knowledge or in the case of revealed truths it would be raised to a higher level to constitute supernatural knowledge. The highest level of intuitive knowledge is that achieved by the mystics. Thus the active role of God in illumination [31] intensifies the higher we ascend in knowledge. Cayré claims that his theory has all the merits of the others and can be justified by the different texts in Augustine. However, it would seem that a more precise elaboration of intuition, both direct and indirect, is required to satisfy all the problems of the theory of the divine illumination.

A third major problem of the theory of the divine illumination is that of accounting for the nature of the illumination itself. Here most commentators are agreed that the light is not a quality of the mind. That is, it has no connaturality with the mind as does corporeal light with the body. Rather it is a created spiritual light, a proper or natural light of reason which is given to all men. On the other hand, for the illumination of the mind to revealed truths, for the acquisition of religious wisdom, a supernatural light is necessary. Such a light is uncreated and identified with the divine wisdom as Truth itself. We are in accord here with Allers who says:

"It is particularly important that one bear in mind the distinction between the created and the uncreated intelligible light. The latter is strictly supernatural. It is identified with divine wisdom and that immutable truth which 'shines like the sun into man's soul' and which, therefore, is not of the same nature as the soul. But this is not the created incorporeal light in which 'all intelligible things are relucent.' " [32]

In concluding this account of the Augustinian theory of knowledge it is important to note the distinction between knowledge and wisdom. Knowledge is the generic term and wisdom may be regarded as the highest form of knowledge. The distinction is based in part upon the distinction between the inferior reason and the superior reason. Inferior reason is that function of the mind which governs the practical life of the individual. It gives him a knowledge of the corporeal and temporal world of things. Superior reason is that function of mind which is concerned with the contemplative life. It gives the individual a knowledge of incorporeal things, of the eternal rules or ideas that exist in the mind of God.[33] Knowledge in this sense is wisdom and its ultimate end is the attainment of God and the beatific vision.

There is no derogation of the life of knowledge and practical activity by Augustine, but this form of life is always subordinated by him to the life of wisdom. The lower must be ordered to the higher, and in the moral and religious context in which he considers knowledge and wisdom the proper task of the individual becomes one of progressing through the various stages of knowledge to wisdom and to God. Wisdom is essentially religious wisdom and the final stage in the journey of the soul to God.

Such an itinerary of the soul is a favorite theme of Augustine and of medieval writers. One description of it will be found at the conclusion of the selection from *The Greatness of the Soul* in the topic on the Psychology of Augustine.

The Created Universe

Few exegetical tasks more delighted and preoccupied the genius of Augustine than the opening lines of Genesis: "In the beginning God created the heaven and the earth." The later books of the *Confessions* are an extended elaboration of the meaning of this statement, and the *City of God* supplements substantially this account. In the *Confessions* Augustine develops first a rather subtle and often original analysis of the meaning of time. It is an analysis that has attracted the attention of such contemporary philosophers as Wittgenstein and Russell. Too frequently, however, the discussion is taken out of the religious context and thus the major significance of the Augustinian treatment of time is overlooked.

The Augustinian analysis may be considered as an important supplement to the more limited Aristotelian treatment of time. For cosmological reasons, Augustine would no doubt accept the Aristotelian notion of time as a measurement of motion. But Augustine is more concerned with the problem of time in relation to the human experience rather than its relation to the physical universe. With Plotinus he would object to Aristotle's treatment as constituting the entire answer; this would be to minimize the spiritual nature of time in favor of time as an accidental attribute.

For Augustine, then, time may be said to be a relational notion, one that emphasizes time as a relation founded upon human experience and more ultimately upon man's relation to God. In a certain respect, the Augustinian analysis may be termed introspective, subjective, and psychological, provided that the limitations of such an interpretation are recognized. The Augustinian philosophy is always God-oriented rather than self-centered; consequently, the psychological treatment of time, like the physical, must always culminate in something higher. The ultimate explanation of the mystery of time is to be found only in God. The objectivity of time has its source in God and the created universe. Time is a part of creation, it is a creature, an image of eternity, and a "distension" of the soul. It is a phenomenon of our consciousness and our memory, but its true nature lies beyond us. In our opinion the puzzlement over time in Book XI of the *Confessions* is more a means to develop the spiritual and religious significance of time than to offer any theory for its explanation. The mystery of what time is in itself is never cleared up, but its larger significance is brought out in the last books of the *Confessions* and its treatment in the *City of God*.

Two problems stand out here: One is to give meaning to the truth of faith that "In the beginning God created the heaven and the earth." "Beginning" means that time itself, as a creature, had a beginning. The world is not created "in time," for this would imply that there was a time before the world began and this would raise such vexatious questions as "What did God do *before* the universe was created?" Auguatine's answer is that there is no *before* and *after* in God. Hence God does not create in time, but rather created time with the universe. Nor does he create the universe in eternity, for this would deny the truth of Scripture that the universe had a beginning.

The second problem turns upon the rejection of the cyclical conception of history. This view asserts an eternal universe in which the same events will recur again and again without end. Augustine is bitterly critical—"those who maintain this are strangely deceived, and rage in the incurable madness of impiety." The cyclical conception of history contradicts the Old Testament teaching on creation and the Messiah. Even more significantly for Augustine it contradicts the Christian teaching that the Incarnation is the central point in history. ("For once Christ died for our sins; and rising from the dead he dieth no more.") The advent of Christ with the promise of salvation and ultimate beatitude gives meaning to history, and substance to man's hopes and expectations. And time assumes a reality with the idea of the possibility of man's progress toward an achievable and ultimate goal. The persistent theme of the *City of God* is this Christian optimism and this hope for an eternal beatitude.

Turning next to the nature of creation itself, its meaning involves an explanation of the exegesis of "heaven" and "earth" in Genesis 1:1. Philosophically the basis for the explanation of creation lies in the Platonic notion of the Ideas or Forms. For Augustine, as we have seen, such Ideas have no independent existence apart from the Creator. As *Exemplars* they exist in the mind of God, and from them God created the things of this universe. "This world could not be known to us unless it existed, but it could not have existed unless it had been known to God." (*City of God* XI, 10)

Creation is *ex nihilo* and its sole motive is the will of

God for which there can be no cause. What God creates is good in so far as it has being. Creation is freely willed by God; the power to create is reserved to God alone, and intermediaries are rejected. The creative action is instantaneous and the biblical account of the six days is not taken in a strictly literal sense. In the order of creation the angelic beings are said to represent the spiritual matter denoted by "heaven," whereas "earth" denotes physical matter, which, since it exists at the greatest distance from God, is said by Augustine to be at least a "something nothing" (*aliquid nihil*). It is not the pure potency of Aristotelian prime matter but does possess some actuality. It is not subject to time, for it is so formless that it does not possess that which can be changed from one form into another and thus become subject to time. On the other hand, the angelic beings are created fully formed and preserved from change. Both types of matter transcend the order of time, their priority to their forms is ontological rather than temporal.[34]

In stating that creation is instantaneous, that all things are created simultaneously by God, it might seem that this would allow for no new creative activity by God. However, with the constant insistence of Augustine upon the providence of God and the dependence of all creation upon Him, there is no place for any *Deus ex machina* theory of the universe. The description of God's creative activity during the first "six days" might seem to imply that all creative activity by God has since ceased.[35] The original work of creation may be said to have ceased, but the divine governance of the universe continues.

To account for the continual coming into being of creatures after the creation of the six days, Augustine turns to the Stoic theory of the Seminal Reasons (*spermatakoi logikoi*). Some created beings Augustine holds were fixed in their forms from the first moment of creation, these were the angels, the souls of men, the elements, and the firmament. But others are composed of all forms of living beings, including human bodies. The species of all things are fixed with the original creation, and hence Augustine's doctrine of seminal reasons is not a theory of evolution. On the other hand, his doctrine does afford him a means of explaining the origin and development of certain classes of creatures after the creation of the six days. The seminal reasons are not seeds or cells, but rather physical powers or causes (the three words *rationes*, *causae*, and *semina* are used by Augustine to indicate such powers). Their resemblance to seeds lies only in their potentiality to become things, but they are actually active powers or secondary causes implanted in matter by God for the further development of individual living creatures. Just as the eternal reasons exemplify creation on the highest level by the direct action of God Himself, so the seminal reasons reflect a continuing creation or a second moment of creation emerging from the lowest level of creation—matter. Such a doctrine also emphasizes the twofold place that man occupies in creation. For the soul of man is created directly by God; the body indirectly, for it develops from the seminal reasons or seeds within the human species.

Evil. "What eloquence," says Augustine, "can suffice to detail the miseries of this life . . . who can enumerate all the great grievances with which human society abounds in the misery of this mortal state? Who can weigh them?" (*City of God* XIX, 4) Given a created universe and a creator who is infinitely wise and good, Augustine faces the problem of reconciling in some manner the wisdom and goodness of God with the very evident evil in the universe. Why, if God is great and good and wise, should any man or any other living creature suffer pain and sickness and death? Why should nature be ordered as it is, why not a far better world around us?

A simple solution often voiced in Augustine's time was that of the Manicheans who stated that God is responsible for all the good in the universe, but that the evil should be attributed to a supremely evil being or principle. Augustine declares, however, that "there is no being contrary to God, the Supreme Being, and Author of all beings whatsoever." God, he argues, could not share the order and the creation of the universe with another being and still be the omnipotent and omniscient creator that we know Him to be. Now, since all beings are created by God who is infinitely good, then all that such a being creates must be good. "What then," we may well ask with Augustine, "is evil, if it is not a being, nor the creation of a principle of evil?"

The answer of Augustine is that evil is a lack, a privation of being. Thus blindness is an evil; it is a privation of what we normally expect a being to possess—sight. Examples can easily be multiplied: death is an evil, lameness is an evil, cancer is an evil. In each instance some form of good or being has been taken away.

The orgin or source of evil must be the good and indirectly God who created the good. Evil cannot exist by itself because it is a privation of being and hence must exist within being. Physical evil is a deficiency or privation of physical being; moral evil is a deficiency of man's will.

Physical evil may be explained away as due to our lack of understanding of the divine purposes and the order intended by God in nature. What appears evil to us is ordained and permitted by God for the attainment of His ends. If we could see things *sub specie aeternatis* the deficiencies of being and order would all appear as good to us. Augustine cautions that we are too prone to consider all nature as merely a convenience for ourselves. "What more useful," he says, "than fire for warming, restoring, cooking, though nothing is more destructive than fire burning and consuming? The same thing, then, when applied in one way is destructive, but when applied suitably, is most beneficial." And speaking of poisons: ". . .even poisons, which are destructive when used injudiciously, become wholesome and medicinal, when used in conformity with their qualities and design . . . for no nature at all is evil, and this is a name for nothing but the want of good." (*City of God* XI, 22)

Yet why could not man have been created in a state of relative perfection, so that he would not be subject to illness and disease and death? Faith, of course, tells us that this became the fallen state of man, but now we seek a philosophical answer. As a philosopher Augustine argues that creation means coming into existence from nothing. This implies that the creature is less than the creator, for if the creature were to possess absolute perfection, it would be identical with God. Therefore, that which is created and has its source in nothingness is naturally subject to imperfection and evil. But why this particular creation and not another? Why not a different order of nature? The ultimate answer here is simply that the present order and creation of things is the will of God and that in His secret understanding all things have been ordered for the fulfillment of His purposes. This universe is not necessarily the best of all possible universes, for this would limit the freedom of God, but it is a good universe and that which best suits His purposes.

True evil, that which cannot be reconciled in any way with the goodness of God is for Augustine moral evil. The source of moral evil lies in the will of man which, like all created things, is subject to privation and hence imperfection or evil. Like other beings man is created from nothing and like them subject to corruption and evil. But unlike other beings man is free in his actions and choices; he can accept or reject the good, he can knowingly and freely choose that which is evil. All other beings less than man are determined in their actions and ordered only to that which is good, although it may seem to be evil to us.

To the objection that man would be better off if he were not free, Augustine replies that free will is a perfection in man and that God should be praised for having given man this perfection. "We must not blame God," he says, "for having given man eyes, if man often uses these to serve some base passions." Furthermore, through free will man can choose God as the highest good or he may turn to lesser goods. The ability to choose God as his end marks the higher perfection of the human will. Yet such a will is not an absolute good, for it can be used for evil purposes. Why God does not grant everyone the power to choose Him as his end is a problem in the theology of grace. Philosophy has no solution.

Finally we may observe that moral evil or sin cannot be as readily explained away as physical evil. The reason is that moral evil is basically our responsibility, the evil that we do is a part of our very being. The sense of guilt that a man may feel provides a far more intense degree of reality than any physical evil.

Moral Philosophy

In no other respect does Augustine's philosophy show itself more rooted within a Christian context than does his moral philosophy. It is difficult, if not impossible, to abstract and to understand the moral issues in his philosophy apart from his Christian faith. For Augustine's religious experience and conversion led him to effect the subordination of intellectual and moral truths to religious truths. Such an experience taught him that morally it is not enough to know what ought to be done; a man must also have the ability to do that which is prescribed by a law or an ethical principle. The Socratic ethics that knowledge leads to virtue must yield to a Christian ethics and the requirement of grace; the Law of the Old Testament must be supplemented by the salvific grace and teaching of the Christ of the New Testament. An additional and significant difference between the Greek ethics and the ethics of Augustine lies in the conception of the chief good of man. For Augustine the chief good lies not in the mere quest for truth, nor in any form of human perfection or good, but rather in the possession of God alone. As in all other aspects of his philosophy God stands at the center; nothing has value or meaning except in relation to God.

To attain God as his beatitude, to enjoy God as his highest end, it is necessary that the will of man be directed to that end. To accomplish what we ought to do or pursue is not, however, in our power alone to decide. Such an ability comes with the grace of God, a grace which does not determine the free will of man but rather frees such a will and gives it that power needed to obey the law, to accomplish the good, and attain beatitude.

This orientation of the will toward God is likened by Augustine to the principle of Greek physics that physical bodies are drawn by their own weight to their proper or natural resting places in the universe. In the *Confessions* he writes:

> The body inclines by its weight towards its own place. A weight is not necessarily an inclination toward the lowest level but to its proper place. Fire inclines upward; a stone, downward. They are moved by their own weights; they seek their proper places. . . . My weight is my love; by it I am carried wherever I am carried. By Thy Gift we are inflamed and are carried upward; we are set on fire and we go." (XIII, 9, 10)

To know God, then, and to attain Him as our end, we must first love Him. Only God can be the end of an unquiet will. "Our hearts are not at rest until they find rest in Thee, O God."

But to love God He must first love us. The love that unites us to God is not a natural love that draws us toward God like a natural weight draws a body to its place. Rather the love of God is a supernatural gift that God bestows upon us. Love, or charity, thus becomes the cardinal principle of the Augustinian ethics. Such a principle consists simply in loving that which we ought to love and in the correct order of love.

> . . . every man is to be loved as a man for God's sake; but God is to be loved for His own sake. And if God is to be loved more than any man, each man ought to love God more than himself. Likewise we ought to love another man better than our own body, because all things are to be loved in reference to God, and another man can have fellowship with us in the enjoyment of God; whereas our body cannot; for the body only lives through the soul, and it is by the soul that we enjoy God. . . . (*Christian Doctrine,* chapter 27)

Furthermore, charity transcends justice in the social order and it culminates in the injunction "love God and do what thou wilt." For if we truly love God than our wills will always be in conformity with His, and evil will be impossible for us. In this way the principle of charity or love lies at the very center of the moral life.

27

The religious aspects of the Augustinian ethics become even more prominent in those difficult disputations centering around the issues of man's free will, God's grace, salvation, and predestination. In all these disputes, which occupied so much of the saint's time and writings, he maintained unswervingly his basic convictions of the freedom of man and the necessity of grace, even though it may occasionally appear in his zealous defense of Christian doctrine against the Pelagians that he leaves too little to man and too much to God. Despite the difficulties dependent upon the interpretation of the Augustinian texts, it is necessary to keep in mind these fundamental convictions of Augustine, both of which he regarded as true, paradoxical though this may seem. In any event these convictions presented no contradiction to Augustine. A similar problem arises with respect to God's love for man and the predestination of man. For Augustine it was evident that not all men are chosen for salvation. But why some are chosen or elected for salvation and others not lies in the secret judgments of God. Predestination remains a great mystery, but in the face of this mystery Augustine never denied the love of God for man. The overwhelming manifestation of God's love for man in the Incarnation far overshadows the perplexity occasioned by any attempt to explain why God elects some men for salvation and not others. God could have chosen all for salvation; why He permits some to sin and reject His grace remains a profound mystery. Yet God wills that all men be saved and grants sufficient grace to all to achieve such an end. The rejection or acceptance of such grace is the responsibility of man and the act of his free will.

Charity or love is not only the center of the moral life of the individual; it is also the center and moving principle of the social order. Such an order is defined by Augustine as "an association of rational beings united by a unanimous agreement upon the things they love." Hence, if the predominant love of a people is for wealth, then their political constitution will be reflected by such a love. Basically, Augustine will say, there are two loves: one is directed to God and spiritual things, the other to the world and material things. Consequently there will be two cities:

Two cities have been formed by two loves: the earthly city by the love of self, even to the contempt of God; the heavenly by the love of God, even to the contempt of self. The former glories in itself, the latter in the Lord. . . .

The one city consist of those who wish to live after the flesh, the other of those who wish to live after the spirit. The citizens of the city of God live according to the spirit, i.e. God; the others live according to the flesh, i.e. according to man. (*City of God* XIV, 28)

The characteristics of the heavenly city are self-sacrifice, humility, and truth. The earthly is characterized by expediency, pride, ambition, and vanity. "The one," he says, "lives by natural generation, the other by supernatural regeneration, the one is temporal and mortal, the other eternal and immortal, the one determined by love of self, the other by love of God."

It is tempting to look for identifying examples of each of the two cities, and frequently some have interpreted Augustine to mean that the earthly city is Rome and the heavenly city the Church. However, the texts will not yield any such precise interpretation. The most that can be said is that Rome may be symbolical of the earthly city and that faith and the Church may be symbolical of the heavenly city. Actually the Church is an earthly institution, for it appears in history and contains not only the elect but also the reprobate.

Hence it is an error to think that Augustine is concerned with the solution of the problems of the Church and the State and their relationship. His true concern is with the two kinds of love that men have and the societies that are the products of such loves. This means that the two cities, the earthly and the heavenly, cannot in this temporal life be absolutely separated. For the elect, those who love God above all else, live in the earthly city with others. But they do not regard the earthly city and the happiness it can bring as their highest end; rather they look upon the earthly city as a means to the achievement of the heavenly city. Their place upon earth is likened to that of pilgrims who are progressing toward their fatherland. As long as they abide in the earthly city, they will accept its laws and its justice, they will "render unto Caesar the things that are Caesar's," but always with the prospect before them of the heavenly city in which their true beatitude lies. Through their faith they can be considered as members of the heavenly city. On the other hand, those of the earthly city who live without such a faith, treat the earthly city and the happiness it affords as an end rather than as a means. Loving the world and the self rather than God, their ultimate end is one of eternal punishment. Loving God and the heavenly city, the ultimate end of the elect is an eternal happiness with God.

The separation of the two cities and the final consummation of history will come on the Day of Judgment. Then Christ will judge the living and the dead, and the two cities of the elect and the reprobate will be constituted in an eternal existence. Thus all history is but a preparation for eternity, the earthly city but a step in the progress and pilgrimage of man toward the heavenly city.

Such is Augustine's theology of history. Augustine did not envision history as a series of recurring cycles, but as a development of God's purpose in creation. What knowledge we have of God's purpose and the ultimate end for mankind, must come from revelation rather than philosophy. Instead of a secular philosophy of history based upon the speculations of a Marx or a Hegel, we have a religious interpretation of history based upon the word of God. Hence God's purposes in history can be seen in the account of creation, in the history of the Jewish peoples, and in the Incarnation and the promise of salvation for man. Beyond that we cannot go.

NOTES (Introduction)

[1] L. Grandgeorge, *Saint Augustin et le Néo-Platonisme*, Paris: Ernest Leroux, 1896, p. 32.

[2] E. Portalié, *A Guide to the Thought of Saint Augustine*, translated by Ralph J. Bastian, S. J., Chicago: Henry Regnery, 1960, p. 95.

[3] According to a tradition cited by Cicero (*Acad.*, I, 12, 45–46, Arcesilaus was a member of the New Academy rather than the Middle Academy.

[4] P. Alfaric, *L'Evolution intellectuelle de saint Augustin*, Paris: 1918.

[5] John Joseph O'Meara, *The Young Augustine*, New York: Longmans, 1954.

[6] Reason (*ratio*) and understanding (*intellectus*) are both faculties of the mind (*mens*). Reason is a mental operation which we may use for a knowledge or understanding of higher things. Understanding is the higher of the two faculties. It is that insight by which we perceive the truths revealed in the divine illumination.

[7] *Tractates on the Gospel According to St. John, Works of Aurelius Augustine*, ed. by Marcus Dods, Vol. X., p. 406.

[8] Boyer, C. *L'idée de vérité dans la philosophie de Saint Augustin*, Beauchesne, Paris, 1940, p. 65.

[9] Cf. *Confessions* VII, 10, 16; *Eighty-three Different Questions*, 54; *City of God* XI, 4.

[10] "The Augustinian Argument for the Existence of God," *Philosophical Studies,* Maynooth, Ireland, 1963, Vol. XII, p. 106.

[11] *The Advantage of Believing* XVI, 34.

[12] *The Trinity* VII, 4, 7.

[13] In his later works Augustine stresses the dual nature of man.

[14] This explains why Augustine rejected any theory of innate ideas, for such a theory might too readily imply a Platonic doctrine of the recollection of ideas and a previous existence for the soul.

[15] *The Immortality of the Soul* 16, 25.

[16] For a more exhaustive discussion of this difficult problem, see especially E. Gilson, *The Christian Philosophy of St. Augustine,* New York, 1960, and the articles by Charles Couturier, S. J., and E. Fortin in *Augustinus Magister,* Vol. III, Paris, 1954.

[17] See the first two selections under this topic and also the selections from *The True Religion* (xxxix, 73) and *Freedom of the Will* (III, 7) from the topic The Existence of God.

[18] Note the following statement: ". . . who would doubt that he lives, remembers, understands, wills, thinks, knows, and judges? For even if he doubts, he lives; if he doubts, he remembers why he doubts; if he doubts, he understands that he doubts; if he doubts, he wishes to be certain; if he doubts, he thinks; if he doubts, he knows that he does not know; if he doubts, he judges that he ought not to consent rashly." (*The Trinity* X, 19, 14)

[19] For an excellent and detailed analysis of this theory see the article "The Active Theory of Sensation in St. Augustine," by Sister Mary Ann Ida, in *The New Scholasticism,* April, 1956.

[20] Vernon J. Bourke, *Augustine's Quest for Wisdom,* Milwaukee: Bruce Publishing Co., 1945, pp. 111-112.

[21] With respect to the sensation of hearing, the analysis is somewhat the same except that sound is transmitted to the ear instead of being projected like the ray of light from the eye or a stick wielded by the body. Cf. *Music* VI, 5, 11.

[22] In the selection from *The Literal Meaning of Genesis,* observe that the functions of the soul are divided into *Sensus, Spiritus,* and *Mens. Sensus* (sense, sensation) has already been described. *Mens* (mind) is the highest part of the rational soul and includes reason (inferior and superior), intellectual memory, and understanding.

[23] Images are of two kinds: (1) *phantasma* or arbitrary images and (2) *phantasia,* images reproduced and retained in memory.

[24] Spirit is also used by Augustine in the Scriptural sense and identified with mind (Cf. *The Literal Meaning of Genesis* XII, 24).

[25] This is exemplified in the following statement from *Music:* "And so, even in hearing the shortest syllable, unless memory help us have in the soul that

motion made when the beginning sounded, at the very moment when no longer the beginning but the end of the syllable is sounding, then we cannot say we have heard anything. . . ." (VI, 8, 21)

[26] Cf. *Confessions* X, 9-16.

[27] Cf. *Confessions* X, 17 ff. For the function of memory in the image of the Trinity in the mind see the last of the selections in this section from *The Trinity*.

[28] Johannes Hessen, *Augustins Metaphysik Der Erkenntnis*, Leiden: E. J. Brill, 1960, p. 216

[29] Gilson, *The Christian Philosophy* . . ., p. 95.

[30] F. Cayré, *Initiation à la Philosophie de Saint Augustin*, Paris: Desclée de Brouwer, 1947, pp. 234 ff.

[31] "illumination" is identified with "intuition."

[32] Rudolph Allers, "St. Augustine's Doctrine on Illumination," *Franciscan Studies*, March, 1952, p. 36

[33] This distinction does not mean that inferior reason and superior reason are separate and distinctive *faculties* of the mind. The mind for Augustine is one, but it may be directed outwardly as with inferior reason or inwardly toward God as in superior reason.

[34] For a brief account of the Plotinian element in Augustine's account of creation, see Hilary Armstrong's article in *Augustinus Magister*, "Etudes Augustiniennes," Paris: 1954, pp. 278-83

[35] Note that the work of creation takes place during the six days, but that the creation of heaven and earth, the spiritual and physical matter, takes place "before" the six days. The priority is causal.

✠ ✠ ✠

A PRAYER OF ST. AUGUSTINE

✠ ✠ ✠

The following selection is taken from Book I., chapter 1 of the *Soliloquies*. It is a prayer of some length, moving and deep in its sincerity and scope, and one of the finest of the many prayers that appear so frequently in the writings of the saint.

Soliloquies ✠ BOOK I ✠ CHAPTER 1

(2) O God, the Founder of the Universe, grant me first of all that I may fittingly supplicate Thee; next, that I may so act that I may be worthy of a hearing from Thee; finally, I beg Thee to set me free.

O God, through whom all those things, which of themselves would not exist, strive to be.

O God, who dost not permit to perish even that which is self-destructive.

O God, who from nothing hast created this world which every eye sees to be most beautiful.

O God, who dost not cause evil, and who dost cause that it become not most evil.

O God, who, to those few who have their refuge in that which truly is, dost show that evil is nothing.

O God, through whom the universe, even with its sinister side, is perfect.

O God, by whose ordinance the uttermost discord is as naught, since the less perfect things are in harmony with the more perfect.

O God, whom everything loves which is capable of loving whether knowingly or unknowingly.

33

O God, in whom are all things—and yet the shamefulness of every creature does not shame Thee, their wickedness does not harm Thee, nor does their error deceive Thee.

O God, who hast not willed that any save the pure should know the True.

O God, the Father of Truth, the Father of Wisdom, Father of True and Supreme Life, Father of Happiness, Father of the Good and the Beautiful, Father of Intelligible Light, Father of our watching and our enlightenment, Father of the covenant by which we are admonished to return to Thee.

(3) I call upon Thee, O God the Truth, in whom and by whom and through whom all those things are true which are true.

O God, Wisdom, in whom and by whom and through whom all those are wise who are wise.

O God, True and Supreme Life, in whom and by whom and through whom all those things live which truly and perfectly live.

O God, Happiness, in whom and by whom and through whom all those things are happy which are happy.

O God, the Good and the Beautiful, in whom and by whom and through whom all those things are good and beautiful which are good and beautiful.

O God, Intelligible Light, in whom and by whom and through whom all those things which have intelligible light have their intelligible light.

O God, whose domain is the whole world unknown to sense.

O God, from whose realm law is promulgated even in these regions.

O God, from whom to turn away is to fall, to whom to turn is to rise again, in whom to abide is to stand firm.

O God, from whom to depart is to die, to whom to return is to be revived, in whom to dwell is to live.

O God, whom no one loses unless deceived, whom no one seeks unless admonished, whom no one finds unless he is purified.

O God, whom to abandon is to perish, whom to heed is to love, whom to see is to possess.

O God, to whom Faith moves us, Hope raises us, Charity unites us.

O God, through whom we overcome the enemy, Thee do I pray.

O God, through whom we obtain that we do not altogether perish.

O God, by whom we are admonished to be ever watchful.

O God, through whom we discern the good from the evil.

O God, through whom we flee evil and follow after good.

O God, through whom we are not overcome by afflictions.

O God, through whom we fittingly serve and fittingly rule.

O God, through whom we learn that that is alien to us which once we thought was meet for us, and that is meet which we used to think was alien.

O God, through whom we cling not to the charms and lures of evil.

O God, through whom deprivations do not abase us.

O God, through whom what is better in us is not under the dominion of our lower self.

O God, through whom death is swallowed up in victory.

O God, who dost convert us, stripping us of that which is not and clothing us with that which is.

O God, who makest us worthy to be heard.

O God, who strengthenest us; who leadest us into all truth.

O God, who speakest to us of all good things; who dost not drive us out of our mind, nor permittest that anyone else do so.

O God, who callest us back to the way; who leadest us to the gate; who grantest that it is opened to those who knock.

O God, who givest us the bread of life.

O God, through whom we thirst for the cup, which when it is drunk we shall thirst no more.

O God, who dost convince the world of sin, of justice, and of judgment.

O God, through whom we are not shaken by those who have no faith.

O God, through whom we denounce the error of those who think that the merits of souls are naught before Thee.

O God, through whom we do not serve weak and beggarly elements.

O God, who dost cleanse us, who dost make us ready for divine rewards, graciously come to me.

(4) Whatever I have said, come to my aid, Thou, the one God, the one, eternal, true substance in whom there is no strife, no disorder, no change, no need, no death; where there is supreme harmony, supreme clarity, supreme permanence, supreme fullness, supreme life; where there is no deficiency and no excess; where the One begetting and the One begotten is One.

O God, who art served by all things which serve, who art obeyed by every good soul.

O God, by whose laws the poles revolve, the stars follow their courses, the sun rules the day, and the moon presides over the night; and all the world maintains, as far as this world of sense allows, the wondrous stability of things by means of the orders and recurrences of seasons: through the days by the changing of light and darkness, through the months by the moon's progressions and declines, through the years by the successions of spring, summer, autumn, and winter, through the cycles by the completion of the sun's course, through the great eras of time by the return of the stars to their starting points.

O God, by whose ever-enduring laws the varying movement of movable things is not suffered to be disturbed, and is always restored to a relative stability by the controls of the encompassing ages.

O God, by whose laws the choice of the soul is free, and rewards to the good and chastisements to the wicked are meted out in accord with inexorable and universal destiny.

O God, from whom all good things flow even unto us, and by whom all evil things are kept away from us.

O God, above whom, beyond whom, and without whom nothing exists.

O God, under whom everything is, in whom everything is, with whom everything is.

O God, who hast made man to Thine image and likeness, a fact which he acknowledges who knows himself.

Hear, hear, O hear me, my God, my Lord, my King, my Father, my Cause, my Hope, my Wealth, my Honor, my Home, my Native Land, my Salvation, my Light, my Life.

Hear, hear, O hear me, in that way of Thine well known to a select few.

(5) Thee alone do I love; Thee alone do I follow; Thee alone do I seek; Thee alone am I ready to serve, for Thou alone hast just dominion; under Thy sway do I long to be.

Order, I beg Thee, and command what Thou wilt, but heal and open my ears, so that with them I may hear Thy words.

Heal and open my eyes so that with them I may perceive Thy wishes.

Banish from me my senselessness, so that I may know Thee.

Tell me where I should turn that I may behold Thee; and I hope I shall do all Thou hast commanded me.

Look, I beseech Thee, upon Thy prodigal, O Lord, kindest Father; already have I been punished enough; long enough have I served Thine enemies whom Thou hast beneath Thy feet; long enough have I been the playthings of deceits. Receive me Thy

36

servant as I flee from them, for they took me in a stranger when I was fleeing from Thee.

I realize I must return to Thee. Let Thy door be open to my knocking. Teach me how to come to Thee. Nothing else do I have but willingness. Naught else do I know save that fleeting and perishable things are to be spurned, certain and eternal things to be sought after. This I do, O Father, because this is all I know, but how I am to reach Thee I know not. Do Thou inspire me, show me, give me what I need for my journey.

If it is by faith that they find Thee who have recourse to Thee, give me faith; if it is through virtue, give me virtue; if it is by knowledge, give knowledge to me. Grant me increase of faith, of hope, and of charity.

O how marvelous and extraordinary is Thy goodness.

(6) To Thee do I appeal, and once more I beg of Thee the very means by which appeal is made to Thee. For, if Thou shouldst abandon us, we are lost; but Thou dost not abandon us, because Thou art the Supreme Good whom no one ever rightly sought and entirely failed to find. And, indeed, every one hast rightly sought Thee whom Thou hast enabled to seek Thee aright. Grant that I may seek Thee, my Father; save me from error. When I seek Thee, let me not find aught else but Thee, I beseech Thee, Father. But, if there is in me any vain desire, do Thou Thyself cleanse me and make me fit to look upon Thee.

With regard to the death of this my mortal body, so long as I am ignorant of its usefulness to me or to those whom I love, I entrust it to Thee, O wisest and best of Fathers, and I shall pray for it as Thou shalt in good time advise me. This only I shall ask of Thine extreme kindness, that Thou convertest me wholly to Thee, and that Thou allowest nothing to prevent me when I wend my way to Thee. I beg Thee to command, while I move and bear this my body, that I may be pure generous, just, and prudent; that I may be a perfect lover and knower of Thy Wisdom; that I may be worthy of Thy dwelling place, and that I may in fact dwell in Thy most blessed kingdom. Amen. Amen.

✠ ✠ ✠

FAITH AND UNDERSTANDING

✠ ✠ ✠

The following selections represent some of the more significant aspects of the Augustinian analysis of the meaning of faith, its relation with the understanding, its priority over reason and its justification by reason, and its origin as a gift or grace from God.

Sermon 43 is one of Augustine's many sermons dealing with the exegesis of Scripture. This particular sermon is a commentary on the second epistle of St. Peter, chapter 1, v. 17-19. Portalié refers to it as "a remarkable résumé" of the thesis "Unless you believe you shall not understand." [1]

The Predestination of the Saints was written in 428 and directed against the Semipelagians. The selection emphasizes that faith is from God, that faith is not a blind assent of reason, but that rather "to believe is to think with assent."

Sermon 126 is another of close to four hundred sermons that Augustine delivered on a variety of topics, ranging from the interpretation of Scripture to the analysis of moral and dogmatic issues. The present sermon offers a brief definition of faith, emphasizes the importance of reason in the understanding of faith, and expounds the meaning of the words of the prophet: "Unless you believe, you shall not understand." (Isa. 7:9)

Letter 120 was written in 410 to Consentius, a monk residing off the south coast of France in a monastery at Lerins or St. Victor. This letter develops in more analytical detail the relationship between faith and reason. It stresses the primacy of faith, the value of reason, and the distinction between seeing and believing.

The Spirit and the Letter was written in 412 and is one of a number of treatises concerned with the problem of grace and freedom and directed against the Pelagians. This particular excerpt endeavors to show that <u>faith</u> is not something within our power, but that it is a form of grace given to the individual by God. The will to believe, Augustine insists, is a power given to us by God. The notion of faith is being used here almost exclusively in the religious sense.

The Advantage of Believing was written shortly after Augustine's ordination to the priesthood in 391. It is addressed to Honoratius, a friend who, like Augustine, had been deceived by the Manicheans. The first part of the work is principally a refutation of the Manichean attacks upon the Old Testament. The second part of the work is devoted to a defense of faith and the advantages of faith, the authority of the Church, and the justification of the priority of faith over reason. The selected excerpts are taken from the second part. Of the several topics discussed, Augustine justifies religious belief by noting its many advantages. His account of the different classes of persons who are to be praised or disapproved or detested for their attitude toward religious belief anticipates a similar analysis by Pascal. In the concluding pages he observes that just as a fool cannot follow the way of the wise man unless he first possesses knowledge enough to know a wise man, so man needs the grace of God to attain wisdom and religious truth.

S ERMON 43 [2] ✠ *On the words of the blessed apostle Peter: We heard a voice coming down from heaven: this is my beloved son; and in the message of the prophets we have something still more certain.* 1. The beginning of the good life, a life which merits even eternal life, is true faith. Faith, moreover, is to believe that which you do not yet see, the reward of that faith is to see that which you believe. In the time of faith, therefore, as in the time of sowing, let us not weaken, and let us not weaken until the very end, but persevere until we reap that which we have sown. When the human race had turned away from God and was prostrate in its sins, just as we needed a creator to be brought into being, so we needed a savior in order to revive. A just God condemned man, a merciful God liberated him. *The God of Israel is he who will give power and strength to his people. Blessed be God.* (Ps. 67:36) But this only the believers receive, not the scornful.

2. However, we are not to glory in the faith as in something of our own achievement. Faith is no trifle, but something great; which, if you have it, is certainly because you have received it. *What have you that you have not received?* (I Cor. 4:7) See, beloved, why you ought to render thanks to the Lord God, lest you prove ungrateful for any of his gifts, and by reason of this ingratitude you lose what you received. It is altogether beyond me to voice adequate praise of faith, but it can be imagined by believers. But if in some degree it may be thought worthy, what can be thought more desirable than the many gifts of God than God Himself? And if we ought to acknowledge God's lesser gifts to us, how much more must we acknowledge the gift that surpasses these?

3. To God we owe our existence. What are we unless what we are is from God? But what are wood and stones unless they are from God? What more therefore are we? Wood and stones are without life, we live. Still, mere life we share with trees and shrubs. Vines, for example, are said to live. If they did not live, no one would have written: *He destroyed their vineyards with hail.* (Ps. 77:47) When the vine is green, it lives; when it dries, it dies. But such life is without sensation. Yet what more have we? We sense. The bodily senses are known to be fivefold. We see, we hear, we smell, we taste, even by touch our whole body distinguishes soft and hard, rough and smooth, warm and cold. Accordingly there are in us five senses. Beasts have these too. Therefore we have something more. Still, my brethren, if we reflect on these qualities of ours we have mentioned, how grateful ought we to be for them, what praise do we owe the creator for them? Yet what more do we have? Mind, reason, deliberation, which neither beasts nor birds nor fishes have. It is in this that we are made in the likeness of God. Finally, in the narrative of our creation, Scripture declares that we are not only placed ahead of the beasts but above them; that is, they are subject to us: *Let us make,* it says, *man to our image and likeness, and let him have dominion over the fishes of the sea, and the fowls of the air, and the beasts and the whole earth, and every creeping thing that moveth upon the earth.* (Gen. 1:26) What is the source of

40

this power? The fact that man is the image of God. Hence by way of reproach it is said to some: *Do not become like the horse and the mule, who have no understanding.* (Ps. 31:9) But understanding is one thing, reason another. For we have reason even before we are able to understand, but we cannot understand unless we have reason. Hence, man is an animal endowed with reason, or, to speak more precisely and briefly, a rational animal whose very nature is to reason, and who has reason before he understands. What makes him eager to understand is the fact that he is endowed with the gift of reason.

4. Therefore we ought to cherish above all the faculty in virtue of which we excel beasts; we ought to refashion and, as it were, reform it. But who can do this except the creator who fashioned it. We were able to deform the image of God in us, but we cannot reform it. We share, then, to sum it up briefly, being with wood and stones, life with trees, sensation with beasts, understanding with angels. We discern colors by sight, sounds by hearing, odors by smelling, tastes by tasting, warmth by touch, morals by understanding. Every man desires to be understood, no one does not desire to understand, but not every one desires to believe. If someone says to me: "I would understand in order that I may believe," I answer: "Believe so that you may understand." When this sort of controversy arises between us, with him saying to me, "Let me understand in order to believe," and me answering, "Rather, believe, so that you may understand"—going to a judge with this sort of controversy neither of us should anticipate a decision in his favor. Where shall we find a judge? After considering everybody I doubt that we can find a better judge than the man through whom God spoke. Consequently in this dispute between us let us not turn to secular authors. The prophet, not the poet, shall be our judge.

5. When the blessed apostle Peter and two other disciples of the Lord Christ, James and John, were on the mountain with our Lord Himself, he heard a voice coming down from heaven: *This is my beloved Son in whom I am well pleased: hear ye him."* (II Pet. 1:17) In relating this the aforementioned apostle said in his letter: *We heard this voice coming down from heaven when we were on the holy mountain.* After saying: *We heard this voice coming down from heaven,* he added: *And in the message of the prophets we have something still more certain.* (II Pet. 1:18–19) The voice sounded from heaven, but the message of the prophet was more certain. Pay attention, dearly beloved, and may the Lord help both my will and your expectation, so that I may say what I

41

wish to say as I wish to say it. Who of us may not wonder that the word of the prophet is declared by the apostle to be more convincing than the voice coming from heaven? To be sure, he says more certain—more certain, not better nor truer. How much more true indeed is that word from heaven, than the prophetical word, how much more good and useful. What then is the meaning of "more firm" except that by it the hearer is confirmed? But how can this be? Because there are unbelievers who slander Christ by saying that what he did he did by magic. In this way these unbelievers, through human guesses and illicit speculations, can ascribe the voice from heaven to the arts of magic. But the prophets existed before, not I say before that voice, but before the Incarnation. Christ was not yet a man when He sent the prophets. As for anyone who calls him a magician, even supposing that by magic he brought about the cult of himself though dead, was he a magician before he was born? Behold why the apostle Peter says: *In the message of the prophets we have something still more certain.* (II Pet. 1:19) The voice from heaven admonishes believers, the voice of the prophets condemns unbelievers. It seems to me, dearly beloved, that we now perceive why the apostle Peter said: *In the message of the prophets we have something still more certain,* after the voice came down from heaven.

6. And how great is the condescension of Christ? This Peter who speaks thus was a fisherman, and now a rhetorician has great praise if a fisherman can be understood by him. Hence the apostle Paul speaking to the first Christians says: *Consider brethren, the circumstances of your own calling; not many of you are wise, in the world's fashion, not many powerful, not many well-born. No, God has chosen what the world holds foolish, so as to abash the wise, God has chosen what the world holds weak, so as to abash the strong. God has chosen what the world holds base and contemptible, nay, has chosen what is nothing, so as to bring to nothing what is now in being."* (I Cor. 1:26–28) If in the first place Christ had chosen an orator, the orator would have said: "My eloquence entitled me to be chosen." If he had chosen a senator, the senator would have said: "Because of my dignity I have been chosen." Finally if he had chosen an emperor, the emperor would have said: "Because of my power I was chosen." Let all these be silent and passed over for the time being, let them be silent, not given up nor disdained, but passed over for a while to give them time to bask in their glory as self-made men. "Give me this simple, unskilled fisherman," he says, "give me this fellow whom the senator will not condescend to speak to, even when he buys fish. Give

me him," he says. "It will be manifest that his power comes from me. Granted that I shall be fashioning a senator, an orator, and an emperor: from time to time I shall indeed fashion a senator, but more certainly a fisherman. A senator can take pride in himself; so may an orator and an emperor. The fisherman cannot except from Christ. Let him stand as a wholesome lesson in humility. First let the fisherman come. Through him it will be easier to lead the emperor on."

7. Remember, therefore, that fisherman, holy, righteous, good, filled with Christ, by whose nets cast about the world even those who already belonged there were destined to be taken. Remember he said: *In the message of the prophet we have something still more certain.* Consequently for the resolution of this controversy give me the prophet as judge. What was the question between us? You were saying: "Let me understand in order that I may believe." I was saying, *Unless you believe, you will not understand.*

8. Do you suppose, dearly beloved, that even he who says "Let me understand in order to believe" is saying nothing? What are we doing now except aiming at faith, not in those who have no faith, but in those in whom faith is still weak. If they had no faith at all, they would not be here. It is faith that drew them here to listen. The word of God has brought them to faith, but this very faith that has taken root must be watered, nourished, strengthened. This is what we are doing now. As we have heard said: *I planted the seed, and Apollo watered it; but God made it grow. Thus it is not the gardeners with their planting and watering who count, but God, who makes it grow.* (I Cor. 3:6–7) Through speech, encouragement, teaching, and exhortation we can plant and water, but we cannot give growth. That man was fully aware of whom he was speaking to, when, begging help for a nascent faith, still tender and weak, to a large extent wavering, but still faith, he said to him, *Lord, I believe.* (Mark 9:23)

9. A little while ago when the Gospel was being read you heard the Lord Jesus saying to the father of the boy: *If you can believe, everything is possible to him who believes.* (Mark 9:22) And he, turning his eye inward and gazing at himself, not in a spirit of rash confidence but first examining his conscience, sees in himself some faith, and he sees also some wavering. Both these things he sees. He declares that he has the one, and he begs help for the other. *I believe, Lord,* he says. What followed from this except "Help my faith"? But he did not say this. *I believe, Lord.* I see here something about which I did not lie. I believe, I am telling the truth. But I also see here something or other that dis-

43

pleases me. I wish to stand, but I waver. I speak standing, I have not fallen down because I believe. But still I waver: *Help my unbelief.* (Mark 9:23) Therefore, dearly beloved, my opponent too, by reason of whose dispute between us I demanded the prophet as judge, has something when he says: "I would understand in order that I may believe." Certainly, what I am now saying, I say with the object that those may believe who do not yet believe. Nevertheless unless they understand what I am saying, they cannot believe. Hence what he says is in some part true, "I would understand in order that I may believe." And I, too, am right when I say, as does the prophet: "Nay, believe in order that thou mayest understand." We both speak the truth; we are in agreement. Therefore, understand in order to believe; believe in order to understand. Here is a brief statement of how we can accept both without controversy. Understand in order that you may believe my word; believe, in order that you may understand the word of God.

THE PREDESTINATION OF THE SAINTS [3] ✝ And, there- fore, commending that grace which is not given according to any merits, but is the cause of all good merits, he says, "Not that we are sufficient to think anything as of ourselves, but our sufficiency is of God." Let them give attention to this and well weigh these words, who think that the beginning of faith is of ourselves and the supplement of faith is of God. For who cannot see that that thinking is prior to believing? For no one believes anything unless he has first thought that it is to be believed. For however suddenly, how- ever rapidly, some thoughts fly before the will to believe, and this presently follows in such wise as to attend them, as it were, in closest conjunction, it is yet necessary that everything which is believed should be believed after thought has preceded; although even belief itself is nothing else than to think with assent. For it is not everyone who thinks that believes, since many think in order that they may not believe; but everybody who believes, thinks— both thinks in believing and believes in thinking. Therefore in what pertains to religion and piety if we are not capable of thinking anything as of ourselves, but our sufficiency is of God, we are certainly not capable of believing anything of ourselves, since we

44

cannot do this without thinking; but our sufficiency, by which we begin to believe, is of God. Wherefore, as no one is sufficient for himself, for the beginning or the completion of any good work whatsoever . . . so no one is sufficient for himself, either to begin or to perfect faith; but our sufficiency is of God. Because if faith is not a matter of thought, it is of no account; and we are not sufficient to think anything as of ourselves, but our sufficiency is of God.

SERMON 126 ✢ 1. The mysteries and secrets of the kingdom of God first seek for believing men, that they make them understanding. For faith is understanding's step; and understanding, faith's attainment. This the prophet expressly says to all who prematurely and in undue order look for understanding and neglect faith. For he says, *Unless ye believe, ye shall not understand.* Faith itself then also hath a certain light of its own in the Scriptures, in Prophecy, in the Gospel, in the Lessons of the Apostles. For all these things which are read to us in this present time are lights in a dark place, that we may be nourished up unto the day. . . .

2. Ye see then, brethren, how exceedingly unregulated and disordered in their haste are they who like immature conceptions seek an untimely birth before the birth; who say to us, "Why dost thou bid me believe what I do not see? Let me see something that I may believe. Thou biddest me believe whilst yet I see not; I wish to see and by seeing to believe, not by hearing." Let the Prophet speak. *Unless ye believe ye shall not understand.* Thou wishest to ascend and dost forget the steps. Surely, out of all order. O man, if I could show thee already what thou mightest see, I should not exhort thee to believe.

3. Faith, then, as it has been elsewhere defined, is the *firm support of those who hope, the evidence of things which are not seen.* If they are not seen, how are they evidenced to be? What! Whence are those things which thou seest but from That which thou seest not? To be sure thou dost see somewhat that thou mayest believe somewhat, and from what thou seest, mayest believe what thou seest not. Be not ungrateful to Him Who hath made thee see, whereby thou mayest be able to believe what as yet thou canst not see. God hath given thee eyes in the body, reason in the

45

heart; wake up the interior inhabitant of thine interior eyes, let it take to its windows, examine the creature of God. For there is one within who sees by the eyes. For when thy thoughts within thee are on any other subject, and the inhabitant within is turned away, the things which are before thine eyes thou seest not. For to no purpose are the windows open, when he who looks through them is away. It is not then the eyes that see, but some one sees by the eyes; awake him, arouse him. For this hath not been denied thee; God hath made thee a rational animal, set thee over the cattle, formed thee after His own image. Oughtest thou to use them as the cattle do; only to see what to add to thy belly, not to thy soul? Stir up, I say, the eyes of reason, use thine eyes as a man should, consider the heaven and earth, the ornaments of the heaven, the fruitfulness of the earth, the flight of the birds, the swimming of the fish, the virtue of the seeds, the order of the seasons; consider the works, and seek for the Author; take a view of what thou seest, and seek Him Whom thou seest not. Believe on Him Whom thou seest not, because of these things which thou seest. And, lest thou think it is with mine own words that I have exhorted thee, hear the Apostle saying, *For the invisible things of God from the creation of the world are clearly seen by those things which are made.*

4. These things thou disregardest, nor didst look upon them as a man, but as an irrational animal . . . God's daily miracles were disesteemed, not for their easiness but their constant repetition. For what is more difficult to understand than a man's birth, that one who was in existence should by dying depart into darkness, and that one who was not, by being born should come forth to light? What so marvellous, what so difficult to comprehend? But with God easy to be done. Men wondered that our Lord God Jesus Christ filled so many thousands with five loaves; and yet they do not wonder that through a few grains the whole earth is filled with crops. When the water was made wine, men saw it and were amazed; what else takes place with the rain along the root of the vine? He did the one, He does the other; the one that thou mayest be fed, the other that thou mayest wonder. . . .

5. . . .Attend, I say, to what thou seest, believe what thou seest not. He hath not abandoned thee, Who hath called thee to believe; though He enjoin thee to believe that which thou canst not see; yet hath He not given thee up to see nothing whereby thou mayest be able to believe what thou dost not see. Is the creation itself a small sign, a small indication of the Creator? He also came, He did miracles. Thou couldest not see God, a man

thou couldest; so God was made Man, that in One thou mightest have both what to see and what to believe. . . .

LETTER 120 ✠ God forbid that He should hate in us that faculty by which He made us superior to all other living beings. Therefore, we must refuse so to believe as not to receive or seek a reason for our belief, since we could not believe at all if we did not have rational souls. So, then, in some points that bear on the doctrine of salvation, which we are not yet able to grasp by reason—but we shall be able to sometime—let faith precede reason, and let the heart be cleansed by faith so as to receive and bear the great light of reason; this is indeed reasonable. Therefore the Prophet said with reason: "If you will not believe, you will not understand" (Isa. 7:9) ; thereby he undoubtedly made a distinction between these two things and advised us to believe first so as to be able to understand whatever we believe. It is, then, a reasonable requirement that faith precede reason, for, if this requirement is not reasonable, then it is contrary to reason, which God forbid. But, if it is reasonable that faith precede a certain great reason which cannot yet be grasped, there is no doubt that, however slight the reason which proves this, it does precede faith.

That is why the Apostle warns us that we ought to be ready to give an answer to anyone who asks us a reason for our faith and hope, since if an unbeliever asks me a reason for my faith and hope, and I see that he cannot accept it until he believes, I give him that very reason, so that he may see how absurd it is for him to ask a reason for things which he cannot grasp until he believes. But if a believer asks a reason that he may understand what he believes, his mental ability is to be considered, and then, when the reason for his faith has been given according to it, he may draw as much understanding as he can, more if he is capable of more, less if he is less capable, but with the provision that, to the extent that he attains to the fullness and perfection of knowledge, he does not withdraw from the way of faith. . . . If, then, we are faithful now, we shall attain to the way of faith, and if we do not leave it, we shall unfailingly come not only to a great understanding of incorporeal and unchanging things, such as cannot be reached by all in this life, but even to the height of contemplation, which the Apostle calls "face to face." For some have very little

47

knowledge, yet by walking with great perseverance in the way of faith they attain to that most blessed contemplation; whereas others, although they know even now what the invisible, unchanging, and incorporeal nature is and what way leads to the abode of such happiness, cannot attain to it because the way, which is Christ crucified, seems foolish to them, and they refuse to withdraw to the innermost chamber of that repose by whose light their mind is stunned as by a far-shining radiance.

There are, however, some things which we are not able to believe when we hear them, because we do not apply our faith to them, yet when a reason for them is given, we recognize it as true. Thus, none of the miracles of God is believed by infidels because the reason for them is not evident; as a matter of fact, there are things for which no reason can be given, but that does not mean there is none, for God made nothing in the universe without reason. Of certain of His wonderful works it is better sometimes for the reason to be hidden; otherwise, our minds, weighed down with weariness, might hold them cheap if we had knowledge of their causes. There are others, and they are many, who are more impressed by wonder at the objects than by a knowledge of their causes, and, when miracles cease to be wonderful, they have to be roused to faith in the invisible by visible wonders. Thus they may be cleansed and purified by charity, and may return to the point they had left when they ceased to wonder, through familiarity with truth. In the theatre, men wonder at the rope-dancer, and take pleasure in the musicians: in the former case, the difficulty of the act rouses awe; in the latter, pleasure sustains and nourishes them.

I should like to say these things to rouse your faith to a love of understanding to which true reason leads the mind and for which faith prepares it. For that reasoning which argues about the Trinity, which is God, that the Son is not co-eternal with the Father, or that He is of another substance, and that the Holy Spirit is unlike Him in some way and therefore inferior, and that reasoning which claims that the Father and the Son are of one and the same substance, but that the Holy Spirit is of another, are to be avoided and detested, not because they are reasoning but because they are false reasoning; for if the reasoning were true, it would surely not go wrong. Therefore, just as you ought not to give up all speech because there is false speech, so you ought not to turn against all reasoning because there is false reasoning. I would say the same of wisdom: that wisdom is not to be avoided because there is also false wisdom, to which Christ crucified is foolishness, though

He is "the power of God and the wisdom of God," and, therefore, "by the foolishness of our preaching it pleased God to save them that believe; for the foolishness of God is wiser than men." (I Cor. 1:18, 24, 21, 25) This truth could not be made acceptable to some of the philosophers and orators who followed a way that was not the true one, but an imitation of the true one, and who deceived themselves and others on it. But by others it could be accepted, and to those who could accept it Christ crucified was neither a stumbling block nor foolishness: among them are those that are called, both Jews and Greeks, "to whom he is the power of God and the wisdom of God." (I Cor. 1:24) In this way, that is, in the faith of Christ crucified, those who were able by the grace of God to embrace His upright code of conduct, even though they are called philosophers or orators, certainly confessed with humble piety that the fishermen who preceded them were far superior to themselves, both in the steadfast strength of their belief and in the unerring truth of their understanding. For when they had learned that the foolish and weak things of the world had been chosen for this purpose that the wise and strong things might be confounded, and when they understood that their own wisdom was folly and their strength weakness, they were confounded for their own salvation and made foolish and weak, that by the foolish and weak thing of God, which is wiser and stronger than men, they might be chosen among the foolish and weak things and might become truly wise and effectually strong.

But the devout believer is ashamed of any but the truest reasoning; therefore, let us not be slow to overthrow a sort of idolatry which the frailty of human thought is prone to set up in our hearts, in consequence of our customary dealing with visible things, and let us not make bold to believe that the Trinity, which we worship as invisible, incorporeal, and unchangeable, is like three great living objects, which, though immense and beautiful, are bounded by the proper limits of their own spaces, touching each other because they are ranged so close together, either with one of them in the middle, so as to separate the two joined to it on either side, or in the fashion of a triangle, with each one touching the other two, and none separated from any. Let us not believe, either, that the huge mass of these three great Persons, which are limited on however large a scale from above and below and round about, have a single Godhead as if it were a fourth person, not like any one of them, whereas it is common to all as the divinity of all and in all and wholly in each one; through which sole Godhead the same Trinity is said to be God. And we must not believe that

His three Persons are nowhere but in heaven, while that Divinity is not in any one place but is present everywhere, and for that reason it would be right to say that God is in heaven and on earth, because of the Godhead which is everywhere and is common to the Three, but it would not be right to say that the Father is on earth or the Son or the Holy Spirit, since the abode of this Trinity is only in heaven. When true reasoning begins to break down that train of carnal thought, that vain imagining, with His interior help and light—since He does not dwell in our hearts with such idols—we make haste to shatter them and, so to speak, to shake our faith free of them, so that we do not allow even the dust of such fancies to remain there.

Therefore, should we not listen in vain to what is true, unless faith which clothes us with piety had preceded reason, through whose outward argument, together with the light of truth within us, we are roused to perceive that these idols are false? Thus, when faith acts in its own sphere, reason following after finds something of what faith was seeking, and true reason is to be preferred to false reason because it makes us understand what we believe, but faith in things not yet understood is undoubtedly even more to be preferred. It is better to believe in something true but not yet seen than to take the false thing one sees for true. For faith has its own eyes with which it sees, so to speak, that what it does not yet see is true, and with which it most certainly sees that it does not yet see what it believes. Moreover, he who now understands by a true reasoning what he only believed a while ago is emphatically to be preferred to the one who wishes to understand now what he believes, but if he does not also have a desire for the things which are to be understood, he considers them an object of belief only, and he fails to grasp the advantage of faith, for a devout faith does not wish to be without hope and without charity. So, then, a faithful man ought to believe what he does not yet see, so as to hope for and love the fulfillment of vision.

As a matter of fact, we hold things visible but past by faith alone, since there is no hope of seeing again what has slipped away with time. They are regarded as finished and gone by, as it is expressed in the words: "Christ died once for our sins, and rose again and dieth now no more: death shall no more have dominion over him." (I Pet. 3:18) The things which are not yet in existence but are to come, such as the resurrection of our spiritual bodies, are believed in such wise that we hope to see them, but they cannot be experienced now. And of the things which are such that they are neither past nor future, but remain forever, some are invisible,

50

like justice and wisdom, and some are visible, like the Body of Christ, now immortal. But, "the invisible things are clearly seen, being understood," (Rom. 1:20) and in that way they are also seen in a special and appropriate manner. And when they are seen, they are much more certain than the objects of the bodily sense, but they are said to be visible because they cannot, in any way, be seen by these mortal eyes. On the other hand, those living things which are visible and perpetual can be seen even by these mortal eyes, if they are made manifest; as the Lord showed Himself to the disciples after His Resurrection, and even after His Ascension, to the Apostle Paul and to the Deacon Stephen.

Therefore, we believe in those visible and perpetual things in such wise that even if they are not manifested to us, we hope we shall see them some day, and we do not make an effort to understand them by reasoning and thought, except that we make a distinction in our thought between these visible things and invisible ones, and we imagine to ourselves in thought what they are like, although we know quite well that they are not known to us. Thus, I think in one way of Antioch, a city unknown to me, and in another way of Carthage, which I do know; my mind makes an image of the former but recalls the latter. There is, however, no doubt in my mind that my belief about the former is based on the evidence of numerous witnesses; but about the latter, on my own sense-impressions. Nevertheless, we do not form an image of justice and wisdom or anything else of this sort in any other way, but we see them differently; we behold these invisible qualities by a simple intellectual attention of the mind and reason, without any forms or physical bulk, without any features or appearance of parts, without any locality, whether limited or of unbounded space. The light itself by which we distinguish all this, by which we are made aware of what we believe without knowing it, that we hold as objects of knowledge, what physical shape we recall, what one we imagine, what the sense-organ perceives, what the mind imagines in the likeness of a body, what is present to the intellect as certain yet totally unlike any physical object, this light by which all these mental acts are differentiated is not diffused in any special place, like the brilliance of this sun or of any physical light, and does not illumine our mind as if it were a visible brightness, but it shines invisibly and indescribably, yet intelligibly, and it is as certain a fact itself as are the realities which we see as certain by means of it.

We have, then, three classes of objects which are seen: the first, of material things, such as heaven and earth and everything the physical sense-organ perceives or experiences in them; the second, of representations of material things, such as those we picture to ourselves in thought by means of our imagination, whether we behold them inwardly as remembered or as imagined objects. In this class are visions, such as occur either in sleep or in some state of ecstasy and are presented in these spatial dimensions. The third class is different from both the former and consists of things which are not corporeal and have no corporeal representation: for example, wisdom, which is perceived by the understanding and by whose light all these other things are correctly estimated. But, in which class are we to believe that the Trinity, which we wish to know about, is included? Obviously, in some one of them or in none. If in some one, it must be the one which is superior to the other two, namely, the one in which wisdom is included. But if His gift is in us, and if it is a lesser thing than that supreme and unchangeable wisdom which is said to be of God—I suppose we should not rate the giver as lower than his gift—if some of His light is in us and is called our wisdom, in so far as we can grasp anything of Him, "through a glass in a dark manner," then we must distinguish that wisdom from all material objects and from all representations of material objects.

But if the Trinity is not to be included in any of those classes, and if it is so far invisible that it is not seen by the mind, we have no reason at all to believe that it is not seen by the mind, we have no reason at all to believe that it is like either material objects or the representations of material objects. It is not in the beauty of its shape nor in its immensity that it surpasses material things but in the difference and complete dissimilarity of its nature. It is also remote from any comparison with our spiritual goods, such as wisdom, justice, charity, chastity, and other like qualities, which we certainly do not value for their physical size, nor do we endow them in out thoughts with bodily shapes, but when we understand them properly, we behold them by the light of our mind without bodily attributes or any likeness of bodily attributes. How much more, then, must we refrain from any comparison of physical qualities and dimensions in thinking of the Trinity! But the Apostle is witness that our mind is not to shrink away from it entirely, when he says: "For the invisible things of him from the creation of the world are clearly seen, being understood by the things that are made; his eternal power also and divinity." (Rom. 1:20) Consequently, since the same Trinity created both body and soul, it is evidently superior to both. And if the soul so considered, especially the human, rational, and intellectual soul, which was made in His image, does not elude our thoughts and understanding; if, by mind and understanding, we are able to grasp its excellence, which is to say, the mind itself and the understanding, it will not perhaps be unreasonable for us to try to raise our soul to the understanding of its Creator, with His help. But if it fails in that and falls back on itself, let it be satisfied with devout faith, as long as it is a wanderer from the Lord, until He acts to fulfill His promise in man, as the Apostle says: "Who is able to do all things more abundantly than we desire or understand." (Eph. 3:20)

THE SPIRIT AND THE LETTER ✤ *Whether Faith Be in a Man's Own Power.*[4] Attend now to the point which we have laid down for discussion: whether faith is in our own power. We now speak of that faith which we employ when we believe anything, not that which we give when we make a promise; for this too is called *faith*. We use the word in one sense when we say, "He had no faith in me," and in another sense when we say, "He did not keep faith with me." The one phrase means, "He did not believe what I said"; the other, "He did not do what he promised." According to the faith by which we believe, we are faithful to God; but according to that whereby a thing is brought to pass which is promised, God Himself even is faithful to us; for the apostle declares, "God is faithful, who will not suffer you to be tempted above that ye are able." (I Cor. 10:13) Well, now, the former is the faith about which we inquire, Whether it be in our power, even the faith by which we believe God or believe on God. For of this it is written, "Abraham believed God, and it was counted unto him for righteousness." (Rom. 4:3) And again, "To him that believeth on Him that justifieth the ungodly, his faith is counted for righteousness." (Rom. 4:5) Consider now whether anybody believes, if he be unwilling; or whether he believes not, if he shall have willed it. Such a position, indeed, is absurd (for what is believing but consenting to the truth of what is said? and this consent is certainly voluntary) : faith, therefore, is in our own power. But, as the apostle says: "There is no power but comes from God," (Rom. 13:1) what reason, then, is there why it may not be said to us even of this: "What hast thou which thou hast not received?" (I Cor. 4:7) —for it is God who gave us even to believe. Nowhere, however, in Holy Scripture do we find such an assertion as, There is no volition but comes from God. And rightly is it not so written, because it is not

true: otherwise God would be the author even of sins (which Heaven forbid!), if there were no volition except what comes from Him; inasmuch as an evil volition alone is already a sin, even if the effect be wanting—in other words, if it has not ability. But when the evil volition receives ability to accomplish its intention, this proceeds from the judgment of God, with whom there is no unrighteousness. (Rom. 9:14) He indeed punishes after this manner; nor is His chastisement unjust because it is secret. The ungodly man, however, is not aware that he is being punished, except when he unwillingly discovers by an open penalty how much evil he has willingly committed. This is just what the apostle says of certain men: "God hath given them up to the evil desires of their own hearts, . . . to do those things that are not convenient." (Rom. 1:24, 28) Accordingly, the Lord also said to Pilate: "Thou couldest have no power at all against me, except it were given thee from above." (John 19:11) But still, when the ability is given, surely no necessity is imposed. Therefore, although David had received ability to kill Saul, he preferred sparing to striking him. (I Sam. 24:7; 26:9) Whence we understand that bad men receive ability for the condemnation of their depraved will, while good men receive ability for trying of their good will.

The Will to Believe is From God [5] Let this discussion suffice, if it satisfactorily meets the question we had to solve. It may be, however, objected in reply that we must take heed lest some one should suppose that the sin would have to be imputed to God which is committed by free will, if in the passage where it is asked, "What hast thou which thou didst not receive?" (I Cor. 4:7) the very will by which we believe is reckoned as a gift of God, because it arises out of the free will which we received at our creation. Let the objector, however, attentively observe that this will is to be ascribed to the divine gift, not merely because it arises from our free will, which was created naturally with us; but also because God acts upon us by the incentives of our perceptions, to will and to believe, either externally by evangelical exhortations, where even the commands of the law also do something, if they so far admonish a man of his infirmity that he betakes himself to the grace that justifies by believing; or internally, where no man has in his own control what shall enter into his thoughts, although it appertains to his own will to consent or to dissent. Since God, therefore, in such ways acts upon the reasonable soul in order that it may believe in Him (and certainly there is no ability whatever in free will to believe, unless

54

there be persuasion or summons towards some one in whom to believe), it surely follows that it is God who both works in man the willing to believe and in all things prevents us with His mercy. To yield our consent, indeed, to God's summons, or to withhold it, is (as I have said) the function of our own will. And this not only does not invalidate what is said, "For what hast thou that thou didst not receive?" (I Cor. 4:7) but it really confirms it. For the soul cannot receive and possess these gifts, which are here referred to, except by yielding its consent. And thus whatever it possesses, and whatever it receives, is from God; and yet the act of receiving and having belongs, of course, to the receiver and possessor. Now, should any man be for constraining us to examine into this profound mystery, why this person is so persuaded as to yield, and that person is not, there are only two things occurring to me, which I should like to advance as my answer: "O the depth of the riches!" (Rom. 11:33) and "Is there unrighteousness with God?" (Rom. 9:14) If the man is displeased with such an answer, he must seek more learned disputants; but let him beware lest he find presumptuous ones.

THE ADVANTAGE OF BELIEVING ✠ CHAPTER 10: 23. But you will say, consider now whether we ought to believe in religion. For although we grant that it is one thing to believe, another to be credulous, it does not follow that it is no fault to believe in matters of religion. For what if it be a fault both to believe and to be credulous, as it is to be drunk and to be a drunkard? Now he who thinks this certain, it seems to me, can have no friend; for if it is base to believe anything, either he acts basely who believes a friend, or, in not believing a friend at all I see not how he can call either him or himself a friend. Here perhaps you may say, I grant that we must believe something at some time; now make plain, how in the case of religion it be not base to believe before one knows. I will do so, if I can. Wherefore I ask of you, which you esteem the graver fault, to deliver religion to one unworthy, or to believe what is said by them who deliver it. If you understand not whom I call unworthy, I call him unworthy who approaches it with hypocrisy. You grant, as I suppose, that it is more blameable to unfold to such an one whatever holy secrets there are than to believe religious men affirming any thing on the matter of religion itself. For it would be unbecoming you to make any other answer. Wherefore now suppose him present, who is about to deliver to you a religion, in what way shall you assure him that you approach with a true mind and that, so far as this matter is concerned, there is in you no fraud or feigning? You will say with your own good conscience that you are no way feigning, asserting this with words as strong as you can, but yet with words. For you cannot lay open man to man the hiding places of your soul, so that you may be thoroughly known. But if he shall say, Lo, I believe you, but is it not more fair that you also believe me, when, if I hold any truth, you are about to receive, I about to give, a benefit? what will you answer, save that you must believe?

24. But you say, Were it not better that you should give me a reason, that, wherever that shall lead me, I may follow without any rashness? Perhaps it were: but, it being so great a matter, that you are by reason to come to the knowledge of God, do you think that all are qualified to understand the reasons by which the human soul is led to know God, or many, or few? Few I think, you say. Do you believe that you are in the number of these? It is not for me, you say, to answer this. Therefore you think it is for him to believe you in this also: and this indeed he does: only do you remember that he has already twice believed you saying things uncertain; that you are unwilling to believe him even once admonishing you in a religious spirit. But suppose that it is so, and that you approach with a true mind to receive religion, and that you are one of few men in such sense as to be able to take in the reasons by which the Divine Power is brought into certain knowledge; what? do you think that other men, who are not endowed with so serene a disposition, are to be denied religion? or do you think that they are to be led gradually by certain steps unto those highest inner recesses? you see clearly which is the more religious. For you cannot think that anyone whatever, in a case where he desires so great a thing, ought by any means to be abandoned or rejected. But do you not think that unless he first believes that he shall attain his goal and reveals the mind of a suppliant, submitting to certain great and necessary precepts and purging himself by a certain way of life, that he will not otherwise attain the things that are purely true? Certainly you think so. What, then, is the case of those (of whom I already believe you to be one) who are able most easily to receive divine secrets by sure reason? Will it be of any hindrance to them if they come as do they who at first believe? I think not. But yet, you say, what need to delay them? Because although they will in no way harm themselves by what is done, yet they will harm the rest

by the precedent. For there is hardly one who has a just notion of his own power: but he who has a less notion must be roused; he who has a greater notion must be checked: that neither the one be broken by despair, nor the other carried headlong by rashness. And this is easily done, if even they, who are able to fly (that they may not allure others into danger) are forced for a short time to walk where the rest also may walk with safety. This is the forethought of true religion: this the command of God: this what has been handed down from our blessed forefathers: this what has been preserved even unto us: to wish to distrust and overthrow this is nothing else than to seek a sacrilegious way unto true religion. As to those who do this, not even if what they wish be granted to them, are they able to arrive at the point at which they aim. For whatever kind of excellent genius they have, unless God be present, they creep on the ground. But He is then present, if they, who are aiming at God, have a regard for their fellow men. Than which step there can be found nothing more surely Heavenward. I for my part cannot resist this reasoning, for how can I say that we are to believe nothing without certain knowledge? For there can be no friendship at all, unless there be believed something which cannot be proved by some reason. Frequently stewards, who are slaves, are trusted by their masters without any fault on their part. But in religion what can there be more unfair than that the ministers of God believe us when we promise an unfeigned mind and we are unwilling to believe them when they enjoin us any thing. Lastly, what way can there be more healthful, than for a man to become fitted to receive the truth by believing those things which have been appointed by God to serve for the previous culture and treatment of the mind? Or, if you be already perfectly fitted, rather to make some little circuit where it is safest to tread, than both to cause yourself danger and to be a precedent for rashness to other men?

CHAPTER 11:25. Wherefore it now remains to consider, in what manner we ought not to follow these, who profess that they will lead by reason. For how we may without fault follow those who bid us to believe, has already been said: but to these who make promises of reason, certain men think that they can come, not only without blame but also with some praise. But this is not so, for there are two classes of persons praiseworthy in religion: one of those who have already found, whom also we must judge most blessed; another of those who are seeking with all earnestness and in the right way. The first, therefore, are already in actual possession, the other on the way, yet on that way whereby they are most sure to arrive. (cf. *Retractions* I, 14, 2) There are three other kinds of men altogether to be disapproved of and detested. One is of those who hold an opinion, that is, of those who think that they know what they know not. Another is of those who are indeed aware that they know not but do not so seek as to be able to find. A third is of those who neither think that they know nor wish to seek. There are also three things, as it were bordering upon one another, in the minds of men well worth distinguishing: understanding, belief, opinion. And, if these be considered by themselves, the first is always without fault, the second sometimes with fault, the third never without fault. For the understanding of matters great, and honorable, and even divine, is most blessed. (cf. *Retractions* I, 14, 2) But the understanding of things unnecessary is not harmful; but perhaps the learning was harmful, in that it took up the time of necessary matters. But on the matters themselves that are harmful, it is not the understanding but the doing or suffering them that is wretched. For not, in case any one understand how an enemy may be slain without the danger to himself, is he guilty from the understanding, not the wish; and if the wish be absent, what can be called more innocent? But belief is then worthy of blame, when either any thing is believed of God which is unworthy of Him, or any thing is too readily believed of man. But in all other matters if any believe aught, provided he understand that he knows it not, there is no fault. For I believe that very wicked conspirators were formerly put to death by the virtue of Cicero; but this I not only know not, but also I know for certain that I can by no means know. But opinion is on two accounts very base; in that both he who has persuaded himself that he already knows, cannot learn; provided only it may be learnt; and in itself rashness is a sign of a mind not well disposed. For even if anyone suppose that he knows what I said of Cicero (although it be no hindrance to him from learning, in that the matter itself is incapable of being grasped by any knowledge) ; yet (in that he understands not that there is a great difference, whether anything be grasped by sure reason of mind, which we call understanding, or whether for practical purposes it be entrusted to common fame or writing, for posterity to believe it) he assuredly errs, and no error is without what is base. What then we understand, we owe to reason; what we believe, to authority; what we have an opinion on, to error. (cf. *Retractions* I, 14, 3) But everyone who understands also believes, and also everyone who has an opinion believes; not everyone who believes understands, no one who has an opinion understands. Therefore if these three things be referred to the five kinds of men, which we mentioned a little above; that is, two kinds to be approved, which we set first, and three that remain faulty; we find that the first kind, that of the blessed, believe the truth itself; but the second kind, that of such as are earnest after, and lovers of, the truth, believe authority. In which kinds, of the two, the act of belief is praiseworthy. But in the first of the faulty kinds, that is, of those who have an opinion that they know what they know not, there is an altogether faulty credulity. The other two kinds that are to be disapproved believe nothing, both they who seek the truth despairing of finding it, and they who seek it not at all. And this only in matters which pertain to any system of teaching. For in the other business of life, I am utterly ignorant by what means a man can believe nothing. Although in the case of those also, they who say that in practical matters they follow probabilities, would seem rather to be unable to know than unable to believe. For who believes not what he approves? or how is what they follow probable, if it be not approved? Wherefore there may be two kinds of such as oppose the truth: one of those who assail knowledge alone, not faith; the other of those who condemn both: and yet again, I am ignorant whether these can be found in matters of human life. These things have been said, in order that we might understand, that, in retaining faith, even of those things which as yet we comprehend not, we are set free from the rashness of such as have an opinion. For they, who say that we are to believe nothing but what we know, are on their guard against that one name 'opinion,' which must be confessed to be base and very wretched. But, if they consider carefully that there is a very great difference, whether one thinks that he knows, or moved by some authority believes that which he understands that he knows not, surely he will escape the charge of error and inhumanity and pride.

26. For I ask if what is not known must not be believed, in what way may children do service to their parents and love with mutual affection those whom they believe not to be their parents? For it cannot, by any means, be known by reason. But the authority of the mother comes in, that it be believed of the father; but of the mother it is usually not the mother that is believed, but midwives, nurses, servants. For she, from whom a son may be stolen and another put in his place, may she not being deceived deceive? Yet we believe, and believe without any doubt, what we confess we cannot know. For who but must see that unless it be so, filial affection, the most sacred bond of the human race, is violated by extreme pride of wickedness? For what madman even would think him to be blamed who discharged the duties that were due to those whom

he believed to be his parents, although they were not so? Who, on the other hand, would not judge him to deserve banishment, who failed to love those who were perhaps his true parents, through fear lest he should love pretended. Many thing may be alleged whereby to show that nothing at all of human society remains safe, if we shall determine to believe nothing, which we cannot grasp by full apprehension.

27. But now hear what I trust I shall by this time more easily persuade you of. In a matter of religion, that is, of the worship and knowledge of God, they are less to be followed, who forbid us to believe, making most ready professions of reason. For no one doubts that all men are either fools or wise. (cf. *Retractions* I 14, 4) But now I call wise, not clever and gifted men, but those, in whom there is, so much as may be in man, the knowledge of man himself and of God most surely received, and a life and manners suitable to that knowledge; but all others, whatever be their skill or want of skill, whatever their manner of life, whether to be approved or disapproved, I would account in the number of fools. And, this being so, who of moderate understanding but will clearly see that it is more useful and more healthful for fools to obey the precepts of the wise than to live by their own judgment? For everything that is done, if it be not rightly done, is a sin, nor can that anyhow be rightly done which proceeds not from right reason. Further, right reason is virtue itself. But to whom of men is virtue at hand, save to the mind of the wise? Therefore the wise man alone sins not. Therefore every fool sins, save in those actions in which he has obeyed a wise man: for all such actions proceed from right reason, and, so to say, the fool is not to be accounted master of his own action, he being, as it were, the instrument and that which ministers to the wise man. Wherefore, if it be better for all men not to sin than to sin, assuredly all fools would live better, if they could be the slaves of the wise. And if no one doubts that this is better in lesser matters, as in buying and selling, and cultivating the ground, in taking a wife, in undertaking and bringing up children, lastly, in the management of household property, much more in religion. For both human matters are more easy to distinguish between than divine; and in all matters of greater sacredness and excellence, the greater obedience and service we owe them, the more wicked and the more dangerous is it to sin. Therefore you see henceforth that nothing else is left us, so long as we are fools, if our heart be set on an excellent and religious life, but to seek wise men, by obeying whom we may be enabled both to lessen the great

feeling of the rule of folly, while it is in us, and at the last to escape from it.

28. Here again arises a very difficult question. For in what way shall we fools be able to find a wise man, whereas this name, although hardly any one dare openly, yet most men lay claim to indirectly by so disagreeing with one another in the very matters in the knowledge of which wisdom consists, that either none of them is wise or some certain one? But when the fool inquires, who is that wise man? I do not at all see in what way he can be distinguished and perceived. For by no signs whatever can one recognize any thing, unless he shall have known that thing, whereof these are signs. But the fool is ignorant of wisdom. For though it is allowed, as in the case of gold and silver and other things of that kind, both to know them when you see them and not to have them, wisdom may not be seen by the mind's eye of him who has it not. For whatever things we come into contact with by bodily sense are presented to us from without; and therefore we may perceive by the eyes what belong to others, when we ourselves possess not any of them or of that kind. But what is perceived by the understanding is within the mind, and to have it is nothing else than to see. But the fool is void of wisdom, therefore he knows not wisdom. For he could not see it with the eyes; but he cannot see it and not have it, nor have it and be a fool. Therefore he knows it not, and, so long as he knows it not, he cannot recognize it in another place. No one, so long as he is a fool, can by most sure knowledge find out a wise man, by obeying whom he may be set free from so great evil of folly.

NOTES (Faith and Understanding)

[1] E. Portalié, S. J., *A Guide to the Thought of St. Augustine,* Chicago, 1960, p. 118.

[2] Translated from the *Corpus Christianorum,* Vol. 41.

[3] II, 5.

[4] Chapter 54.

[5] Chapter 60.

✠ ✠ ✠

THE EXISTENCE OF GOD

✠ ✠ ✠

Of the selections that follow *The True Religion* was composed at Tagaste between 389 and 391 during a period of seclusion in which Augustine founded his first monastery. The treatise is addressed to the friend of his father and his patron Romanianus. Although the principal theme is the refutation of the Manichean religion and the vindication of the truth of the Catholic religion, this apologetic treatise is particularly rich in its anticipation and development of other themes of the Augustininian philosophy. The use and references to history, the contrast between the "old man" and the "new man," and the description of the progress of the soul anticipate similar themes in the *City of God*. As an apologetic treatise developing various arguments in defense of the faith it anticipates what is developed more fully in other apologetic treatises, e.g. *The Advantage of Believing*. In this connection the meaning and justification of authority and its relation to reason will be found to be a valuable supplement to some of the selections in the topic on Faith and Understanding. Similarly there is material on sense knowledge and intellectual knowledge which may be studied in connection with the topic on the Problem of Knowledge.

All of this may suggest that perhaps this treatise should not be included in a topic on the Existence of God. It is also true that no attempt here is made toward a formal demonstration of God's existence. In a letter (#162) written to Evodius (circa 414) Augustine declares that if Evodius would read this book on religion, he would not think that reason could ever prove God's existence. However, the treatise is valuable in reference to this problem principally because it contains a very marked anticipation of the basic argument of *Freedom of the Will* that it is necessary to advance in reason from the temporal to the eternal and that there exists a standard of truth higher than our minds, a truth that is immutable and eternal. *Freedom of the Will* develops this argument in more detail and establishes a more explicit identification of such truth with God.

Freedom of the Will is a dialogue divided into three books. It was begun at Rome in 388 and not completed until the end of 395. The dialogue is principally devoted to the problems of the freedom of the will and the origin of evil or sin. It appears to be the outgrowth of a conversation between Augustine and his friend Evodius on the origins of evil. In the course of their conversation the question of the existence of God is raised and the selection from Book II presents the only explicit attempt on the part of Augustine to prove God's existence. The demonstration is neither effective nor adequate and was rejected by Thomas Aquinas * who questioned the validity of the inference from the existence of the eternal and immutable truths known by man to the existence of God as Truth itself. As Aquinas stated his objection: "The existence of truth in general is self-evident, but the existence of a Primal Truth is not self-evident to us." (*Summa Theologiae*, I.-I., Q. 2. a. 1. ad. 3)

THE TRUE RELIGION ✢ CHAPTER 24:45.

The treatment of the soul, which God's providence and ineffable loving-kindness administers, is most beautiful in its steps and stages. There are two different methods, authority and reason. Authority demands belief and prepares man for reason. Reason leads to understanding and knowledge. But reason is not entirely absent from authority, for we have got to consider whom we have to believe, and the highest

---

* His knowledge of the argument was derived from Anselm.

authority belongs to truth when it is clearly known. But because we dwell among temporal things and love of them is an obstacle to our reaching eternal things, a kind of temporal medicine, calling not those who know but those who believe back to health, has priority by the order, not of nature or its inherent excellence, but of time. Wherever a man falls there he must lie until he is raised up. So we must strive, by means of the carnal forms which detain us, to come to know those of which carnal sense can bring us no knowledge. And by carnal sense I mean eyes, ears, and other bodily senses. To carnal or corporeal forms boys must necessarily and lovingly adhere; adolescents, almost necessarily. But with increasing years the necessity disappears.

CHAPTER 25:46. Divine providence not only looks after individuals as it were privately but also after the whole human race publicly. How it deals with individuals God knows, who does it, and they also know, with whom he deals. But how he deals with the human race God has willed to be handed down through history and prophecy. The trustworthiness of temporal things whether past or future can be believed rather than known by the intelligence. It is our duty to consider what men or what books we are to believe in order that we may rightly worship God, wherein lies our sole salvation. Here the first decision must be this: Are we to believe those who summon us to the worship of many gods or those who summon us to worship one God? Who can doubt that we ought rather to follow those who summon us to worship one God, especially since the worshippers of many gods agree that there is one God who rules all things? At least the numerical series begins from the number one. Those, therefore, are to be followed who say that the one most high God is the only true God and is to be worshipped alone. If the truth does not shine out brightly among them, then, but not till then, must we go elsewhere. In the realm of nature there is a presumption of greater authority when all things are brought into unity. In the human race a multitude has no power unless by consent, i.e., agreement in unity. So in religion the authority of those who summon us to unity ought to be greater and more worthy of being believed.

47. Another thing which must be considered is the dissension that has arisen among men concerning the worship of the one God. We have heard that our predecessors, at a stage in faith on the way from temporal things up to eternal things, followed

visible miracles. They could do nothing else. And they did so in such a way that it should not be necessary for those who came after them. When the Catholic Church had been founded and diffused throughout the whole world, on the one hand miracles were not allowed to continue till our time, lest the mind should always seek visible things, and the human race should grow cold by becoming accustomed to things which when they were novelties kindled its faith. On the other hand we must not doubt that those are to be believed who proclaimed miracles, which only a few had actually seen, and yet were able to persuade whole peoples to follow them. At that time the problem was to get people to believe before anyone was fit to reason about divine and invisible things. No human authority is set over the reason of a purified soul, for it is able to arrive at clear truth. But pride does not lead to the perception of truth. If there were no pride there would be no heretics, no schismatics, no circumcised, no worshippers of creatures or of images. If there had not been such classes of opponents before the people was made perfect as promised, truth would be sought much less eagerly.

CHAPTER 26:48. This is the tradition concerning God's temporal dispensation and his providential care for those who by sin had become deservedly mortal. First, consider the nature and education of any individual man who is born. His first age, infancy, is spent in receiving bodily nourishment, and it is to be entirely forgotten when he grows up. Then follows childhood when we begin to have some memories. To this adolescence succeeds, when nature allows propagation of offspring and fatherhood. After adolescence comes young manhood, which must take part in public duties and be brought under the laws. Now sins are more strictly forbidden, and sinners have to undergo the servile coercion of penalty. In carnal souls this of itself causes more dreadful onsets of lust, and wrong-doing is redoubled. For sin has a double aspect. It is not merely wrong-doing. It is disobedience. After the labors of young manhood, a little peace is given to old age. But it is an inferior age, lacking in lustre, weak and more subject to disease, and it leads to death. This is the life of man so far as he lives in the body and is bound by desires for temporal things. This is called "the old man" and "the exterior or earthly man," even if he obtain what the vulgar call felicity in a well-ordered earthly city, whether ruled by kings or princes or laws or all of them together. For without these things no people can be well-ordered, not even a people that pursues earthly goods. Even such a people has a measure of beauty of its own.

49. I have described "the old or exterior or earthly man." He may be a moderate man after his kind, or he may transgress the measure of servile justice. Some live thus from the beginning to the end of their days. But some begin in that way, as they necessarily must, but they are reborn inwardly, and with their spiritual strength and increase of wisdom they overcome "the old man" and put him to death and bring him into subjection to the celestial laws, until after visible death the whole is restored. This is called "the new man," "the inward and heavenly man," whose spiritual ages are marked, not according to years but according to his spiritual advance. In the first stage he is taught by the rich stores of history which nourish by examples. In the second stage he forgets human affairs and tends towards divine things. He is no longer kept in the bosom of human authority, but step by step by the use of reason he strives to reach the highest unchangeable law. In the third stage he confidently marries carnal appetite to strong reason and inwardly rejoices in the sweetness of the union. Soul and mind are joined together in chaste union. There is as yet no compulsion to do right, but even though no one forbids sin, he has no pleasure in sinning. The fourth stage is similar, only now he acts much more firmly and springs forth as the perfect man, ready to endure and overcome all the persecutions, tempests and billows of this world. In the fifth stage he has peace and tranquillity on all sides. He lives among the abundant resources of the unchangeable realm of supreme ineffable wisdom. The sixth stage is complete transformation into life eternal, a total forgetfulness of temporal life passing into the perfect form which is made according to the image and likeness of God. The seventh is eternal rest and perpetual beatitude with no distinguishable ages. As the end of "the old man" is death, so the end of "the new man" is eternal life. The "old man" is the man of sin, but the "new man" is the man of righteousness.

CHAPTER 27:50. No one doubts that these two lives are related as follows: A man can live the whole of this life as "the old and earthly man." But no one in this life can live as "the new and heavenly man"; he must associate with the "old man." For he must begin there and must so continue till death, though the old grows weaker and the new progresses. Similarly, the entire human race, whose life, like the life of an individual from Adam

66 ·

to the end of the world, is so arranged by the laws of divine providence that it appears divided among two classes. In one of these is the multitude of the impious who bear the image of the earthly man from the beginning to the end of the world. In the other is the succession of the people devoted to the one God. But from Adam to John The Baptist they live the life of the earthly man under a certain form of righteousness. Their history is called the Old Testament, having the promise of a kind of earthly kingdom, which is nothing but the image of the new people, and the New Testament, with the promise of the kingdom of heaven. Meantime the life of this people begins with the coming of the Lord in humility and goes on till the day of judgment, when he will come in all clearness. After the judgment the "old man" will come to an end, and there will take place the change that betokens the angelic life. For we shall all be raised, but we shall not all be changed. (I Cor. 15:51) The pious people will be raised as they transform the remnants of the "old man" that cling to them into the "new man." The impious people, who have kept the "old man" from the beginning to the end, will be raised in order to be precipitated into the second death. Those who read diligently can make out the divisions of the age. They have no horror of tares or chaff. For the impious lives with the pious, and the sinner with the righteous, so that, by comparing the two, men may more eagerly rise to seek perfection.

CHAPTER 28:51. If any of the earthly people at any time had the merit of reaching the illumination of the inward man, he gave to the human race in his day his aid showing it what that age required, hinting by prophecy what it was not opportune to show clearly. Such were the patriarchs and the prophets. So those discover who do not behave like children, but who diligently and piously handle this good and great secret of the divine human-relations. In the time of the new people I see that this has been most carefully provided by great and spiritual men for the nurse-lings of the Catholic Church. They are not to treat publicly of what they know is not seasonable to be handled before the people. They earnestly feed the multitude of those who are weak and needy with copious supplies of milky food; and the few who are wise they feed with stronger meats. They speak wisdom among the perfect, but from the carnal and the psychics, though they be "new men," they keep some things back, because they are still children, but they never lie. They do not look to vain honors and vain praise for themselves but to the advantage of those with whom they have deserved to be associated in this life. This is the law of divine providence that no one is to receive assistance from his superiors to know and grasp the grace of God, unless he is prepared with a pure affection to assist his inferiors to the same. So out of our sin, which our nature committed in the first sinful man, the human race is made the great glory and ornament of the world and is so properly governed by the provisions of divine providence that the art of God's ineffable healing turns even the foulness of sin into something that has a beauty of its own.

CHAPTER 29:52. We have said enough for the present about the benefit of authority. Let us see how far reason can advance from visible to invisible things in its ascent from temporal to eternal things. We should not vainly behold the beauty of the sky, the order of the stars, the brightness of light, the alternations of day and night, the monthly courses of the moon, the fourfold seasons of the year, the meeting of the four elements, the life-force of seeds begetting forms and numbers, and all things that keep their nature and their appropriate measure each in its own kind. In considering these things there should be no exercise of vain and perishing curiosity, but a step should be taken towards immortal things that abide for ever. The first thing to notice is living nature which senses all these things. Because it gives life to the body it must necessarily excel the body. No mass of matter, however great or bright, is to be held of much account if it is without life. Any living substance is by the law of nature to be preferred to any inanimate substance.

53. No one doubts that irrational animals also live and feel. So in the human mind the most excellent part is not that which perceives sensible objects but that which judges of sensible objects. Many animals see more sharply and have a keener sense of corporeal objects than men have. But to judge of bodies belongs not to life that is merely sentient but to life that has also the power of reasoning. Where the animals are lacking, there is our excellence. It is easy to see that that which judges is superior to that which is judged. For living reason judges not only of sensible things but also of the senses themselves. It knows why the oar dipped in water must appear crooked though it is really straight, and why the eyes must see it in that way. Ocular vision can only tell us that it is so but cannot judge. Wherefore it is manifest that as the life of sense excels the body, the life of reason excels both.

68

CHAPTER 30:54. If rational life judges by itself alone, then there is nothing more excellent. But clearly it is mutable, since it can be skilled at one moment and unskilled at another. The more skilled it is the better it judges, and its skill is in proportion to its participation in some art, discipline or wisdom. Now we must ask what is the nature of an art. By an art in this context I would have you understand not something that is observed by experience but something that is found out by reason. There is nothing very remarkable in knowing that sand and lime bind stones more securely together than mud, or that he who would build elegantly, must put a feature that is to be unique in the middle of the building, and, if there are several features, they must be made to correspond, like with like. That is sense-knowledge, but it is not far from reason and truth. We must indeed inquire what is the cause of our being dissatisfied if two windows are placed not one above the other but side by side, and one of them is greater or less than the other, for they ought to have been equal; while, if they are placed one directly above the other, even though they are unlike, the inequality does not offend us in the same way. Why don't we notice very much how much the one is greater or less than the other? If there are three windows, sense itself seems to demand either that they should not be unequal, or that between the largest and the smallest there should be an intermediate one as much larger than the smallest as it is smaller than the largest. In this way we take counsel with nature, as it were, to see what she approves. And here we must observe how that which displeases us only a little when we simply look at it, is rejected when we compare it with what is better, Thus we discover that art in the popular sense is nothing but the memory of things we have experienced and which have given us pleasure, with the addition of some skilled bodily activity. If you lack the skill you can still judge of the works produced even though you cannot produce them. And the power of judging is much better.

55. In all the arts it is symmetry that gives pleasure, preserving unity and making the whole beautiful. Symmetry demands unity and equality, the similarity of like parts, or the graded arrangements of parts which are dissimilar. But who can find absolute equality or similarity in bodily objects? Who would venture to say, after due consideration, that any body is truly and simply one? All are changed by passing from form to form or from place to place and consist of parts each occupying its own place and extended in space. True equality and similitude, true and primal unity, are not perceived by the eye of flesh or by any

bodily sense, but are known by the mind. How is equality of any kind demanded in bodies, and how are we convinced that any equality that may be seen there is far different from perfect equality, unless the mind sees that which is perfect? If indeed that which is not made (*facta*) can be called perfect (*perfecta*).

56. All things which are beautiful to the senses, whether they are produced by nature or are worked out by the arts, have a spatial or temporal beauty, as for example the body and its movements. But the equality and unity which are known only by the mind, and according to which the mind judges of corporeal beauty by the intermediary of the senses, are not extended in space or unstable in time. It would be wrong to say that a wheel can be judged to be round by this standard, while a little jar cannot, or a jar can but a penny cannot. So in the case of times and motions of corporeal things, it would be ridiculous to say that years can be judged by any standard to be of equal length but months cannot, or that months can and days cannot. Whether a proper movement occupies a larger space of time or is measured by hours or brief minutes, all are judged by one and the same standard of changeless equality. If greater and smaller movements and spatial figures are all judged according to the same standard of equality or similitude or fitness, the standard is greater than all of them in potency. But it is neither greater nor less in a spatial or a temporal sense. If it were greater we should not use the whole of it to judge things that are less. If it were smaller we could not use it to judge things that are larger. As it is, we use the absolute standard of squareness to judge the squareness of a marketplace, a stone, a table or a gem. And we use the absolute standard of equality to judge the movements of the feet of a running ant and those of an elephant on the march. Who then can doubt that it is neither greater nor less in a spatial or temporal sense, but in potency surpasses all else? This standard of all the arts is absolutely unchangeable, but the human mind, which is given the power to see the standard, can suffer the mutability of error. Clearly, then, the standard which is called truth is higher than our minds.

CHAPTER 31:57. We must not have any doubt that the unchangeable substance which is above the rational mind is God. The primal life and primal essence is where the primal wisdom is. This is unchangeable truth which is the law of all the arts and the art of the omnipotent artificer. In perceiving that it cannot judge

70

by itself the form and movement of bodies, the soul ought at the same time to realize that its nature excels the nature of what it judges, but also that it is excelled by the nature according to which it judges and concerning which it cannot judge. I can say why the corresponding members of a single body, one on the one side and the other on the other, ought to be alike, because I delight in absolute equality which I behold not with the bodily eyes but with the mind. And therefore I judge that things seen with the eyes are better the nearer they are in their own kind to the things which I know with my mind. No one can say why these intelligible things should be as they are; and no one in his sober senses should say that they ought to be as they are, as if they could be otherwise.

 58. No one, if he rightly understands the matter, will venture to say why intelligible things please us, and why when we are wise we earnestly love them. As we and all rational souls rightly judge of inferior creatures when we judge according to truth, so truth alone judges of us when we cleave to it. Not even the Father judges of truth, for it is not less than he is. What the Father judges he judges by means of the truth. All things which seek unity have this rule, or form or example, or whatever it is to be called. For unity alone bears the whole similitude of him from whom it has received existence, if it is not incongruous to say "it has received existence" in view of the significance which attaches to the word Son. In any case it derives its existence not from itself but from the first and highest principle which is called the Father: "from whom the whole family in heaven and on earth is named." (Eph. 3:15) "The Father therefore judgeth no man, but hath given all judgment to the Son." (John 5:22) "The spiritual man judgeth all things and is himself judged of none" (I Cor. 2:15), that is by no man, but only by the law according to which he judges all things. Wherefore it is most truly said "we must all appear before the judgment throne of Christ." (II Cor. 5:10) He judges all things because he is above all when he is with God. He is with God when he knows most purely and loves what he knows with all charity. Accordingly, the law is that according to which he judges all things and concerning which no man can judge. In the case of temporal laws, men have instituted them and judge by them, and when they have been instituted and confirmed no judge may judge them but must judge according to them. He who draws up temporal laws, if he is a good and wise man, takes eternal life into account, and that no soul may judge. He determines for the time being what is to be commanded and for-

71

bidden according to the immutable rules of eternal life. Pure souls may rightly know the eternal law but may not judge it. The difference is that, for knowing, it is enough to see that a thing is *so* and not *so*. For judging, it is necessary in addition to see that a thing can be thus or not thus; as when we say it ought to be thus, or to have been thus, or to be thus in the future, as workmen do with their works.

CHAPTER 32:59. But many stop with what delights men and are unwilling to rise to higher things, so that they may judge why visible things give pleasure. If I ask a workman why, after constructing one arch, he builds another like it over against it, he will reply, I dare say, that in a building like parts must correspond to like. If I go further and ask why he thinks so, he will say that it is fitting, or beautiful, or that it gives pleasure to those who behold it. But he will venture not further. He will bow and direct his eyes downward and not understand the cause for all this. But if I have to do with a man with inward eyes who can see the invisible, I shall not cease to press the query why these things give pleasure, so that he may dare to be the judge of human pleasure. He transcends it and escapes from its control in judging pleasure and not according to pleasure. First I shall ask him whether things are beautiful because they give pleasure, or give pleasure because they are beautiful. Then I shall ask him why they are beautiful, and if he is perplexed, I shall add the question whether it is because its parts correspond and are so joined together as to form one harmonious whole.

60. When he sees that that is so, I shall ask whether they completely achieve the unity they aim at, or fall far short of it, and in a measure misrepresent it. No one who is put on his guard can fail to see that there is no form or material thing which does not have some trace of unity, or that no material thing however beautiful can possibly achieve the unity it aims at, since it must necessarily have its parts separated by intervals of space. If this is so, I shall ask him to tell me where he sees that unity, and what is its source; and if he cannot see it, how does he know what it is that material things imitate but cannot completely achieve? If he says of material things: You would not exist unless some kind of unity held you together, but on the other hand if you were unity itself you would not be material things. The correct reply would be: Whence have you acquired the knowledge of unity according to which you judge material things? Unless

you had seen it you would not be able to judge that they come short of it. You would not be right to say that you see it with your bodily eyes, although things do show traces of it, but they come nowhere near it. With the bodily eyes you see nothing but corporeal things. Therefore it is with the mind that we see true unity. But where? If it were here where our body is, it would not be visible to a man who in eastern parts judges in the same way about corporeal things. It is not, then, circumscribed by space. It is present wherever anyone judges in this way. It is nowhere present spatially, but its potency is nowhere absent.

CHAPTER 33:61. If corporeal things are deceptive of unity, we must not trust things that deceive, lest we fall into the vanities of them that are vain. Since they deceive by appearing to show to the eye of flesh the unity which is seen by the mind alone, we must rather ask whether they deceive by resembling unity or in failing to achieve unity. If they achieved it they would be completely identical with what they imitate. In that case there would be no difference at all. If that were so there would be no deception. They would be exactly what unity is. In any case, if you consider the matter closely they do not actively deceive. He is a deceiver who wants to appear what he is not. He who, without willing it, is thought to be other than he is, is not a deceiver but simply causes mistakes. This is how a deceiver is distinguished from one who causes mistakes. Every deceiver has the will to deceive, whether he is believed or not. But mistakes can be caused by one who has no intention to deceive. Therefore a corporeal form, which can have no will of its own, does not deceive. Nor does it cause mistakes if it is not thought to be what is is not.

62. Even the eyes do not cause mistakes, for they can report nothing to the mind except what they actually see. If not only the eyes but also all bodily senses report simply as they are affected, I know not what more we ought to expect of them. If there are no vain people there will be no vanity. Anyone who thinks that the oar is broken in the water and is restored when it is taken out has nothing wrong with his senses, but he is a bad judge of what they convey to him. By nature he could have seen nothing else in the water, nor ought he to have seen anything else. Air and water differ, so it is proper that sensations should be different according as they relate to things in air and in water. So the eye does its duty correctly, for it was made simply to see. But the mind operates perversely, for it and not the eye was made

to contemplate supreme beauty. Such a man as we have been speaking of wants to turn his mind to corporeal things and his eyes to God. He seeks to know carnal things and to see spiritual things. But that is impossible.

CHAPTER 34:63. That perversity must be corrected. Otherwise things are all out of order, up is down and down is up. Such a man will not be fit for the kingdom of heaven. Do not let us seek the highest in the lowest, nor cleave to the lowest. Let us judge these things lest we be judged along with them. Let us attribute to them no more than, as lowest forms, they deserve, lest seeking the first in the last, we be numbered with the last instead of with the first. That is no disadvantage to these lowest things but is a great disadvantage to us. The divine providential government is not on that account any less fitting because the unjust are put in their just place and the foul are fairly dealt with. If the beauty of visible things causes us to make mistakes because it consists in unity but does not completely achieve unity, let us understand if we can that the mistake arises not from what they are but from what they are not. Every corporeal thing is a true body but a false unity. For it is not supremely one and does not completely imitate unity. And yet it would not be a body either if it did not have some unity. Besides it could have no unity unless it derived it from supreme unity.

64. . . . If there is one sun, that is a false one which I conjure up in thought, for the real sun pursues its course in its appointed place and time. The imaginary sun I place where and when I will. If my friend is one, I conjure up a false image. I do not know where the real one is, but the imaginary one is where I like to put him. I myself am one person, and I feel that my body is here, but in imagination I go where I like and speak to whom I like. These imaginary things are false, and what is false cannot be known. When I contemplate them and believe in them, I do not have knowledge, because what I contemplate with the intelligence must be true, and not by any possibility what are commonly called phantasms. Whence, then, is my mind full of illusions? Where is the truth which the mind beholds? It can be replied to one who thinks in this way that that is the true light which enables you to know that these things are not true. By the true light you see the unity whereby you judge whatever you see to be one. But it is quite a different thing from any mutable thing you can see. . . .

CHAPTER 36:66. Whoever clearly sees that falsehood is thinking something is what it is not, knows that truth is that which declares what it is. If material things deceive us in so far as they fall short of the unity which they demonstrably imitate, we naturally approve them; for that is the principle from which all unity derives, and to resemble which all things strive. We equally disapprove all that departs from unity and tends towards its opposite. We can understand that there is something so resembling the sole unity and principle of all unity that it coincides with it and is identical with it. This is truth, the Word that was in the beginning (*in principio*), the divine Word that was with God. If falsehood springs from things which imitate unity, not in so far as they imitate it but in so far as they cannot achieve it, the truth which does achieve it, and is identical with it, is unity and manifests unity as it is in reality. Hence, it is rightly called unity's Word and Light. Other things may be said to be like unity in so far as they have being, and so far they are also true. But this is itself the complete likeness of unity and is therefore truth. Truth makes all things true which are true, and likeness makes things like which are alike. Truth is the form of all things which are true, and likeness of all things which are alike. Since things are true in so far as they have being and have being in so far as they resemble the source of all unity, that is, the form of all things that have being, which is the supreme likeness of the principle. It is also perfect truth because it is without any unlikeness.

67. Falsehood arises not because things deceive us, for they can show the beholder nothing but their form, and that they have received according to their position in the scale of beauty. Nor do the senses deceive us, for when they are in contact with natural objects they report to their presiding mind nothing but the impression formed upon them. It is sin which deceives souls, when they seek something that is true but abandon or neglect truth. They love the works of the artificer more than the artificer or his art and are punished by falling into the error of expecting to find the artificer and his art in his works, and when they cannot do so they think that the works are both the art and the artificer. God is not offered to the corporeal senses and transcends even the mind. . . .

CHAPTER 39:72. What obstacle then remains to hinder the soul from recalling the primal beauty which it abandoned, when it can make an end of its vices? The wisdom of God extends from end to end with might. By wisdom the great Artificer knit his works together with one glorious end in view. His goodness has no grudging envy against any beauty from the highest to the lowest, for none can have being except from him alone. So that no one is utterly cast away from the truth who has in him the slightest vestige of truth. What is it about bodily pleasure that holds us fast? You will find that it is agreeableness. Disagreeable things beget grief and agreeable things beget pleasure. Seek therefore the highest agreeableness. Do not go abroad. Return within yourself. In the inward man dwells truth. If you find that you are by nature mutable, transcend yourself. But remember in doing so that you must also transcend yourself even as a reasoning soul. Make for the place where the light of reason is kindled. What does every good reasoner attain but truth? And yet truth is not reached by reasoning but is itself the goal of all who reason. There is an agreeableness than which there can be no greater. Agree, then, with it. Confess that you are not as it is. It has to do no seeking, but you reach it by seeking, not in space but by a disposition of mind, so that the inward man may agree with the indwelling truth in a pleasure that is not low and carnal but supremely spiritual.

73. If you do not grasp what I say and doubt whether it is true, at least make up your mind whether you have any doubt about your doubts. If it is certain that you do indeed have doubts, inquire whence comes that certainty. It will never occur to you to imagine that it comes from the light of the sun, but rather from that "true light which lighteth every man that cometh into the world." It cannot be seen with these eyes, nor with the eyes which seem to see the phantasms of the brain, but with those that can say to phantasms: You are not the thing I am seeking. Nor are you the standard by which I put you in your rightful place, disapproving of all that is base in you, and approving of all that is beautiful. The standard according to which I approve and disapprove is still more beautiful, so I approve more highly of it and prefer it not only to you but to all those bodily shapes from which you spring. Now think of the rule in this way. Everyone who knows that he has doubts knows with certainty something that is true, namely, that he doubts. He is certain, therefore, about *a* truth. Therefore everyone who doubts whether there be such a thing as *the* truth has at least *a* truth to set a limit to his doubt; and nothing can be true except truth be in it. Accordingly, no one ought to have doubts about the existence of *the* truth, even if

doubts arise for him from every possible quarter. Wherever this is seen, there is light that transcends space and time and all phantasms that spring from spatial and temporal things. Could this be in the least destroyed even if every reasoner should perish or grow old among inferior carnal things? Reasoning does not create truth but discovers it. Before it is discovered it abides in itself; and when it is discovered it renews us.

FREEDOM OF THE WILL ✠ BOOK II ✠ CHAPTER 2:

5 ... *A.* At least you are certain that God exists?
E. Even that I do not hold by reason but by steadfast faith.
A. If then one of those fools of whom it is written: *The fool hath said in his heart, There is no God* (Ps. 13:1) should say this to you and not be willing to believe what you believe but want to know whether you were believing the truth would you leave the man, or would you think that in some way he should be persuaded of what you so firmly believe, especially if he had the will not to oppose it obstinately but wished eagerly to know?
E. What you said last advises me well enough as to how I should answer him. For however unreasonable he might be, he would admit that nothing whatever, and least of all so great a matter, should be argued about insincerely or with obstinacy. This granted, he would first try to convince me that he was asking in good faith, and that he had no hidden guile or obstinacy about the matter.

Then I should show (as I think anyone could easily do) that since he himself was demanding that matters hidden in his own mind be believed by another who did not know them, that it would be only reasonable for him to believe that God exists, from the books of those great men who have left written testimony that they lived with the Son of God and who have written also of things seen by them which could not possibly be if there were no God: and he would be a simple fellow indeed to criticize me for believing those men when he wanted me to believe him. But that which he could not rightly object to he could in no wise make an excuse for his unwillingness to imitate.
A. If then, as to whether God exists, it is enough for you that it should not seem unreasonable to believe those great men, why, pray, do you not think we should likewise take on the authority

77

of those same men all those other things which we subjected to inquiry as if they were unsure and not clearly known? We should then have to trouble no further to examine them.

E. But that which we believe, we desire also to know and to understand.

6. *A.* You remember rightly; we cannot go back on the position we took at the beginning of our former discussion. For believing is one thing; and understanding, another; and we must first believe whatever great and divine matter we desire to understand. Else would the Prophet have said in error, *Except ye believe, ye shall not understand.* (Isa. 7:9) Then too our Lord himself, both by His words and His acts, exhorted those whom He called to salvation to first believe. But afterwards, when He spoke of the gift itself that was to be given to believers, He did not say, "This moreover is eternal life, that ye believe," but, *This is life eternal, that they might know thee the only true God, and Jesus Christ, whom thou has sent.* (John 17:3) Again, He says to believers, *Seek, and ye shall find.* (Matt. 7:7) But one cannot speak of that being found which is believed without knowledge, nor does anyone become prepared to find God who does not first believe that which he is afterward to know. Wherefore, following our Lord's precepts, let us seek earnestly. For what He himself encourages us to seek, that same shall we find by His showing, so far as such things may be found in this life and by such as we. For it is to be believed that these things are seen more clearly and known more perfectly by those better than we, even while they live on earth, and certainly by the good and pious after this life. And so we must hope it will be with us, and despising things earthly and mortal must love and desire these things in every way.

CHAPTER 3 *That it may become evident that God exists, it is inquired what is most excellent in man.*

7. *A.* Let us then pursue the following order of inquiry: first, how it is manifest that God is; next, whether goods, whatsoever their kind or degree, are from Him; finally, whether free will is to be accounted a good. When we have answered these it will be clear enough, I think, whether free will was rightly given to man. Wherefore, in order that we may take our start from the most obvious things, I ask you whether you yourself exist, or whether you think you may be under an illusion as to that; although surely if you did not exist, you could not possibly have an illusion.

E. Go on rather to other matters.

A. It is evident, then, that you exist; and since that could not be evident unless you were living, it is also evident that you live. Do you understand that these two things are very true?

E. I understand thoroughly.

A. Therefore this third thing is evident; you understand.

E. It is evident.

A. Which of these three do you think is most excellent?

E. Understanding.

A. Why do you think so?

E. Because while there are three things: to exist, to live, to understand; even a stone exists, and a beast lives, yet I do not think that a stone lives, or that a beast understands. But he who understands assuredly both exists and lives; wherefore, I do not hesitate to judge that one more excellent, in which all three are present, than that in which two or one are lacking. For though what lives certainly also exists, it does not follow that it also understands: of such sort, I judge, is the life of the beast. If something exists, moreover, it by no means follows that it lives and understands; for I may acknowledge that a corpse exists, but no one would say that it lives. But if the thing does not live, much less does it understand.

A. We see then that of these three, two are wanting to the corpse, one to the beast, and none to man.

E. True.

A. We also hold that to be most excellent of the three which man has with the two others; namely, understanding, whose possession implies both existence and life.

E. Surely.

8. *A.* Tell me now, whether you know that you have those everyday bodily senses: seeing, and hearing, and smelling, and tasting, and touching.

E. I do.

A. What do you think pertains to the sense of sight; I mean what do you think we perceive by sight?

E. Anything corporeal.

A. Do you think we also perceive hardness and softness by sight?

E. No.

A. What then properly pertains to the eyes, and is perceived by them?

E. Color.

A. What to the ears?

E. Sound.

A. What to smell?

E. Odor.

A. What to taste?

E. Flavor.

A. What to touch?

E. Softness and hardness, smoothness and roughness, and many such things.

A. How about the shapes of bodies: large, small, square, round, and such? Do we not perceive them both by touch and by sight, so that we cannot properly assign them either to touch or sight alone but only to both?

E. That is clear.

A. You see then that certain senses have individually their own proper objects about which they tell us, and that certain others have some objects in common.

E. I see that too.

A. Now can we by means of any of these senses distinguish what is proper to each sense, and what all or certain senses have in common?

E. By no means: we judge that by a sort of interior sense.

A. Is that perhaps reason itself, which the beasts have not? For it is by reason, I think, that we grasp these things, and so know that we have senses.

E. I think rather that by reason we comprehend that there is a certain interior sense, to which all things are referred by the five ordinary senses. For the sense by which a beast sees is one thing; and that by which it seeks or avoids what it perceives by sight, is another; for the first sense is in the eyes, but that other is in the soul itself. By it animals seek and appropriate what they like and avoid and reject what they do not; not only what they see, but what they hear or perceive by the other senses. Nor can this sense be called sight or hearing or smell or taste or touch; it is something other that presides over all of them together. While we comprehend this by reason, as I have said, we cannot nevertheless call it reason, since the beasts also evidently have it.

9. *A.* I recognize that, whatever it is, and do not hesitate to call it the interior sense. But unless it goes beyond what is brought to us by our bodily senses, it cannot attain to knowledge. For

what we know, we hold in the grasp of reason. But, not to mention other things, we know that we cannot perceive colors by hearing nor voices by sight. And when we know this, we know it neither by our eyes nor by our ears nor by that interior sense which the beasts also have. For one cannot believe that they know that ears do not perceive light nor eyes voices, since we discern such things only by rational attention and thought.

E. I cannot say that I see that clearly. For what if they do discern also by that interior sense, which you admit they have, that colors cannot be perceived by hearing nor voices by sight?

A. Well, do you think that they can distinguish from one another the color that is perceived and the sense that is in the eye and that interior sense within the soul and the reason by which these are defined and enumerated one by one?

E. By no means.

A. Could reason, then, distinguish these four from one another and set bounds to them by definitions, if color were not referred to it by the sense of the eyes and that sensation again by the interior sense by itself, assuming that there is not yet another something interposed?

E. I do not see how else it could.

A. And do you see that color is perceived by the sense of the eyes, but that the sensation itself is not perceived by the same sense? For you do not see the seeing itself by the same sense by which you see color.

E. Not at all.

A. Try also to distinguish these; for I think you will not deny that color is one thing; and seeing color, another, and that it is yet another, when color is not present, to have the sense by which it could be seen if it were present.

E. I distinguish those too and grant that they are different.

A. Do you see any of these three with your eyes, except color?

E. Nothing else.

A. Tell me then how do you see the other two; for if you did not see them, you could not distinguish them.

E. I know nothing further. I know that I do, nothing more.

A. You do not know then whether this is reason itself or that life which we call the interior sense, which is superior to the bodily senses, or something else?

E. No.

A. You know at least that these things can be defined only by reason and that reason cannot do this unless they are presented to it for examination.

E. That is true.

A. Whatever, therefore, that other thing is, by means of which we perceive everything that we know, it is in the service of reason, to which it presents and reports whatever it touches, so that the things perceived may be distinguished by their properties and grasped not merely for perception but for knowledge as well.

E. That is so.

A. Well, how about this reason, which distinguishes from one another its servants and the things they bring before it, and likewise recognizes the difference between itself and these things and assures itself of its superiority to them? Does it comprehend itself by means of anything other than itself, that is, reason? Or would you know that you had reason if you did not perceive it by reason?

E. Most true.

A. So then, when we perceive a color we do not likewise by the sense itself perceive that we perceive; nor when we hear a sound do we also hear our hearing; nor when we smell a rose has the smelling fragrance too; nor tasting something does the tasting itself have flavor in the mouth; nor touching a thing can we also touch the sense of touch. Therefore it is clear that those five senses cannot be perceived by any one sense among them, although by them all corporeal things are perceived.

E. That is clear.

CHAPTER 4 *The interior sense perceives that it perceives; whether it also distinguishes itself or not.*

10. *A.* I think it is clear that the interior sense perceives not only the things referred to it by the five senses but also the sensations themselves. For otherwise an animal would not stir, either to pursue or to run away from anything, if it did not perceive that it had the sensation—not as knowledge, for that is reason's province, but only in order to move—which it certainly does not perceive by any one of those five. If this is still not clear, it will become clear by considering some one sense, say sight. For one could not open his eyes or turn his gaze upon what he seeks to see, unless when his eyes were closed, or not turned toward it, he perceived that he did not see. But if, not seeing, he perceives that he does not see, he must also perceive that he sees when he

does see; for the fact that when he sees a thing he does not move his eyes in search of it shows that he perceives both.

But whether this life that perceives that it perceives corporeal things perceives itself too, is not so clear; except that anyone who looks within himself finds that every living thing flees death. But since death is the opposite of life, it must be that life perceives itself, since it flees its own opposite. But if this be still not clear, let us pass it over, so that we may move on toward our goal only by evidence that is certain and manifest. For this much is clear: we perceive corporeal things by our bodily senses, but we cannot by the sense itself perceive a sense. By the interior sense we perceive both that we are perceiving corporeal things through the bodily sense and also the bodily sense itself. But by reason all those other things and also reason itself become known and are held together in knowledge. Is this clear to you?

E. Perfectly clear.

A. Tell me now, how did this problem arise, over which, in our search for a solution, we have tarried so long on this road?

CHAPTER 5 *The interior sense is superior to the external senses, of which it is a regulator and judge.*

11. *E.* So far as I recall, we are still considering the first of those three questions which we proposed a little while ago in arranging the order of this discussion; namely, how can that be made evident which we must anyhow believe most firmly and steadfastly—that God exists.

A. You are quite right. But I want you also to keep carefully in mind that when I asked you whether you knew that you yourself existed, not only was that clear to us but also two other propositions.

E. I remember that too.

A. See now to which of those three you think pertains everything that is touched by our bodily senses; that is, under which head would you put whatever reaches our senses through the eyes or through any other instrument of the body. Is it in the class which just exists or in that which also lives or in that which also understands?

E. In that which just exists.

A. How about the sense itself? In which class of the three do you think it is?

E. In that which lives.

A. Which now of these two do you judge to be the better: the sense itself or what the sense perceives?

E. The sense, of course.

A. Why?

E. Because that which lives is better than that which merely is.

12. *A.* How about the interior sense? It is below reason, to be sure, and our earlier investigations have shown that we share it with the beasts. But would you hesitate to rank it above the senses by which we perceive bodies and which you have just said are to be ranked above the bodies themselves?

E. I should not hestiate at all.

A. I should like also to hear from you why you do not hesitate. For you will not be able to say now that the interior sense should be put in that one of the three classes which also understands, but it must still go in the class that exists and lives, albeit without understanding; for the beasts, who have no understanding, have this sense. This being the case, I ask why you prefer the interior sense to the sense by which bodies are perceived, since both belong to the class that lives. For you placed the sense by which we perceive bodies above those bodies because they are in the class that merely exists, while it is in the class that also lives; so that when you find the interior sense also in that class, tell me why you think it superior. For you say it is because the one perceives the other, I do not believe you will be able to find a rule by which we can establish that everything that perceives is better than that which is perceived by it, lest perhaps we should thence be constrained to say that everything that understands is better than that which is understood by it. But this is false: because man understands wisdom, but he is not better than wisdom itself. See, therefore, for what reason it appears to you that the interior sense is to be preferred to those senses by which we perceive bodies.

E. Because I perceive the former to be a sort of regulator and judge of the latter. For if anything is lacking in the performance of its office, it is demanded of it as a service owing, as was argued a little while ago. For the sense of the eyes does not see that it sees or that it does not see; and not seeing this, cannot judge what is lacking or what is sufficient. But the interior sense tells the soul of the beast when to open closed eyes, and perceives when they are supplied with what was lacking. But there is no doubt that he who judges is superior to him whom he judges.

A. Do you see too that those bodily senses also judge of bodies after a fashion? For pleasure and pain are their affairs, as when they are touched gently or roughly by a body. For just as the interior sense judges what is lacking or sufficient in the sense of the eyes, so the sense itself of the eyes judges what is lacking or sufficient in colors. So too, just as the interior sense judges our hearing, whether or not it be sufficiently alert, our hearing itself judges of voices, when they breathe softly, and when they grate harshly. There is no need to run through the other bodily senses, for now you perceive, I think, what I want to say: namely, that the interior sense judges those bodily senses, approving their integrity or demanding what they owe; and in like manner the bodily senses themselves judge of bodies, appropriating their light touch and rejecting the opposite.

E. I see clearly and most heartily agree.

CHAPTER 6 *Reason is more excellent than all else in man: if there is anything more excellent, it is God.*

13. *A.* Consider now whether reason judges the interior sense. For I do not ask whether you think it is better, because I have no doubt that you do—though for that matter I do not think it need be asked whether reason judges this sense. For in those very things that are below it, that is, in bodies and the bodily senses and in the interior sense, what indeed but reason tells us how one thing is better than another, and that it itself is superior to them; and this it certainly could not do if it did not judge them.

E. That is evident.

A. Since, therefore, a nature that neither lives nor understands but only is, such as a dead body, is surpassed by a nature such as the soul of a beast, which not only is but lives too, though it does not understand; and this again is surpassed by one that is and lives and understands, such as the rational mind of man; do you think you can discover in us, that is, among those things that go to make up our nature as men, anything more excellent than that which we have placed highest among these three? For it is clear that we have a body and a certain vital principle by which that body lives and grows, which two we recognize also in the beasts; and a third something which the beast's nature has not—a sort of head or eye of the soul, not to think of a more appropriate name for reason and understanding. So pray see whether you can find anything in man's nature higher than reason.

E. I see nothing at all better.

14. *A.* What if we could find something of which you were sure,

not only that it exists, but also that it is more excellent than our reason? Would you hesitate, whatever it might be, to call it God?

E. I do not see why, if I can find something that is better than what is best in my own nature, I should say that it is God: for I do not like to call that God which to my own reason is inferior, but only Him than Whom none is higher.

A. Clearly so: for He himself has given to this reason of yours the power to feel thus reverently and truly about Him. But, I would ask, if you find nothing above our reason but what is eternal and changeless, would you hesitate to call that God? For you know that bodies are changeable; and clearly the very life that animates the body is subject to change with changing conditions; and reason itself, now striving to attain the truth and anon not striving, sometimes attaining it and again not attaining it, is clearly shown to be mutable. So, if without the use of any of the body's instruments—not touch, nor taste, nor smell, nor ears, nor eyes, nor any sense inferior to it, but by itself alone—reason discovers something eternal and immutable, and sees itself as lower, it should acknowledge that to be its God.

E. That one will I plainly acknowledge to be God, than Whom nothing is proved to be higher.

A. Well said. It will be enough then if I show that there is something of that sort, so that you will acknowledge it to be God; or if there is something higher, you will grant that that is God. So that whether there be anything higher or not, it will be proved that God exists when I shall have shown you, with His help, what I assured you was higher than reason.

E. Show me then what you promise.

CHAPTER 7 *How the same thing may be perceived by many, either entire or not entire, and at the same time by different persons.*

15. *A.* I will do so. But I would first ask whether my bodily senses are the same as yours, or whether mine are in fact mine alone; and yours, yours alone; for if this were not the case I could not see anything with my eyes which you did not see.

E. I concede fully that though they are the same in kind, we have each of us his own personal senses—sight, hearing, and all the others. For one man can not only see but hear what another does not and perceive by any other sense you will what another does not perceive. Whence it is evident that your senses are yours alone, and mine are mine alone.

A. Would you say the same about the interior sense too, or is there a difference?

E. No difference, surely. For certainly my own interior sense perceives my sensations, and yours perceives yours; so that I am frequently asked by someone who sees something whether I too see it, because only I perceive whether I see it or not, not he who asks me.

A. How about reason: has not each one of us his own? For it may happen that I understand something that you do not; and you cannot know whether I understand, but I know.

E. It is evident that we have each of us individually his own rational mind.

16. *A.* But now will you be able to say too that we have each individual suns which we see or moons or morning stars or such like things; even though it be true that each sees them through his own individual sense?

E. I would never say that.

A. Many of us, therefore, can see one thing at the same time, while the senses through which we perceive the one thing that we see together are separate and individual; so that while my sense is one and yours is another, it can nevertheless happen that what we see is not one mine and another yours, but a single thing, appearing to both of us and seen simultaneously by both.

E. That is very evident.

A. Also we may hear simultaneously some one voice; and although my hearing is one and yours another, yet the voice we hear is not one voice for me and another for you, but whatever has sounded is simultaneously present to both of us as a single and undivided thing to be heard.

E. That too is evident.

17. *A.* But now as to the other bodily senses you must note what we are saying: that in what touches this matter they neither act altogether like those two of the eyes and ears, nor altogether unlike them. For you and I can fill our nostrils from the same air and perceive its condition by its odor, and likewise can both taste of one honeycomb or any other food or drink, and perceive its condition by its flavor; and though it is one, our sensations are separate, yours for you and mine for me, so that while we both perceive the same odor or flavor, you do not perceive by my sense

nor I by yours, nor by any sense that might be common to both of us; but my sense is utterly mine, and yours is yours, although one odor or one flavor is perceived by both. In this respect, therefore, these two senses are found to have something like those other two, seeing and hearing. But in what pertains to the matter in hand they differ in this: that although we both draw in one air through our nostrils or take one food in tasting, I do not nevertheless breathe that part of the air which you breathe nor take the same part of the food as you, but I take one part and you another; so that when I breathe of the whole air I draw in a part such as suffices me, and you likewise from the whole draw in another sufficiency for yourself; and though one entire repast is eaten by both of us, nevertheless it cannot be eaten entire by me and also entire by you, in the way that I hear a whole word and you the same whole word at the same time, or as what I see of any view you too see at the same time; but of food or drink one part must pass into me and another into you. But perhaps this is not clear to you!

E. Nay, rather it is most clear and indubitable.

18. *A.* Do you think now that the sense of touch is to be compared to the senses of the eyes and ears, as regards the question before us? For not only can we both perceive one body by touching it, but you too can touch the same part of the body I have touched, so that we can both perceive by our touch not only the same body but the same part of that body. For with touching it is not the case as with something edible set before us, where you and I cannot both take all when we both eat of it; but the same undivided thing that I touch you too can touch, so that we both touch not each a part but each the whole.

E. I admit that in this way the sense of touch is very like those other two. But it seems unlike in this respect; namely, that both of us can at one and the same time see or hear one entire thing: we can indeed also touch at the same time one entire object but in different parts—the same part, however, only at different times; for I can put my touch on no part which you are touching until you remove your hand.

19. *A.* Carefully answered—but since, of all the things that we perceive, there are some which both, some which each one individually may perceive, you ought to see this too: our sensations themselves are indeed perceived only individually, so that neither I perceive your sensation, nor you mine. As regards those things which we perceive with our bodily senses, what we cannot perceive

both, but only individually, is only that which so becomes our own that we can change it and turn it into ourselves; like food and drink, of which no part that I digest can you too digest. . . .

Other sensible things we may perceive as we will, without thereby destroying them and changing them into our bodies. There we may both perceive, either at the same time or by turns at different times, so that either the whole or the part that I perceive is perceived by you also; such are light or sound or bodies that we touch without injuring them.

E. I understand.

A. It is clear, then, that those things which we do not change and yet perceive by our bodily senses do not belong to the nature of our senses and hence are more our common possession, because they are not changed into something that is ours exclusively.

E. I thoroughly agree.

A. Therefore that is to be regarded as our own and as it were private possession which is of each one of us alone, and which he alone perceives within himself because it pertains properly to his own nature. That, however, is common and, so to speak, public, which is perceived by all percipients without any change or destruction.

E. Just so.

CHAPTER 8 *The reason of numbers is perceived by no bodily sense; by anyone who understands it, it is perceived as one and immutable.*

20. *A.* Consider now and tell me whether you can find anything which all men, each reasoning with his own mind and reason, may see in common; while that which they see is present to all and is not converted to the use of those to whom it is present, as are food and drink, but remains whole and uncorrupted, whether they see it or do not see it. Or would you perhaps think that there is nothing of this sort?

E. On the contrary, I think there are many, of which it is enough to mention one. For the reason and truth of numbers waits upon all who reason, so that every calculator may see it, each with his own reason and endeavor to grasp it with his understanding. And one will do so easily, another with more difficulty, and yet another will be quite unable; although notwithstanding it offers itself to all who have the power to grasp it; nor is it changed and transmuted when anyone perceives it into nutriment as it were for the perceiver, nor when one makes a mistake in it is it thereby less; but while it remains true and whole, he is the more in error the less he perceives it.

21. *A.* Quite right: but I see that you answered readily as if not unversed in these things. Nevertheless, if some one should say that these numbers are as it were certain images of visible things impressed on our mind, not by any nature of their own but by those things that are reached by the senses of the body,—what would you answer? Or do you too think that?

E. I should by no means think that. For even if I have perceived numbers by a bodily sense, I cannot thereby perceive by a bodily sense the ratios of partition and combination of numbers. For by this light of the mind I refute him who gives a false result in calculation, either by addition or subtraction. And I do not know for how long will endure anything that I touch with my bodily senses, such as this sky and this earth, and whatever other bodies I perceive in them. But seven and three are ten, not only now but always; nor was there ever a time when seven and three were not ten, nor will ever be a time when seven and three will not be ten. I say, therefore, that this incorruptible truth of number is common to me and to any reasoning person whatsoever.

22. *A.* I do not oppose you when you answer so truly and indisputably. But you may also easily see that numbers are not derived from our bodily senses, if you will consider, as to any number, that as many times as it contains one, so many is it called. For example, if it contains one twice it is called two; if thrice, three; and if it contains one ten times it is called ten; and the number of times any number whatever contains one gives it its name, and it is called so much. But anyone who considers the matter aright will certainly find that we cannot perceive one by our bodily senses. For whatever reaches us through such a sense is clearly seen to be not one but many; for it is body, and therefore has innumerable parts. For—not to trace out finer and even finer divisions—however tiny a particle that body may be, it has certainly a right part and a left part, a top and a bottom, a front and a back, or an outside and an inside; for we might acknowledge that these are present in any body, however tiny its dimensions, and hence we must concede that no body is truly and simply one; although we nevertheless could not enumerate such a many without a separate and distinct knowledge of one. For when I look for one in a body and when I have no doubt that I do not find it, I know assuredly what I seek there, and what I do not

find there, and what cannot be found there, or rather what is not there at all. But whenever I know one, I certainly do not know this through my bodily senses, because by the bodily senses we know only body, which we have proved to be not one, pure and simple.

Moreover, if we do not perceive one by a sense of the body, we do not perceive any number by that sense, so far at least as concerns those numbers that we discern by our understanding. For there is no one of them that does not get its name from the number of times it contains one; and one is not perceived by the bodily sense. For the half of any particle makes up a whole of two such halves and has also its half; therefore, those two parts are in the body in such a way that they are not simply two. But on the other hand the *number* that we call two because it contains twice that which is simply one, its half part, is something which is itself simply one, and cannot have a half or a third or any part whatsoever, because it is simply and truly one.

23. Then again, whereas taking the numbers in order, after one we get two, which comparing with one we find to be its double; the double of two does not follow in immediate succession, but four, which is the double of two, follows after the interposition of three. And this rule extends to all the other numbers by a most certain and immutable law: that after one, that is after the first of all the numbers, itself excepted, the first is that which contains it twice; for two follows one. But after the second number, that is after two, it is the second, itself excepted, that is the double of it; for the first after two is three and the second four, the double of the second number. After the third, that is after three, it is the third, itself excepted, that is the double of it; for after the third, that is to say three, the first is four, the second five, and the third six, which is the double of three. So again after the fourth it is the fourth, itself excepted, that is its double; for after the fourth, that is four, the first is five, the second six, the third seven, and the fourth eight, which is the double of four. And so throughout all the other numbers you will find this that has been found in the first pair of numbers, that is, in one and two: that the double of any number is just as many numbers after it as that number itself is from the very beginning.

But now when we perceive this thing to be for all numbers fixed and inviolate, whence comes this perception? For no one has touched all numbers by any sense of the body, for they are innumerable. Whence then do we know this for all or by what so sure an appearance or image do we know so confidently this truth of number throughout things innumerable, if we do not perceive it by that inner light which the sense of the body knows not?

24. By this and many like proofs, those to whom God has given an inquiring mind and who are not blinded by obstinacy, are compelled to acknowledge that the reason and truth of numbers is not related to the bodily sense, and that it is established pure and unalterable for all reasoning men to see in common. Wherefore, while many other things might be thought of which are present and as it were public to reasoning men, and which remain inviolate and changeless while they are perceived by the mind and reason of each individual perceiver; I was yet by no means sorry that the reason and truth of numbers was what first came to your mind when you wished to answer my question. For not for nothing is number joined to wisdom in the Sacred Books, where it is said: *I and my heart have gone round, that I might know, and consider, and inquire the wisdom and the number.* (Eccles. 7:25)

CHAPTER 9 *What wisdom is, without which no one is happy; whether it is one in all wise men.* 25. But I would like to know how you think wisdom itself is to be regarded. Do you think that individual men have each their individual wisdoms, or that one wisdom is present to all in common, and that each is wise in the measure that he partakes of it?

E. I do not know what you call wisdom; for I see, forsooth, that what is said or done wisely seems different to different men. For those who go to war seem to themselves to be acting wisely; and those who, disdaining war, devote their care and labor to the cultivation of the land, praise this more highly and attribute it to wisdom; and those who are shrewd in devising ways to make money think themselves wise; and those who disregard or put from them all these and suchlike temporal things, and devote all their zeal to the investigation of truth, that they may know themselves and God, judge this to be the great reward of wisdom; and those who are loath to give themselves to this leisure of seeking and contemplating truth, but prefer to busy themselves with exacting cares and duties, that they may take counsel with men and be employed in the control and just government of human affairs, think themselves wise; and those who do both of these things and live partly in the contemplation of truth and partly in official labors, which they think they owe to human society, seem to themselves to hold the palm of wisdom. I omit innumerable sects, of which there is none that, placing its own adherents above all others, does not hold that they alone are wise. Wherefore, since the question before us demands an answer, not as to what we believe but as to what we hold with clear understanding, I shall be quite unable to reply to your question until I know also by contemplating and discerning reason that which by believing I hold wisdom to be.

A. Do you think that there is any wisdom other than the truth in which the supreme good is discerned and held? For all those sectarians that you have mentioned seek the good; but they are split into different sects because different things seem good to different men. Whoever therefore seeks what he should not seek, even though he seeks what to him seems good, errs notwithstanding. But he who seeks nothing cannot err, nor can he who seeks that which he should seek. In so far, therefore, as all men seek a happy life, they do not err. But in so far as anyone does not hold to that way of life which leads to happiness, though he acknowledges and professes that he wants only to attain happiness, he errs. For it is error when we follow something which does not lead to that which we wish to attain. And the more anyone strays in the path of life, the less wise is he; for he is that much farther from the truth in which the supreme good is discerned and known. But if anyone has pursued and attained the supreme good, he is happy; which indisputably we all desire. Therefore, as it is certain that we wish to be happy, so also is it certain that we wish to be wise, because no one is happy without wisdom. But no one is happy except by the supreme good, which is discerned and known in that truth which we call wisdom. And so, just as before we are happy the notion of happiness is yet impressed on our minds, so also before we are wise we have impressed on our minds a notion of wisdom; so that each of us, if he were asked whether he wished to be wise, would reply without a shade of hesitation that he so wished.

27. Wherefore, since we are now agreed as to what wisdom is, albeit you were not able to explain it in words (for if you were quite unable to see this with your mind, you could never know both that you wish to be wise, and that you ought so to wish). I would have you tell me whether you think that like the reason and truth of numbers wisdom offers itself to all reasoning men in common; or whether, since there are as many minds as there are men, so that I perceive nothing of your mind, nor you of mine, you think there are also as many wisdoms as there are wise men.

E. If the supreme good is one for all, the truth also in which it is discerned and known, that is wisdom, should be one and common for all.

A. But do you doubt that the supreme good, whatever it be, is for all men one?

E. I doubt it indeed; because I see different men taking delight in different things as if they were their supreme goods.

A. I should have wished indeed that no one were in doubt as to the supreme good, just as no one doubts that whatever it is a man cannot be happy until he has attained it. But since this is a large question and requires perhaps a long discourse, let us assume that there are just as many supreme goods as there are different things themselves, which by different men are sought as their supreme goods; does it then follow that wisdom itself is not one to all in common, because those goods which men discern and choose in it are many and diverse? For if you think this, you may also doubt that the light of the sun is one, because the things we discern by it are many and diverse: from which things each one selects at will that which he would enjoy through his sense of sight; and one man is pleased to look upon the height of some mountain and rejoices in that sight; another, the level surface of a field; another, the slopes of the valleys; another, the greenness of the woods; another, the inconstant evenness of the sea; and another, brings together in one view all of these things, or certain of them that are fair, for the joy of regarding them. Just as, therefore, those things are many and diverse which in the light of the sun men behold and choose for their enjoyment, although that light itself is one in which the gaze of each beholder sees and dwells upon that which rejoices it; even so are the goods many and diverse from which each one chooses what he will, and seeing it and holding it for his enjoyment rightly and truly makes it his supreme good; but it may yet be that the light itself of wisdom, in which these things are seen and held, is one and common to all wise men.

E. I admit that it may be, and that there is nothing to prevent there being one wisdom common to all, even though the supreme goods be many and various; but I would like to know whether it is so. For what we concede may be so, is not thereby conceded to be so.

A. In the meanwhile we know that there is wisdom; but whether it be one and common to all, or whether individual wise men have their separate wisdoms, as they have their own souls and minds, we do not yet know.

E. That is so.

CHAPTER 10 *The light of wisdom is one to all wise men in common.*

28. *A.* Where then do we see this that we know, whether it be that there is wisdom, or that there are wise men, or that all men wish to be wise and happy? For I do not doubt at all that you see it, and that it is true. Do you see this then as your own thought in such wise that if you did not tell me I should be completely ignorant of it, or so that you may understand it, and this truth may be seen by me even though you have not told it to me?

E. Nay, I do not doubt that it can also be seen by you, even were I unwilling.

A. But then if we both see one truth with our individual minds, is not that truth common to both of us?

E. Evidently.

A. Again, I believe you do not deny that wisdom should be sought after and concede that this is true.

E. I do not question that at all.

A. Can we then deny that this is likewise true and one and to be seen in common by all who know it; although each one sees it, not with my mind nor with yours, nor with the mind of any other, but with his own mind; while what he sees is there for all to see in common?

E. Surely not.

A. Again—We should live justly, put worse things below better, and compare equal things with equal, and give to each man what is properly his: do you not acknowledge this to be most true, and to be present in common to me and to all who see it, as well as to you?

E. I agree.

A. Can you deny that an uncorrupted thing is better than a corrupted thing, an eternal thing than a temporal thing, an inviolable than a violable?

E. Who can deny it?

A. Can anyone then call this truth his private possession, when it is changelessly present for the contemplation of all who are able to contemplate it?

E. No one can truly say that it is his exclusively, since it is as much one and common to all as it is true.

A. Again, who denies that the soul should be turned away from corruption and toward incorruption; that is, that no corruption, but incorruption should be loved? Or who, when he acknowledges that this is true, does not also understand it to be immutable and see that it stands there for all minds in common that are able to contemplate it?

E. Most true.

A. And does anyone doubt that that life which can be shaken by no adversity in its true and honest opinions is better than that which is easily ruined and broken by transient misfortune?

E. Who would doubt that?

29. *A.* I will ask no more questions of this sort now; for it is enough that you see as well as I and concede it to be most certain that these rules, and as it were lights of virtue, are true and immutable and singly or all together are present for the common contemplation of those who, each with his own mind and reason, are able to perceive them. But I do ask whether you think that these rules pertain to wisdom. For I believe that he who has attained wisdom will seem wise to you.

E. He certainly will.

A. Well, could he who lives justly so live if he did not see what lower things to subordinate to what higher, and what equal things to join to each other, and how to distribute to each what is properly his own?

E. He could not.

A. Will you then deny that he who sees this sees wisely?

E. I do not deny it.

A. And does not he who lives prudently choose incorruption and see that it is to be preferred to corruption?

E. Clearly so.

A. When, therefore, he chooses that which no one doubts should be chosen as the object toward which he should turn his soul, can it be denied that he chooses wisely?

E. I should certainly not deny it.

A. Therefore, when he turns his soul to that which he chooses wisely, he turns his soul wisely.

E. Surely.

A. And he who is not driven away by any fears or penalties from that to which he wisely turns himself, without doubt acts wisely.

E. Without doubt indeed.

A. It is very clear, therefore, that all these things, which we have called rules and lights of the virtues, pertain to wisdom; inasmuch as the more one uses them in the conduct of life and lives his life according to them, the more he lives and acts wisely. But what is done wisely cannot rightly be said to be separated from wisdom.

E. Just so.

A. Just as, therefore, there are true and immutable rules of numbers, the reason and truth of which you have said is immutably present to all perceivers in common; so there are true and immutable rules of wisdom, concerning a few of which, when you were just now asked about them one by one, you answered that they were true and manifest and conceded that they are present for the common contemplation of all who are able to regard them.

CHAPTER 11 *Whether wisdom and number are the same, or whether one arises from the other, or exists in the other.*

30. *E.* I cannot doubt it. But I would much like to know whether these two, wisdom and number, are contained in some one genus, as you have mentioned that they are also joined together in the holy Scriptures; or whether one arises from the other or consists in the other, as number from wisdom or in wisdom. For I should not have ventured to say that wisdom arises from number or consists in number, for I know not how this could be; for wisdom strikes me as far more venerable than number, because I have known many calculators or computers, or whatever else you may call them, who reckon superbly and marvellously—but of wise men only a very few or possibly none.

A. You say something at which I too often wonder. For when I reflect upon the immutable truth of numbers and upon its lair, as it were, or shrine or region or whatever else we may appropriately call the dwelling place and seat as it were of numbers, I am far removed from the body; and finding maybe something which I can think, but not finding anything which I can put into words, I return as if wearied to this world of ours, so that I may speak and may talk of those things that are not set before our eyes as they are wont to be talked of. This happens to me too, when as best I can I think very carefully and intently about wisdom. And because of this I wonder much, since these two are in the most mysterious and certain truth, and the testimony of the Scriptures is added also, in which, as I have noted, they are placed together—I wonder greatly, as I have said, why to the multitude of men number is held of small account and wisdom dear.

But doubtless it is this, that there is one, and as it were the same thing; but yet, since it is nonetheless said of wisdom in the divine Books that it *reaches from the end unto the end mightily, and disposes all things sweetly* (Wisd. of Sol. 8:1), that power by which it *reaches from the end unto the end mightily* is perhaps called number, but that which *disposes all things sweetly* is wisdom strictly so called; while both are of one and the same wisdom.

31. But because God gave numbers to all things, even to the lowest, and to those placed in the end of things—for all bodies, though they are among things the meanest, have their numbers—yet to be wise He did not grant to bodies, or even to all souls, but only to rational souls, as if He placed in them a seat for Himself, from which He disposes all those lowest things to which He gave numbers. And so since we judge easily of numbers, as of the things which are ordered beneath us, on which we perceived the impressed numbers as beneath us, we therefore hold them also of less account. But when we begin to turn back, and as it were upwards, we find that they too transcend our minds and remain immutable in truth itself. And because few can be wise, whereas to count is granted even to fools, men admire wisdom and despise numbers. The learned, however, and the studious, the more remote they are from earthly blemish, the more they look upon both number and wisdom in truth itself and hold both dear; and in comparison with its truth, not for them are gold and silver and other things for which men contend, but even their own selves grow unimportant.

32. Nor should you wonder that numbers are held cheap by men and wisdom dear, because they can more easily count than be wise; when you see them hold gold dearer than the light of a lamp and laugh to see gold compared with it. But a far inferior thing is honored, because even a beggar lights himself a lamp, but few have gold: although wisdom may be lacking, so that in comparison with number it is found inferior, while it is the same, but seeks the eye by which it can be seen.

But just as brightness and heat are perceived consubstantial, so to speak, in one fire, and yet the heat reaches only those things that are brought close, while the brightness is diffused farther and more widely; in like manner by the power of understanding that is present in wisdom the nearer things, such as the rational souls, grow warm, but the more remote things, such as bodies, are not reached by the heat of being wise, but are suffused by the light of numbers. This is perhaps obscure to you; for no visible thing can be made a perfect analogy of something invisible. Only note this, which is enough for the question in hand and which reveals itself even to humbler minds like ours; that even if it cannot be clear to us whether number is in wisdom or from wisdom, or wisdom itself is in number or from number, or whether it can be shown that they are names for one thing; it is certainly manifest that both are true and true immutably.

CHAPTER 12 *There is a single immutable truth in all understandings, and it is superior to our minds.* 33. Wherefore you will certainly not deny that there is an immutable truth, containing all things that are immutably true, which you cannot say is yours or mine or any one man's; but that in some wonderful way a mysterious and universal light, as it were, proffers itself to all in common. But who would say that that which is commonly present to all who reason and understand belongs properly to the nature of any one of them? For you remember, I think, what we said a little while ago about the bodily senses; namely, that those things which we perceive in common by the sense of the eyes or ears, such as colors and sounds, do not pertain to the nature of our eyes or ears but are there for all to perceive in common. So too it will not do for you to say that those things which we see in common, each with his own mind, pertain to the nature of the mind of either one of us. For what the eyes of two persons see at the same time cannot be said to be the eyes of this man or that but is some third thing to which the gaze of both is turned.

E. That is manifestly true.

34. *A.* Do you think then that this truth, which we have been discussing at such length and in which, single though it be, we have discerned so many things, is more excellent than our minds or equal to them or is it even inferior?

But if it were inferior we would judge not according to it but concerning it; just as we judge of bodies because they are below us, and say commonly not only that they are so or not so, but that they ought to be so or not so. So too of our minds we know not only that the mind is so, but frequently also that it should be so. And of bodies to be sure we judge thus when we say: this is not as white as it should be, or not as square, and many similar things. But of minds: it is less apt than it should be, or less gentle, or less vehement; according as the manner of our character shows itself. And we judge of these things according to those inner rules of truth that we discern in common; but no one judges in any way of the rules themselves. For when anyone says that eternal things are better than temporal or that seven and three are ten, no one says that it ought to be so; but knowing that it is so, he does not correct it as an examiner but rejoices in it as a discoverer.

If again the truth were equal to our minds, it would be also mutable. For our minds perceive it sometimes more and sometimes less, and thereby acknowledge themselves mutable, while it, continuing in itself is neither enhanced when we see it more, nor diminished when we see it less, but whole and uncorrupted it makes glad those who turn to it and punishes with blindness those who turn away. But what then, if also we judge of those same minds according to that truth, while we can in no way judge of it? For we say of our mind: it understands less than it should or it understands as much as it should. But a mind should understand in the measure that it is able to draw near to and cleave to immutable truth. Wherefore, if that truth be neither inferior nor equal to our minds, it remains that it is higher and more excellent.

CHAPTER 13 *Exhortation to embrace truth, which alone makes men happy.* 35. I promised however, as you will remember, that I would show you something more sublime than our mind and reason. Behold, it is truth! Embrace it, if you can, and enjoy it and delight in the Lord, and He will give you the desires of your heart. (Ps. 37:4) For what do you desire more than to be happy? And who is so happy as he who enjoys truth—unshaken and immutable and also excellent?

Do men, forsooth, proclaim themselves happy, when lusting with great desire they embrace the fair bodies of wives or even harlots: and shall we doubt that we are happy in the embrace of truth?

Men proclaim themselves happy, when with heat-parched throats they reach a pure and abundant spring; or famished, find an elaborate and bountiful repast: and will we deny that we are happy who are watered and fed by truth?

We are wont to hear the voices of those who proclaim

themselves happy, when they lie among roses and other flowers, or even if they enjoy sweet-smelling unguents: but what is more fragrant, more delicious, than the inspiration of truth? And do we hesitate when we are inspired by it to call ourselves happy?

Many make for themselves a happy life in the song of voices, and of strings and flutes; and when these are wanting they deem themselves miserable, but when they are present they are transported by joy: and when without, so to speak, any din of songs, a kind of eloquent silence of truth steals upon our minds, shall we seek another happy life, and not enjoy the one so instant and so sure?

Men who love the gleam of gold and silver, the sparkle of gems or bright colors, or the clarity and pleasantness of the light itself that reaches these eyes—be it in earthly fires or stars or moon or sun—think themselves happy when they are not recalled from that pleasure by any vexation or need, and for these would fain live always: and do we fear to place a happy life in the light of truth?

36. Yea, truly, since in truth the supreme good is perceived and held secure and that truth is wisdom, let us descry the supreme good in it and grasp it and enjoy it. For he is indeed happy who enjoys the supreme good. For this truth spreads before us all those goods that singly or together men of understanding, each to the measure of his grasp, choose for themselves and enjoy. But just as men in the light of the sun choose that which they would fain gaze upon and are gladdened by the sight; whereas if there were perchance any of more robust health and endowed with stronger eyes, these would look upon nothing more willingly than the sun itself, which lights up also all those other things that delight weaker eyes: so the keen vision of a strong and active mind, when with sure reason it has looked upon many things true and unchanging, turns toward truth itself, through which all things are made evident; and cleaving, as it were, to that truth, forgets all things else and in it at once enjoys them all. For whatever is pleasant in other truths is surely present in truth itself.

37. This is our freedom, when we are submissive to that truth; and it itself is our God, who frees us from death, that is from the state of sin. For Truth itself, speaking as man to men, has said to those who believe in Him: *If ye continue in my word, then are ye my disciples indeed; and ye shall know the truth, and the truth shall make you free.* (John 8:31-32) For the soul enjoys no thing with freedom, except that which it enjoys with security.

CHAPTER 14 *Truth is possessed with security.* But no one is secure in those things which he can lose against his will. No one unwilling, however, loses truth and wisdom. For one cannot be separated from it by occasions, but what is called separation from truth and wisdom is a perverse will, by which inferior things are chosen; but no one wills anything unwillingly. We have therefore that which all may enjoy in common; there are no difficulties and no defects in it. It takes to itself all lovers, with none the least envious, and is common to all and chaste to each. No one says to another: Move back, that I too may draw near; remove your hands, that I too may embrace. All cling to it; all touch the thing itself. No portion of its food is torn away; you drink naught of it that I cannot drink: for by that common participation in it you do not convert anything to your private possession; but what you take from it remains whole for me. I do not wait for what is inspired by it; for naught of it is at any time made the property of any one, or of a few, but the whole is at one time common to all.

38. Less like this truth therefore are those things that we touch or taste or smell; and more like it, those that we see and hear; because every word is heard entire by all those by whom it is heard and heard entire by each at the same time, and every visible object that is before the eyes is seen at the same time as much by one as by another. But even these are like it at a great remove; for not all of any voice sounds at one time, but some of it sounds earlier and some later; and every visible object swells out, so to speak, through space and is not everywhere whole. And assuredly all of these are taken from us despite our will, and difficulties of one sort or another stand in the way of our enjoying them. For even if the sweet singing of someone should last forever, and people vied with one another to listen to it, they would crowd together and fight for places, there would be such a multitude, that each might be nearer the singer; and in hearing they would hold nothing that would remain with them but would be touched by sounds that all vanish. Moreover, if I wished to look at the sun and could do so persistently, it would desert me in its setting or when veiled by a cloud, and by many other obstacles would I lose unwillingly the pleasure of seeing it. Finally, even were this sweetness of seeing light and hearing voices ever present to me, it were no great thing, seeing that it would be common to me and to the brutes. But the beauty of truth and wisdom, so long as there is a steadfast will to enjoy it, does not shut off comers by the thronged multitude of listeners, nor does it play through time nor wander to places, nor is it interrupted by night or shut off by shadows, nor

is it subject to the senses of the body. To those who from the whole world have turned to it for their delight, it is very near to all, to all everlasting; it is in no place, it is never away; it admonishes openly; it teaches inwardly; it changes all who see it to better, by none is it changed to worse; no one judges of it, without it no one judges well. And from this it is manifest beyond doubt that it is superior to our minds, which are each made wise by it; and of it you may not judge, but through it you may judge all things else.

CHAPTER 15 *That God exists is shown fully by reason and is now certainly known.* 39. You conceded, however, that if I should show you something higher than our minds, you would confess that it is God, if there were nothing yet higher. Accepting this concession of yours I said that it would be enough if I should prove this. For if there is something yet more excellent than truth, that rather is God; but if not, then truth itself is God. Whether therefore there is this more excellent thing, or whether there is not, you cannot deny that God is, which was the question set for our discussion and treatment. For if you are disturbed by what we have received in faith from the sacred teaching of Christ, that God is the Father of Wisdom, remember that we have also accepted in faith that equal to the eternal Father is the Wisdom begotten of Him. Wherefore nothing more need be asked but only held with steadfast faith. For God is; and He is truly and supremely. This, I think, we not only hold now undoubted by faith but know also by a sure albeit still rather tenuous form of knowledge; which for the question in hand is enough to explain the other things that pertain to the matter. Unless, that is, you have something to say in objection.
E. Nay, I accept these things, and am completely filled with an incredible joy, which I cannot express in words, and I cry out that they are most sure. I cry out moreover with an inner voice by which I wish to be heard by truth itself and to cleave to it, because I concede it to be not only good but the supreme good and the maker of happiness.
A. Rightly so; and I too rejoice greatly. But I would ask whether we are now wise and happy, or whether we as yet only incline that way, so that it may come forth and be ours?
E. I think rather that we incline to it.
A. Whence then do you understand these things, at whose certainty and truth you cried our that you rejoiced? And do you

grant that they pertain to wisdom? Or is any fool able to know wisdom?

E. So long as he is a fool he cannot.

A. You, then are wise; or else you do not know wisdom.

E. I am certainly not yet wise, but neither would I call myself a fool insofar as I know wisdom; since these things which I know are certain, and I cannot deny that they pertain to wisdom.

A. Tell me, pray, will you not admit that he who is not just is unjust, and he who is not prudent is imprudent, and he who is not temperate is intemperate? Can there be any doubt as to this?

E. I admit that when a man is not just he is unjust; and would give the same reply as to the prudent and temperate man.

A. Why, then, when he is not wise, is he not foolish?

E. I admit that too: when one is not wise, he is a fool.

A. Well then, which of these are you?

E. Whichever you call me; I should not dare to call myself wise, and I see that it follows from those things that I conceded, that I should not hesitate to say I am a fool.

A. Therefore the fool knows wisdom. For he would not be sure, as we said just now is the case, that he wished to be wise, and that he ought to wish it, if there were not inherent in his mind a notion of wisdom as having to do with those matters concerning which you answered when asked about them separately, and which pertain to wisdom, and in the knowledge of which you rejoiced.

E. It is as you say.

✠ ✠ ✠

THE AUGUSTINIAN PSYCHOLOGY

✠ ✠ ✠

L*etter 143* was written in 412 to Marcellinus, a special legate of the Emperor Honorious, appointed to adjudicate the dispute between Catholics and Donatists. The letter raises certain issues regarding the origin of the soul. Augustine notes four possible theories regarding the origin of the soul. It may be contended, he argues, that all souls are generated from Adam or that each soul is created. On the latter supposition it is possible to hold that each soul is created at the moment that it is united with the body, that all souls are created by God at the beginning of the world and then united with the body because of sin, and finally that all souls are created by God at the beginning of the world and then are sent out successively to the bodies at birth. Any theory of special creation raises difficulties regarding the transmission of original sin, and the theory that all souls were generated in Adam has materialistic implications. Augustine reached no definitive solution of this problem, and although he apparently favored a view of the special creation of the soul at birth, he remained uncertain. In 426 he wrote in the *Retractions:* "I did not know then and I still do not know." (I, 1, 3)

The dialogue with Evodius on *The Greatness of the Soul* was written in Rome either in 387 or 388. It is primarily a discussion of the nature of the soul in which Augustine is concerned to show that the powers of the soul reveal its spirituality, that the nature of the soul is incompatible with any conception of physical quantity or magnitude, that extension cannot be an attribute of the soul. The spirituality or incorporeality of the soul is exemplified in its definition and particularly in the analysis of sensation in which sensation is revealed as an activity of the soul rather than of the body. The last several pages of the selection further exemplify the powers of the soul and its spirituality by noting the several stages in the progress of the soul to God as Unchanging Wisdom. These stages of the soul—which were influential in the development of medieval mysticism—find their complement in the brief selection from the treatise *Christian Doctrine*. This exegetical treatise is devoted largely to an interpretation of the Bible as the source for Christian doctrine. The greater part of the treatise was written after 397 and it was not completed until 426.

Further material on the nature of the soul, particularly on the meanings of such terms as 'soul,' 'spirit,' 'intellect,' and 'mind' will be found in the selection from *The Literal Meaning of Genesis* in section four dealing with the problem of knowledge.

The brief selection from *Letter 137* written to Volusian in 412 exemplifies the problem of the unity of soul and body in man by drawing an analogy between such a union and that of God and man in the Incarnation. A belief in the latter offers less difficulty, Augustine maintains, because it is a union of one immaterial substance with another, than a belief in the union of soul and body (which involves a union of a *material* substance—the body—with an *immaterial* substance—the soul). Hence if we can accept the former belief, then we should be able to accept the latter belief.

The Trinity was written between 400 and 416 and in the opinion of many Augustinian scholars is one of the most profound and original works of Augustine. A masterly treatise on the theology of the Trinity, it also contains a wealth of material on a variety of topics, both philosophical and theological, that arise out of Augustine's exemplification of the mystery of the Trinity. The brief selection we have included here touches on the immortality of the soul and represents the more mature view of Augustine on this subject. It emphasizes that immortality is more a matter of faith than of reason. True beatitude depends on our faith in immortality rather than in philosophical argumentation. Augustine had written an earlier essay entitled *The Immortality of the Soul* in which he had restated some of the arguments from Plato's *Phaedo:* for example, the contention that since the essence of the soul is to live, then its contrary, which is death, cannot be admitted. To such an argument Augustine added the Christian conception of God as having created and conserved the soul in existence. The essay is rather ineffective and Augustine himself did not approve of it. He remarked of it in the *Retractions:* "It is so obscure that it is tiresome even to my reading, and it is with difficulty that it is intelligible to me!" (I, 5, 1)

For an account of the soul as an image of the Blessed Trinity, a favorite theme of Augustine's and one highly popular in the Middle Ages, the reader is referred to the selection from Book IX of *The Trinity* in the topic on the Problem of Knowledge.

LETTER 143 ✠ 3. Cicero, the prince of Roman orators, says of some one, "He never uttered a word which he would wish to recall." This commendation, though it seems to be the highest possible, is nevertheless more likely to be true of a consummate fool than of a man perfectly wise; for it is true of idiots that the more absurd and foolish they are, and the more their opinions diverge from those universally held, the more likely they are to utter no word which they will wish to recall; for to regret an evil or foolish or ill-timed word is characteristic of a wise man. If, however, the words quoted are taken in a good sense, as intended to make us believe that some one was such that, by reason of his speaking all things wisely, he never uttered any word which he would wish to recall, this we are, in accordance with sound piety, to believe rather concerning men of God, who spoke as they were moved by the Holy Ghost, than concerning the man whom Cicero commends. For my part, so far am I from this excellence that if I have uttered no word which I would wish to recall, it must be because I resemble more the idiot than the wise man. The man whose writings are most worthy of the highest authority is he who has uttered no word, I do not say which it would be his desire, but which it would be his duty to recall. Let him that has not attained to this occupy the second rank through his humility, since he cannot take the first rank through his wisdom. Since he has been unable, with all his care, to exclude every expression whose use may be justly regretted, let him acknowledge his regret for anything which, as he may now have discovered, ought not to have been said.

5. Notwithstanding what I have just said, I am prepared to defend the sentence in the third book of my treatise on *Free Will*, in which, discoursing on the rational substance, I have expressed my opinion in these words: "The soul, appointed to occupy a body inferior in nature to itself after the entrance of sin, governs its own body, not absolutely according to its free will but only insofar as the laws of the universe permit." (III, 11, 34) I bespeak the particular attention of those who think that I have here fixed and defined, as ascertained concerning the human soul, either that it comes by propagation from the parents or that it has, through sins committed in a higher celestial life, incurred the penalty of being shut up in a corruptible body. Let them, I say, observe that the words in question have been carefully weighed by me, that while they hold fast what I regard as certain, namely, that after the sin of the first man, all other men have been born and continue to be born in that sinful flesh, for the healing of which "the likeness of sinful flesh" [1] came in the person of the Lord, they are also so chosen as not to pronounce upon any one of those four opinions which I have in the sequel expounded and distinguished—not attempting to establish any one of them as preferable to the others but disposing in the meantime of the matter under discussion and reserving the consideration of these opinions, so that whichever of them may be true, praise should unhesitatingly be given to God.

6. For whether all souls are derived by propagation from the first, or are in the case of each individual specially created, or being created apart from the body are sent into it, or introduce themselves into it of their own accord, without doubt this creature endowed with reason, namely, the human soul—appointed to occupy an inferior, that is, an earthly body—after the entrance of sin, does not govern its own body absolutely according to its free will.[2] For I did not say, "after his sin," or "after he sinned," but after the entrance of sin, that whatever might afterwards, if possible, be determined by reason as to the question whether the sin was his own or the sin of the first parent of mankind, it might be perceived that in saying that "the soul, appointed, after the entrance of sin, to occupy an inferior body, does not govern its body absolutely according to its own free will," I stated what is true; for "the flesh lusteth against the spirit,[3] and in this we groan, being burdened,"[4] and "the corruptible body weighs down the soul."[5] In short, who can enumerate all the evils arising from the infirmity of the flesh, which shall assuredly cease when "this corruptible shall have put on incorruption," so that "that which is mortal shall be swallowed up of life?"[6] In that future condition, therefore, the soul shall

govern its spiritual body with absolute freedom of will; but in the meantime its freedom is not absolute but conditioned by the laws of the universe, according to which it is fixed, that bodies having experienced birth experience death and having grown to maturity decline in old age. For the soul of the first man did, before the entrance of sin, govern his body with perfect freedom of will, although that body was not yet spiritual but animal; but after the entrance of sin, that is, after sin had been committed in that flesh from which sinful flesh was thenceforward to be propagated, the reasonable soul is so appointed to occupy an inferior body, that it does not govern its body with absolute freedom of will. That infant children, even before they have committed any sin of their own, are partakers of sinful flesh, is, in my opinion, proved by their requiring to have it healed in them also, by the application in their baptism of the remedy provided in Him who came in the likeness of sinful flesh. But even those who do not acquiesce in this view have no just ground for taking offence at the sentence quoted from my book; for it is certain, if I am not mistaken, that even if the infirmity be the consequence not of sin but of nature, it was at all events only after the entrance of sin that bodies having this infirmity began to be produced; for Adam was not created thus, and he did not beget any offspring before he sinned.

7. Let my critics, therefore, seek other passages to censure, not only in my other more hastily published works but also in these books of mine on *Free Will*. For I by no means deny that they may in this search discover opportunities of conferring a benefit on me; for if the books, having passed into so many hands, cannot now be corrected, I myself may, being still alive. Those words, however, so carefully selected by me to avoid committing myself to any one of the four opinions or theories regarding the soul's origin, are liable to censure only from those who think that my hesitation as to any definite view in a matter so obscure is blameworthy; against whom I do not defend myself by saying that I think it right to pronounce no opinion whatever on the subject, seeing that I have no doubt either that the soul is immortal—not in the same sense in which God is immortal, who alone hath immortality,[7] but in a certain way peculiar to itself—or that the soul is a creature and not a part of the substance of the Creator, or as to any other thing which I regard as most certain concerning its nature. But seeing that the obscurity of this most mysterious subject, the origin of the soul, compels me to do as I have done, let them rather stretch out a friendly hand to me confessing my ignorance and desiring to know whatever is the truth on the subject; and let them, if they can, teach or demonstrate

to me what they may either have learned by the exercise of sound reason or have believed on indisputably plain testimony of the divine oracles. For if reason be found contradicting the authority of the Divine Scriptures, it only deceives by a semblance of truth, however acute it be, for its deductions cannot in that case be true. On the other hand, if, against the most manifest and reliable testimony of reason, anything be set up claiming to have the authority of the Holy Scriptures, he who does this does it through a misapprehension of what he has read and is setting up against the truth not the real meaning of Scripture, which he has failed to discover, but an opinion of his own; he alleges not what he has found in the Scriptures, but what he has found in himself as their interpreter.

8. Let me give an example, to which I solicit your earnest attention. In a passage near the end of Ecclesiastes, where the author is speaking of man's dissolution through death separating the soul from the body, it is written, "Then shall the dust return to the earth as it was, and the spirit shall return unto God who gave it."[8] A statement having the authority on which this one is based is true beyond all dispute and is not intended to deceive any one; yet if any one wishes to put upon it such an interpretation as may help him in attempting to support the theory of the propagation of souls, according to which all other souls are derived from that one which God gave to the first man, what is there said concerning the body under the name of "dust" (for obviously nothing else than body and soul are to be understood by "dust" and "spirit" in this passage) seems to favour his view; for he may affirm that the soul is said to return to God because of its being derived from the original stock of that soul which God gave to the first man, in the same way as the body is said to return to the dust because of its being derived from the original stock of that body which was made of dust in the first man, and therefore may argue that, from what we know perfectly as to the body, we ought to believe what is hidden from our observation as to the soul; for there is no difference of opinion as to the original stock of the body, but there is as to the original stock of the soul. In the text thus brought forward as a proof, statements are made concerning both, as if the manner of the return of each to its original was precisely similar in both—the body, on the one hand, returning to the earth as it was, for thence was it taken when the first man was formed; the soul, on the other hand, returning to God, for He gave it when He breathed into the nostrils of the man whom He had formed the breath of life, and he became a living soul,[9] so

110

that thenceforward the propagation of each part should go on from the corresponding part in the parent.

9. If, however, the true account of the soul's origin be that God gives to each individual man a soul not propagated from that first soul but created in some other way, the statement that "the spirit returns to God who gave it" is equally consistent with this view. The two other opinions regarding the soul's origin are, then, the only ones which seem to be excluded by this text. For in the first place, as to the opinion that every man's soul is made separately within him at the time of his creation, it is supposed that, if this were the case, the soul should have been spoken of as returning not to God who gave it but to God who made it; for the word "gave" seems to imply that that which could be given had already a separate existence. The words "returneth to God" are further insisted upon by some, who say, How could it return to a place where it had never been before? Accordingly they maintain that if the soul is to be believed to have never been with God before, the words should have been "it goes" or "goes on" or "goes away," rather than it "returns" to God. In like manner, as to the opinion that each soul glides of its own accord into its body, it is not easy to explain how this theory is reconcilable with the statement that God gave it. The words of this scriptural passage are consequently somewhat adverse to these two opinions, namely, the one which supposes each soul to be created in its own body and the one which supposes each soul to introduce itself into its own body spontaneously. But there is no difficulty in showing that the words are consistent with either of the other two opinions, namely, that all souls are derived by propagation from the one first created, or that, having been created and kept in readiness with God, they are given to each body as required.

10. Nevertheless, even if the theory that each soul is created in its own body may not be wholly excluded by this text—for if its advocates affirm that God is here said to have given the spirit (or the soul) in the same way as He is said to have given us eyes, ears, hands, or other such members, which were not made elsewhere by Him, and kept in store that He might give them, i.e. add and join them to our bodies, but are made by Him in that body to which He is said to have given them—I do not see what could be said in reply, unless, perchance, the opinion could be refuted, either by other passages of Scripture, or by valid reasoning. In like manner, those who think that each soul flows of its own accord into its body take the words "God gave it" in the sense in

which it is said, "He gave them up to uncleanness through the lusts of their own hearts."[10] Only one word, therefore, remains apparently irreconcilable with the theory that each soul is made in its own body, namely, the word "returneth," in the expression "returneth to God," for in what sense can the soul return to Him with whom it has not formerly been? By this one word alone are the supporters of this one of the four opinions embarrassed. And yet I do not think that this opinion ought to be held as refuted by this one word, for it may be possible to show that in the ordinary style of scriptural language it may be quite correct to use the word "return," as signifying that the spirit created by God returns to Him not because of its having been with Him before its union with the body but because of its having received being from His creative power.

11. I have written these things in order to show that whoever is disposed to maintain and vindicate any one of these four theories of the soul's origin must bring forward, either from the Scriptures received into ecclesiastical authority, passages which do not admit of any other interpretation, as the statement that God made man, or reasonings founded on premises so obviously true that to call them in question would be madness, such as the statement that none but the living are capable of knowledge or of error; for a statement like this does not require the authority of Scripture to prove its truth, as if the common sense of mankind did not of itself announce its truth with such transparent cogency of reason that whoever contradicts it must be held to be hopelessly mad. If any one is able to produce such arguments in discussing the very obscure question of the soul's origin, let him help me in my ignorance; but if he cannot do this, let him forbear from blaming my hesitation on the question.

THE GREATNESS OF THE SOUL ✠ CHAPTER 13 *Knowledge of abstract quantities shows the soul is immaterial. Definition of the soul.*

Aug. . . . As to what the soul actually is, I am surprised that you have forgotten that we discussed this topic previously. You must remember that the first question you asked was where the soul comes from; and I recall that we considered that question in two ways: first, we devoted to the soul a regional inquiry, as it were; secondly, we inquired whether it was derived from earth or fire or any other of the elements or from all of them together or from a combination of some of them. But on this problem we agreed that there is no more sense in asking what the soul is derived from than in asking from what earth or any other single element is derived. For it must be understood that although God made the soul, it has a certain essence of its own, which is not composed of earth nor of fire nor of air nor of water; or we may be forced to the conclusion that God gave earth its own exclusive individuality but failed to give to the soul that which makes it soul and nothing else. But if you want a definition of the soul, and so ask me—what is the soul? I have a ready answer. It seems to me to be a special substance, endowed with reason, adapted to rule the body.

Ev. . . . Wherefore, please take up now the problem in which I am intensely interested: if the soul does not have a spatial magnitude commensurate with that of the body, why is it that it feels wherever the body is touched?

CHAPTER 23 *Tentative definition of sensation. How sight operates.*

41. *Aug.* All right, let us tackle that problem, as you wish, but you will have to give me much closer attention than you may think necessary. So, collect your wits as best you can and answer me what is your idea of "sensation" which the soul exercises through the body. For "sensation" is the proper term to use here.

Ev. I have always heard that there are five senses: seeing, hearing, smelling, tasting, and touching. I do not know what more to answer.

Aug. That division is very ancient, and it is the usual popular presentation of it. But I would have you define what sensation itself is, so that all these may be included in one simple definition, and nothing else that is not sensation may be understood under it. However, if you cannot do this, I shall not press you. This one thing you can do—and that will be enough—you can either disprove or approve my definition.

Ev. With that method I shall perhaps not fail you, so far as I am able. But even that is not always easy.

Aug. Now then, listen: I think sensation is the soul's not being unaware of the body's experience.

Ev. That definition satisfies me.

Aug. Stand by it as your own, then, and defend it while I disprove it briefly.

Ev. I shall defend it, all right, if you will stand by me; but if you do not, I am through with it already. Evidently you have good reason for deciding to refute it.

Aug. Do not rely too much upon authority, especially mine, which does not exist. Also, to quote Horace, "Have the courage to think for yourself," lest fear defeat you before an argument does.

Ev. I have no fear at all, no matter what the issue, for you will not suffer me to be in error. But begin if you have anything to say, lest I be worn out by delay rather than by your objections.

42. *Aug.* Tell me, then, what effect does your body undergo when you see me?

Ev. It does experience something, for, if I mistake not, my eyes are part of my body; and if they experienced nothing, how could I see you?

Aug. But it is not enough for you to prove that your eyes experience some effect, unless you also show me what they experience.

Ev. Well, what could it be but sight itself? For they see. If you were to ask me what a sick person experiences, I should answer, sickness; a lustful person, lust; a fearful person, fear; a joyful person, joy. Why, then, when you ask me what someone experiences when he sees, should I not answer that it is sight itself?

Aug. But a joyful person senses joy. Or do you deny that?

Ev. No, indeed, I agree.

Aug. I should say the same about the other emotions.

Ev. So should I.

Aug. But whatever the eyes sense, they see.

Ev. I should not say that at all. For who sees pain, even though the eyes often sense it?

Aug. Evidently you are concerned with the eyes. You are wide awake. See, then, whether, just as a joyful person senses joy by being joyful, so also one who sees senses sight by seeing.

Ev. Can it be otherwise?

Aug. But whatever the one who sees senses in the act of seeing, he must also see.

Ev. No, that does not follow. For, suppose he has a sensation of love when he sees: he does not see love, does he?

Aug. A very cautious and shrewd observation! I am glad you are not easily deceived. But now, note this: we agree that we do not see everything which the eyes sense, nor everything we sense in the act of seeing; but do you think that at least this is true—that we sense everything that we see?

114

Ev. Indeed, if I did not grant that, how could the fact that we see be called sensation?

Aug. Well, are we not also acted upon by everything of which we have a sensation?

Ev. That is right.

Aug. Then, if we have a sensation of everything we see and if we are acted upon by everything of which we have a sensation, we are acted upon by everything we see.

Ev. I have no objection to make.

Aug. Therefore, you are acted upon by me, and I in turn am acted upon by you, when we see each other.

Ev. So I think, and for me this is an instant dictate of reason.

43. *Aug.* Take what follows, for I believe you would regard it as quite absurd and foolish if anyone should say that you are acted upon by a body, where that body which affects you is not present.

Ev. It does seem absurd, and I believe it is just as you say.

Aug. Well, now, is it not evident that my body is in one place; and yours, in another?

Ev. Yes.

Aug. Just the same, your eyes have a sensation of my body, and if they have a sensation, they certainly are being acted upon; and they cannot be acted upon where that which acts is not present. Yet, your eyes are not there where my body is. Therefore, they are subjected to action where they are not present.

Ev. Well, I granted all those points which it seemed unreasonable not to grant; but this last which flows from the rest is so very absurd that I would rather own that I have made a rash concession somewhere along the line than admit that this conclusion is true. Not even in my sleep would I dare to say that my eyes have sensation where they are not present.

Aug. Then, see where you have dozed off. What would you have been too cautious to let slip by, if you had been as wide awake as you were a little while ago?

Ev. To be sure, that is what I am carefully retracing and reconsidering. Still, it is not quite clear to me that a concession should be regretted, except perhaps this, that our eyes have sensation when we see; for it is possibly sight itself that has the sensation.

Aug. Yes, that is it. Sight extends itself outward and through the eyes darts forth far in every possible direction to light up what we see. Hence it happens that it seems rather in the place where the object seen is present, not in the place from which it goes out to see.

115

Therefore, is it not you that see, when you see me?

Ev. Who but a crazy person would say this? By all means—it is I who see, but I see by the emission of sight through the eyes.

Aug. But, if you see, you have a sensation. If you have a sensation, you are acted upon. And you cannot be acted upon at a place where you are not present. But you see me where I am. Therefore, you are acted upon where I am. But if you are not there where I am, I do not know at all how you dare to say that you see me.

Ev. I say that by means of sight, reaching out to that place where you are, I see you where you are. But that I am not there, I admit. Still, let us suppose that I were to touch you with a stick: I certainly would be the one doing the touching and I would sense it; yet I would not be there where I touched you. In the same way, because I say that I see by means of sight, even though I am not there, I am not thereby compelled to admit that it is not I who see.

44. *Aug.* Then you have made no rash concession. For your eyes can be defended in this way also: their sight is, as you say, like the stick. And your conclusion that your eyes see where they are not present, is not absurd. Or do you think otherwise?

Ev. It is just as you say, certainly. In fact, I now realize that if the eyes should see where they are present, they would also see themselves.

Aug. It would be more correct for you to say, not that they would see *also* themselves, but that they would see *only* themselves. For where they are, that is, the place they occupy, they alone occupy. The nose is not where they are nor is anything else that is near them. Otherwise you would also be where I am, because we are near each other. Consequently, if the eyes were to see only where they are, they would see only themselves. But since they do not see themselves, we are compelled to agree not only that they can see where they are not but even that they cannot see at all, except where they are not.

Ev. Nothing can make me doubt that.

Aug. Then you do not doubt that the eyes are acted upon where they are not present. For where they see, there they have a sensation, for seeing itself is a sensation, and to have a sensation is to undergo an action. Hence, where they have a sensation, there they are acted upon. But they actually see in another place than that in which they are. Therefore, they are subjected to an action where they are not present.

Ev. I am surprised how I consider all this to be true.

45. *Aug.* Perhaps you are right in thinking so. But tell me, please, do we see everything that we recognize by means of sight?

Ev. I think so.

Aug. Do you also believe that we recognize by means of sight everything we recognize by the act of seeing?

Ev. Yes, I believe that also.

Aug. Why, then, when we see only smoke, do we generally recognize that beneath it there is hidden fire which we do not see?

Ev. You are right. [Your question is in order.] And now I do not think we see everything we recognize by means of sight, for we can, as you have shown, by seeing one thing, recognize another which is out of the range of sight.

Aug. Well, is it possible not to see what we sense by means of sight?

Ev. No, not at all.

Aug. Therefore, sense perception and recognition are two different things.

Ev. They are entirely different. For example, we have sense perception of the smoke which we see, and from that we recognize that beneath it there is fire which we do not see.

Aug. You understand that correctly. But you surely see that when this happens, our body, that is, our eyes are in no wise affected by the fire but by the smoke which is all they see. For we have already agreed that to see is to have sensation, and to have sensation is to be acted upon.

Ev. I grasp that and I agree.

Aug. When, therefore, as a result of an impression received by the body the soul is not unaware of something, this is not at once identifiable with one of the five senses mentioned; but this latter holds only when it is aware of the bodily experience itself. That fire, for example, is not seen nor heard nor smelled nor tasted nor touched by us; yet, the sight of smoke makes the soul aware of it. And, while this awareness is not called sensation, because the body is not affected by the fire, it is nevertheless termed recognition through sensation, because the fire is conjectured and established from an experience of the body, though the experience was something different, that is, the sight of a different reality.

Ev. I understand, and I see very well that this harmonizes with, and supports, that definition of yours which you gave me to defend as my own. For I remember that you defined sensation as "the soul's not being unaware of the body's experience." Therefore, the fact that smoke is seen we call a sensation, for by seeing the smoke the eyes experience it, and the eyes are parts of the body, and themselves are bodies; but the fire, of which the body had no experience at all, although its presence became known, we do not term an object of sensation.

46. *Aug.* I commend you on your memory and the intelligence that is yours to serve it. But your defense of the definition is tottering.

Ev. Will you tell me why?

Aug. Because you do not deny, I think, that the body undergoes some effect when we are growing, or when we become old. At the same time it is clear that we do not perceive it by any of the senses; and yet it does not escape the soul. Therefore, there is one effect on the body of which the soul is not unaware, though this cannot be called sensation. Plainly, by seeing those things to be larger which formerly we had seen smaller and seeing men grown old who obviously had been young men and boys, we infer that our own bodies are undergoing some such change, even now while we are talking. Nor are we mistaken in this, I am sure; for I am more likely to make a mistake saying that I *see* than saying that I *understand* that my hair is growing now or that my body undergoes constant change. And if this change is an effect on the body, which no one denies, and if we do not actually perceive it by the senses, yet the soul is not unaware of it because we are not unaware of it, then, as I said, the body undergoes an effect of which the soul is not unaware, and yet it is not sensation. Wherefore, that definition which should include nothing which is not sensation, is certainly defective, since it did include this.

Ev. I see the only thing remaining for me to do is to ask you to give another definition or to revise this one, if you can; for in the light of your reasoning, perfectly convincing to me, I must own that it is defective.

Aug. It is an easy matter to correct this, and I want you to try it. Take my word for it—you will do it, once you grasp well where it is at fault.

Ev. There is no other possibility, is there, than that it includes something that does not belong there?

Aug. How, then?

Ev. Because of the fact that the body ages, even in its youth, it cannot be denied that it undergoes some change. And when we know that, we have an experience of the body of which the soul is not unaware. And yet it is imperceptible to each and every sense; for neither do I see that I am aging at this moment, nor do I perceive it by hearing or smelling or tasting or touching.

Aug. How, then, do you know it?

Ev. I infer it by reason.

Aug. On what arguments is your reasoning based?

Ev. On the fact that I see other people old, who, as I now am, were once young.

Aug. Is it not by a sense faculty that you see them—one of the five?

Ev. Who denies that? But from the fact that I see them, I infer that I, too, am growing old, though I do not actually see it.

Aug. What words, then, do you think should be added to the definition to make it perfect, considering that sensation is present only when the soul is not unaware of an effect produced in the body, yet not in such a way that the soul recognizes it through another effect or through any other factor at all.

Ev. Kindly state that a little more clearly.

CHAPTER 25 *Rules for definition. Application to definition of sensation.*

47. *Aug.* I shall comply with your wish, and that the more willingly if you go slowly rather than hurry. At any rate, give me your complete attention, for what I shall say will be applicable in many respects.

A definition contains nothing less, nothing more, than what is up for explanation; otherwise, it is in reality a bad definition. Now, whether it is free from such defects is determined by conversion; and that this is so, the following examples will make clearer to you. If, for instance, you were to ask me what man is, and I should give this definition: "Man is a mortal animal," you should not, just because what is said is true, approve it as a definition. But, by prefixing one little word, namely, "every," change the proposition and see whether the simple converse is also true; that is to say, whether, just as it is true that "every man is a mortal animal," it is also true that "every mortal animal is a man." When you find that this is not the case, you should reject the definition because of the fault that it includes something extraneous. For, not only man but every beast as well is a mortal animal. Hence, it is usual to complete this definition of man by adding "rational" to "mortal"; for man is a rational mortal animal; and, just as every man is a mortal rational animal, so also every mortal rational animal is a man. The previous definition, then, was faulty because it included too much, applying to the beast as well as to man; the present one, embracing every man, and nothing besides man, is perfect.

Again, if it embraces too little, if, for example, you add "grammarian," it is likewise defective. For, even though every rational mortal animal that is a grammarian is a man, yet there are many men who are not grammarians and so are not embraced by this definition; and for this reason the statement in the first proposition is false, though its converse is true. For it is false that every man is a rational, mortal, grammarian animal; but it is true that every rational, mortal, grammarian animal is a man. When, however, neither the statement of the proposition as such nor that of its converse is true, the defect obviously is greater than when only one is false. Take these two propositions: "Man is a white animal"; again, "Man is a four-footed animal." For, whether you say, "Every man is a white animal" or "Every man is a four-footed animal," the statements are false; and the converse statements are also false. But there is this difference, that the first applies to some men, for a great many men are white; the second does not apply to any man, for there is no man who is a quadruped. For the present, you might learn these points testing definitions, how to judge of them in the proposition and in conversion. There are many other things of this kind offered in instructions, both verbose and vague, which I shall try to teach you by an by, at the right moment.

48. Now turn your attention to that definition of ours and, applying your added experience to a study of it, correct it. Well, we had discovered that while it was a definition of sensation, it included something besides sensation, and, therefore, was not true when converted. Perhaps it is true that every sensation is an effect on the body that does not escape the awareness of the soul, just as it is true that "every man is a mortal animal." But just as it is false that "every mortal animal is a man"—for a beast is also that—so is it false that "every effect on the body that does not escape the awareness of the soul is a sensation," because our fingernails are growing now and the soul is not unaware of that, for we know it; yet we learn of it not by sensation but by inference. In the same way, therefore, as "rational" was added to the definition of man to make it exact, and the addition ruled out the beasts which had also been found included, so that we understand the definition in this form to embrace man only and all men—do you not think that our present definition requires some addition by which to exclude any

foreign item it contains and to make it stand for sensation only and for all that is sensation?

Ev. Yes, I think so; but what addition can be made, I do not know.

Aug. Every sensation is certainly an effect on the body of which the soul is not unaware. But this proposition cannot be converted, because of that action on the body as a result of which it grows or shrinks, with our knowing it—that is, the soul is aware of it.

Ev. That is right.

Aug. Now, does the soul become aware of this through the action itself or through something else?

Ev. Obviously, through some other factor. It is one thing to see that the nails are longer; another to know that they grow.

Aug. Since, then, growth itself is an action which we do not experience by any of the senses, while the increase in size which we do know by the senses is a result of the same action but is not the action itself, it is obvious that we know such an action not through itself but through something else. Therefore, if it were not through something else that the soul is aware of it, would it not be known by the senses rather than by inference?

Ev. I understand.

Aug. Why, then, do you hesitate regarding what is to be added to the definition?

Ev. I see now that sensation is to be defined thus: it is a bodily experience that of itself does not escape the soul's awareness; for every sensation is just that, and each time you have that, you have, I believe, sensation.

49. *Aug.* If that is true, I admit the definition is perfect. But let us put it to a test, if you will, to see whether it is not shaky because of that second fault, as was the definition of man to which "grammarian" was added. You recall, of course, that it was said that "man is a mortal rational grammarian animal," and that this definition is faulty, because, though the converse of it is true, the original proposition is false. For it is false that "every man is a rational, mortal, grammarian animal," though it is true that "every rational, mortal, grammarian animal is a man." Wherefore, this definition is unsound for the reason that although it applies to man alone, it does not apply to every man. And it may be that the definition we are boasting of as perfect, is like that. For, although the body's every experience directly entering the awareness of the soul is a sensation, still not every sensation is such. You may understand that in this way: brute animals have sense experience, and practically all of

them have the use of the five senses, so far as nature has endowed them. You will not deny that, will you?

Ev. Certainly not. . . .

CHAPTER 33 *The seven levels of the soul's greatness. Its significance in the body, its significance to itself, its significance before God.*

The First Level of the Soul

70. *Aug.* Oh, would that the two of us could put our questions on this topic to a man of great learning—not only that, but one of great eloquence, too; yes, to one wise and perfect in every respect! What efforts he would make to explain, by statement and proof, what the soul means to the body, what it means to itself, what it means before God, to whom it is very near, provided it is perfectly undefiled, and in whom it finds its supreme and complete perfection! But now, since I have no one else to do this for me, I venture this—not to fail you. This, at all events, will be my reward, that while I endeavor to explain to you, untutored as I am, what powers the soul has, I may confidently experience what powers I myself have. But from the start let me rid you of any far-flung and boundless expectations you may have. Do not think that I shall speak of every soul, but only of the human soul, which should be our only concern, if we have concern for ourselves.

In the first place, then, as anyone can easily observe, the soul by its presence gives life to this earth- and death-bound body. It makes of it a unified organism and maintains it as such, keeping it from disintegrating and wasting away. It provides for a proper, balanced distribution of nourishment to the body's members. It preserves the body's harmony and proportion not only in beauty but also in growth and reproduction. Obviously, however, these are faculties which man has in common with the plant world; for we say of plants, too, that they live; we see and acknowledge that each of them is preserved to its own generic being, is nourished, grows, and reproduces itself.

The Second Level of the Soul

71. So, go up another level and see what power the soul has in the senses, which offer a plainer and clearer understanding of what life is. Of course, we should pay no attention to a certain kind of utterly crude perversion which is more wooden than the very

trees it takes under its wing and which believes that the vine suffers pain when a grape is plucked and that such things not only feel it when they are cut but even that they see and hear. Of this impious error this is not the place to speak. Now, then, following the scheme I proposed, look at what power the soul has in the senses and in the entire nobility of the higher living organism, by reason of which we cannot possibly belong in the same category with things which are held down by roots.

The soul directs itself to the sense of touch and through it feels and distinguishes hot and cold, rough and smooth, hard and soft, light and heavy. Then again, it distinguishes countless varieties of savors, odors, sounds, and shapes, by tasting, smelling, hearing, and seeing. And in all these the soul seeks and selects whatever suits the nature of its own body; it rejects and shuns what is unsuited. At certain intervals it withdraws itself from the senses and, by giving them time off, so to say, gives their activities an opportunity to recuperate their strength, the while it lumps together in manifold combinations, and mulls over, the images of realities it has taken in through the senses; and all this constitutes sleep and dreams. Frequently, too, it takes advantage of the mobility present to delight in making gestures and unusual motions, and without effort it sets the parts of the body in harmony. For sexual union it does what it can, and by companionship and love it strives to forge two natures into one. It cooperates not merely to beget offspring but also to foster it, to protect and nourish it. It attaches itself by habit to things among which the body acts and by which it sustains the body, and from these, as if they were of its own constitution, it is reluctant to be separated; and this force of habit which is not terminated even by separation from the realities themselves and by the passing of time is called memory. But again, no one denies that the soul can produce all these effects even in brute animals.

The Third Level of the Soul

72. Advance, then, to the third level, which belongs to man exclusively. Think of memory, not of things that have become habituated by repeated acts, but of the countless things that have been attained and retained by observation and illustration—all the arts of craftsmen, the tilling of the soil, the building of cities, the thousand-and-one marvels of various buildings and undertakings, the invention of so many symbols in letters, in words, in gesture, in sound of various kinds, in paintings and statues; the languages of so many peoples, their many institutions, some new and some re-

vived; the great number of books and records of every sort for the preservation of memory and the great concern shown for posterity; the gradations of duties, prerogatives, honors, and dignities, in family life and in public life—whether civilian or military—in profane and sacred institutions; the power of reason and thought, the floods of eloquence, the varieties of poetry, the thousand forms of mimicries for the purpose of entertainment and jest, the art of music, the accuracy of surveying, the science of arithmetic, the interpretation of the past and future from the present. These things bear the mark of greatness and they are characteristically human. But here we still have a capacity shared by both the learned and the unlearned, by both the good and the wicked.

The Fourth Level of the Soul

73. Take hold now and swing yourself onto the fourth level, which goodness and all true worth call their home. Here it is that the soul ventures to take precedence not only over its own body, acting some part in the universe, but even over the whole body of the universe itself. The goods of the world it does not account its own, and comparing them with its own power and beauty, it keeps aloof from them and despises them. Hence, the more the soul turns to itself for its own pleasure, the more does it withdraw from sordid things and cleanse itself and make itself immaculately clean through and through. It steels itself against every effort to lure it away from its purpose and resolve. It shows high consideration for human society and desires nothing to happen to another which it does not wish to happen to itself. It submits to the authority and the bidding of wise men and is convinced that through them God speaks to itself. Yet this performance of the soul, noble as it is, still requires strenuous effort, and the annoyances and allurements of this world engage it in a mighty struggle, bitterly contested. In this work of purification there is an underlying fear of death, sometimes not strong, but sometimes all-pervading. It is scarcely present when one has a very vigorous faith that—and to see the truth of this is granted only to the purified soul—all things are so governed by the great providence and justice of God that death cannot come as an evil to anyone, even though someone may inflict it with evil intentions. But on this level there is a great fear of death, when, on the one hand, confidence in God's justice is so much the weaker the more anxiously one seeks for it; and when, on the other hand, corresponding to the lack of tranquillity in the presence of fear, there is a greater lack of understanding; for tran-

quillity is absolutely necessary for the study of matters shrouded in mystery.

Further, as the soul in the course of its progress realizes more and more what great difference there is between its state of purity and its state of defilement, the greater is its apprehension that when it has sloughed off this body, God may find it less endurable than it finds itself when defiled. There is, moreover, nothing more difficult than to fear death and to refrain from the allurements of this world in a degree commensurate with the jeopardies involved. Yet, so great is the soul that it can do even this, by the help, of course, of the goodness of the supreme and true God—that goodness which sustains and rules the universe, that goodness by which it has been brought about not only that all things exist but that they exist in such a way that they cannot be any better than they are. It is to this divine goodness that the soul most dutifully and confidently commits itself for help and success in the difficult task of self-purification.

The Fifth Level of the Soul

74. When this has been accomplished, that is, when the soul will be free from all corruption and purified of all its stains, then at last it possesses itself in utter joy and has no fears whatever for itself nor any anxiety for any reason. This, then, is the fifth level. For it is one thing to achieve purity, another to be in possession of it; and the activity by which the soul restores its sullied state to purity and that by which it does not suffer itself to be defiled again are two entirely different things. On this level it conceives in every way how great it is in every respect; and when it has understood that, then with unbounded and wondrous confidence it advances toward God, that is, to the immediate contemplation of truth; and it attains that supreme and transcendent reward for which it has worked so hard.

The Sixth Level of the Soul

75. Now, this activity, namely, the ardent desire to understand truth and perfection, is the soul's highest vision: it possesses none more perfect, none more noble, none more proper. This, therefore, will be the sixth level of activity. For it is one thing to clear the eye of the soul so that it will not look without purpose and without reason and see what is wrong; it is something else to protect and strengthen the health of the eye; and it is something else again to direct your gaze calmly and squarely to what is to be seen.

Those who wish to do this before they are cleansed and healed recoil so in the presence of that light of truth that they may think there is in it not only no goodness but even great evil; indeed, they may decide it does not deserve the name of truth, and with an amount of zest and enthusiasm that is to be pitied, they curse the remedy offered and run back into the darkness engulfing them and which alone their diseased condition suffers them to face. Hence, the divinely inspired prophet says most appositely: *Create a clean heart in me, O God, and renew a right spirit within my bowels.* The spirit is "right," I believe, if it sees to it that the soul cannot lose its way and go astray in its quest for truth. This spirit is not really "renewed" in anyone unless his heart is first made clean, that is to say, unless he first controls his thoughts and drains off from them all the dregs of attachment to corruptible things.

The Seventh Level of the Soul

76. Now at last we are in the very vision and contemplation of truth, which is the seventh and last level of the soul; and here we no longer have a level but in reality a home at which one arrives via those levels. What shall I say are the delights, what the enjoyment, of the supreme and true Goodness, what the everlasting peace it breathes upon us? Great and peerless souls—and we believe that they have actually seen and are still seeing these things—have told us this so far as they deemed it should be spoken of. This would I tell you now: if we hold most faithfully to the course which God enjoins on us and which we have undertaken to follow, we shall come by God's power and wisdom to that supreme Cause or that supreme Author or supreme Principle of all things or whatever other more appropriate appellative there may be for so great a reality. And when we understand that, we shall see truly how *all things under the sun are the vanity of the vain.* For "vanity" is deceit; and "the vain" are to be understood as persons who are deceived, or persons who deceive, or both. Further, one may discern how great a difference there is between these and the things that truly exist; and yet since all the other things have also been created and have God as their Maker, they are wonderful and beautiful when considered by themselves, although in comparison with the things that truly exist, they are as nothing. Then shall we acknowledge how true are the things we have been commanded to believe, and how excellently we have been nurtured in perfect health by Mother Church, and how nourishing is that milk which the Apostle Paul declared he gave as drink to children. To take such

food when one is fed by a mother is most proper; to do so when one is already grown would be shameful; to refuse it when needed would be regrettable; to find fault with it at any time or to dislike it would be wicked and impious; but to discuss it and communicate it in kindness betokens a wealth of goodness and charity.

We shall also see such great changes and transformations in this physical universe in observance of divine laws that we hold even the resurrection of the body, which some believe with too many reservations and some do not believe at all, to be so certain that the setting of the sun is no greater certainty to us. Then, indeed, shall we condemn those who ridicule the assumption of human nature by the almighty, eternal, immutable Son of God as a warranty and as first fruits of our salvation and His birth from a Virgin and the other marvels of that historic account. We shall condemn them for acting like boys who, when they see an artist painting with other pictures set up before him so that he can follow them closely, cannot believe it possible to draw a man unless the painter looks at another picture.

Furthermore, in the contemplation of truth, no matter what degree of contemplation you reach, the delight is so great, there is such purity, such innocence, a conviction in all things that is so absolute, that one could think he really knew nothing when aforetime he fancied he had knowledge. And that the soul may not be impeded from giving full allegiance to the fullness of truth, death—meaning complete escape and acquittal from this body—which previously was feared, is now desired as the greatest boon.

CHRISTIAN DOCTRINE ✠ *Steps to Wisdom*[11] 9. First of all, then, it is necessary that we should be led by the *fear of God* to seek the knowledge of His will, what He commands us to desire and what to avoid. Now this fear will of necessity excite in us the thought of our mortality and of the death that is before us and crucify all the motions of pride as if our flesh were nailed to the tree. Next it is necessary to have our hearts subdued by *piety* and not to run in the face of Holy Scripture, whether when understood it strikes at some of our sins or when not understood, we feel as if we could be wiser and give better commands ourselves. We must rather think and believe that whatever is there written, even though it be hidden, is better and truer than anything we could devise by our own wisdom.

10. After these two steps of fear and piety, we come to the third step, *knowledge*, of which I have now undertaken to treat. For in this every earnest student of the Holy Scriptures exercises himself to find nothing else in them but that God is to be loved for His own sake and our neighbour, for God's sake; and that God is to be loved with all the heart, and with all the soul, and with all the mind, and one's neighbor as one's self—that is, in such a way that all our love for ourselves should have reference to God. And on these two commandments I touched in the previous book when I was treating about things.[12] It is necessary, then, that each man should first of all find in the Scriptures that he, through being entangled in the love of this world—that is, of temporal things—has been drawn far away from such a love for God and such a love for his neighbor as Scripture enjoins. Then that fear which leads him to think of the judgment of God and that piety which gives him no option but to believe in and submit to the authority of Scripture, compel him to bewail his condition. For the knowledge of a good hope makes a man not boastful but sorrowful. And in this frame of mind he implores with unremitting prayers the comfort of the Divine help that he may not be overwhelmed in despair, and so he gradually comes to the fourth step—that is, *strength* and *resolution* (fortitudo)—in which he hungers and thirsts after righteousness. For in this frame of mind he extricates himself from every form of fatal joy in transitory things and turning away from these, fixes his affection on things eternal, to wit, the unchangeable Trinity in unity.

11. And when, to the extent of his power, he has gazed upon this object shining from afar and has felt that, owing to the weakness of his sight, he cannot endure that matchless light, then in the fifth step—that is, in the *counsel of compassion* (consilium misericordiae)—he cleanses his soul, which is violently agitated and disturbs him with base desires, from the filth it has contracted. And at this stage he exercises himself diligently in the love of his neighbor; and when he has reached the point of loving his enemy, full of hopes and unbroken in strength, he mounts to the sixth step, in which he *purifies the eye itself which can see God*, so far as God can be seen by those who as far as possible die to this world. For men see Him just so far as they die to this world; and so far as they live to it they see Him not. But yet, although that light may begin to appear clearer, and not only more tolerable but even more delightful, still it is only through a glass darkly that we are said to

see, because we walk by faith and not by sight, while we continue to wander as strangers in this world, even though our conversation be in heaven. And at this stage, too, a man so purges the eye of his affections as not to place his neighbor before, or even in comparison with, the truth, and therefore not himself, because not him whom he loves as himself. Accordingly, that holy man will be so single and pure in heart that he will not step aside from the truth, either for the sake of pleasing men or with a view to avoid any of the annoyances which beset this life. Such a son ascends to *wisdom,* which is the seventh and last step, and which he enjoys in peace and tranquillity. For the fear of God is the beginning of wisdom. From that beginning, then, till we reach wisdom itself, our way is by the steps now described.

L ETTER 137 ✠ 10. But where in all the varied movements of creation is there any work of God which is not wonderful, were it not that through familiarity these wonders have become small in our esteem? Nay, how many common things are trodden under foot, which, if examined carefully, awaken our astonishment! Take, for example, the properties of seeds: who can either comprehend or declare the variety of species, the vitality, vigour, and secret power by which they from within small compass evolve great things? Now the human body and soul which He took to Himself was created without seed by Him who in the natural world created originally seeds from no pre-existent seeds. In the body which thus became His, He who, without any liability to change in Himself, has woven according to His counsel the vicissitudes of all past centuries, became subject to the succession of seasons and the ordinary stages of the life of man. For His body, as it began to exist at a point of time, became developed with the lapse of time. But the Word of God, who was in the beginning and to whom the ages of time owe their existence, did not bow to time as bringing round the event of His incarnation apart from His consent but chose the point of time at which He freely took our nature to Himself. The human nature was brought into union with the divine; God did not withdraw from Himself.

11. Some insist upon being furnished with an explanation of the manner in which the Godhead was so united with a human soul and body as to constitute the one person of Christ, when it was necessary that this should be done once in the world's history, with

as much boldness as if they were themselves able to furnish an explanation of the manner in which the soul is so united to the body as to constitute the one person of a man, an event which is occurring every day. For just as the soul is so united to the body in one person so as to constitute man, in the same way is God united to man in one person so as to constitute Christ. In the former personality there is a combination of soul and body; in the latter there is a combination of the Godhead and man. Let my reader, however, guard against borrowing his idea of the combination from the properties of material bodies, by which two fluids when combined are so mixed that neither preserves its original character; although even among material bodies there are exceptions, such as light, which sustains no change when combined with the atmosphere. In the person of man, therefore, there is a combination of soul and body; in the person of Christ there is a combination of the Godhead with man; for when the Word of God was united to a soul having a body, He took the union with Himself both the soul and the body. The former event takes place daily in the beginning of life in individuals of the human race; the latter took place once for the salvation of men. And yet of the two events, the combination of two immaterial substances ought to be more easily believed than a combination in which the one is immaterial and the other material. For if the soul is not mistaken in regard to its own nature, it understands itself to be immaterial. Much more certainly does this attribute belong to the Word of God; and consequently the combination of the Word with the human soul is a combination which ought to be much more credible than that of soul and body. The latter is realized by us in ourselves; the former we are commanded to believe to have been realized in Christ. But if both of them were alike foreign to our experience, and we were enjoined to believe that both had taken place, which of the two would we more readily believe to have occurred? Would we not admit that two immaterial substances could be more easily combined than one immaterial and one material; unless, perhaps, it be unsuitable to use the word combination in connection with these things, because of the difference between their nature and that of material substances, both in themselves and as known to us?

T HE TRINITY ✛ BOOK XIII ✛ CHAPTER 7 *Faith is necessary, that man may at some time be blessed, which he will only attain in the future life. The blessedness of proud philosophers ridiculous and pitiable.* 10. And on this account, faith, by which men believe in God, is above all things necessary in this mortal life, most full as it is of errors and hardships. For there are no good things whatever, and above all, not those by which any one is made good, or those by which he will become blessed, of which any other source can be found whence they come to man, and are added to man, unless it be from God. But when he who is good and faithful in these miseries shall have come from this life to the blessed life, then will truly come to pass what now is absolutely impossible—namely, that a man may live as he will. For he will not will to live badly in the midst of that felicity, nor will he will anything that will be wanting, nor will there be wanting anything which he shall have willed. Whatever shall be loved, will be present; nor will that be longed for, which shall not be present. Everything which will be there will be good, and the supreme God will be the supreme good and will be present for those to enjoy who love Him; and what altogether is most blessed, it will be certain that it will be so for ever. But now, indeed philosophers have made for themselves, according to the pleasure of each, their own ideals of a blessed life; that they might be able, as it were by their own power, to do that, which by the common condition of mortals they were not able to do—namely, to live as they would. For they felt that no one could be blessed otherwise than by having what he would and by suffering nothing which he would not. And who would not will that the life, whatsoever it be, with which he is delighted and which he therefore calls blessed, were so in his own power that he could have it continually? And yet who is in this condition? Who wills to suffer troubles in order that he may endure them manfully, although he both wills and is able to endure them if he does suffer them? Who would will to live in torments, even although he is able to live laudably by holding fast to righteousness in the midst of them through patience? They who have endured these evils, either in wishing to have or in fearing to lose what they loved, whether wickedly or laudably, have thought of them as transitory. For many have stretched boldly through transitory evils to good things which will last. And these doubtless, are blessed through hope, even while actually suffering such transitory evils, through which they arrive at good things which will not be transitory. But he who is blessed through hope is not yet blessed: for he expects, through patience, a blessedness which he does not yet grasp. Whereas he, on the other hand, who is tormented without any such hope, without any such reward, let him use as much endurance as he pleases, is not truly blessed but bravely miserable. For he is not on that account not miserable, because he would be more so if he also bore misery impatiently. Further, even if he does not suffer those things which he would not will to suffer in his own body, not even then is he to be esteemed blessed, inasmuch as he does not live as he wills. For to omit other things, which, while the body remains unhurt, belong to those annoyances of the mind, without which we should will to live, and which are innumerable; he would will, at any rate, if he were able, so to have his body safe and sound, and so to suffer no inconveniences from it, as to have it within his own control, or even to have it with an imperishableness of the body itself; and because he does not possess this, and hangs in doubt about it, he certainly does not live as he wills. For although he may be ready from fortitude to accept and bear with an equal mind, whatever adversities may happen to him, yet he had rather they should not happen and hinders them if he is able; and he is in such way ready for both alternatives that, as much as is in him, he wishes for the one and shuns the other; and if he have fallen into that which he shuns, he therefore bears it willingly, because that could not happen which he willed. He bears it, therefore, in order that he may not be crushed; but he would not willingly be even burdened. How, then, does he live as he wills? Is it because he is willingly strong to bear what he would not will to be put upon him? Then he only wills what he can, because he cannot have what he wills. And here is the sum-total of the blessedness of proud mortals, I know not whether to be laughed at or not rather to be pitied, who boast that they live as they will, because they willingly bear patiently what they are unwilling should happen to them. For this, they say, is like Terence's wise saying—

"Since that cannot be which you will, will that which thou canst." (Andreia Act, II. Scene 1, v. 5, 6) That this is aptly said, who denies? But it is advice given to the miserable man, that he may not be more miserable. And it is not rightly or truly said to the blessed man, such as all wish themselves to be, "that cannot be which you will." For if he is blessed, whatever he wills can be; since he does not will that which cannot be. But such a life is not for this mortal state, neither will it come to pass unless when immortality also shall come to pass. And if this could not be given at all to man, blessedness too would be sought in vain, since it cannot be without immortality.

CHAPTER 8 *Blessedness cannot exist without immortality.* 11. As, therefore, all men will to be blessed, certainly, if they will truly, they will also to be immortal; for otherwise they could not be blessed. And further, if questioned also concerning immortality, as before concerning blessedness, all reply that they will it. But blessedness of what quality soever, such as is not so but rather is so called, is sought, nay indeed is feigned, in this life, whilst immortality is despaired of, without which true blessedness cannot be. Since he lives blessedly, as we have said before and have sufficiently proved and concluded, who lives as he wills and wills nothing wrongly. But no one wrongly wills immortality, if human nature is by God's gift capable of it; and if it is not capable of it, it is not capable of blessedness. For, that a man may live blessedly, he must needs live. And if life quits him by his dying, how can a blessed life remain with him? And when it quits him, without doubt it either quits him unwilling or willing, or neither. If unwilling, how is the life blessed which is so within his will as not to be within his power? And whereas no one is blessed who wills something that he does not have, how much less is he blessed who is quitted against his will, not by honor nor by possessions nor by any other thing but by the blessed life itself, since he will have no life at all? And hence, although no feeling is left for his life to be thereby miserable (for the blessed life quits him, because life altogether quits him), yet he is wretched as long as he feels, because he knows that against his will that is being destroyed for the sake of which he loves all else and which he loves beyond all else. A life therefore cannot both be blessed and yet quit a man against his will, since no one becomes blessed against his will; and hence how much more does it make a man miserable by quitting him against his will, when it would make him miserable if he had it against his will! But if it quit him with his will, even so how was that a blessed life, which he who had it willed should perish? It remains for them to say that neither of these is in the mind of the blessed man; that is, that he is neither unwilling nor willing to be quitted by a blessed life, when through death life quits him altogether; for that he stands firm with an even heart, prepared alike for either alternative. But neither is that a blessed life which is such as to be unworthy of his love whom it makes blessed. For how is that a blessed life which the blessed man does not love? Or how is that loved, of which it is received indifferently, whether it is to flourish or to perish? Unless perhaps the virtues, which we

love in this way on account of blessedness alone, venture to persuade us that we do not love blessedness itself. Yet if they did this,
we should certainly leave off loving the virtues themselves, when we
do not love that on account of which alone we loved them. And
further, how will that opinion be true, which has been so tried
and sifted and thoroughly strained and is so certain, viz. that all
men will to be blessed, if they themselves who are already blessed
neither will nor do not will to be blessed? Or if they will it, as
truth proclaims, as nature constrains, in which indeed the supremely good and unchangeably blessed Creator has implanted that
will; if, I say, they will to be blessed who are blessed, certainly they
do not will to be not blessed. But if they do not will not to be
blessed, without doubt they do not will to be annihilated and
perish in regard to their blessedness. But they cannot be blessed except they are alive; therefore they do not will so to perish in regard to their blessedness. Therefore, whoever are either truly blessed
or desire to be so will to be immortal. But he does not will
blessedly who has not that which he wills. Therefore it follows
that in no way can life be truly blessed unless it be eternal.

CHAPTER 9 *We say that future blessedness is truly eternal, not
through human reasonings, but by the help of faith. The immortality of blessedness becomes credible from the incarnation
of the Son of God.* 12. Whether human nature can receive this,
which yet it confesses to be desirable, is no small question. But if
faith be present, which is in those to whom Jesus has given power
to become the sons of God, then there is no question. Assuredly,
of those who endeavor to discover it from human reasonings, scarcely
a few, and they endued with great abilities and abounding in
leisure and learned with the most subtle learning, have been able
to attain to the investigation of the immortality of the soul alone.
And even for the soul they have not found a blessed life that is
stable, that is true, since they have said that it returns to the
miseries of this life even after blessedness. And they among them
who are ashamed of this opinion and have thought that the purified soul is to be placed in eternal happiness without a body
hold such opinions concerning the backward eternity of the world
as to confute this opinion of theirs concerning the soul: a thing
which here it is too long to demonstrate, but it has been, as I
think, sufficiently explained by us in the twelfth book of the *City
of God.* But that faith promises not by human reasoning but by
divine authority, that the whole man, who certainly consists of soul

and body, shall be immortal and on this account truly blessed. And so when it had been said in the Gospel that Jesus has given "power to become the sons of God to them who received Him"; and what it is to have received Him had been shortly explained by saying, "To them that believe on His name" and when it was further added in what way they are to become sons of God, viz., "Which were born not of blood, nor of the will of the flesh, nor of the will of man, but of God";—lest then that infirmity of men which we all see and bear should despair of attaining so great excellence, it is added in the same place, "And the Word was made flesh, and dwelt among us"; so that, on the contrary, men might be convinced by contrast of that which seemed incredible. For if He who is by nature the Son of God was made the Son of man through mercy for the sake of the sons of men—for this is what is meant by "The Word was made flesh, and dwelt among us" men— how much more credible is it that the sons of men by nature should be made the sons of God by the grace of God and should dwell in God, in whom alone and from whom alone the blessed can be made partakers of that immortality, of which that we might be convinced, the Son of God was made the partaker of our mortality?

NOTES (The Augustinian Psychology)

[1] Rom. 8:3

[2] The text being here obscure, we have followed the MSS., which omit the words "interim quod constat peccatum primi hominis."

[3] Gal. 5:17

[4] II Cor. 5:4

[5] Wisd. of Sol. 9:15

[6] I Cor. 15:53

[7] I Tim. 6:16

[8] Eccles. 12:7

[9] Gen. 2:7

[10] Rom. 1:24

[11] *Christian Doctrine* II, 7, 9-11

[12] *Christian Doctrine* I, 22, 21

✠ ✠ ✠

THE PROBLEM OF KNOWLEDGE

✠ ✠ ✠

The first selection, the dialogue *Against the Academics,* is dedicated to Romanianus the friend of Augustine and was written in the first year of his conversion. One of the most pressing problems at this time for Augustine was his need to be assured of the possibility of attaining certitude and truth, for he had only recently accepted for a time the position of the Academics and their scepticism. Of the importance of this problem of doubt and certitude at this time he writes: "This doubt was the source of my writing three books at the very beginning of my conversion, so that I might not be hindered at the very threshold of faith by this opposing doctrine." [1] The dialogue covers several aspects of the problem of knowledge. The material selected is taken entirely from Book III. Book I is concerned largely with the identification of the happy life with wisdom, for happiness is a life in conformity with reason. More explicitly, Augustine maintains that happiness consists in the knowledge of truth and not in the mere pursuit of it. In Book II he develops in more detail the various aspects of the sceptical philosophy and aside from certain historical observations the discussion turns upon the problem of truth and its relation to probabilism. The brunt of Augustine's criticism here is that the Academics assert that they follow the "truth-like" or that which resembles the true; they do not know what truth itself is and thus are limited to judgments of probability. Book III returns to a discussion and review of the nature of wisdom. The sceptical position is then summed up in the statement that "nothing is understood and that assent is not to be given to anything." Augustine's refutation of scepticism begins with a review of the various fields of knowledge in which he endeavors to discover truths that may be considered as necessary, immutable, and eternal. Such truths, he maintains, are to be found in mathematics—"even if the whole human race were fast asleep, it would still be necessarily true that three times three are nine"—and in dialectic.[2] Concerning dialectic or logic, Augustine notes especially the necessary truth of disjunctive propositions, e.g. that the soul cannot be both mortal and immortal, that there cannot be both one sun and two, that a man cannot be both happy and miserable at the same time. Such truths of dialectic, as well as the truths of mathematics, he terms *rationes* or *veritates aeternae* because they are beyond time and change. That such truths exist, he is convinced, is a sufficient answer to the scepticism of the Academics and establishes the validity of human reason. He concludes by noting some of the practical and moral consequences of probabilism and doubt.

The *City of God* is undoubtedly familiar to most readers and needs little introduction. Probably the most influential book of the middle ages, it ranks with *The Trinity* and the *Confessions* as the greatest of Augustine's intellectual achievements. Written between 413 and 426, it is concerned in the first ten book with the refutation of the pagan charge that "Rome fell in Christian days." The more positive achievement of the work is covered in the last twelve books with a defense and exposition of the Christian faith which culminates by contrasting the ideals of the City of God with those of the Earthly City and the wisdom of Christianity over against the most notable philosophies and religions of the pagan world. The brief selection taken from Book XI is illustrative of what may be termed the Augustinian *Cogito*. The principal theme of the selection is the *Si fallor sum,* if I am deceived then I am. This may be compared with Descartes' famous *Cogito, ergo sum;* but as we have pointed out in the general introduction there are significant differences in the Augustinian and the Cartesian *Cogito*.

The selection from Book XV of *The Trinity* is directed against the Academic philosophy. It repeats the theme of the previous selection, but expounds it in more detail. More important it reveals the fundamental conviction of Augustine that a certain knowledge does exist. Augustine's position is not one of declaring 'let us see how much we can doubt' but rather "far be it from us to doubt" as do the Academics.

The selection from Book XI of *The Trinity* is an analysis of sensation or perception with the objective of developing the three elements in sense knowledge: the object, the sense act, and the activity of mind or attention. The analysis of sensation in this manner affords Augustine the opportunity to utilize the notion of the Trinity in relation to sensation in a manner similar to the exposition of intellectual knowledge as a reflection of the activity of the Trinity. This analysis may also be compared with the treatment of sensation in *The Greatness of the Soul,* cited in the previous topic on the Psychology of Augustine, and with the selection from *The Literal Meaning of Genesis* which immediately follows.

The Literal Meaning of Genesis consists of twelve books dealing largely with the explanation of creation as revealed in *Genesis.* As an account of creation it supplements considerably that given in the *Confessions,* and is the more comprehensive of the several commentaries that Augustine wrote on Genesis. The work was carried out over a period of fifteen years, from 401 to 415, and it contains, as well as the account of creation, studies on astrology, psychology, and anthropology, an essay on the knowledge of angels, and an exegesis of the statement of St. Paul: "I know a man in Christ who fourteen years ago—whether in the body I do not know, or out of the body I do not know, God knows—such a one was caught up to the third heaven. And I know such a man—whether in the body or out of the body I do not know, God knows—that he was caught up into paradise and heard secret words that man may not repeat." (II Cor. 12:2-4) It is this exegesis that leads Augustine to the subject of visions, and he proceeds in the selection chosen here to study the three kinds of vision: corporeal, spiritual, and intellectual. Particular attention is given to the meaning of the term "spirit," the nature of spiritual vision, and its relation to the other two forms of vision. An analysis of sensation supplements the account of corporeal vision and shows more specifically the function of spirit in sensation.

The Teacher is another of the earlier philosophical dialogues of Augustine. It was written circa 389, at least two years after his conversion. The participants in the dialogue are Augustine and his son Adeodatus who was to die in that year at the age of 18. The first several chapters of the dialogue are devoted to a study of the symbolism of language, following which Augustine proceeds to the development of his famous paradox *nusquam discere*—nothing can be learned. In explaining the paradox Augustine observes that in the relation between teacher and student there are three possible alternatives for the communication of ideas: (1) The teacher may fail to convince or persuade the student that what he, the teacher, has said is true, and hence nothing is learned. (2) The student may be convinced that the teacher is in error and again nothing is learned. (3) Assuming that the student accepts as correct what the teacher has said, there is still nothing learned, for the student has seen for himself that what has been said is true. Learning is a process of discovering that which already exists within the mind.[3] The outcome of the analysis is that in order that we may discover the truth we must look within to the Interior Master. Christ is the Interior Master and only through His Word and by His help can man gain a comprehension of the truth and attain the highest knowledge.

Between 393 and 396, shortly before he became bishop of Hippo, Augustine participated in a series of discussions on a variety of philosophical and theological questions at Tagaste and Hippo. After he became bishop he arranged all his notes and replies to these questions in the form of a book which he entitled *Eighty-three Different Questions*. Question 46 is entitled *The Ideas* and is perhaps the best and most explicit statement of Augustine on the Platonic Ideas. The selection is significant for the status that it gives to such Ideas, namely, that they have an existence as *Exemplars* in the mind of God, rather than as Plato taught an independent existence in an intelligible world of their own. The selection provides then an essential account of what has been termed Augustine's exemplarism, an integral part of his theory of the Divine Illumination and the role the Ideas play in our knowledge and the divine creativity.

The last three selections are from *The Trinity*. The selection from Book XII deals fairly explicitly with the theme of the relation between knowledge and wisdom, but out of this discussion several significant statements are made relevant to Augustine's doctrine of the Divine Illumination. The brief selection from Book XIV of *The Trinity* deals with one aspect of the theory of the Divine Illumination, namely, the existence of the eternal rules and how we may obtain a knowledge of them.

The selection from Book IX of *The Trinity* is concerned principally with a theme that was of considerable interest to Augustine—the exposition of the existence of different possible trinities in the mind of man as an exegesis of the biblical statement that man was created in the image of God. The selection is an exposition of the existence of a trinity of mind, knowledge, and love that exists in us and which is revealed in the analysis of the mind's knowledge and love of itself. As revealing a conception of the nature of man, the selection might have been included with those dealing with the nature of the soul. However, the present selection also has considerable relevance for Augustine's theory of the Divine Illumination, his conception of wisdom, and the analysis of self-knowledge.

AGAINST THE ACADEMICS ✠ BOOK III ✠ CHAPTER

3. *The difference between the Wise Man and the Philosopher*
5. "I would like you," I said, "to tell me briefly what you think to be the difference between the wise man and the philosopher."

"In my opinion," he said, "the wise man differs in no way from the philosopher except that the wise man in a certain way possesses those things which can only be longed for—however eagerly—by the philosopher."

"Now, then," I asked, "what are these things? For my part, I see no difference except that one knows wisdom and the other wants to know."

"If," he said, "you give us a simple definition of knowledge, your point already becomes more clear."

"No matter how I define it," I replied, "all are agreed that there cannot be knowledge of what is not true."

"In my remark," he said, "I purposed to limit that question for you, in order to prevent an unconsidered concession of mine from allowing your oratory to gallop unrestrained over the plains of this cardinal question."

I replied: "To be sure, you have left me no galloping space at all! Indeed, if I mistake not, we have arrived at that for which I have been striving all the time—the end. For it, as you stated so acutely and truly, there is no difference between the philosopher and the wise man except that the former loves, the latter possesses, wisdom—for which reason you did not hesitate to use the term proper here, 'possess'; and since no one can possess wisdom in his mind, if he has not learned anything; and since no one can learn anything, if he does not know anything; and since no one can know what is not true: therefore, the wise man knows truth, you yourself have just admitted that he has wisdom, that is to say, its 'possession,' in his mind."

"I may," he said, "seem to be impertinent, but I do wish to deny that I admitted that the wise man has the 'possession' of the power of inquiring into divine and human things. I do not see why you should think that it is not the 'possession' of discovered probabilities that he has."

"Do you concede to me," I asked, "that no one knows what is not true?"

"Certainly," he replied.

"Assert, if you can," I said, "that the wise man does not know wisdom."

"But why" said, he, "do you in this way restrict the whole question? Could he not believe that he has grasped wisdom?"

"Give me your hand," I said. "If you recall, this is the point which I said yesterday that I would prove; and now I am happy that it was not I who expressed this conclusion, but that you offered it to me spontaneously on your own. For I said that between the Academics and myself there was this difference: that while they thought it probable that truth could not be perceived, I believed that, though I myself had not yet found it, it could be found by the wise man. You now, when pressed by my question as to whether or not the wise man did not know wisdom, reply: 'He thinks that he knows'."

"Well," he asked, "what follows from that?"

"This," I replied: "that if he thinks that he knows wisdom, he does not think that the wise man cannot know anything. Or, if wisdom is nothing, then say so."

6. "I should indeed believe," he replied, "that we had arrived at our final object but that suddenly, as we joined hands, I realized that we are very far apart and separated by a long distance. For, obviously, the only point at issue between us was, whether or not the wise man could arrive at the perception of truth. You asserted that he could. I denied it. But I do not think that I have now conceded to you anything except that the wise man can believe that he has achieved the wisdom of probabilities. That wisdom I understood to be concerned with the investigation of things human and divine. We are, I take it, agreed on that."

"You will not," I said, "evolve a method of escape by involving the issue! For the moment, it would seem to me, you are arguing merely to try your skill. You know well that these young men can scarcely as yet follow subtle and acute reasoning. You abuse, then, the ignorance of your jury. It is a case of your saying as much as you like simply because no one will protest. Now, a few moments ago, when I was questioning you as to whether or not the wise man knew wisdom, you said that he believed that he knew. But he who believes that the wise man knows wisdom, certainly cannot believe that the wise man knows nothing. Such a proposition is impossible, unless a man dares to say that wisdom is nothing. From this it follows that in this your view is identical with mine. For my view that the wise man knows something, is, I believe, also yours, since you believe that the wise man believes that he knows wisdom."

He replied: "I think that you wish to exercise your powers just as much as I do. I am surprised at that, for you have no need of any practice in this matter at all. I may, of course, still be blind in seeing a difference between 'believing-one-knows' and 'knowing,' and between the wisdom bound up with investigation and truth itself. I do not see how these opinions expressed by each of us can be squared with one another."

As we were being called to lunch, I said: "I am not displeased that you should be so obstinate. Either both of us do not know what we are talking about, and we must, therefore, take steps to avoid such a disgrace; or this is true of only one of us, and to leave him so and neglect him, is equally disgraceful. We shall, however, have to meet again in the afternoon; for, just when I thought that we had finished, you began to indulge in fisticuffs with me."

They all laughed at this and we departed.

CHAPTER 4 *The Wise Man Knows Truth* 7. When we returned, we found Licentius, whose thirst for Helicon could never be quenched, eagerly trying to think out verses. For he had quietly arisen without having had anything to drink, in the middle of lunch, even though this was over almost as quickly as it begun. I remarked to him: "I certainly hope that some day you will realize your heart's desire and master poetry. Not that I take such pleasure in the art; but I see that you are so obsessed by it that you cannot escape from this infatuation except through tiring of it, and this is a common experience when one has reached perfection. And another thing, since you have a good voice, I would prefer that you would ply our ears with your verses than that you should sing, like poor little birds that we see in cages, from those Greek tragedies words which you do not understand. But I suggest that you go, if you wish, and drink something and then return to our school, provided the *Hortensius* and philosophy still mean something to you. To her you have already dedicated the tender first fruits of your mind in your recent discussion—a discussion which inflamed you even more than does poetry for the knowledge of great and truly fruitful things. But while I endeavor to bring you back to the circle of those studies by which the mind is developed, I fear lest it become a labyrinth to you, and I almost repent of having held you back from your first impulse."

Licentius blushed and went away to drink. He was very thirsty. Moreover, he could thus avoid me, who seemed likely to have more and sharper things to say to him.

8. When he had come back, I began as follows, while all paid close attention: "Alypius, can it be that we disagree on a matter which to me seems really very evident?"

"It is not surprising," he said, "if what you say is manifest to you should be obscure to me. After all, many things evident enough in themselves can be more evident to some than to others; so, too, some things obscure in themselves can be still more obscure to some people. For, believe me, that if this matter is evident to you, there is some one else to whom it is even more evident, and still another person to whom it is more obscure than it is to me. But I beg you to make what is evident still more evident, so that you may cease to regard me as a diehard in argument."

"Please, listen closely," I said, "and do not bother for the moment to reply to my question. Knowing you and myself well, I feel that with a little attention my point will become clear and one of us will quickly convince the other. Now, then, did you not say—or, perhaps, I did not hear rightly—that the wise man thought that he knew wisdom?"

He said that this was so.

"Let us," I said, "forget about the wise man for the moment. Are you yourself wise or are you not?"

"I am anything but that," he replied.

"But," said I, "do give me your own personal opinion about the Academic wise man. Do you think that he knows wisdom?"

He replied: "Is thinking that one knows the same as, or different from, knowing? I am afraid lest confusion on this point might afford cover to either of us."

9. "This," I said, "has become what they call a Tuscan argument: for this is the name they gave to an argument when instead of answering the difficulty, a man proposes another. It was this

that our poet—let us win the attention of Licentius for a moment —in his Eclogues judged fairly to be rustic and downright countryish: when one asks the other, where the heavens are no more than three ells broad, the other replies: 'In what lands do flowers grow engraved with the names of kings?' Please, Alypius, do not think that we can allow ourselves that merely because we are on the farm! At least, let these little baths serve you as a reminder of the decorum that is expected in places of learning. Kindly answer my question: Do you think that the Academic wise man knows wisdom?"

"Not to lose ourselves," he replied, "parrying words with words—I think that he thinks that he knows wisdom."

"Therefore," I said, "you think that he does not know wisdom? I am not asking you what you think the wise man thinks, but if you think that the wise man knows wisdom. You can, I take it, say either yes or no, here and now."

"I do wish," he returned, "that the matter were either as easy for me as it is for you or as difficult for you as it is for me; and that you were not so insistent and put such great store in these points. For, when you asked me what I thought about the Academic wise man, I replied that in my opinion it seemed to him that he knew wisdom: I did not wish to assent rashly that I knew or, what would be just as rash, say that he knew."

"I shall be greatly obliged," I said, "if you will be good enough, first, to answer the question I put to you, and not those you yourself put to yourself. Secondly, you may disregard for the moment what satisfaction I expect to receive from this: I know that you are as interested in it as in your own expectations. Obviously, if I deceive myself by this line of questioning, I shall promptly come over to your side and we shall finish the dispute. Finally, banish the anxiety which I note is somehow gripping you, and pay close attention so that you will have no trouble in understanding what I want you to reply.

"Now, you said that you did not give your assent or denial— but this is just what you should do with my question—for the reason that you did not wish to state rashly that you knew what you did not know. As if I were to ask you what you know, and not what you think! And now I ask the same question more plainly—if, indeed, I can ask it any more plainly: is it, or is it not, your opinion that the wise man knows wisdom?"

"If it is possible," he replied, "to find a wise man such as reason conceives of, I can believe that he knows wisdom."

"Reason, therefore," I said, "indicated to you that the wise

144

man is such that he knows wisdom. So far you are right. You could not properly have held any other opinion."

10. "And now I ask you if the wise man can be found. If he can, then he can also know wisdom and our discussion is finished. But if you say that he cannot be found, then the question will be, not if the wise man knows anything, but rather if any one can be a wise man. Answering this in the affirmative, we must take leave of the Academics, and go over this point with you as far as we can, and with great care and attention. For the Academics maintained, or rather opined, at one and the same time that the wise man could exist, but that, nevertheless, man could not attain to knowledge. Therefore, they actually claimed that the wise man knows nothing. But you believe that he knows wisdom, which certainly is not identical with knowing nothing. For we are agreed, as are all the ancients and even the Academics themselves, that no one can know what is not true. Accordingly, there remains now that you either maintain that wisdom is nothing, or admit that the wise man as described by the Academics is such as is unknown to reason, and then, dropping that question, agree to investigate if man can possess such wisdom as is conceived by reason. For there is no other wisdom which we should, or can, rightly call by that name."

CHAPTER 5 *The Question of Assent* 11. "Even though I should concede," he said, "what you are so anxiously striving for, namely, that the wise man knows wisdom and that between us we have discovered something which the wise man can know, nevertheless, I do not at all think that the whole case of the Academics has been undermined. Indeed, I notice that they can fall back on a stronghold that is by no means weak and that their line of retreat has not been cut off. They can still withold assent. In fact, the very point in which you think they have been vanquished helps their cause. For they will say that it is so true that nothing can be known and that assent must be withheld from everything, that even this their principle of not being able to know anything, which practically from the very beginning until you came along, they had maintained as probable, is now wrested from them by your argument. Your argument may be in fact invincible or may seem so to me in my stupidity, but as before, so now, it cannot dislodge them, when they can still with confidence assert that even now assent must be withheld from everything. It is possible, they will say, that perhaps some day they themselves or some one else will discover some argument which can be urged with point and probability against this second principle of theirs also. They would have us notice that their behavior is illustrated and mirrored, so to speak, by that of Proteus who, it is said, could be caught only by means which invariably did not result in his capture. His pursuers were never sure that what they had was still he, unless some divinity informed them. May that divinity be present to us and may he deign to show us that truth for which we strive so hard! I, too, shall then confess, even if the Academics do not agree—though I think they will—that they have been overcome."

12. "Good!" I said, "that was all I wanted. For look, I beg you, at all the great gains I have made! First, we can say that the Academics are so far vanquished that they have now no defense left except the impossible. Indeed, who could in any way understand or believe that a man who is beaten, by the very fact that he has been beaten, boasts that he has won. And so, if we have any further dispute with them, if it is not on the score of their assertion that nothing can be known but on the score of their maintaining that one must not assent to anything.

"Consequently, we are now in agreement. For both they and I believe that the wise man knows wisdom. But they advise, all the same, that assent should not be given to this. They say that they *believe* only but do not at all *know*. As if I should profess that I *know!* I say that I also *believe* this. If they do not know wisdom, then they, and I with them, are stupid. But I think that we should approve of something, namely, truth. I ask them if they deny this, that is to say, if they declare that one must not assent to truth. They will never say this; but they will maintain that truth cannot be found. Consequently, in this I am to a great extent at one with them in so far as both of us do not object and, therefore, necessarily agree to the proposition that one must assent to truth.

" 'But who will indicate truth for us?' " they ask. "On that point I shall not trouble to dispute with them. I am satisfied, since they consider it no longer probable that the wise man knows nothing. Otherwise, they would be forced to maintain a most absurd proposition, that either wisdom is nothing, or the wise man does not know wisdom."

CHAPTER 6 *Truth Revealed only by a Divinity* 13. "You, Alypius, have told us who it is that can point out truth—and I must take pains to disagree with you as little as possible. You remarked that only some divinity could reveal truth to man. Your words were brief but full of piety. There has been nothing in our discussion which has given me more delight, nothing more profound, nothing more probable, and, provided, so I trust, that divinity be present to us, nothing more true. With what profound understanding and sensitiveness to what is best in philosophy did you direct our attention to Proteus! Proteus, of whom you all know, is introduced as a symbol of truth. You will see, young men, from this that the poets are not entirely despised by philosophy. Proteus, as I say, plays in poetry the role of truth which no one can hold if, deceived by false representations, he slackens or lets loose the bonds of understanding. It is these representations which, because of our association with corporeal things, do their best to fool and deceive us through the senses which we use for the necessities of this life, even when we have already grasped truth and hold it, so to speak, within our hands.

"Here, then, is the third blessing which has come upon me, and I cannot find words to express how highly I value it. I find my most intimate friend agreeing with me not only on probability as a factor in human life but also on religion itself—a point which is the clearest sign of a true friend; for friendship has been rightly and with just reverence defined as 'agreement on things human and divine combined with goodwill and love.'"

CHAPTER 7 *Augustine's Refutation of the New Academy* 14
"Nevertheless, lest the arguments of the Academics should seem somewhat to cloud the issue, or we ourselves seem to some to dispute arrogantly the authority of highly learned men, among whom Tullius especially must always have weight with us, I shall with your leave first put forward a few considerations against those who would believe that the arguments referred to stand in the way of truth. Then I shall show why, as it seems to me, the Academics concealed their real doctrine. Now, then Alypius, although I see that you are entirely on my side, nevertheless take a brief for them for a few moments, and answer my question."

"Since," he replied, "you have, as they say, got off on the right foot today, I shall not do anything to hinder your complete victory. I shall with the greater confidence attempt to defend their side, seeing that the task is one imposed by yourself. All the same, I would prefer you, if you find it convenient, to achieve the result you aim at rather by means of an uninterrupted discussion than by this questioning, lest, although already your prisoner, I should be tormented, as being in fact an unyielding enemy, by the rack of all your detailed arguments. Such cruelty is not at all in accordance with your humanity!"

15. And so I, when I noticed that the others, too, wanted this, began, as it were anew. "I shall do as you wish," I said, "although I had hoped that after my toil in the rhetoric school, I should find some rest in this light armour—that is, I should conduct these enquiries by question and answer rather than by exposition—nevertheless, since we are so few and it will not be necessary for me to raise my voice beyond what is good for my health and since I have also wished that the pen should, so to speak, guide and control my discourse—also on account of my health, lest I become more excited mentally than is good for my body—listen, then, to my opinion, given to you, as you wish in continuous exposition.

"In the first place, however, let us examine a point about which the enthusiastic supporters of the Academics are very boastful. There is in the books which Cicero wrote in support of them a certain passage that to me seems seasoned with rare wit, while some think it a passage of great power and conviction. It would be hard to imagine that any man should not be impressed by what is there written."

Everybody of every other school that claims to be wise gives the second place to the wise man of the Academy. It is inevitable, of course, that each claims the first place for himself. From this one can conclude with probability that the Academic rightly judges himself as holding the first place, since in the judgment of all the others he holds the second.

16. Suppose, for example, that there is a Stoic wise man present. It was against the Stoics especially that the Academics felt called upon to pit their wits. If Zeno or Chrysippus be asked who is the wise man, he will reply that it is the man whom he himself has described. But Epicurus or some other adversary will deny this and maintain that his own representative, rather, is the wise man. The fight is on! Zeno shouts, and the whole Porch is in uproar: man was born for nothing else but virtue; she draws souls to herself merely by her grandeur, without resorting to the bait of any external advantage and, as it were, of a pandering reward; the pleasure vaunted by Epicurus is a thing received in common by beasts and by them alone; to pitch out man—and the wise man!—into such company is abominable.

But over against this, Epicurus, like another Bacchus, calling from his Gardens a horde to aid him, who, though drunk, yet look for someone whom in their Bacchic frenzy, they can tear to pieces with their long nails and savage fangs, and exploiting the popular approval of pleasure and an easy-going and quiet life, maintains passionately that without pleasure nobody could appear to be happy.

Should an Academic chance upon their quarrel, he will listen to each side as it attempts to win him over to itself. But if he joins one side or the other, he will be shouted down by the side he is leaving in the lurch, as crazy, ignorant, and reckless. Accordingly, when he has given an attentive ear now to this side, now to that, and is asked his opinion, he will say that he is in doubt. Now ask the Stoic, which is the better—Epicurus who declares that the Stoic is talking nonsense or the Academic who gives the verdict that he must give further consideration to a matter of such moment—and no one doubts but that the Academic will be preferred. And next turn to Epicurus and ask him which he prefers—Zeno by whom he is called a beast or Arcesilas who tells him: "Perhaps what you say is true, but I shall have to look into the matter more closely." Is it not clear that Epicurus will decide that the whole Porch is crazy, and that in comparison with them, the Academics are unassuming and judicious people?— *Acad.*, Frag. XX (Müller)

"Quite similarly, regarding practically all the other philosophical sects Cicero treats his readers to what we might call a delightful piece of theatre. He shows, as it were, that there is none of those sects which, having of necessity put itself in the first place, does not proclaim that it allots the second place to the one which it sees is not in opposition to, but merely undecided about, its own position. On that point I shall not oppose them in any way or deprive them of glory."

CHAPTER 8 17. "Some people, to be sure, may think that in this passage Cicero was not poking fun, but rather that because he was appalled by the levity of these Greeklings, he purposed to dig up and collect some of their banalities and rantings. But if I wished to join issue with such pretence, could I not easily show how much less an evil it is to have no knowledge than to be incapable of receiving any? Thus it happens that if this petty boaster of the Academics offers himself as a pupil to the various sects, and none of them succeeds in convincing him of what it thinks it knows, they will then all come together with a will and make a mockery of him. For now each of them will judge that every other adversary has not indeed learnt anything, but that the Academic is *incapable* of learning anything. After that he will be driven from one school after the other not with the rod, which would cause him a little more shame than hurt, but by the clubs and cudgels of the men of the mantle. For there will be no trouble in calling in the help of the Cynics, as one would call in Hercules, to overcome the common scourge.

"And if I, who may be more easily allowed to do so, seeing that though I practice philosophy I am not yet wise, wish to compete with the Academics for the contemptible glory that is theirs, how can they halt me? Suppose that an Academic and myself together came upon the conflict of philosophers described before. Let all be present. Let them expound their opinions briefly in the time allowed. Ask Carneades his opinion. He will reply that he is in doubt. Promptly each will prefer him to all the others; that is to say, all will prefer him among all the others—truly a distinction great and remarkable!

"Who would not like to achieve a like distinction? And so, when I am asked my opinion, I, too, shall give the same answer. I shall be equally commended. That is to say, the glory which the wise man is reaping is of the sort that equates him with the blockhead! But suppose the latter easily beats him in his distinction: will not the Academic be put to shame? As he is trying to slip off from the trial, I shall pull him back—for stupidity surpasses itself in craving for a victory of this kind. Holding him tight, I shall tell the judges something which they do not know, and say: 'Gentlemen, there is much in common between this fellow and myself that neither of us knows which of you follows truth. But we have also individual opinions of our own, about which I ask you to enter a judgment. I, for my part, am uncertain, although I have heard your expositions, as to where truth is, for the simple reason that I do not know which of you is the wiser. But this fellow denies that even the wise man knows anything, even wisdom itself to which he owes it that he is called wise!'

"Can anybody fail to see who will win the palm? If my opponent admits my charge, I shall best him in glory. But if he blushes for shame and confesses that the wise man does know wisdom, then my opinion carries the day."

CHAPTER 9 18. "However, let us now retire from this courthouse with its wranglings and betake ourselves somewhere where no crowd will disturb us. If only it could be the school of Plato, which is said to have received its name from the fact that it was cut off from the public! But let us no longer talk about glory, which is a thing of little and trifling account, but rather, so far as we can, of life itself and what hope there is of happiness.

"The Academics deny that anything can be known. How have you established this, you men of learning and scholarship? 'Zeno's definition,' they say, 'taught us that.' But why I beg of you? If it is true, then a man who knows merely it itself, knows some truth. If it is not true, then it should not have upset men of such calibre. But let us examine what Zeno says: according to him that object of sense can be comprehended and perceived which manifests itself by signs that cannot belong to what is not true. Was it this that moved you, my dear Platonist, to use every endeavor to draw those interested away from the hope of learning so that, aided as they were by a shameful lethargy of mind, they might give up the whole business of philosophy?

19. "But why should it not have influenced him profoundly, if nothing such can be found, and unless it be such, cannot be perceived? If this be so, it would have been better to say that man could not possess wisdom than that the wise man should not know why he lives, should not know how he lives, should not know if he lives, and finally—than which nothing more perverse, silly and crazy could be said—that he should be wise and at the same time ignorant of wisdom. Which is the more shocking statement to bear: that man cannot be wise or that the wise man does not know wisdom? There can be no use in discussing the point further, if the matter itself so explained does not offer the necessary basis for a decision. But the chance is that if the former statement were made, men would be driven away entirely from philosophy. In view of this are they to be attracted to her by the august and alluring name of wisdom that later, having wasted their lives and learnt nothing, they may only heap upon you their greatest curses? For forsaking the pleasures of the body which they might have had, they followed you only into tortures of the mind!

20. "But let us see who it is that most frightens men away from philosophy. Is it he who will say: 'Listen, friend, by philosophy we mean not wisdom itself but rather the study of wisdom. If you devote yourself to her, you will never indeed be wise while you live here on earth—for wisdom is with God and man cannot possess her—but when you will have sufficiently exercised and purified yourself in this kind of study, your spirit will enjoy wisdom unencumbered after this life, that is, when you will have ceased to be a man?' Or is it he who will say: 'Come, mortal men, to philosophy. Here there is much to be gained. After all, what can be dearer to man than wisdom? Come, then, so that you may become wise—and not know wisdom?' 'I,' he says, 'shall not put it like that.' That is to say, you will deceive; because that exactly represents your position. So it happens that if you do put it like that, they will shun you like a madman; and if you should win them over in some other way, you would make them mad. But let us take it that men would be equally discouraged from philosophy by either view, if my friend Zeno's definition did necessitate some conclusion damaging to philosophy, which should a man be told—something that would grieve him or something that would lead him to make a laughingstock of you?

151

21. "Nevertheless, let us discuss as best we can—granted that we are not wise—Zeno's definition. 'That sense object,' he says, 'can be comprehended, which so manifests itself that it cannot manifest itself as not true. It is clear that nothing else can be perceived.' 'I, too,' says Arcesilas, 'see this, and it is precisely on this account that I teach that nothing is perceived. For nothing so described can be found.'

"That may be true for you, Arcesilas, and for others who are not wise; but why could it not be found by the wise man? I think, however, that you could give no satisfaction to one—even though he be not wise—who bids you employ your remarkable genius in exploding Zeno's definition, and showing that it, too, can be not true. If you cannot do that, then you have something which you can perceive. But if in fact you do explode it, there is nothing to hinder you from perception. For my part I do not see how it can be exploded and I judge it to be entirely true. Consequently, once I know this much, even though I be not wise, I know something. But suppose it yields to your cleverness: I shall employ the safest disjunction. It must be either true or not true. If it is true, then I am in sound possession of it. If it is not true, then something can be perceived, even though it manifest itself by signs which are shared in common with what is not true. 'But that is impossible,' he says. Well, then, Zeno's definition is entirely true, and anyone who has agreed with him even in this one point only is not guilty of error. Surely, that definition is worthy of the greatest praise and confidence which, while it indicated—in opposition to those who wanted to advance many arguments against the possibility of perception—what kind of thing it was that could be perceived, showed itself at the same time to be that kind of thing. And so it is both a definition and example of things capable of being comprehended. 'Whether or not it be itself true,' says Arcesilas, 'I do not know. But since it is probable, I follow it and in doing so show that there is nothing such as can, according to it, be comprehended.' You show perhaps that there is nothing such except itself, and you see, I believe, what that means. In any case, even if we were uncertain of it, too, knowledge still does not desert us. For we do know that the definition itself is either true or not true; that is, we know something.

"All the same, Arcesilas will never make me appear ungrateful. It is my considered judgment that that definition is in fact true. For either things which are not true can also be perceived—which the Academics are very much afraid of and which, in fact, is absurd—or, granted that they cannot be perceived, neither can those things be perceived which are very like things which are not true. From which it follows that that definition of Zeno's is true. But now let us turn to what remains to be considered."

CHAPTER 10 *The Two Principles of the Academy* 22. "Although, unless I am mistaken, what I have said is enough to bring about victory, perhaps I should say more in order to drive my victory home. There are two points put forward by the Academics against which, in so far as we can, we have decided to advance: 'Nothing can be perceived' and 'one must not assent to anything.' We shall come later on to the question of assent. For the moment we shall say a few more things about perception.

"Do you people insist that nothing whatever can be comprehended? At this point Carneades woke up—for none of those men slept as lightly as he—and surveyed the evidence of things. As one speaks to oneself, so he, I believe, went on somewhat like this: 'Now, Carneades, are you really going to claim that you do not know whether you are a man or an insect? Will you allow Chrysippus to gloat over you? Let us say that the things that we do not know are those about which *philosophers* inquire. As to *other* things, they do not concern us. If I then stumble in plain, broad daylight, I shall be able to appeal to those obscurities that are impenetrable to the unskilled and penetrable only to a certain few gifted with eyes that are divine. They, even though they see me in difficulties and falling, cannot betray me to those who are blind, especially when they are also arrogant and too proud to learn.'

"You are getting on nicely, O Greek subtlety, well equipped and prepared as you are! But you overlook the fact that that principle is at once the formulation of a philosopher and is placed firmly at the entrance to philosophy. If you attempt to undermine it, the axe with double edge will rebound on to your shins. For if once you shake it, not only can something be perceived, but that, too, can be perceived which is very like that which is not true. Your only chance is to have the courage to do away with it altogether. But it is your lurking-place from which you jump out and pounce fiercely upon the unwary who wish to pass on their way. Some Hercules will strangle you, half-human as you are, in your cave, and will crush you with the weight of that principle. For he will show you that there is something in philosophy which cannot be demonstrated by you to be uncertain on the plea that it is like to what is not true.

"I was, it is true, in a hurry to go on to other considerations. Whoever presses me to do so, casts a great slur on you yourself, Carneades, for he supposes that you are as good as dead and can be routed by me on any and every front. But if he does not suppose any such thing, then he is pitiless. For then he leads me on to abandon my fortifications everywhere and to come down to do battle with you on the level plain. Just as I had begun to come down against you, terrified by your mere name, I drew back and cast from my lofty position some kind of a shaft. Whether it reached you or what it did, let them judge who preside over our conflict. But what a fool am I to have such fear! If I recollect aright, you are dead, and Alypius does not choose to fight as he might in defense of your grave; and God will readily help me against your ghost.

23. "You say that in philosophy nothing can be perceived, and so that you may give your contention wide publicity, you seize upon the disputes and disagreements of philosophers and think with them to furnish arms to yourself against the philosophers themselves. For how, you argue, shall we be able to settle the dispute between Democritus and his predecessors in physics as to whether there is one or innumerable worlds, when Democritus himself and his heir, Epicurus, could not agree? When this latter voluptuary allows the atoms, as it were his little handmaids, those little bodies which he joyfully embraces in the dark, to deviate from their course and turn aside wherever they like into the domain of others, he is quarrelling and he has thus dissipated all his patrimony.

"But this is no concern of mine. If it is part of wisdom to know something of these things, then all this will certainly not escape the attention of the wise man. But if wisdom consists in something different, then it is *that*, that the wise man knows and the other is despised by him. Even I, however, who am still far from being anyway near a wise man, know something at any rate in physics. I am certain, for instance, that there is one world or not one. If there is not one world, then the number of worlds is finite or infinite. Carneades may say, if he likes, that this opinion is like one that is not true. Likewise, I know that this world of ours is ordered as it is, either by the intrinsic nature of corporeal matter or by some providence; that it either always was and always will be or began to be and will never cease or never exist forever. I know countless things about physics of a similar nature, but these disjunctions are true, and no one can refute them by pointing to any likeness in them to what is not true.

" 'But elect for one member of the disjunction,' bids the Academic. No. I shall not. You are asking me not to assert what I do know and assert what I do not know. 'But your assertion hangs in the air.' It is better that it should hang there than that it should be dashed to the ground. You see, it is adequate for our purpose; that is to say, as an assertion it can be pronounced either true or not true. I assert that this is something that I know. Let you, who cannot deny that such matter pertains to philosophy and who assert that none of these things can be known, demonstrate to me that I do not know these things. Assert that these disjunctions are either not true or have something in common with what is not true, so that, as a consequence, they are incapable of being distinguished from what is not true."

CHAPTER 11 *Something Can be Perceived* 24. " 'But,' he asks, 'how do you know that the world you speak of exists at all? The senses may deceive.' No matter how you argued, you were never able to repudiate the value of the senses to the extent that you could convince us that nothing appears to us to be. Indeed, you have never in any way ventured to try to do so. But you have done your very best to convince us that the reality could be different from the appearance. By the term 'world,' then, I mean all this, whatever kind of thing it be, which surrounds and nourishes us and which presents itself to my eyes and seems to me to hold earth and sky or quasi earth and quasi sky. If you say that nonreality presents itself to me, I shall still be free from error. It is he who rashly judges that which presents itself to him to be actual reality that falls into error. But while you do say that what is not true can present itself to sentient beings, you do not say that nonreality so presents itself. Indeed, all ground for disputation—wherein you love to reign supreme—is entirely removed if not only we know nothing, but if no appearance presents itself to us. If, however, you deny that that which presents itself to me is the world, you are raising a question merely about a word; for I have stated that I do call that appearance the 'world.'

25. "But you will ask me: 'If you are asleep, does the world which you now see exist?' I have already said that whatever presents itself to me in that way, I call 'world.' But if you wish that only to be called 'world' which presents itself to those who are awake or, even better, those who are sane, then maintain also, if you can, that those who are asleep or insane are not insane and asleep in the world! Accordingly, I make this statement: all that

mass and contrivance in which we are, whether we be sleeping or insane or awake or sane, is either one or not one. Explain how that judgment can be not true. If I am asleep, possibly I have made no statement at all. Or, if in my sleep the words have, as happens, escaped my mouth, possibly I have not spoken them here, sitting as I am and with this audience. But the proposition itself that I have mentioned cannot be not true.

"And I am not saying that I have perceived this on condition of my being awake. For you could say that in my sleep, too, this could have presented itself to me, and, consequently, can be very like what is not true. But it is manifest that no matter in what condition I am, if there is one world and six worlds, there are in all seven worlds, and I unhesitatingly assert that I know this. Now, then, convince me that this combination or the above-mentioned disjunctions can be not true by reason of sleep, madness, or the unreliability of the senses; and if being awakened from my slumber I recall them, I shall allow that I am vanquished. I feel sure that it is now sufficiently clear what appearances, although not true, can because of sleep or insanity present themselves as true; they are those which pertain to bodily senses. For that three times three makes nine, and that this is the squaring of rational numbers, must be true even though the human race were snoring! All the same, I notice that much can be said in defense even of the senses themselves—things which we do not find to be questioned by the Academics. The senses are not, I take it, blamed for the fact that insane people have illusions, or that we see in our dreams things that are not true. If the senses give reports that are true to those who are awake and sane, then they will not be involved in what the mind of one who is asleep or insane conjures up.

26. "There remains to ask if, when the senses report, they report what is true. Now, then, if an Epicurean says: 'I have no complaint to make about the senses. It is unjust to demand from them more than that of which they are capable. When the eyes see anything, they see what is true': is, then, what the eyes see of an oar in water true? Certainly, it is true. A cause has intervened so that it should present itself so. If when an oar was dipped under water it presented itself as straight, then in that case I would convict my eyes of giving a report that was not true. For they would not see what, given the existing circumstances, should have been seen. What need is there of developing the theme? The same thing can be said of towers that appear to move, of the changing colors on the feathers of birds, and of countless other cases.

" 'But,' says someone, 'I am deceived, if I give my assent.' Do not assent more than that you know that it appears so to you. There is then no deception. I do not see how the Academic can refute him who says: I know that this presents itself to me as white; I know that this delights my ear; I know that this has a sweet smell for me; I know that this feels cold to me. 'Tell me, rather, are the leaves of the wild olive tree, of which the goat is so passionately fond, *per se* bitter?' You rascal! The goat himself is more reasonable! I do not know how cattle find them. Anyway, I find them bitter. Does that satisfy you? 'But there is perhaps among men one to whom they are not bitter.' You are trying to make a nuisance of yourself. Have I said that all men found them bitter? I said that I found them bitter now, and I do not even assert that they will always be so for me. Could it not happen that at different times and for different reasons a thing could taste in one's mouth now sweet, now bitter? This I do assert: that when a man tastes something, he can swear in all good faith that he knows that to his palate a given thing is sweet or the contrary. No Greek sophistry can steal such knowledge from him. Who would be so impertinent as to say to me as I savor with delight the taste of something: 'Perhaps there is nothing to taste; you are only dreaming?' Do I stop my savoring? No! I reply that even though I were dreaming, it would still delight me. Accordingly, no likeness to what is not true can prove that which I said I knew was wrong. Moreover, an Epicurean or the Cyrenaics may perhaps say many other things in defense of the senses, and I am not aware that the Academics have said anything to refute them. But what is that to me? If they want to, and if they can, let them refute these things. I shall even help them.

"Certainly, their arguments against sense perception are not valid against all philosophers. There are some philosophers, for example, who maintain that whatever the spirit receives by way of bodily sense can generate opinion, indeed, but not knowledge. They insist that the latter is found only in the intelligence and, far removed from the senses, abides in the mind. But we shall talk about this at another time. Now let us turn to the points that remain. In view of what has already been said, we shall, if I mistake not, be able to deal with them in a few words."

CHAPTER 12 27. "What help or hindrance can bodily sense be in the consideration of ethics? Those who put man's true and greatest good in pleasure are not prevented, by the dove's neck or the cry that is doubtful or the weight that is heavy for a man but light for a camel or a thousand other such things, from saying that they know that they find pleasure in that in which they find pleasure and are displeased by that by which they are displeased— and I do not see how this can be refuted. Can it be that these things influence him who places the ultimate good in the mind?

" 'Which of these two opinions do you yourself choose?' If you ask me my opinion, I think that in the mind is to be found man's supreme good. Now, however, we are talking about knowledge. Go, then, and question the wise man, who must know wisdom. But in the meantime I, who am such a dullard and ignoramus, am able to know the ultimate good of man, wherein is happiness: either there is none or it is in the spirit or in the body or in both. Prove, if you can, that I do not know this. Your celebrated arguments can do nothing. And if you cannot do this—for you will not be able to find anything not true to which it bears likeness— shall I hesitate to conclude that my opinion that the wise man knows whatever in philosophy is true is correct, since I myself already know in philosophy many things that are true?

28. " 'But perhaps the wise man is afraid lest he should choose the ultimate good while he is asleep.' No danger at all! When he awakes, he will, if it displeases him, repudiate it, and if it pleases, retain it. Who can justly blame him for having seen in a dream something that was not true? Or perhaps you will be afraid lest while he is asleep, if he assents to what is not true as true, he lose his wisdom? Indeed, not even one who is asleep would dare to dream that he should call a man wise if he were awake, but deny that he is such if he were to sleep.

"The same things hold for the question of insanity. Though I am anxious to hurry on to other things, I shall, however, before I go, leave an irrefutable statement on the point: either a man's wisdom is lost because of his madness, in which case he will no longer be the wise man, who, you insist, does not know truth; or his knowledge remains in his intellect, even though the rest of his mind represents as if in a dream what it has received from the senses."

CHAPTER 13 29. "There remains dialectics. The wise man certainly knows this well, and no one can know what is not true. But if he does not know dialectics, then the knowledge of dialectics does not pertain to wisdom, seeing that he can be wise without it. Moreover, it is superfluous for us to ask whether it be true or can be perceived.

"Someone may say to me at this point: 'Well, stupid, you usually tell us whatever you know. Were you not able to know anything about dialectics?' I know more about it than about any other part of philosophy. In the first place, it was dialectics that taught me that all the propositions which I have indicated already were true. Again, through dialectics I have come to know many other true things. 'Enumerate them for us, if you can.' If there are four elements in the world, there are not five. If there is one sun, there are not two. The same soul cannot both die and be immortal. A man cannot at the same time be happy and not happy. Here and now there is not day and night at the same time. We are now either awake or asleep. What I seem to see is either body or not body. These and many other things which would take too long to mention, I have learned through dialectics to be true. They are true in themselves no matter what state our senses are in. Dialectics taught me that if of any one of the conditional statements which I have just mentioned the first part be assumed as true, it necessarily involves the truth of the dependent part. But the propositions involving contrariety or disjunction which I enunciated are of this nature that when a part is taken away, whether that be composed of one or more things, something is left which by the removal is made certain. Dialectics also taught me that when there is agreement about the matter on account of which words are employed, then one should not dispute about the words. If one does that through inexperience, then one should be taught. If one does it through malice, then one should be ignored. If one is incapable of being taught, one should be advised to do something else than waste one's time and labor in trifling. If one does not take the advice, then one should be abandoned to one's fate.

"Concerning specious and fallacious reasonings there is a short principle of behavior: if they come about as a result of an unwise concession, then one should return to what one has conceded. If truth and falsehood are found in conflict in one and the same statement, one should conclude on what one understands and not bother about what cannot be explained. But if the 'how' of certain things escapes man entirely, then one should not seek the knowledge of it.

"All these things and many others, which it is unnecessary to recall, dialectics has taught me, and certainly I must not be ungrateful. The wise man either ignores all these or, if a thorough knowledge of dialectics is the knowledge itself of truth, he will know it so well that in contempt, and without any weakening, he will destroy, if only by ignoring it, that most fallacious sophism of the Academics: 'If it is true, it is not true; if it is not true, it is true.'

"I think this will be enough on the question of perception, especially since the whole case will be dealt with again when I come to speak of the matter of assent."

CHAPTER 14 *Assent Can be Given* 30. "And now, therefore, let us come to a point on which Alypius still seems to be in doubt. First, let us see what it is that makes you so careful and exacting. 'If the opinion of the Academics that the wise man knew nothing, confirmed as it was' —these are your own words— 'by so many powerful arguments, is overthrown by your discovery, whereby we are compelled to admit that it is much more probable that the wise man knows wisdom, then all the more should we refuse to assent. For by this itself is it demonstrated that nothing can be advocated—even though the arguments used be ever so copious and neatly pointed—which cannot also, granted sufficient ingenuity, be controverted with equal if not greater acuteness. And so it happens that the moment he is beaten, the Academic has won.'

"Would that he were beaten! No matter what Pelasgic trick he uses, he will never succeed in leaving the field victorious when he has been beaten by me. Of course if nothing else can be found to counter this argument, of my own free motion I, too, allow that I am beaten. For we are not interested in covering ourselves with glory but in the finding of truth. I am content if by any means I can cross over that barrier which confronts those who are beginning philosophy. It piles up darkness from some hidden source and warns that the whole of philosophy is obscure and does not allow one to hope that any light will be found in it.

"For my part, I desire nothing more if it is now probable that the wise man knows something. It seemed probable that he should withhold his assent for no other reason than that it was probable that nothing could be perceived: when that reason has disappeared—the wise man perceives, as is conceded, at least wisdom herself—no reason any longer will remain why the wise man should not assent at least to wisdom. Obviously, it is without any doubt even more monstrous that the wise man should not assent to wisdom than that he should not know her.

31. "But let us now, if you will and if that be possible, picture to ourselves the spectacle of a fight, so to speak, between the wise man and wisdom. Wisdom says (and what else should she say?) that she is wisdom. He replies, 'I do not believe it.' Who is it that says to wisdom, 'I do not believe that you are wisdom?' Who, but he with whom she could talk and in whom she deigned to dwell— that is to say, the wise man?

"Now go and fetch me to engage in a conflict with the Academics. There! a new fight is on! The wise man and wisdom are fighting! The wise man does not want to give in to wisdom! I shall stand aside with you and await the issue without anxiety; for who does not believe that wisdom is invincible? All the same, let us strengthen our position with some argument. In this conflict either the wise man of the Academics conquers wisdom, in which case he will be conquered by me—for he will not be the wise man; or he will be conquered by her, in which case we shall teach that the wise man assents to wisdom. That is to say, either the Academic wise man is not a wise man at all, or the wise man will assent to something—unless, of course, he who was ashamed to say that the wise man did not know wisdom, will not be ashamed to say the wise man does not assent to wisdom! But if it is now probable that the wise man perceives at least wisdom herself, and there is no longer any reason why he should not assent to that which he can perceive, I conclude that what I wanted is probable, namely, that the wise man will assent to wisdom.

"If you ask me where he will find wisdom herself, I shall reply: in his own very self. If you say that he does not know what is in himself, you are returning once again to the ridiculous proposition that the wise man does not know wisdom. If you say that the wise man himself cannot be found, then our dispute will be not with the Academics but with you, whoever you are that hold this, and on another occasion. When these men engage in this type of discussion, they deal with it as certainly referring to the case of the wise man. Cicero exclaims that, as for himself, he is a man of many opinions only but that he is discussing the case of the wise man. If you were unaware of this, young men, you must have read in the *Hortensius*: 'If, then, nothing is certain and the wise man must not have opinion merely, the wise man will never give assent.' From this it is clear that in those disputations of theirs against which we are contending, they are dealing with the case of the wise man.

32. "I, therefore, think that the wise man has sure possession of wisdom, that is to say, that the wise man has perceived wisdom,

and, consequently, that he does not have opinions merely, when he assents to wisdom. For he assents to that which if he did not perceive, he would not be a wise man. The Academics, in fact, do not prohibit anyone from assenting except to things which cannot be perceived. Wisdom is not nothing. When, then, the wise man knows wisdom and assents to wisdom, he does not know nothing and does not assent to nothing.

"Do you wish for more? Shall we discuss briefly that error which the Academics say can be entirely avoided if assent does not draw the mind to anything at all? They say that not only he errs who assents to what is not true, but also he errs who assents to what is doubtful, even though it be in fact true. For my part, I find nothing that is doubtful. But the wise man finds, as we were saying, wisdom herself."

CHAPTER 15 *The "Probable" Insufficient and Dangerous* 33. "But perhaps, you are now asking me to leave my own ground. One should be careful about leaving a position that is safe. We are dealing with men who are crafty indeed. Nevertheless, I shall do as you bid me. But what shall I say at this point? Indeed, what am I to say? Tell me, what can I say? I shall have to use the old stock argument for which they have a stock reply. What else can I do, seeing that you have compelled me to leave my stronghold? Shall I appeal to the help of the learned, so that if I am vanquished in their company, I shall perhaps be less ashamed of being beaten? I shall with all my strength, then, hurl at them a weapon which though now rusty and musty with age, is, unless I am mistaken, all the same a very effective one: 'He who does not assent to anything, does nothing.' 'You ignoramus! What about the "probable"? What about "what-is-like-truth"?' There you are! That is what you were looking for! Do you hear the clash of Grecian shields? The shock of my weapon, great as it was, has been withstood; and with what force did we hurl it! And my supporters can offer me nothing more potent; and, as far as I can see, we have inflicted no trace of a wound. I shall turn for help to the homely weapons offered me by the farm. The heavier ones only weigh me down and are of no help to me.

34. "When at my leisure here in the country I had been thinking for a long time how it was that what they call 'probable' or 'what-is-like-truth' could prevent our acts from error, at first it seemed to me—as it had seemed when I taught such things for

money—that the matter was nicely established and defended against attack. But then as I examined the whole position more carefully, I thought I saw one way by which error could come in upon those who felt so secure. For I think that not only does he err who follows the wrong track but he also who does not follow the right one.

"To illustrate, let us picture two men travelling to one place. One of them has resolved not to believe anyone; the other believes everyone. They come to a place where the road forks. The credulous traveller addresses a shepherd or some rustic standing on the spot: 'Hello, my good man. Tell me, please, which is the best way to that place?' The reply: 'If you take this road, you will not go wrong.' He says to his companion: 'What he says is correct. Let us go this way.' The careful traveller laughs and makes a fool of the other for having given assent so quickly. While the other takes his way, he remains at the junction of the roads. He is beginning to feel foolish himself because of his hesitation, when from the road not taken by his companion there appears and draws near an elegant and refined gentleman riding on horseback. The traveller rejoices. He salutes the man as he approaches, and tells him what is on his mind. He asks him the way. No only that—he tells him why he has delayed so that by indicating his preference for him rather than for the shepherd, he may make him the better disposed to himself. He, however, happens to be an arrant knave, one of those fellows now commonly called *sam ardoci*. The scoundrel indulges in his usual practice, and that, too, without charging a penny: 'Go this way,' he says, 'I have just come from there.' So, he deceives him and passes on his way.

"But our traveller would not be deceived! 'Indeed,' he says, 'I shall not assent to his information as true. But since it is probable and since to do nothing here is neither proper nor useful, I shall go the way he indicates.' Meanwhile he who erred in assenting, too quickly judging that the shepherd's words were true, is already resting in the place for which they set out. But he who has not erred, since he follows the 'probable,' is lost in some woods and has not yet found anybody who knows the place where he proposed to go!

"Really, I must tell you that when I was thinking over these things, I could not keep from laughing. To think that the doctrine of the Academics somehow brings it about that he should err, who is on the right road—even though it be by chance—but that he, who following probability is led over impassable mountains and does not get where he wants to go, should not seem to err!

To show, quite justly, my disapproval of rash assent, I should say that both erred, rather than that the second traveller did not err. And so being more on my guard against the Academic doctrine, I began to consider the deeds of men and their principles of behavior. Then, indeed, I discovered so many and such fundamental grounds against the Academics that I could no longer laugh; I was half angry and half sorrowful that men so learned and intelligent should have descended to such criminal and shameful doctrine."

CHAPTER 16 35. "It may be, indeed, that not everyone who errs commits sin. It is conceded, however, that everyone who sins either errs or does something worse. Well, then, if some young man, hearing the Academics say: 'It is shameful to err, and, consequently, we ought not to assent to anything; when, however, a man does what seems probable to him, he neither sins nor errs. All he need remember is that he is not to assent to as true anything that comes before his mind or senses'—if, I say, he hears this, what if the young man will lay siege to the chastity of another's wife?

"I am asking you, Marcus Tullius—yes, you—for your opinion. We are dealing with the morals and lives of young men, with whose formation and instruction all your writings are concerned. What can you say but that it is not probable to *you*, that the young man would do such a thing? But to *him*, it is probable. For if he were to live by what seemed probable to another, you ought not to have governed in the state, since Epicurus thought that one should not do such a thing. That young man will, then, commit adultery with another's wife. If he is caught, where will he find you to defend him? And even if he does find you, what will you say? You will deny outright that the thing happened. But if it is so clear that it is useless to deny it? Of course, you will try to convince your opponents, as if you were in a scholastic establishment at Cumae or Naples, that he had committed no sin, in fact, had not even erred. He did not assent to the proposition that 'I should commit adultery' as true. But then it occurred to him as probable: he followed it—he did the deed. Or, perhaps, he did not do it but thinks he has done it! The husband in his simplicity is causing general confusion by his litigation and the clamor he raises about his wife's chastity—with whom he is perhaps now sleeping without being aware of it!

"If the jury is able to follow this, they will either ignore the Academics and mete out punishment on the crime as having been actually committed; or, being convinced by the same gentlemen, they will, acting according to what is likely and probable, condemn the man, so that his advocate will now be at a complete loss as to what course to take. He will not have cause to get angry with any of them, since all say that they have not fallen into error. For, while not assenting, they had done what seemed probable. In these circumstances he will lay aside the role of advocate and assume that of the consoling philosopher. He can thus readily persuade the young man, who has already made such progress in the Academy, to think that he is condemned only in a dream.

"But you think I am making fun! I am prepared to swear by all that is holy that I am completely at a loss to know how that young man sinned, if one who does what seems probable to him does not sin. The only possible answer I find is that they may say that to err and to sin are two entirely different things and that by their principles they had in mind that we should not err, while they considered sinning itself to be of no great consequence.

36. "I pass over homicide, parricide, sacrilege, and every type of crime and evil-doing that can be committed or thought of—all can be justified by a few words and, what is worse, before judges that are wise: 'I did not assent, and therefore I did not err. How could I not have done what seemed probable?' If anyone thinks that such arguments cannot be made to seem probably conclusive, let him read the speech of Catiline wherein he sought to commend the parricide of one's country, in which is embodied all crime.

"But what follows is merely ridiculous. The Academics themselves say that they act only on the probable. Nevertheless, they make great efforts in searching for truth, although they have already made up their minds that it is probable that it cannot be found. What a marvellous absurdity! But let us forget about it: it does not affect us or endanger our lives or belongings. But the other point is of the greatest importance: it is fraught with the most serious consequences and must cause the greatest anxiety to every upright man. For if this reasoning of the Academics is probable, then one may commit every crime without being blamed for an error—since one thought that one should act on the probable without assenting to anything as true. Well, then, did the Academics not see this? Indeed, they did see it—for they were clever and careful. I would never think of claiming that I came anyway near Marcus Tullius in hard work, prudence, capacity, or learning. Yet, when

165

he says that one cannot know anything, if this only were replied: 'I know that it seems to me that he can,' he would not be able to refute it."

THE CITY OF GOD ✛ BOOK XI ✛ CHAPTER 26 *Of the Image of the Supreme Trinity, which we find in some sort in Human Nature even in its Present State.* And indeed we recognize in ourselves the image of God, that is, of the supreme Trinity, an image which, though it be not equal to God or, rather, though it be very far removed from Him—being neither co-eternal nor, to say all in a word, consubstantial with Him—is yet nearer to Him in nature than any other of His works and is destined to be yet restored, that it may bear a still closer resemblance. For we both are and know that we are and delight in our being and our knowledge of it. Moreover, in these three things no true-seeing illusion disturbs us; for we do not come into contact with these by some bodily sense, as we perceive the things outside of us—colors, e.g. by seeing, sounds by hearing, smells by smelling, tastes by tasting, hard and soft objects by touching—of all which sensible objects it is the images resembling them, but not themselves, which we perceive in the mind and hold in the memory and which excite us to desire the objects. But without any delusive representation of images or phantasm, I am most certain that I am and that I know and delight in this. In respect of these truths, I am not at all afraid of the arguments of the Academicians, who say, What if you are deceived? For if I am deceived, I am. For he who is not, cannot be deceived; and if I am deceived, by this same token I am. And since I am, I am deceived, how am I deceived in believing that I am? For it is certain that I am, if I am deceived. Since, therefore, I , the person deceived, should be, even if I were deceived, certainly I am not deceived in this knowledge that I am. And, consequently, neither am I deceived in knowing that I know. For, as I know that I am, so I know this also; that I know. And when I love these two things, I add to them a certain third thing, namely, my love, which is of equal moment. For neither am I deceived in this, that I love, since in those things which I love I am not deceived; though even if these were false, it would still be true that I *loved* false things. For how could I justly be blamed and prohibited from loving false things, if it were false that I loved them? But, since they are true and real, who doubts that when they are loved, the

166

love of them is itself true and real? Further, as there is no one who does not wish to be happy, so there is no one who does not wish to be. For how can he be happy, if he is nothing?

THE TRINITY ✛ BOOK XV ✛ CHAPTER 12 *The Academic Philosophy*. First, of what sort and how great is the very knowledge itself that a man can attain, be he ever so skillful and learned, by which our thought is formed with truth, when we speak what we know? For to pass by those things that come into the mind from the bodily senses, among which so many are otherwise than they seem to be, that he who is overmuch pressed down by their resemblance to truth, seems sane to himself but really is not sane—whence it is that the Academic philosophy has so prevailed as to be still more wretchedly insane by doubting all things— passing by, then, those things that come into the mind by the bodily senses, how large a proportion is left of things which we know in such manner as we know that we live? In this, indeed, we are absolutely without any fear, lest perchance we are being deceived by some resemblance of the truth; since it is certain that he too who is deceived, yet lives. And this again is not reckoned among those objects of sight that are presented from without, so that the eye may be deceived in it; in such way as it is when an oar in the water looks bent, and towers seem to move as you sail past them, and a thousand other things that are otherwise than they seem to be: for this is not a thing that is discerned by the eye of the flesh. The knowledge by which we know that we live is the most inward of all knowledge, of which even the Academic cannot insinuate. Perhaps you are asleep and do not know it, and you see things in your sleep. For who does not know that what people see in dreams is precisely like what they see when awake? But he who is certain of the knowledge of his own life does not therein say, I know I am awake but I know I am alive; therefore, whether he be asleep or awake, he is alive. Nor can he be deceived in that knowledge by dreams; since it belongs to a living man both to sleep and to see in sleep. Nor can the Academic again say, in confutation of this knowledge, perhaps you are mad and do not know it: for what madmen see is precisely like what they also see who are sane; but he who is mad is alive. Nor does he answer the Academic by saying, I know I am not mad but, rather, I know

I am alive. Therefore he who says he knows he is alive can neither be deceived nor lie. Let a thousand kinds, then, of deceitful objects of sight be presented to him who says, I know I am alive; yet he will fear none of them, for he who is deceived yet is alive. But if such things alone pertain to human knowledge, they are very few indeed; unless that they can be so multiplied in each kind, as not only not to be few, but to reach in the result to infinity. For he who says, I know I am alive, says that he knows one single thing. Further, if he says, I know that I know I know I am alive, now there are two; but that he knows these two is a third thing to know. And so he can add a fourth and a fifth, and innumerable others, if he holds out. But since he cannot either comprehend an innumerable number by additions of units or say a thing innumerable times, he comprehends this at least, and with perfect certainty, viz. that this is both true and so innumerable that he cannot truly comprehend and say its infinite number. This same thing may be noticed also in the case of a will that is certain. For it would be an impudent answer to make to any one who should say, I will to be happy, that perhaps you are deceived. And if he should say, I know that I will this, and I know that I know it, he can add yet a third to these two, viz. that he knows these two; and a fourth, that he knows that he knows these two, and so on *ad infinitum*. Likewise, if any one were to say, I will not to be mistaken; will it not be true, whether he is mistaken or whether he is not, that nevertheless he does will not to be mistaken? Would it not be most impudent to say to him, perhaps you are deceived? when beyond doubt, whereinsoever he may be deceived, he is nevertheless not deceived in thinking that he wills not to be deceived. And if he says he knows this, he adds any number he chooses of things known and perceives that number to be infinite. For he who says, I will not to be deceived, and I know that I will not to be so, and I know that I know it, is able now to set forth an infinite number here also, however awkward may be the expression of it. And other things too are to be found capable of refuting the Academics, who contend that man can know nothing. But we must restrict ourselves, especially as this is not the subject we have undertaken in the present work. There are three books of ours on that subject,[4] written in the early time of our conversion, which he who can and will read, and who understands them, will doubtless not be much moved by any of the many arguments which they have found out against the discovery of truth. For whereas there are two kinds of knowable things—one, of those things which the mind perceives by the bodily senses; the other, of those which it perceives by itself—these philosophers have babbled much against the bodily senses but have never been able to throw doubt upon those most certain perceptions of things true, which the mind knows by itself, such as is that which I have mentioned, I know that I am alive. But far be it from us to doubt the truth of what we have learned by the bodily senses; since by them we have learned to know the heaven and the earth and those things in them which are known to us, so far as He who created both us and them has willed them to be within our knowledge. Far be it from us to deny, that we know what we have learned by the testimony of others: otherwise we know not that there is an ocean; we know not that the lands and cities exist which most copious report commends to us; we know not that those men were, and their works, which we have learned by reading history; we know not the news that is daily brought us from this quarter or that, and confirmed by consistent and conspiring evidence; lastly, we know not at what place or from whom we have been born: since in all these things we have believed the testimony of others. And if it is most absurd to say this, then we must confess that not only our own senses but those of other persons also have added very much indeed to our knowledge.

THE TRINITY ✝ BOOK XI ✝ CHAPTER 2 *A certain trinity in the sight. That there are three things in sight, which differ in their own nature. In what manner from a visible thing vision is produced, or the image of that thing which is seen. The matter is shown more clearly by an example. How these three combine in one.* 2. When, then, we see any corporeal object, these three things, as is most easy to do, are to be considered and distinguished: First, the object itself which we see; whether a stone, or flame, or any other thing that can be seen by the eyes; and this certainly might exist also already before it was seen; next, vision or the act of seeing, which did not exist before we perceived the object itself which is presented to the sense; in the third place, that which keeps the sense of the eye in the object seen, so long as it is seen, viz. the attention of the mind. In these three, then, not only is there an evident distinction but also a diverse nature. For, first, that visible body is of a far different nature from the sense of the eyes, through the incidence of which sense upon it vision arises. And what plainly is vision itself other than perception informed by that thing which is perceived? Although there is no vision, if the visible object be withdrawn, nor could there by any vision of the kind at all if there were no body that could be seen; yet the body by which the sense of the eyes is informed, when that body is seen, and the form itself which is imprinted by it upon the sense, which is called vision, are by no means of the same substance. For the body that is seen is, in its own nature, separable; but the sense, which was already in the living subject, even before it saw what it was able to see, when it fell in with something visible—or the vision which comes to be in the sense from the visible body when now brought into connection with it and seen—the sense, then, I say, or the vision, that is, the sense informed from without belongs to the nature of the living subject, which is altogether other than that body which we perceive by seeing, and by which the sense is not so formed as to be sense, but as to be vision. For unless the sense were also in us before the presentation to us of the sensible object, we should not differ from the blind, at times when we are seeing nothing, whether in darkness, or when our eyes are closed. But we differ from them in this, that there is in us, even when we are not seeing, that whereby we are able to see, which is called the sense; whereas this is not in them, nor are they called blind for any other reason than because they have it not. Further also, that attention of the mind which keeps the sense in that thing which we see, and connects both, not only differs from that visible thing in its nature; in that the one is mind, and the other body; but also from the sense and the vision itself: since this attention is the act of the mind alone; but the sense of the eyes is called a bodily sense for no other reason than because the eyes themselves also are members of the body; and although an inanimate body does not perceive, yet the soul commingled with the body perceives through a corporeal instrument, and that instrument is called sense. And this sense, too, is cut off and extinguished by suffering on the part of the body, when any one is blinded; while the mind remains the same; and its attention, since the eyes are lost, has not, indeed, the sense of the body which it may join by seeing to the body without it, and so fix its look thereupon and see it, yet by the very effort shows that, although the bodily sense be taken away, itself can neither perish nor be diminished. For there remains unimpaired a desire of seeing, whether it can be carried into effect or not. These three, then, the body that is seen and vision itself and the attention of mind which joins both together, are manifestly distinguishable not only on account of the properties of each but also on account of the difference of their natures.

3. And since, in this case, the perception does not proceed from that body which is seen, but from the body of the living being that perceives, with which the soul is tempered together in some wonderful way of its own; yet vision is produced, that is, the sense itself is informed, by the body which is seen; so that now, not only is there the power of sense, which can exist also unimpaired even in darkness, provided the eyes are sound, but also a sense actually informed, which is called vision. Vision, then, is produced from a thing that is visible; but not from that alone, unless there be present also one who sees. Therefore vision is produced from a thing that is visible, together with one who sees; in such way that, on the part of him who sees, there is the sense of seeing and the intention of looking and gazing at the object; while yet that information of the sense, which is called vision, is imprinted only by the body which is seen, that is, by some visible thing; which being taken away, that form remains no more which was in the sense so long as that which was seen was present: yet the sense itself remains, which existed also before anything was perceived; just as the trace of a thing in water remains so long as the body itself, which is impressed on it, is in the water; but if this has been taken away, there will no longer be any such trace, although the water remains, which existed also before it took the form of that body. And therefore we cannot, indeed, say that a visible thing produces the sense; yet it produces the form, which is, as it were its own likeness, which comes to be in the sense, when we perceive anything by seeing. But we do not distinguish, through the same sense, the form of the body which we see, from the form which is produced by it in the sense of him who sees; since the union of the two is so close that there is no room for distinguishing them. But we gather by reason that we could not perceive at all, unless some similitude of the body was wrought in our own sense. For when a ring is imprinted on wax, it does not follow that no image is produced, because we cannot discern it, unless when it has been separated. But since, after the wax is separated, what was made remains, so that it can be seen; we are on that account easily persuaded that there was already also in the wax a form impressed from the ring before it was separated from it. But if the ring were imprinted upon a fluid, no image at all would appear when it was withdrawn; and yet none the less for this ought the reason to discern that there was in that fluid before the ring was withdrawn a form of the ring produced from the ring, which is to be distinguished from that form which is in the ring, whence that form was produced which ceases to be when the ring is withdrawn, although that in the

ring remains, whence the other was produced. And so the perception of the eyes may not be supposed to contain no image of the body, which is seen as long as it is seen; because, when that is withdrawn, the image does not remain. And hence it is very difficult to persuade men of duller mind that an image of the visible thing is formed in our sense, when we see it, and that this same form is vision.

4. But if any perhaps attend to what I am about to mention, they will find no such trouble in this inquiry. Commonly, when we have looked for some little time at a light, and then shut our eyes, there seem to play before our eyes certain bright colors variously changing themselves and shining less and less until they wholly cease; and these we must understand to be the remains of that form which was wrought in the sense, while the shining body was seen, and that these variations take place in them as they slowly and step by step fade away. For the lattices, too, of windows, should we happen to be gazing at them, appear often in these colors; so that it is evident that our sense is affected by such impressions from that thing which is seen. That form therefore existed also while we were seeing, and at that time it was more clear and express. But it was then closely joined with the species of that thing which was being perceived, so that it could not be at all distinguished from it; and this was vision itself. Why, even when the little flame of a lamp is in some way, as it were, doubled by the divergent rays of the eyes, a twofold vision comes to pass, although the thing which is seen is one. For the same rays, as they shoot forth each from its own eye, are affected severally, in that they are not allowed to meet evenly and conjointly, in regarding that corporeal thing, so that one combined view might be formed from both. And so, if we shut one eye, we shall not see two flames but one as it really is. But why, if we shut the left eye, that appearance ceases to be seen, which was on the right; and if, in turn, we shut the right eye, that drops out of existence which was on the left, is a matter both tedious in itself, and not necessary at all to our present subject to inquire and discuss. For it is enough for the business in hand to consider, that unless some image, precisely like the thing we perceive, were produced in our sense, the appearance of the flame would not be doubled according to the number of the eyes; since a certain way of perceiving has been employed, which could separate the union of rays. Certainly nothing that is really single can be seen as if it were double by one eye, draw it down, or press, or distort it as you please, if the other is shut.

5. The case then being so, let us remember how these three things, although diverse in nature, are tempered together into a kind of unity; that is, the form of the body which is seen and the image of it impressed on the sense, which is vision or sense informed, and the will of the mind which applies the sense to the sensible thing, and retains the vision itself in it. The first of these, that is, the visible thing itself, does not belong to the nature of the living being, except when we discern our own body. But the second belongs to that nature to this extent, that it is wrought in the body and through the body in the soul; for it is wrought in the sense, which is neither without the body nor without the soul. But the third is of the soul alone, because it is the will. Although then the substances of these three are so different, yet they coalesce into such a unity that the two former can scarcely be distinguished, even with the intervention of the reason as judge, namely the form of the body which is seen, and the image of it which is wrought in the sense, that is, vision. And the will so powerfully combines these two, as both to apply the sense, in order to be informed, to that thing which is perceived, and to retain it when informed in that thing. And if it is so vehement that it can be called love or desire or lust, it vehemently affects also the rest of the body of the living being; and where a duller and harder matter does not resist, changes it into like shape and color. One may see the little body of a chameleon vary with ready change, according to the colors which it sees. And in the case of other animals, since their grossness of flesh does not easily admit change, the offspring, for the most part, betray the particular fancies of the mothers, whatever it is that they have beheld with special delight. For the more tender, and so to say, the more formable are the primary seeds, the more effectually and capably they follow the bent of the soul of the mother, and the phantasy that is wrought in it through that body, which it has greedily beheld. Abundant instances might be adduced, but one is sufficient, taken from the most trustworthy books; viz. what Jacob did, that the sheep and goats might give birth to offspring of various colors, by placing variegated rods before them in the troughs of water for them to look at as they drank, at the time they had conceived. (Gen. 30:37-41)

THE LITERAL MEANING OF GENESIS ✠ BOOK XII 6.

To see an object not in an image but in itself, yet not through the body, is to see with a vision surpassing all other visions. There are various ways of seeing, and with God's help I shall try to explain them and show how they differ. When we read this one commandment: "Thou shalt love thy neighbor as thyself," we experience three kinds of vision: one through the eyes, by which we see the letters; a second through the spirit, by which we think of our neighbor even when he is absent; and a third through an intuition of the mind, by which we see and understand love itself. Of these three kinds of vision the first is clear to everyone: through it we see heaven and earth and in them everything that meets the eye. The second, by which we think of corporeal things that are absent, is not difficult to explain; for we think of heaven and earth and the visible things in them even when we are in the dark. In this case we see nothing with the eyes of the body but in the soul behold corporeal images: whether true images, representing the bodies that we have seen and still hold in memory, or fictitious images, fashioned by the power of thought. My manner of thinking about Carthage, which I know, is different from my manner of thinking about Alexandria, which I do not know. The third kind of vision, by which we see and understand love, embraces those objects which have no images at once resembling them, yet differing from them. A man, a tree, the sun, or any other bodies in heaven or on earth are seen in their own proper form when present and are thought of when absent, in images impressed upon the soul. There are two ways of seeing them: one through the bodily senses, the other through the spirit, in which images are contained. But in the case of love, is it seen in one manner, when present, in the form in which it exists, and in another manner, when absent, in an image resembling it? Certainly not. But in proportion to the clarity of our intellectual vision, love itself is seen by one more clearly, by another less so. If, however, we think of some corporeal image, it is not love that we behold.

7. These are the three kinds of visions about which we had something to say in the preceding books as occasion arose, though we did not there specify their number. Now that we have briefly explained them, since the question under consideration demands a somewhat fuller discussion of them, we must give them definite and appropriate names, in order to avoid the encumbrance of constant circumlocution. Hence let us call the first kind of vision corporeal, because it is perceived through the body and presented to the senses of the body. The second will be spiritual, for whatever is not a body, and yet is something, is rightly called spirit; and certainly the image of an absent body, though it resembles a body,

174

is not itself a body any more than is the act of vision by which it is perceived. The third kind will be intellectual, from the word intellect, since *mentale* (mental) from *mens* (mind) , because it is just a newly coined word, is too ridiculous for us to employ.

. . . Accordingly it is sufficient to know that a thing is called corporeal either in the proper sense, when it refers to bodies, or in a metaphorical sense, as in the statement: "For in him dwells all the fullness of the Godhead bodily." Now the Godhead is not a body, but because the Apostle calls the religious observances of the Old Testament shadows of what is to come (using the analogy of shadows in the physical world) , he says that the fullness of the Godhead dwells in Christ bodily; for in him was fulfilled all that was prefigured by those shadows, and thus in a certain sense he is the embodiment of the shadows; that is, he is the truth of those figures and symbols. The figures therefore are called shadows in a metaphorical rather than proper sense of the word; and similarly, in saying that the fullness of the Godhead dwells bodily, the Apostle is using a metaphor.

The word spiritual is used in different ways. Even our body, in the state in which it will be in the resurrection of the saints, is called spiritual by the Apostle when he says: "What is sown a natural body shall rise a spiritual body," meaning that it will be subject to the spirit in a wonderful way and possess every facility and incorruption, and without any need of bodily nourishment will be vivified by the spirit alone, but not that it will have an incorporeal substance. Moreover, the body as we have it in this life does not have the essence of a soul, and it cannot be identified with the soul (*anima*) on the ground that is is a living thing (*animale*). Furthermore the air, or a wind (which is the motion of the air) is called spirit, as in the following words: "Fire, hail, snow, ice, and the spirit of the storm." The soul of man or beast also is called a spirit, as in the following passage: "And who knoweth if the spirit of the children of man ascend upward, and the spirit of the beast descend downward into the earth?" The word spirit is also used to designate the rational mind itself, in which there is so to speak an eye of the soul to which the image and knowledge of God pertains. Hence the Apostle urged: "Be renewed in the spirit of your mind, and put on the new man, which has been created according to God"; and elsewhere he speaks of the interior man, . . . "which is being renewed unto the knowledge of God according to the image of his Creator." So too, after he had said: "Therefore I myself with my mind serve the law of God, but with my flesh the law of sin," he returned to the same thought in another place and added: "The flesh lusts against the spirit and the spirit against the flesh, so that you do not do what you would"; thus he indifferently gave to the same thing the name mind or spirit. God also is called a spirit, as our Lord declares in the Gospel: "God is spirit, and they who worship him must worship in spirit and in truth."

8. It is not from any of these meanings we have mentioned, in which spirit is used, that we take the word spiritual to designate the kind of vision we are now treating. It is rather from that singular use of the word, found in the *Epistle to the Corinthians,* in which spirit is obviously distinguished from mind. "For," says the Apostle, "if I pray in a tongue, my spirit prays, but my understanding is unfruitful." By the word tongue in this passage he is to be understood to refer to obscure and mystical signs, which profit no man if the understanding of his mind is removed from them, for he hears what he does not understand. Hence he also says: "For he who speaks in a tongue does not speak to men but to God; for no one understands, though the spirit is speaking mysteries." Thus he makes it clear enough that in this passage he is speaking of the sort of tongue in which there are signs, such as the images and likenesses of things, which demand an intuition of the mind to be understood; and when they are not understood he says they are in the spirit, not in the mind. And so he declares more plainly: "If thou givest praise with the spirit, how shall he who fills the place of the uninstructed say 'Amen' to thy thanksgiving? For he does not know what thou sayest." Hence in view of the fact that signs of things, and not the things themselves, are given forth by the tongue, the member of the body which is moved in the mouth in speech, the Apostle, using a metaphor, designated as tongue any production of signs before they are understood. But once the understanding has grasped the sign (and this activity is proper to the mind), then there is revelation or knowledge or prophecy or teaching. Accordingly he says: "If I come to you speaking in tongues what shall I profit you, unless I speak to you either in revelation, or in knowledge, or in prophecy, or in teaching?" And he means to say that this happens when the intellect grasps the signs, or, in other words, the tongue; so that what is done is done not by the spirit alone but also by the mind.

9. Hence those to whom signs were manifested in the spirit by means of certain likenesses of corporeal objects had not yet the gift of prophecy, unless the mind had performed its function, in order that the signs might be understood; and the man who interpreted what another had seen was more a prophet than the

man who had seen. Thus it is obvious that prophecy belongs more to the mind than to the spirit, in the rather special sense in which the word spirit is taken, namely, in the sense of a certain power of the soul inferior to the mind, wherein likenesses of corporeal objects are produced. And so Joseph, who understood the meaning of the seven ears of corn and the seven kine, was more a prophet than Pharaoh, who saw them in a dream; for Pharaoh saw only a form impressed upon his spirit, whereas Joseph understood through a light given to his mind. And for this reason the former had a gift of tongues; the latter, the gift of prophecy. In the one there was the production of the images of things; in the other, the interpretation of the images produced. Less a prophet, therefore, is he who, by means of the images of corporeal objects, sees in spirit only the signs of the things signified, and a greater prophet is he who is granted only an understanding of the images. But the greatest prophet is he who is endowed with both gifts, namely, that of seeing in spirit the symbolic likenesses of corporeal objects and that of understanding them with the vital power of the mind. Such a one was Daniel. His pre-eminence was tested and established when he not only told the king the dream he had had but also explained the meaning of it. For the corporeal images themselves were produced in his spirit, and an understanding of them was revealed in his mind. I am using the word spirit, therefore, in the sense in which the Apostle uses it, where he distinguishes it from the mind: "I will pray with the spirit, but I will pray with the mind also." Here he implies that signs of things are formed in the spirit, and that an understanding of the signs shines forth in the mind. According to this distinction, then, I have designated as spiritual the kind of vision by which we represent in thought the images of bodies even in their absence.

10. But the intellectual type of vision, which is proper to the mind, is on a higher plane. The word intellect, as far as I know, cannot be used in a wide variety of meanings, such as we found in the case of the word spirit. But whether we say intellectual or intelligible, we mean one and the same thing, though some have wished to make a distinction between the two, designating as intelligible that reality which can be perceived by the intellect alone, and as intellectual the mind which understands. But whether there exists any being perceivable by the intellect alone, but not itself endowed with intellect—this is a large and difficult question. On the other hand I do not believe there is any one who either thinks or says that there exists a thing which perceives with the intellect and is at the same time incapable of being perceived by

the intellect. For mind is not seen except by mind. Therefore, since it can be seen, it is intelligible, and since it can also see, it is intellectual, according to the distinction just mentioned. Putting aside then the extremely difficult question about a thing which would only be understood but not possess understanding, we here use intellectual and intelligible in the same sense.

11. These three kinds of vision, therefore, namely, corporeal, spiritual, and intellectual, must be considered separately so that the reason may ascend from the lower to the higher. We have already proposed above an example by which all three kinds are illustrated in one sentence. For when we read: "Thou shalt love thy neighbor as thyself," the letters are seen corporeally, the neighbor is thought of spiritually, and love is beheld intellectually. But the letters when absent can also be thought of spiritually, and the neighbor when present can be seen corporeally. But love can neither be seen in its own essence with the eyes of the body nor be thought of in the spirit by means of an image like a body; but only in the mind, that is, in the intellect, can it be known and perceived. Corporeal vision indeed does not oversee any operations of the other two kinds of vision; rather the object perceived by it is announced to the spiritual vision, which acts as an overseer. For when an object is seen by the eyes, an image of it is immediately produced in the spirit. But this representation is not perceived unless we remove our eyes from the object that we were gazing at through the eyes and find an image of it within our soul. And if indeed the spirit is irrational, as in the beasts, the announcement made by the eyes goes just as far as the spirit. But if the soul is rational, the announcement is made also to the intellect, which presides over the spirit. And so, after the eyes have taken their object in and announced it to the spirit, in order that an image of it may be produced there, then, if it is symbolic of something, its meaning is either immediately understood by the intellect or sought out; for there can be neither understanding nor searching except by the functioning of the mind.

Baltassar the king saw the fingers of a hand writing on the wall, and immediately the image of a corporeal object was impressed on his spirit by means of a bodily sensation; and, when the vision was gone, the image remained in his thoughts. It was seen in spirit but not understood. At the same time when the sign was produced in a corporeal manner and was presented to his bodily eyes, Baltassar did not understand it, though even then he understood that it was a sign and knew this from the exercise of his mind. For since he was seeking out its meaning, it was his mind certainly that was conducting the search. When he failed to discover the meaning, Daniel came forward; and, his mind illuminated by the spirit of prophecy, he unfolded to the troubled king the prophetic meaning of the sign. For Daniel, by reason of the sort of vision that is proper to the mind, was more a prophet than the king, who had seen with the eyes of the body a corporeal sign, and in thought had beheld within his spirit the image of the object after its disappearance. But the king could do no more than recognize with his intellect that it was a sign and inquire into its meaning. . . . A careful consideration of these and other similar facts makes it abundantly clear that corporeal vision is ordered to the spiritual and the spiritual to the intellectual. . . .

16. Bodily sensation, therefore, belongs to the visible corporeal world and flows through the channels of the five senses, which are capable of perceiving objects even at a distance. Light, the finest element in bodies and hence more akin to the soul than the others, is first of all diffused in a pure state through the eyes and shines forth in rays from the eyes to behold visible objects. Moreover, it intermingles in some way with pure air, with misty and vaporous air, with a crasser sort of liquid, and with solid matter; and in these four states, as well as in its pure state in ocular vision, in which it is most perfect it brings about the five kinds of sensation. . . .

In this connection there is a remarkable thing to be noted. Spirit takes precedence over body, and the image of a body comes after the real body. But, since that which is second in time is produced in that which is prior in nature, the image of a body in a spirit is more excellent than the body itself in its own substance. It must not, of course, be thought that a body produces something in the spirit, as if the spirit were subjected as matter to the action of a body. For he who produces something is in every respect more excellent than the thing from which he produces it. Now body is in no way more excellent than spirit; indeed spirit is obviously superior to body. Hence, though we first see a body that we had not seen before and thereupon an image of it arises in our spirit, and in this same spirit we recall it when it is absent, nevertheless the body does not produce this image in the spirit, but the spirit produces it within itself. It does this with a wonderful speed that far surpasses the sluggish actions of the body. As soon as the eyes have seen their object, an image of it is formed without a moments's delay in the spirit of the one who sees. And it is the same in the case of hearing. Unless the spirit immediately formed within itself and retained in memory an image of the word perceived by the ears, one could not tell whether the second syllable was actually the second one, since the first would not longer exist once it had impinged upon the ear and passed away. And so all habits of speech, all sweetness of song, all motion in the act of our body would break down and come to nought, if the spirit did not retain a memory of past bodily motions with which to join further operations. And the spirit surely does not retain these motions except in so far as it has formed them in imagination within itself. Furthermore there are within us images of our future actions before the actions themselves begin. For what act do we perform through the body that the spirit has not previously fashioned in thought, first seeing within itself the likenesses of all visible operations and in some way ordering them?

24. . . . In one and the same soul, then, there are different visions: by means of the body it perceives objects such as the corporeal heaven and earth and everything that can be known in them in the degree that they are capable of being known; with the spirit it sees likenesses of bodies, a matter that I have already discussed at length; and with the mind it understands those realities that are neither bodies nor the likenesses of bodies. But there is, of course, a hierarchy in these visions, one being superior to another. For spiritual vision is more excellent than corporeal, and intellectual vision more excellent than spiritual. Corporeal vision cannot take place without spiritual, since at the very moment when we encounter a body by means of bodily sensation, there appears in the soul something not identical with the object perceived but resembling it. If this did not happen, there would be no sensation by which exterior objects are perceived. For it is not the body that perceives, but the soul by means of the body; and the soul uses the body as a sort of messenger in order to form within itself the object that is called to its attention from the outside world. Hence corporeal vision cannot take place unless there is a concommitant spiritual vision; but no distinction is made between the two until the bodily sensation has passed and the object perceived by means of the body is found in the spirit. On the other hand, there can be no spiritual vision without corporeal vision, namely, when the likenesses of absent bodies appear in the spirit, and when many such images are fashioned by the free activity of the soul or are presented to it in spite of itself. Moreover, spiritual vision needs intellectual vision if a judgment is to be made upon its contents; but intellectual vision does not need spiritual, which is of a lower order. And so corporeal vision is inferior to the spiritual, and both are inferior to the

intellectual. When, therefore, we read "The spiritual man judges all things, but he himself is judged by no man," we should not take "spiritual" as pertaining to the spirit which is distinguished from the mind (as in the text, "I will pray with the spirit, and I will pray with the mind also"), but we must understand it as deriving from that other sense as in the following: "But be renewed in the spirit of your mind." For I have already shown above that the name "spirit," in another sense of the word, is given also to the mind itself, to that power, namely, by which the spiritual man judges all things. Hence I believe that spiritual vision can be reasonably and naturally said to occupy a kind of middle ground between intellectual and corporeal vision. For I suppose that a thing which is not really a body, but like a body, can be appropriately said to be in the middle between that which is truly a body and that which is neither a body nor like a body.

THE TEACHER ✠ CHAPTER 7 Aug.—I wish now to have you review what we, in our reasoning, have discovered.
Ad.—I will do that so far as I can. First of all, I remember we were searching why we use language, and it was found that we speak for the purpose either of teaching or recalling; since, even when we ask a question, we do no other thing than that by which he, whom we question, may learn what we want to hear; and in singing, what we seem to do for the sake of delight is not a property of language. In praying to God, of whom we can not think as being taught or reminded by us, words have this force, that by them we either remind ourselves, or others are reminded or taught by us. Then, when it was proved well enough that words are nothing else but signs, and that what does not signify something can not be a sign, you proposed a line, of which I was to try to show what the words, one by one, signify. But this line was: "Si nihil ex tanta superis placet urbe relinqui." The second word of this line (nihil), though its use is most familiar, its meaning clear, yet, as to its exact signification, we were not finding it: And when it appeared to me that we do not give this word a place to no purpose in speaking, but that by it we teach our hearer something, you replied that by this word, perhaps, a state of mind is indicated, when the mind finds not what it seeks, or thinks that it has not found. You, indeed [suggested this]; but yet you

put off the unexplored difficulty of the problem to be cleared up at some other time, avoiding the force of the question by a jest; and do not think that I have forgotten your obligation. Next, then, when I was trying hard enough to explain the third word in the line, I was urged by you not to show what one word meant by another word which might have the same meaning, but rather to make clear the objective reality which is signified by words. And, when I had said that this can not be done by our conversation, we came to those things which can be pointed out by the finger to those who question about them. These objects I thought were all things corporeal, but we found them to be only things visible. From this we passed on to the deaf and to actors, I know not just how, to those who signify by gesture, without a word, not only things that can be seen, but almost everything that we speak: we found, however, that these gestures are signs. Then again we began to study how we might show these very realities, which are known by means of signs, without any symbols; since this wall, and color, and everything visible that is pointed out by extending the finger is proved to be shown by a kind of sign. Here, when I had said, wrongly indeed, that no such thing could be found, it was finally agreed between us that those things can be shown without a sign, which we are not doing when we are questioned, and which we can do straightway after we are interrogated: that language yet does not belong to this class; since it appeared clearly enough, that if we are asked what talking is while we are talking, it is easy to show that by means of itself.

We were reminded then that signs are made manifest by means of signs, or, by means of signs, other things that are not signs; or again, without the medium of a sign, realities [external and visible actions] which we can do following an interrogation about them: and of these three we took up the first to be studied and discussed more carefully. In this discussion it was made clear that there are some signs which are not signified in turn by the signs which they signify, as in this word of four syllables when we say *conjunction*. On the other hand, it was made clear that there are signs also which are signified in turn by the signs which they themselves are, as when we express the word sign, we signify a sign; for sign and word are two signs and also two words. But in this class where signs signify each other mutually, it was shown that some are unequal in force [or comprehension], others are equal, and others again identical. For this word of two syllables which is expressed when we say *signum* (sign) signifies everything absolutely by which anything is signified: but when we say *word* (verbum) it is not the sign of all signs, but of those only that are uttered by articulate voice. Whence it is clear that though a word may be signified by a sign, and a sign by a word, these latter two syllables by the former, and the former by the latter (*verbum* and *signum*), yet *signum* has greater comprehension than *verbum*, since these two syllables (*signum*) signify more objects than the other two (*verbum*). But the general term word and a common noun have the same value. For reason showed that all parts of speech are nouns also, since they can be used in connection with pronouns, and that they get a name can be said of all; and there is not one of them, used in conjunction with a verb, that may not make a complete sentence. But, while a noun and a word may have the same force, for this reason that all words may be used also as nouns, they have not the same comprehension. For it was proved quite clearly enough that words are so called from one cause, nouns from another. Indeed, that one of these is found to refer to the vibration of the ear, the other to noting down the thought of the soul, can be understood also from this, that we say speaking correctly: what is the name of this thing, wishing to give the object to memory; but we are not wont to say: what is the word of this thing. But terms which signify, not only as much [one as the other], but the very same, we found to be *nomen* and *onoma*. This point truly had escaped me in the division where symbols signify each other mutually, that we had found no symbol which among other things that it signifies, signifies also itself. These points I have recalled so far as I could. You now see, perhaps, whether I have set them forth well and in order.

CHAPTER 8 Aug.—You indeed have reviewed from memory well enough all that I wanted: and, I acknowledge to you, these points are now seen more clearly by me than they were when by questioning and arguing we both were drawing them forth from some unknown obscurity. But whereto, by such tortuous ways, I am laboring to reach with you, is not easy to say at present. You think perhaps, indeed, that we are jesting and recreating the mind from more serious subjects by apparently childish questions; or, if you have a suspicion that this problem is to bring forth something great, you are eager now to know, or at least to hear it. But I wish you to be assured that I have not been teaching shallow jests in this conversation, though possibly we do jest, this too is not to be measured in a childish sense, and we are thinking of no little or common good. And yet if I say that there is a certain life of contentment, and that everlasting, whereto, God being our guide, that is, the truth itself leading us.—If I say that thereto I wish to be brought by degrees accommodated to our slow progress, I fear that I may seem to be unwise, because I have begun to enter upon the way not by the study of the very realities themselves, but of symbols only. You will pardon me, then, I make this prelude with you, not for the purpose of amusing, but to exercise the powers and the keenness of the mind, by which we may be enabled not only to endure, but to love the warmth and light of that region where is the life of contentment.

Ad.—Go on rather as you have begun, for never shall I think those things worthy of scorn which you shall have thought deserving of words and action.

Aug.—Come, now, let us study that division where signs do not signify other signs, but rather those other things which are called signifiable. And first of all, tell me whether man is man.

Ad.—Now, indeed, I know not whether you are jesting.

Aug.—Why so?

Ad.—Because you think that I am to be asked whether man is anything other than man.

Aug.—So you would think, I believe, that you are made an object of jest, even if I were to ask if the first syllable of this noun is anything other than *ho,* and the second anything other than *mo.*

Ad.—So indeed.

Aug.—But these two syllables united are *homo:* or do you deny it?

Ad.—Who can deny it?

Aug.—I am asking, therefore, whether you are these two syllables united.

Ad.—Not at all: but I see your purpose.

Aug.—Say it, therefore, so that you may not think of me as offending.

Ad.—The logical inference, you think, is that I am not a man.

Aug.—Why do you not think the same, since you grant that all the foregoing, on which this inference is built, is true?

Ad.—I shall not tell you what I think, until I hear from you whether when you asked if man is man, you were asking about these two syllables (*homo*), or the objective reality which they signify.

Aug.—Suppose you answer how you understood my question. For

184

if the question is ambiguous, you should have been on guard against that, and you should not have answered until you were certain as to how I meant the question.

Ad.—How could that ambiguity trip me, when I have answered both: for *homo* is surely *homo;* and these two syllables are nothing more than two syllables; and that which they signify is nothing other than what it is.

Aug.—Well said! But why did you take the word *homo* only, and not the other words that we uttered for both symbol and object symbolized?

Ad.—How is it proved that I did not so understand the other words?

Aug.—To omit other points, if you had understood that first question of mine only as pertaining to the sounding symbols, you should have answered nothing: it would appear indeed that I had asked nothing: but now, when I have pronounced three words, one of which I have repeated at the center, saying: *utrum homo homo sit,* it is clear that you understood the first word and the last, not the second, as signs: but that you took the second for the objects signified is proved even by this that immediately, and with no real doubt, you thought of answering my question.

Ad.—You say truly.

Aug.—Why, therefore, did you choose to take the word at the center only both according to the way in which it is sounded and according to what it means?

Ad.—Behold, now, I take it only in that sense in which the object is signified, for I agree with you that we cannot carry on a conversation except by means of words, which when they are heard, the mind is directed to the objective realities of which words are the signs. Show me then how it is that I am deceived by that sophism in which the conclusion is that I am not a man.

Aug.—No, but I will ask the question again, in order that you may find your error.

Ad.—You do well.

Aug.—I shall not ask, then, what I asked in the first place, because you have granted that now. See, therefore, more carefully whether the syllable *ho* is nothing other than *ho,* and whether *mo* is nothing else than *mo.*

Ad.—I see here nothing else at all.

Aug.—See also whether *homo* is formed by the union of these two.

Ad.—I should not have granted that at all: for it was decided, and decided correctly, that when the sign is expressed we take note of the object signified; and, from the consideration of that, we assent to what has been said, or we dissent. But these two syllables, pronounced separately, because they have sounded without any signification, are just what they sound. This has been granted.

Aug.—It is granted, therefore, and you hold it fixed in mind that answers should be given only to questions which are concerned with real objects signified by means of words.

Ad.—I do not see why we are not agreed upon that point, provided only that the words be words.

Aug.—I would like to know how you would refute that sophist of whom we are told in jest that the conclusion of the one with whom he was wrangling was that a lion had proceeded from his mouth: For when he had asked whether those things which we speak proceed from our mouth, and the one with whom the dispute was carried on could not deny it, he twisted the subject of the conversation so as to have his opponent name a lion. This done, he began, laughingly, to heckle him, and to force him to admit that because he had granted that what we speak goes forth from our mouth, and he could not deny that he had uttered "lion," it must be clear that a man so meek had thrown out a brute so savage.

Ad.—It would be easy to refute this punster: for I would not grant that whatsoever we speak proceeds from our mouth. Indeed we signify the things that we speak; but from the mouth of the speaker proceeds, not the objective reality which is signified, but a sign which is a symbol of the object; excepting where the very signs themselves are signified, which division we considered just previously.

Aug.—You would be armed quite well indeed against such an opponent: however, what will you answer when I ask whether *man* is a noun.

Ad.—What, but that it is a noun?

Aug.—Now, when I see you, do I see a noun?

Ad.—No.

Aug.—Will you have me tell you what follows as a logical conclusion?

Ad.—No; do not, I beg of you: for I can answer that I am not the man who, I say, is a noun, when you ask whether man is a noun. For it has been settled that we give assent or dissent according to the thing which is signified.

186

Aug.—But it appears to me that your hitting upon this answer has not been a mere accident. Indeed, the very law of reason itself implanted in our minds has established your ability to discriminate. For if I were to ask what man is, you would reply, perhaps, an animal. But if I were to ask what part of speech man is, you could answer correctly only a noun. Wherefore, while *man* is said to be both a noun and an animal, the former is expressed in the sense of a sign, the latter in the sense of the thing which is signified. To anyone therefore who asks whether man is a noun no other answer can be given than the affirmative, for his question indicates that he wishes to be answered in the sense in which *man* is a sign. But if he asks whether man is an animal I will respond in the affirmative even more readily. Because if, expressing neither noun nor animal, he were to ask simply what man is, the mind would turn, by that same fixed law of speech, to the object which is signified by the two syllables, *homo,* and the answer would only be "animal"; or even the full definition might be expressed, namely, a rational and mortal animal. Is this not clear to you?

Ad.—Quite clear; but, since we have granted that man is a noun, how shall we avoid that too flippant reply in which the conclusion is put together that we are not men?

Aug.—How else but by showing that the conclusion is not derived from the sense in which we agreed with the questioner. Or if the questioner acknowledges that he is concerned with a reference to the sign and not the thing, then we need have no apprehension, for what is there to be feared in acknowledging that I am not a man, that is these three syllables—*hominem?*

Ad.—Nothing could be more true. Why then is it offensive when the inference is expressed: "You therefore are not man," when, according to these points granted, nothing is more true or more truly said?

Aug.—Because I cannot but think that the conclusion has reference to that which is signified by these two syllables as soon as the words are expressed, by reason of that law which is naturally very strong, so that the attention is turned to the objects signified immediately as soon as the symbols are perceived.

Ad.—I accept what you say.

CHAPTER 9 Aug.—I want you to understand, therefore, that realities which are signified are to be rated at a higher value than their symbols. Whatsoever, indeed, is on account of something else must be of less worth than that for which it is: unless you think otherwise.

Ad.—It seems to me that assent is not to be granted here too hastily. For when we express the word *filth,* this noun I think is to be ranked far ahead of the reality which it signifies. What offends us when we hear is not the sound of this word; for by the change of one letter *coenum* (filth) becomes *coelum* (the sky); but we see what a difference there is between the objects signified by these nouns. Wherefore I would not attribute to this symbol what we shun in the object it signifies. More readily, indeed, do we hear this than by any one of the organs of sense do we perceive it.

Aug.—Very keen, indeed. Therefore it is untrue that all realities are to be rated as of higher value than their signs.

Ad.—So it seems.

Aug.—Tell me, therefore, what plan you think they followed who gave a name to this object so foul and so much shunned (*coenum*): or whether you approve or disapprove their action.

Ad.—I dare not presume either to approve or disapprove: and I do not know what plan they followed.

Aug.—Can you find, at any rate, what your purpose is when you pronounce this word?

Ad.—I can, yes: My purpose is to signify so that I may teach him, with whom I speak, or remind him about that reality which I think ought to be taught or recalled.

Aug.—How is this? The very fact of teaching or of reminding, or of being taught or reminded, which either you express fittingly by this word, or which is expressed to you—is not that fact itself to be esteemed of higher value than the mere word?

Ad.—I grant that the knowledge itself which comes through this symbol is superior, but I do not think that the real object itself is so ranked.

Aug.—In this, our judgment, therefore, while it may not be true that all objective realities are to be ranked ahead of their symbols; it is not consequently untrue that everything that is on account of another is less excellent than that other for which it is. Indeed, the knowledge of filth, from which this noun has its fixed meaning, is to be esteemed of higher worth than the noun itself, which, we have found, is in turn to be esteemed more excellent than filth. But the one reason why knowledge is preferred before its symbol, of which we are speaking, is that this latter is proved to be on account of the former, not the former on account of the latter. Thus, if a certain glutton, and, as the Apostle has said, "a slave of sensuality," (Rom. 16:18) were to say that therefore he lives in order that he may eat; a temperate man, who has heard his words, has not the patience to endure, and says: How much better would it be to eat in order to live? He says this, indeed, in accordance with that same rule. For he disapproved for no other reason than this, that he (the glutton) should place a value so low upon his life as to esteem it cheaper than the pleasure of the palate, declaring that he lives for feasting. And this one would be approved for no other reason rightly than because, understanding which one was for the other, that is, subordinate to the other, he uttered the admonition that food is to be taken in order that we may live: that we do not live in order to be fed. In like manner you also perhaps, or any man who values things rightly, might answer one who talks and a noisy lover of words, who says that he teaches in order to talk: Why, man, not rather: talk in order to teach? But if these things are true, as you know that they are, you see surely how much less words are to be esteemed than that on account of which we use words; because the very use itself of words is more excellent than words, for words are in order that we may use them, but we use them in order to teach. As teaching, therefore, is better than talking, so is language better than words. Far more excellent, therefore, is teaching than mere words. But I want to hear what you perhaps, think can be said against this.

Ad.—I am quite agreed, indeed, that teaching is better than words. But whether everything, that is on account of something else, is so fixed as a rule, that nothing can contradict it, I do not know.

Aug.—Elsewhere we shall take up that problem more fittingly and more carefully. For the present, the point which you grant is enough for that which I wish to prove. For you grant that knowledge of realities is more excellent than the symbols of realities. Therefore the knowledge of objective realities, which are signified, is to be preferred to the knowledge of their symbols (by which they are signified): or does it not so seem to you?

Ad.—Have I not granted that the knowledge of realities is to be preferred to the knowledge of symbols, and not to the symbols themselves? I fear, therefore to be agreed with you here. For what, if, as the noun *filth* is to be ranked ahead of the objective reality which it signifies, so also the knowledge of this noun

189

should be given a place before the knowledge of its material object, though the noun itself may be less excellent than that knowledge? Indeed there are four points here—the noun, the real object, knowledge of the noun, knowledge of the real object. As the first, therefore, is more excellent than the second, why may not the third also be better than the fourth? But granting that it may not be more worthy, does it follow that it must be counted as less?

Aug.—I see that you have retained quite well what you granted, and explained what you thought. But you understand, I think, that this noun of three syllables, which sounds when we say *vitium* (vice), is more excellent than that which it signifies; while the knowledge of the noun is much less perfect than acquaintance of vices. While, therefore, you may determine these four points, and study them—the noun, the objective reality, the knowledge of the noun and the knowledge of the object; we rightly rank the first ahead of the second. Thus this noun placed properly in its line, where Persius says: "But this one is sotted with vice" (*Satyra* 3, v. 33), not only introduces no vice into the verse, but even adds something of ornament: while yet the objective reality, which is signified by this noun, makes vicious anything whatsoever in which it exists. But not so is the third ranked ahead of the fourth; for the fourth, we see, has a greater value than the third. Indeed the knowledge of this noun is of small importance compared with a knowledge of vices.

Ad.—Think you that the knowledge of this last division is to be preferred even when it makes men more unhappy? For, of all the pains that the heartlessness of tyrants has discovered, or their designs invented, this same Persius gives the first place to that one by which men are tortured, who are forced to acknowledge the vices which they can not avoid.

Aug.—By that reasoning you can say the knowledge even of virtues is not to be preferred to the knowledge of this noun. For to see virtue and not to have it is the punishment by which this same satirist wished to have tyrants tortured.

Ad.—God save us from such unreason. Now I see indeed that knowledge, by which learning nobly enriches the soul, is not to be blamed: but they, of all men are to be esteemed the most unhappy, who, as Persius, I think, also judged, are afflicted by such disease that a remedy so powerful will not relieve it.

Aug.—You understand well: but, whatever the judgment of Persius may be, is not to our point now. For in such problems we do not depend upon the authority of these men (satirists as a class). Then again, whether knowledge on one subject is to be preferred to another, is not to be settled here offhand. I hold what has been proved quite sufficiently: that is, that the knowledge of realities which are signified, while it may not be more excellent than the knowledge of its symbols, is yet more excellent than the symbols themselves. Wherefore let us study more and more thoroughly what is the quality of that class of realities, which we saw, can be shown by themselves, without symbols, as talking, walking, sitting down, reclining, and other things of this kind.

Ad.—I recall now what you say.

CHAPTER 10 Aug.—Does it appear to you that we can show without a sign all things that we can straightway do when we are questioned, or do you make some exceptions?

Ad.—Studying this over and over again, I find nothing yet that can be taught without some sign, except perhaps talking, and possibly if someone were to ask what teaching is. For I see that he, whatsoever I shall have done to make him learn, following his inquiry, does not learn really from the object which he wishes to have made clear to him. For, as has been said, if he questions me about walking when I am not walking, or when I am doing something else, and I, on the spot endeavor to show by walking what he has asked, how shall I prevent his thinking that *to walk* is just so much as I have walked? But if he thinks that he will be deceived; and, indeed, whosoever shall have walked more or less than I did, that one, he will think, has not walked. And what I have said of this one word will be true of all others, which I had thought could be shown without a sign, excepting the two named (talking and teaching).

Aug.—I accept that, indeed: But does it not appear to you that talking is one thing, teaching another?

Ad.—It does seem so truly, for if they were the same, no one would teach except in the fact of speaking; however, we teach many things by means of other signs aside from words. Who, then, will doubt that there is a difference?

Aug.—Are teaching and signifying the same or is there some difference?

Ad.—I think they are the same.

Aug.—Does not he speak correctly who says that we signify in order that we may teach?

191

Ad.—Correctly indeed.

Aug.—What if another one says that we therefore teach in order to signify, is he not easily refuted by the sentence above?

Ad.—So he is.

Aug.—If, therefore, we signify in order to teach, we do not teach in order to signify: teaching is one thing, signifying another.

Ad.—You speak truly; and I answered incorrectly that both are the same.

Aug.—Now answer this, whether he who teaches what teaching is, does that by signifying, or otherwise.

Ad.—I do not see how he could otherwise.

Aug.—Therefore, what you said a while ago is untrue, that when the question is asked what teaching is, the reality can be taught without the means of signs; since we see that not even this can be done without signifying, where you have granted that to signify is one thing, to teach is another. For if they are distinct, as it appears they are, and this latter is shown only by the former, then it is not indeed shown by itself, as it appeared to you. Wherefore nothing has been found, as yet, that can be shown by means of itself, excepting language, which, among other things which it signifies, signifies also itself: which yet, because itself is symbol, shows nothing that stands out clearly that can be taught without means of symbols.

Ad.—I have nothing upon which to disagree.

Aug.—It is established therefore that nothing is taught without symbols; also that the knowledge itself ought to be to us more precious than the symbols by which we know; though all things signified may not have greater worth than their signs.

Ad.—So it does appear.

Aug.—By what a roundabout way have we arrived at so small a point. For, from the time that we began this fencing of words, which we have been doing now for quite some time, it has been worked out that we find these three points: (1) whether nothing can be taught without the means of signs; (2) whether some signs are to be preferred to the objects which they signify; (3) whether the knowledge of things is more excellent than their symbols. But there is a fourth point which I would like to know briefly from you, i.e. whether you think that these points are so cleared up that now you can not doubt about them.

Ad.—I would wish indeed that we had reached some certainty after such doubts and complications, but your question disturbs me, I

192

know not how, and prevents me from agreeing with you. For it appears to me that you would not ask this question if you did not have something to say against it: and the problem is so complex that I cannot explore it thoroughly nor with the assurance you would expect of me. I am fearful lest something may be hidden in such a labyrinthian problem that the keenness of my mind cannot perceive it.

Aug.—I admire your hesitancy, for it indicates a mind not too hasty in its decisions, a most important safeguard of a tranquil mind. For it is very difficult indeed not to be moved at all, when those things which we readily accept and approve are wrenched, as it were from our hands. Wherefore, as it is right to yield to well studied reasons, so it is perilous to accept things unknown as if they were known. For when those things which we presume are going to persist and stand firmly are too frequently upset, it is to be feared that, falling into distrust and hatred of reason, we may lose confidence in truth itself.

But come, now, let us review more thoroughly, and see whether you think we may entertain doubt on any of these points. Consider, for example, if someone who knows nothing of the art of bird-catching, which is done by means of reeds and birdlime, were to meet a birdcatcher, fitted out in his hunting dress and not hunting but walking along. Thus seeing him, the stranger would stop astonished, wondering and reflecting what this make-up of man could mean. But the birdcatcher seeing the astonished observer, with the purpose of making himself known, throws off the reeds, and, by means of the sling and the snare, takes aim, strikes and captures a bird which he sees near by; would not this birdcatcher teach his spectator what he wanted to know by means of no sign made but the very objective reality itself?

Ad.—I fear that there may be something here like that which I said of him who asks what walking is. And, indeed, I see that the whole art of bird-catching is not here set forth.

Aug.—It is easy to free yourself of that care; for I will add that an observer may be so keenly intelligent that he grasps this complete branch of the art from what he sees. For it is sufficient to our purpose if some things, though not all, can be shown, and some men can be taught without a symbol.

Ad.—To that I can also add that if a person is quick to understand, he will know what walking is when walking is shown to him by a few paces.

Aug.—You may do that. I will grant it. And I not only do not oppose, but I favor the solution. Moreover you see that this conclusion is reached by both of us, that, namely, some things can be taught without the means of symbols: and that what appeared right to us a while ago is not true, that, namely, there is nothing absolutely that can be shown without symbols. For of these, not one only or another, but thousands of things come to mind which can be shown, without a sign expressed, but by themselves. Passing over numberless spectacles of men in every theatre, where things are exhibited through themselves and not with signs, does not God and does not nature exhibit and show to those who see them, the sun surely and this light diffusing and clothing all these visible things, the moon also and other planets, the earth and the sea, and whatever lives in them without number.

But if we study more closely perhaps you will find that there is nothing actually learned by means of symbols: for when a sign is given to me, if it finds me now knowing the reality of which it is the sign, that sign can teach me nothing; but if it finds me knowing the reality, what then do I learn by the sign? For when I read: *"And their saraballae were not changed"* (Dan. 3:94), the word saraballae does not show me the reality which it signifies. Indeed if a headdress is called by this name, have I therefore, by the hearing of this word, learned what head is or what dress is? I had known these before; and the knowledge of them came to me, not when they were named by others, but when they were seen by me. Indeed when these two syllables, which we utter when we say *caput,* first struck my ears I knew as little what they meant as when first I heard or read *saraballae.* But when *caput* (the word) was spoken repeatedly, I, remarking and taking note when it was spoken, found that it is the vocal term (the sign) of a reality which was already quite familiarly known to me by sight. But before I made this discovery this word was to me merely sound: I learned, however, that it is a sign, then, when I discovered of what reality it is the sign, which, as I have said, I learned, not by its signification, but the sight of it. Therefore that the sign is learned by means of a known reality is more truly correct than that a reality is learned by means of its given sign.

In order that you may understand this more thoroughly, let us suppose that we hear now for the first time the word *caput,* and not knowing whether it is merely a meaningless sound or whether it signifies something, we ask what *caput* is. (Remember that we want to have a knowledge of the sign and not of that which it signifies, which knowledge we do not have as long as we do not know of what it is a sign.) If therefore to our inquiry, the object is pointed out with the finger, it is by that seeing that we learn the meaning of the sign, which we had heard only before, and not known. In this symbol, however, there are two elements, sound and meaning. We surely do not perceive the sound from the fact that it is a sign, but by the very fact that it strikes the ear; but the meaning we get by noting the reality which is signified. For the pointing of the finger can signify nothing other than that towards which the finger is pointed; but it was pointed at the member which is called the head and not to the sign. Therefore it must be that I have not learned the nature of the thing by that pointing, for I knew that already, nor did I learn the sign in that way, since the pointing is not directed to the sign. But I do not insist too much on the pointing of the finger, for to me it seems to be rather a sign of demonstration than a pointing out of the realities, whatever they may be, which are pointed out; as in the case of the adverb which we express by saying: "lo" or "behold": for with this adverb we are wont to extend the finger, lest one sign of demonstration be not enough. And if I can, I shall try to prove to you that by signs, which are called words, we learn nothing. For it is more correct, as I have said, that we learn the force of the word, that is the meaning which is hidden in its sound by knowledge of the reality, which is signified, than that we perceive the reality by such signification.

Then what I have said about head I might also have said of coverings and of numberless other things. And these I already know, but *saraballae* I do not know up to the present time. If someone were to signify their meaning by gesture or were to make a drawing of them, or indicate something to which they are similar, I will not say that he would not be teaching me (which I could maintain if I wished to talk a little more) ; but I do say, what is very much to the point, that he would not teach me by means of words. But if someone, having seen by chance this headdress (*saraballae*) while I was present, should have brought the fact to my notice saying: "Behold the *saraballae*" I would learn something I did not know. Not by the words which are uttered, but by the sight of that object, by means of which I would know and retain the meaning of that name. For when I learned the very reality of the object I was not giving credit to the words of others, but to my own eyes. Yet perhaps I did believe their words in order to take note, that is, in order to find what was to be seen.

CHAPTER 11 So far words have value (to give them their full credit) to remind us only to look for realities, but they do not so exhibit the realities that we know them. But that person teaches me something, who holds out to my eyes, or to any one of the senses of the body, or even to the mind the things which I desire to know. By means of words, therefore, we learn only words or rather only the sound and noise of words. For if those things which are not signs cannot be words, even though a word may be heard, yet I do not know that it is a word until I know its signification. By means, therefore, of things *known* the knowledge of words also is made perfect; but by means of words *heard,* words are not learned. For we do not *learn* words that we know; nor can we say that we have learned words, which we did not know, except by perceiving their meaning, which is not by the hearing of sounds but by the knowledge of things signified. For it is the truest reason, and most truly said, that when words are uttered, we either know their meaning, or we do not. If we know, then we are said to be recalling rather than learning; but if we know not the meaning, then we are not even said to be recalling, although possibly we are moved to inquire.

But if you say this, we cannot know those head coverings, the name of which we know only as a sound, except by seeing them. On the other hand, we cannot know the name itself more fully except by knowing the thing signified.

But we accept that account from the youths themselves of how they triumphed over the king and over the fires by faith and religion, what praises they sang to God, and what honors they won even from their very enemies. Have we learned all this otherwise than by words? I answer that everything signified by these words had previously been the subject of our knowledge. For what three youths are, what a furnace is, what fire is, what a king is, and finally, what being unhurt by fire and all the rest which these words signify, I knew and held before I had the experience of hearing these words. But Ananias and Azarius and Misael are to me strangers, just as much as this strange word, *saraballae*; and these names have not helped me, and cannot now help me to know these men. But all the facts together, which are described in the account of history, I acknowledge that I *believe* to have been so done as they are described rather than that I *know* them: and they whom we believe too were not in ignorance as to this point of difference (between believing and knowing). For the Prophet says: "Unless you believe you shall not understand"; which he would not have said if he had thought that there is no difference between the two.

What I understand, that also I believe; but not everything that I believe do I also understand. Everything that I understand,

196

however, I also know: I do not know all that I believe. And I do not, therefore, not know how useful it is to take on trust also many things that I do not know. With this advantage of believing I count also this narrative of the three youths. Wherefore, while there is a vast reach of things that I cannot know, I do know what is the advantage of believing.

But, referring now to all things that we understand, we consult, not the one speaking, whose words sound without, but truth within, presiding over the mind, reminded perhaps by words to take note. Moreover He who is consulted teaches, for Christ is He who is said to "dwell in the interior man" (Eph. 3:16-17): that is, the changeless power of God, and the everlasting wisdom, which every rational soul truly consults. But there is revealed to each one as much as he can grasp by reason of a good or a bad habit of life. And if sometimes errors are made, that is not due to a defect in the truth which he has consulted; just as it is also not the fault of this light which is bright without that the eyes of the body are frequently deceived. But we acknowledge that we consult this external light about visible things in order that it may show us such objects so far as we have the power to discern.

CHAPTER 12 But if we consult the light in reference to colors and other properties which we perceive through the body; if we consult the elements of this world and the objects of our senses; if we consult the senses themselves, which the mind uses as interpreters to know such things; and, if in reference to those things that we understand, we consult interior evidence, what can be said to have made it clear that by means of words we learn nothing but the sound that strikes the ear? For everything that we perceive, we perceive either by a corporeal sense organ or by the power of the mind. The former are the objects of the senses, the latter of the understanding: or, to speak after the manner of our own (Christian) authors, we give the name carnal to the former, spiritual to the latter. When we are questioned concerning the former, we answer what we perceive if they are present, as when we are questioned while looking at the new moon as to its size and position. Here he who asks, if he does not see the moon, believes our words, and often he believes not; but he does not learn at all unless he himself sees what is described. Now he learns, not by means of the words which are sounded but by means of the things themselves and from his own senses. For the same words are heard by the one who sees and by the one who does not see. But when there is a question not about things which we presently perceive, but about what we have formerly perceived, we do not speak then of the things themselves but of the images impressed by them and stored in the memory. I do not know how we can speak of these as true if we do not perceive them as true, unless we relate not what we see or perceive, but what we have seen or perceived. Thus do we carry in the inner courts of memory those images, documents of things perceived before. Contemplating these in the mind we utter no falsehood if we speak in good conscience. But these documents belong to us; for he who hears us (telling of past experience), if he has perceived the facts that I tell, and if he was present, does not learn by my words. But he recalls by means of the impressions which he has received from the same facts; and if he did not himself experience what I tell, who does not see that such a one *learns* not, but rather *believes* my words?

But when there is a question of those things which we perceive in the mind, that is, by means of understanding and reason, we speak truly of the things which we behold as present in that interior light of truth, by which he who is called the interior man is enlightened and whence also comes his joy. But then our hearer, if he also himself sees those things with the simple and unseen eye, knows what I say, not by means of my words, but by his own judgment—the vision of his own mind. Therefore, speaking of what is true, I do not *teach* anyone viewing the same true things in his own mind; for he is taught, not by means of my words, but by means of the same mental realities which God, by the natural light of intelligence reveals within the soul. Hence, if he is questioned he might have answered the very same. But what is more unreasonable than to think that he is taught by my speech, when if he were questioned before I spoke, he could have explained the very same things. For, it frequently happens, that being questioned, someone answers in the negative, and then when he is urged by other questions, replies in the affirmative. This happens because he cannot consult this light on the entire problem. He is reminded to do this on particular points when he is questioned on them one by one. That which he cannot do in the entire problem, he can discern in the parts of which the whole is made up. To this he is directed by the words of the questioner, not by mere verbal instruction, but by means of questions put in such a manner that the individual is able to learn by the inner powers of the soul. A good example of this is to be found in the very question on which we are now engaged, namely, whether or not nothing can be taught by means of words. And first it seemed to you unreasonable, because you were unable to see clearly the whole problem. Therefore, I should have put my questions so as to make them correspond to the powers of your mind to hear that master teaching within. Thus I would express what you acknowledge to be true while I am talking, and you are sure, and you affirm that you know these things. Whence did you learn them? You might say, perhaps, that I taught them? Then I would reply: What if I were to say that I had seen a man flying? Would my words give the same certitude as if you were to hear it said that men of understanding are better than fools. You would surely answer in the negative; and you might reply that you do not believe the former; or, even though you were to believe, that you know nothing about it; but this latter, you would say you know most surely. From this discussion you would understand that you have not learned anything by means of my words, neither concerning the flying exploit, of which you knew nothing, nor concerning the relative worth of wise men and fools, of which you had knowledge. And indeed, even though you were to be questioned about each one of these points, you could take an oath that that is unknown, that this is well known to you.

Then, in truth, you would acknowledge all that you had formerly denied, when you knew with clarity and distinctness all the elements of which it consists. For whenever we say anything, either the hearer knows not whether or not they are true, or he knows that they are untrue, or he knows that they are true. In the first of these three he will either believe (take on trust) or he will form an opinion, or he will hesitate. In the second case he will either take a stand against what is said, or he will reject it. In the third he simply witnesses to what has been said (confirming its truth). In no one of these three cases does he therefore learn. For he who, after hearing our words, still remains ignorant as to their objective meaning; as he also, who knows that what he has heard is untrue; and he again who could have expressed the very same thought, if he had been asked, is proved surely to have learned nothing by means of my words.

CHAPTER 13 From the foregoing it follows, therefore, that in the things which are discerned by the mind, one who cannot grasp that which the mind of the speaker discerns, hears his words to no purpose, excepting the case where it is practicable to take a thing on trust so long as it cannot be known. On the other hand, he who can discern those things which are grasped by the mind is inwardly a disciple of the truth; in the world of external things, he is the judge of the one who speaks, or more properly of his speech. Not infrequently the hearer knows what has been said, though the speaker himself perhaps may not know the true meaning of his own words. For example, someone who follows the Epicurean school of philosophy, and who believes that the human soul is mortal, may express the arguments by which more far-seeing thinkers have proved its immortality. A person who can judge of spiritual things and who hears such arguments would consider them true. But he who speaks them does not know that they are true; furthermore, he thinks that they are quite untrue. Is he, therefore, to be thought of as *teaching* what he does not know? But he uses the very same words which one who knows could also use.

Wherefore now not even this is left to words, namely, that they express the mind of the speaker, since it is not certain at least whether he knows what he is talking about. Consider also those who lie and those who deceive, by whom you will easily understand that not only is the mind opened by means of words, but by means of words also the mind is concealed. For I do not by any means call into question the fact that the words of truthful men aim at this and profess to make clear the meaning, the mind of the speaker. They indeed would realize this, as everyone grants, if liars were not allowed to speak.

However, we may have experienced, both in ourselves and in others, that frequently words are expressed which are not the proper terms of the thought actually in mind. This I see can be verified in two ways: (1) either when something which has been committed to memory and frequently repeated is expressed by one who is thinking of other things, which often happens to us when we chant a hymn, (2) or, when aside from our intention, and by a slip of the tongue, some words escape us in place of others which we meant to say. For here too signs are expressed which are not of the things which we have in mind. And indeed those who lie also think of the thing that they are saying. Although we do not know whether or not they speak the truth, we do know that they have in mind what they are saying, if they do not do one of the two things previously mentioned. If someone insists that it does sometimes happen (though frequently it is unknown, and has deceived me often), I do not oppose such a statement.

But in addition to these there is another class (of words that do not convey their meaning), a class far-reaching indeed, and the source of numberless misunderstandings and disputes. It is that class which is involved when he who speaks is thinking of the same things which he utters, but for the most part only to himself and certain others. To the one to whom he is speaking, and to others also, the word has not the same meaning. Let someone say, for example, in our hearing, that by some brute animals man is surpassed in manly force (*virtute*); immediately, we cannot endure such a statement and with considerable feeling we reject the statement as false and repugnant. The speaker, perhaps, is using the term manly force (*virtutem*) to mean the physical strength of the body. And by that word he may be expressing that which he has in mind, neither lying, nor erring, nor putting together words that lingered in his memory, while he was turning over something else in his mind. And he is not, by a slip of the tongue, saying something other than that which he turns over in his mind, but is only calling the thing of which he is thinking by a name other than that which we call it. On this point we would be immediately agreed with him if we could read his mind and see directly the thought he was unable communicate to us. A definition, they say, will remedy this source of error; so that if, in this dispute, the speaker were to define what manly force (*virtus*) is, it would be clear that the disagreement is not about the objective reality but about the meaning of a word. If I am to grant that this is so, how often is one found who makes a good definition? And yet there are many arguments against the systematic teaching of the art of argument; which it is not in line with our purpose to study now, and they are not approved by me in all respects.

I pass over the fact that there are many things that we do not hear distinctly, and yet we insist long and forcefully as if we had heard accurately. For example, just a little while ago you were saying that you had heard that by a certain Punic word piety is understood, according to those to whom this language is quite familiar, while I said that the word means mercy. But I insisted that you had forgotten what you had heard. For it seemed to me that you had said, not piety, but faith, though you were seated quite close to me, and these two words do not by any means deceive the ears because of their similarity in sound. Yet for some time I thought that you knew not what had been said to you, but the truth was that I did not know what you had said. For if I had heard you correctly, it would not have appeared to me at all unreasonable that piety and mercy are signified by the same word in the Punic tongue. These things happen not infrequently, but we shall pass them over in order that I may not appear to be falsifying words, where the carelessness of the hearer is to be blamed, or again the deafness of men. Those points which I referred to above are more difficult, where by means of truly Latin words, clearly perceived, we cannot know the thought of the speaker even though we speak the same language.

But now I retreat and I admit that when words are perceived by the hearing of one who knows their meaning, he may be assured that the speaker has been thinking of those things which the words signify. But does it follow from this that he learns also whether or not the speaker has uttered the truth?

CHAPTER 14 For do teachers make the claim that it is their own thoughts which are perceived and retained by pupils and not rather the branches of learning which they communicate by talking? Who, indeed, is so unreasonably careful as to send his child to school to learn what the teacher thinks? But all these branches of learning, which teachers profess to teach, the doctrine of virtue even and of wisdom itself, they explain through words. Then those who are called pupils consider within the inwardness of the mind whether what has been said is true, that is, in the measure of their own mental power they see the agreement that is within. Thus they learn and when the truth that is within makes known to them that true things have been spoken, they applaud, not knowing that their applause belongs rather to those who are taught than to their teachers, if indeed their teachers know what they are talking about. But men are deceived, so that they call teachers those who are not teachers at all, generally because there is no delay between the time of speaking and the time of thinking. And because after the suggestion of the one who speaks they learn instantaneously within, they think they have learned from him who spoke from without.

But if God so grants, we shall study at some other time the usefulness of words which rightly viewed is no small matter. For the present I have brought to your notice that we must not give to words more than belongs to them. So that now we may not only believe, but we may begin to understand also how truly the word is written on divine authority that we claim no one as our master on earth, because one is the Master of all in heaven. (Matt. 23:8-10) But what "in heaven" means, He will teach us by means of men, through signs and from without, so that we may turning to Him within become learned in the inner life of the soul. He will teach us, to love whom and to know whom is itself the happiness of life; that happiness which all men declare that they seek, but few have rejoiced in finding it. But now I want you to tell me what you think of this whole explanation of mine. For if you have approved all that has been said as true, then if you had been questioned on each statement you would have said that you did know it. You see, therefore, from whom you have learned these points. Surely not from me, to whom you could have given the correct answer if questioned. But if you had not known these things to be true, then neither do I teach you, nor he (the inner man, the judgment of reason from within). But I do not teach, because I never can teach; he (the inner man) does not teach, because you as yet are incapable of learning.

Ad.—But I have learned by the admonition of your words that by the means of words a man can do no more than be admonished to learn; and that is very little, indeed, a fraction only of what a speaker thinks is expressed in his words. Moreover, whether the things that are spoken are true or not, I have learned that he alone can teach who dwells within, who reminds us that he is dwelling within, when words are spoken without. This same dweller within I shall now, by his own favor, love the more ardently as I advance in knowing him better. However, I am grateful for this reasoned explanation of yours which at all times anticipated and turned aside all the objections which occurred to me. Nothing that might cause me to doubt has been left by you, on which that unseen judgment within would not give the same answer to me as was stated by your words from without.

THE IDEAS ✚ *Question Forty-Six* from Saint Augustine's *Book of Eighty-Three Various Questions*⁵ 1. They say it was Plato who first gave the Ideas their name. This does not mean that the realities themselves, which he called Ideas, did not already exist or that no one had ever perceived them, though the word did not exist before he introduced it. But they were given different names, perhaps, by different people. Anyone may impose any name at all upon an unfamiliar object that does not have a commonly accepted name. It is incredible that before Plato's time there were either no wise men or that these had not grasped the very realities, whatever they are, which Plato called the Ideas, as we have stated, since, in fact, so great importance is given them that no one can be wise unless he has an understanding of them.

It is likely that there were found wise men even outside Greece, among the other nations. Plato himself gave evidence of this not only by travelling to deepen his wisdom but by the reference he makes to this fact in his books. We must not suppose, therefore, that these men, if any did exist, were ignorant of the Ideas, even though they may, perhaps, have called them by another name. But enough has been said so far about the name. Let us see about the reality, which deserves our utmost thought and consideration, and, allowing freedom for the use of words, let each one call the thing he knows by whatever name he chooses.

2. Accordingly, we may call the Ideas in Latin, either Forms (*formas*) or Natures (*species*), in order to make it clear that we are translating word for word. Now if we call them Reasons (*rationes*), then, of course, we are departing from the strict meaning of the term, since, in Greek, the Reasons are called λόγοι not *Ideas*. Nevertheless, a person who chooses to employ this term will not find himself in disagreement about the reality itself. Actually, the Ideas are Original Forms (*principales formae*) or fixed and changeless patterns of things which have not been fashioned from the Forms themselves and consequently, being eternal and always the same, are contained in the Divine Mind. And while these themselves neither come to be nor cease to exist, it is maintained that, in accordance with them, everything is fashioned capable of having a beginning and end, as well as whatever actually comes into, or goes out of, existence.

They insist that a soul can not contemplate these Forms unless it is rational and then, only by that part of it which accounts for its excellence, namely, by the mind itself and reason, by a kind of facial view, so to speak, or by its own inner and spiritual eye. They further assert that not even every kind of rational soul is fit for such a vision but only one that is holy and pure, namely, the soul that keeps this eye which sees such realities, pure and serene and akin to the things it is intent upon beholding.

What man, religiously disposed and imbued with true religion, would dare deny this vision, even though he were still incapable of it? On the contrary, would he not proclaim that all things in existence have been created by God, their Cause—all things, that is, whose capacity for existence is determined in kind by their own specific nature; and that it is by this Cause that all living things have their life, and that the entire conservation of things as well as the very order whereby changing realities accomplish their periodic courses in definite directions, are maintained and governed by the laws of the Most-High God?

Once this is established and granted, who can dare to declare that God has made everything in an irrational manner? If one can not really say or believe such a thing, then it follows that all things have been fashioned according to an intelligible principle (*ratione*). Neither has man been made by the same intelligible principle as the horse, since this is an absurd supposition. Each thing, therefore, has been created according to its own intellectual principle. But where are we to suppose that these intelligible principles exist, if not in the very Mind of the Creator? He was not fixing His gaze upon anything located outside Himself to serve as a model when He made the things he created, for such a view is blasphemous. But if the intelligible principles of things created, and of those to be created, are contained in the Divine Mind and if only the eternal and changeless can exist there—Plato called these Original Exemplars the Ideas—then not only are these realities Ideas but they are themselves true, seeing that they are eternal and, as such, remain unchangeable in their existence. It is by participating in these Ideas that a thing comes to exist, whatever its mode of being.

Among the things made by God, the rational soul stands superior to all and, as long as it is undefiled, is close to God. To the degree that it is united to Him by charity, by so much does it contemplate these intelligible principles (*rationes*) through whose vision it is made supremely happy, being bathed, so to speak, and illumined by Him with a spiritual light. Its contemplation is not through the eyes of the body but through the soul's highest power which accounts for its excellence. As we have observed, these intelligible principles may be called either Ideas or Forms or Natures or Reasons. The choice of a name is allowed the many, but the perception of the reality itself is granted to very few.

THE TRINITY ✢ BOOK XII ✢ CHAPTER 14 *What is the difference between wisdom and knowledge. The worship of God is the love of Him. How the intellectual cognizance of eternal things comes to pass through wisdom.* 21. For knowledge also has its own good measure, if that in it which puffs up, or is wont to puff up, is conquered by love of eternal things, which does not puff up but, as we know, edifieth. (1 Cor. 8:1) Certainly without knowledge the virtues themselves, by which one lives rightly, cannot be possessed, by which this miserable life may be so governed, that we may attain to that eternal life which is truly blessed.

22. Yet action, by which we use temporal things well, differs from contemplation of eternal things; and the latter is reckoned to wisdom, the former to knowledge. For although that which is wisdom can also be called knowledge, as the apostle too speaks, where he says, "Now I know in part, but then shall I know even as also I am known" (1 Cor. 13:12) ; when doubtless he meant his words to be understood of the knowledge of the contemplation of God, which will be the highest reward of the saints; yet where he says, "For to one is given by the Spirit the word of wisdom, to another the word of knowledge by the same Spirit," (1 Cor. 12:8) certainly he distinguishes without doubt these two things, although he does not there explain the difference, nor in what way one may be discerned from the other. But having examined a great number of passages from the Holy Scriptures, I find it written in the Book of Job, that holy man being the speaker, "Behold, piety, that is wisdom; but to depart from evil is knowledge." (Job 28:28) In thus distinguishing, it must be understood that wisdom belongs to contemplation, knowledge to action. For in this place he meant by piety the worship of God, which in Greek is called θεοσέβεια. For the sentence in the Greek MSS. has that word. And what is there in eternal things more excellent than God, of whom alone the nature is unchangeable? And what is the worship of Him except the love of Him, by which we now desire to see Him, and we believe and hope that we shall see Him; and in proportion as we make progress, see now through a glass in an enigma, but then in clearness? For this is what the Apostle Paul means by "face to face." (1 Cor. 13:12) This is also what John says, "Beloved, now we are the sons of God, and it doth not yet appear what we shall be; but we know that, when He shall appear, we shall be like Him; for we shall see Him as He is." (1 John 3:2) Discourse about these and the like subjects seems to me to be the discourse itself of wisdom. But to depart from evil, which Job says is knowledge, is without doubt of temporal things. Since it is according to time that we are in evil, from which we ought to abstain, that we may come to those good eternal things. And therefore, whatsoever we do prudently, boldly, temperately, and justly, belongs to that knowledge or discipline wherewith our action is conversant in avoiding evil and desiring good; and so also, whatsoever we gather by the knowledge that comes from inquiry, in the way of examples either to be guarded against or to be imitated, and in the way of necessary proofs respecting any subject, accommodated to our use.

23. When a discourse then relates to these things, I hold it to be a discourse belonging to knowledge, and to be distinguished

from a discourse belonging to wisdom, to which those things belong, which neither have been, nor shall be, but are; and on account of that eternity in which they are, are said to have been, and to be, and to be about to be, without any changeableness of times. For neither have they been in such way as that they should cease to be, nor are they about to be in such way as if they were not now; but they have always had and always will have that very absolute being. And they abide, but not as if fixed in some place as are bodies; but as intelligible things in incorporeal nature, they are so at hand to the glance of the mind, as things visible or tangible in place are to the sense of the body. And not only in the case of sensible things posited in place, there abide also intelligible and incorporeal reasons of them apart from local space; but also of motions that pass by in successive times, apart from any transit in time, there stand also like reasons, themselves certainly intelligible, and not sensible. And to attain to these with the eye of the mind is the lot of few; and when they are attained as much as they can be, he himself who attains to them does not abide in them, but is as it were repelled by the rebounding of the eye itself of the mind, and so there comes to be a transitory thought of a thing not transitory. And yet this transient thought is committed to the memory through the instructions by which the mind is taught; that the mind which is compelled to pass from thence, may be able to return thither again; although, if the thought should not return to the memory and find there what it had committed to it, it would be led thereto like an uninstructed person, as it had been led before, and would find it where it had first found it, that is to say, in that incorporeal truth, whence yet once more it may be as it were written down and fixed in the mind. For the thought of man, for example, does not so abide in that incorporeal and unchangeable reason of a square body, as that reason itself abides: if, to be sure, it could attain to it at all without the phantasy of local space. Or if one were to apprehend the rhythm of any artificial or musical sound, passing through certain intervals of time, as it rested without time in some secret and deep silence, it could at least be thought as long as that song could be heard; yet what the glance of the mind, transient though it was, caught from thence, and absorbing as it were into the belly, so laid up in the memory, over this it will be able to ruminate in some measure by recollection, and to transfer what it has thus learned into systematic knowledge. But if this has been blotted out by absolute forgetfulness, yet once again, under the guidance of teaching, one will come to that which had altogether dropped away, and it will be found such as it was.

CHAPTER 15 *In opposition to the reminiscence of Plato and Pythagoras the Samian. Of the difference between wisdom and knowledge, and of seeking the Trinity in the knowledge of temporal things.* 24. And hence that noble philosopher Plato endeavored to persuade us that the souls of men lived here even before they had these bodies; and that hence those things which are learnt, are rather remembered as having been already known, than taken into knowledge as things new. For he has told us that a boy, when questioned I know not what respecting geometry, replied as if he were perfectly skilled in that branch of learning. For being questioned step by step and skilfully, he saw what was to be seen, and said that which he saw. But if this had been a recollecting of things previously known, then certainly every one, or almost every one, would not have been able so to answer when questioned. For not every one was a geometrician in the former life, since geometricians are so few among men that scarcely one can be found anywhere. But we ought rather to believe, that the intellectual mind is so formed in its nature as to see those things, which by the disposition of the Creator are subjoined to things intelligible in a natural order, by a sort of incorporeal light of an unique kind; as the eye of the flesh sees things adjacent to itself in this bodily light, of which light it is made to be receptive, and adapted to it. For none the more does this fleshly eye, too, distinguish black things from white without a teacher, because it had already known them before it was created in this flesh. Why, lastly, is it possible only in intelligible things that any one properly questioned should answer according to any branch of learning, although ignorant of it? Why can no one do this with things sensible, except those which he has seen in this his present body, or has believed the information of others who knew them, whether somebody's writings or words? For we must not acquiesce in their story, who assert that the Samian Pythagoras recollected some things of this kind, which he had experienced when he was previously here in another body; and others tell yet of others, that they experienced something of the same sort in their minds: but it may be conjectured that these were untrue recollections, such as we commonly experience in sleep, when we fancy we remember, as though we had done or seen it, what we never did or saw at all; and that the minds of these persons, even though awake, were affected in this way at the suggestion of malignant and deceitful spirits, whose care it is to confirm or to sow some false belief concerning the changes of souls, in order to deceive men. This, I say, may be conjectured from this, that if they truly remembered those things which they had seen here before, while occupying other bodies, the same thing would happen to many, nay to almost all; since they suppose that as the dead from the living, so, without cessation and continually, the living are coming into existence from the dead; as sleepers from those that are awake, and those that are awake from them that sleep.

25. If therefore this is the right distinction between wisdom and knowledge, that the intellectual cognizance of eternal things belongs to wisdom, but the rational cognizance of temporal things to knowledge, it is not difficult to judge which is to be preferred or postponed to which. But if we must employ some other distinction by which to know these two apart, which without doubt the apostle teaches us are different, saying, "To one is given by the Spirit the word of wisdom; to another the word of knowledge by the same Spirit"; still the difference between these two which we have laid down is a most evident one, in that the intellectual cognizance of eternal things is one thing, the rational cognizance of temporal things another; and no one doubts but that the former is to be preferred to the latter. As then we leave behind those things which belong to the outer man, and desire to ascend within from those things which we have in common with beasts, before we come to the cognizance of things intelligible and supreme, which are eternal, that rational cognizance of temporal things presents itself. Let us then find a trinity in this also, if we can as we found one in the senses of the body, and in those things which through them entered in the way of images into our soul or spirit; so that instead of corporeal things which we touch by corporeal sense, placed as they are without us, we might have resemblances of bodies impressed within on the memory from which thought might be formed, while the will as a third united them; just as the sight of the eyes was formed from without, which the will applied to the visible thing in order to produce vision, and united both, while itself also added itself thereto as a third. But this subject must not be compressed into this book; that in that which follows, if God help, it may be suitably examined, and the conclusions to which we come may be unfolded.

THE TRINITY ✤ BOOK XIV ✤ CHAPTER 15:21. . . .
For hence it is that even the ungodly think of eternity, and rightly blame and rightly praise many things in the morals of men.

And by what rules do they thus judge, except by those wherein they see how men ought to live, even though they themselves do not so live? And where do they see these rules? For they do not see them in their own [moral] nature; since no doubt these things are to be seen by the mind, and their minds are confessedly changeable, but these rules are seen as unchangeable by him who can see them at all; nor yet in the character of their own mind, since these rules are rules of righteousness and their minds are confessedly unrighteous. Where indeed are these rules written, wherein even the unrighteous recognizes what is righteous, wherein he discerns that he ought to have what he himself has not? Where, then, are they written, unless in the book of that Light which is called Truth? Whence every righteous law is copied and transferred (not by migrating to it, but by being as it were impressed upon it) to the heart of the man that worketh righteousness, as the impression from a ring passes into the wax, yet does not leave the ring. But he who worketh not, and yet sees how he ought to work, he is the man that is turned away from that light, which yet touches him. But he who does not even see how he ought to live, sins indeed with more excuse, because he is not a transgressor of a law that he knows; but even he too is just touched sometimes by the splendor of the everywhere-present truth, when upon admonition he confesses.

THE TRINITY ✚ BOOK IX ✚ *That a kind of trinity exists in man, who is the image of God, viz. the mind, and the knowledge wherewith the mind knows itself, and the love wherewith it loves both itself and its own knowledge; and these three are shown to be mutually equal, and of one essence.*

CHAPTER 1 *In what way we must inquire concerning the Trinity.* 1. We certainly seek a trinity—not any trinity, but that Trinity which is God, and the true and supreme and only God. Let my hearers then wait, for we are still seeking. And no one justly finds fault with such a search, if at least he who seeks that, which either to know or to utter is most difficult, is steadfast in the faith. . . .

. . . For a certain faith is in some way the starting point of knowledge; but a certain knowledge will not be made perfect, except
after this life, when we shall see face to face. (I Cor. 13:12) Let
us therefore be thus minded, so as to know that the disposition to
seek the truth is more safe than that which presumes things unknown to be known. Let us therefore so seek as if we should find,
and so find as if we were about to seek. For "when a man hath done,
then he beginneth." (Ecclus. 18:7) Let us doubt without unbelief
of things to be believed; let us affirm without rashness of things to
be understood: authority must be held fast in the former, truth
sought out in the latter. As regards this question, then, let us believe that the Father, and the Son, and the Holy Spirit is one God,
the Creator and Ruler of the whole creature; and that the Father is
not the Son, nor the Holy Spirit either the Father or the Son, but
a trinity of persons mutually interrelated, and a unity of an equal
essence. And let us seek to understand this, praying for help from
Himself, whom we wish to understand; and as much as He grants,
desiring to explain what we understand with so much pious care
and anxiety, that even if in any case we say one thing for another,
we may at least say nothing unworthy. . . .

CHAPTER 2 *The three things which are found in love must be
considered.* 2. And this being so, let us direct our attention to
those three things which we fancy we have found. We are not
yet speaking of heavenly things, nor yet of God the Father, and
Son, and Holy Spirit, but of that inadequate image, which yet is
an image, that is, man; for our feeble mind perhaps can gaze upon
this more familiarly and more easily. Well then, when I, who make
this inquiry, love anything, there are three things concerned—myself, and that which I love, and love itself. For I do not love love,
except I love a lover; for there is no love where nothing is loved.
Therefore there are three things—he who loves, and that which is
loved, and love. But what if I love none except myself? Will there
not then be two things—that which I love, and love? For he who
loves and that which is loved are the same when any one loves himself, just as to love and to be loved, in the same way, is the very same
thing when any one loves himself. Since the same thing is repeated,
when it is said, he loves himself, and he is loved by himself. For in
that case to love and to be loved are not two different things, just as
he who loves and he who is loved are not two different persons. But
yet, even so, love and what is loved are still two things. For there is
no love when any one loves himself, except when love itself is

loved. And it is one thing to love one's self, another to love one's own love. For love is not loved, unless as already loving something; since where nothing is loved there is no love. Therefore there are two things when any one loves himself—love and that which is loved. For then he that loves and that which is loved are one. Whence it seems that it does not follow that three things are to be understood wherever love is. For let us put aside from the inquiry all the other many things of which a man consists; and in order that we may discover clearly what we are now seeking, as far as in such a subject is possible, let us treat of the mind alone. The mind, then, when it loves itself, discloses two things—mind and love. But what is to love one's self, except to wish to help one's self to the enjoyment of self? And when any one wishes himself to be just as much as he is, then the will is on a par with the mind, and the love is equal to him who loves. And if love is a substance, it is certainly not body, but spirit; and the mind also is not body, but spirit. Yet love and mind are not two spirits, but one spirit; nor yet two essences, but one: and yet here are two things that are one, he that loves and love; or, if you like so to put it, that which is loved and love. And these two, indeed, are mutually said relatively. Since he who loves is referred to love, and love to him who loves. For he who loves, loves with some love, and love is the love of some one who loves. But mind and spirit are not said relatively, but express essence. For mind and spirit do not therefore exist because the mind and spirit of any man exists. For if we withdraw that which is man, which is so called with the conjunction of body; if then we withdraw the body, the mind and spirit remain. But if we withdraw him that loves, then there is no love; and if we withdraw love, then there is no one that loves. And therefore, in so far as they are mutually referred to one another, they are two; but whereas they are spoken in respect to themselves, each are spirit, and both together also are one spirit; and each are mind, and both together one mind. Where, then, is the trinity? Let us attend as much as we can, and let us invoke the everlasting light, that He may illuminate our darkness, and that we may see in ourselves, as much as we are permitted, the image of God.

CHAPTER 3 *The image of the Trinity in the mind of man who knows himself and loves himself. The mind knows itself through itself.* 3. For the mind cannot love itself, except also it know itself; for how can it love what it does not know? Or if anybody says that the mind, from either general or special knowledge, believes itself of such a character as it has by experience found others to be, and therefore loves itself, he speaks most foolishly. For whence does a mind know another mind, if it does not know itself? For the mind does not know other minds and not know itself, as the eye of the body sees other eyes and does not see itself; for we see bodies through the eyes of the body, because, unless we are looking into a mirror, we cannot refract and reflect the rays into themselves, which shine forth through those eyes, and touch whatever we discern—a subject, indeed, which is treated of most subtly and obscurely, until somehow it may be clearly demonstrated whether the fact be so, or whether it be not. But whatever is the nature of the power by which we discern through the eyes, certainly, whether it be rays or anything else, we cannot discern with the eyes that power itself; but we inquire into it with the mind, and if it may be so, understand even this with the mind. As the mind, then, itself gathers the knowledge of corporeal things through the senses of the body, so of incorporeal things through itself. Therefore it knows itself also through itself, since it is incorporeal; for if it does not know itself, it does not love itself.

CHAPTER 4 *The three are one, and also equal, viz. the mind itself, and the love, and the knowledge of it. That the same three exist substantially, and are predicated relatively. That the same three are inseparable. That the same three are not joined and commingled like parts, but that they are of one essence, and are relatives.* 4. But as there are two things, the mind and the love of it, when it loves itself; so there are two things, the mind and the knowledge of it, when it knows itself. Therefore the mind itself, and the love of it, and the knowledge of it, are three things, and these three are one; and when they are perfect they are equal. For if one loves himself less than as he is—as for example, suppose that the mind of a man only loves itself as much as the body of a man ought to be loved, whereas the mind is more than the body—then it is in fault, and its love is not perfect. Again, if it loves itself more than as it is—as if, for instance, it loves itself as much as God is to be loved, whereas the mind is incomparably less than God—here also it is exceedingly in fault, and its love of self is not perfect. But it is in fault more perversely and wrongly still, when it loves the body as much as God is to be loved. Also, if knowledge is less than that which is known, and which can be fully known, then knowledge is not perfect; but if it is greater, then the nature which knows is above that which is known, as the knowledge of the body is greater than the body itself, which is known by that knowledge. For knowledge is a kind of life in the reason of the knower; but the body is not life; and any life is greater than any body, not in bulk, but in power. But when the mind knows itself, its own knowledge does not rise above itself, because itself knows, and itself is known. When, therefore, it knows itself entirely, and no other thing with itself, then its knowledge is equal to itself; because its knowledge is not from another nature, since it knows itself. And when it perceives itself entirely, and nothing more, then it is neither less nor greater. We said therefore rightly, that these three things, when they are perfect, are by consequence equal.

5. Similar reasoning suggests to us, if indeed we can any way understand the matter, that these things exist in the soul, and that, being as it were involved in it, they are so evolved from it as to be perceived and reckoned up substantially, or, so to say, essentially. Not as though in a subject, as color, or shape, or any other quality or quantity, are in the body. For anything of this kind does not go beyond the subject in which it is; for that color or shape of this particular body cannot be also those of another body. But the mind can also love something besides itself, with that love with which it loves itself. And further, the mind does not know itself only, but also many other things. Wherefore love and knowledge are not contained in the mind as in a subject, but these also exist substantially, as the mind itself does; because, even if they are mutually predicated relatively, yet they exist each severally in their own substance. Nor are they so mutually predicated relatively as color and the colored subject are; so that color is in the colored subject, but has not any proper substance in itself, since colored body is a substance, but color is in a substance; but as two friends are also two men, which are substances, while they are said to be men not relatively, but friends relatively.

6. But, further although one who loves or one who knows is a substance, and knowledge is a substance, and love is a substance; but he that loves and love, or he that knows and knowledge, are spoken of relatively to each other, as are friends: but mind or spirit are not relatives, as neither are men relatives; yet he that loves and love, or he that knows and knowledge, cannot exist separately from each other, as men can that are friends. Although it would seem that friends, too, can be separated in body, not in mind, in as far as they are friends: nay, it can even happen that a friend may even also begin to hate a friend, and on this account cease to be a friend, while the other does not know it, and still loves him. But if the love with which the mind loves itself ceases

to be, then the mind also will at the same time cease to love. Likewise, if the knowledge by which the mind knows itself ceases to be, then the mind will also at the same time cease to know itself. Just as the head of anything that has a head is certainly a head, and they are predicated relatively to each other, although they are also substances: for both a head is a body, and so is that which has a head; and if there be no head, then neither will there be that which has a head. Only these things can be separated from each other by cutting off, those cannot.

7. And even if there are some bodies which cannot be wholly separated and divided, yet they would not be bodies unless they consisted of their own proper parts. A part then is predicated relatively to a whole, since every part is a part of some whole, and a whole is a whole by having all its parts. But since both parts and whole are bodies, these things are not only predicated relatively, but exist also substantially. Perhaps, then the mind is a whole, and the love with which it loves itself, and the knowledge with which it knows itself, will be its parts, of which two parts that whole consists. Or are there three equal parts which make up the one whole? But no part embraces the whole, of which it is a part; whereas, when the mind knows itself as a whole, that is, knows itself perfectly, then the knowledge of it extends through the whole of it; and when it loves itself perfectly, then it loves itself as a whole, and the love of it extends through the whole of it. Is it, then, as one drink is made from wine and water and honey, and each single part extends through the whole, and yet they are three things (for there is no part of the drink which does not contain these three things; for they are not joined as if they were water and oil, but are entirely commingled: and they are all substances, and the whole of that liquor composed of the three is one substance) —is it, I say, in some such way as this we are to think these three to be together, mind, love, and knowledge? But water, wine, and honey are not of one substance, although one substance results in the drink made from commingling them. And I cannot see how those other three are not of the same substance, since the mind itself loves itself, and itself knows itself; and these three so exist, as that the mind is neither loved nor known by any other thing at all. These three, therefore, must needs be of one and the same essence; and for that reason, if they were confounded together as it were by a commingling, they could not be in any way three, neither could they be mutually referred to each other. Just as if you were to make from one and the same gold three similar rings, although connected with each other, they are mutually referred to each other, because they

215

are similar. For everything similar is similar to something, and there is a trinity of rings, and one gold. But if they are blended with each other, and each mingled with the other through the whole of their own bulk, then that trinity will fall through, and it will not exist at all; and not only will it be called one gold, as it was called in the case of those three rings, but now it will not be called three things of gold at all.

CHAPTER 5 *That these three are several in themselves, and mutually all in all.* 8. But in these three, when the mind knows itself and loves itself, there remains a trinity, mind, love, knowledge; and this is not confounded together by any commingling; although they are both each severally in themselves and mutually all in all, or whether each severally in each two, or each two in each. Therefore all are in all. For certainly the mind is in itself, since it is called mind in respect to itself: although it is said to be knowing, or known, or knowable, relatively to its own knowledge; and although also as loving, and loved, or lovable, it is referred to love, by which it loves itself. And knowledge, although it is referred to the mind that knows or is known, nevertheless is also predicated both as known and knowing in respect to itself: for the knowledge by which the mind knows itself, is not unknown to itself. And although love is referred to the mind that loves, whose love it is; nevertheless it is also love in respect to itself, so as to exist also in itself: since love too is loved, yet cannot be loved with anything except with love, that is with itself. So these things are severally in themselves. But so are they in each other, because both the mind that loves is in love, and love is in the knowledge of him that loves, and knowledge is in the mind that knows. And each severally is in like manner in each two, because the mind which knows and loves itself, is in its own love and knowledge: and the love of the mind that loves and knows itself, is in the mind and in its knowledge: and the knowledge of the mind that knows and loves itself is in the mind and in its love, because it loves itself that knows, and knows itself that loves. And hence also each two is in each severally, since the mind which knows and loves itself, is together with its own knowledge in love, and together with its own love in knowledge; and love too itself and knowledge are together in the mind, which loves and knows itself. But in what way all are in all, we have already shown above; since the mind loves itself as a whole, and knows itself as a whole, and knows its own love wholly, and loves its own knowledge wholly, when these three things are perfect in respect to themselves. Therefore these three things are marvellously inseparable from each other, and yet each of them is severally a substance, and all together are one substance or essence, whilst they are mutually predicated relatively.

CHAPTER 6 *One knowledge of the thing in the thing itself, and another in eternal truth itself. That corporeal things, too, are to be judged by the rules of eternal truth.* 9. But when the human mind knows itself and loves itself, it does not know and love anything unchangeable: and each individual man declares his own mind by one manner of speech, when he considers what takes place in himself; but defines the human mind in another by special or general knowledge. And so, when he speaks to me of his own individual mind, as to whether he understands this or that, or does not understand it, or whether he wishes or does not wish this or that, I believe; but when he speaks the truth of the mind of man generally or specially, I recognize and approve. Whence it is manifest, that each sees one thing in himself, such that another person may believe what he says of it, yet may not see it; but another in the truth itself, such that another person also can gaze upon it; of which the former undergoes changes at successive times, the latter consists in an unchangeable eternity. For we do not gather a generic or specific knowledge of the human mind by means of resemblance, by seeing many minds with the eyes of the body: but we gaze upon indestructible truth, from which to define perfectly, as far as we can, not of what sort is the mind of any one man, but of what sort it ought to be upon the eternal plan.

10. Whence also, even in the case of the images of things corporeal which are drawn in through the bodily sense and in some way infused into the memory, from which also those things which have not been seen are thought under a fancied image, whether otherwise than they really are, or even by chance as they are—even here too, we are proved either to accept or reject, within ourselves, by other rules which remain altogether unchangeable above our mind, when we approve or reject anything rightly. For both when I recall the walls of Carthage which I have seen, and imagine to myself the walls of Alexandria which I have not seen, and, in preferring this to that among forms which in both cases are imaginary, make that preference upon grounds of reason; the judgment of truth from above is still strong and clear, and rests firmly upon the utterly indestructible rules of its own right; and

if it is covered as it were by cloudiness of corporeal images, yet is not wrapt up and confounded in them.

11. But it makes a difference, whether, under that or in that darkness, I am shut off as it were from the clear heaven; or whether (as usually happens on lofty mountains), enjoying the free air between both, I at once look up above to the calmest light, and down below upon the densest clouds. For whence is the ardor of brotherly love kindled in me, when I hear that some man has borne bitter torments for the excellence and steadfastness of faith? And if that man is shown to me with the finger, I am eager to join myself to him, to become acquainted with him, to bind him to myself in friendship. And accordingly, if opportunity offers, I draw near, I address him, I converse with him, I express my good-will towards him in what words I can, and wish that in him too in turn should be brought to pass and expressed goodwill towards me; and I endeavor after a spiritual embrace in the way of belief, since I cannot search out so quickly and discern altogether his innermost heart. I love therefore the faithful and courageous man with a pure and genuine love. But if he were to confess to me in the course of conversation, or were through unguardedness to reveal about himself in any way, that either he believes anything unseemly of God, and desires too somewhat carnal in Him, and that he bore these torments on behalf of such an error, or from the desire of money for which he hoped, or, from empty greediness of human praise: immediately it follows that the love with which I was borne towards him, displeased, and as it were repelled, and taken away from an unworthy man, remains in that form, after which, believing him such as I did, I had loved him; unless perhaps I have come to love him to this end, that he may become such, while I have found him not to be such in fact. And in that man, too, nothing is changed: although it can be changed, so that he may become that which I had believed him to be already. But in my mind there certainly is something changed, viz. the estimate I had formed of him, which was before of one sort, and now is of another; and the same love, at the bidding from above of unchangeable righteous-ness, is turned aside from the purpose of enjoying, to the purpose of taking counsel. But the form itself of unshaken and stable truth, wherein I should have enjoyed the fruition of the man, believing him to be good, and wherein likewise I take counsel that he may be good, sheds in an immovable eternity the same light of incorrupti-ble and most sound reason, both upon the sight of my mind, and upon that cloud of images, which I discern from above, when I think of the same man whom I had seen. Again, when I call back

to my mind some arch, turned beautifully and symmetrically, which, let us say, I saw at Carthage; a certain reality that had been made known to the mind through the eyes, and transferred to the memory, causes the imaginary view. But I behold in my mind yet another thing, according to which that work of art pleases me; and whence also, if it displeased me, I should correct it. We judge therefore of those particular things according to that [form of eternal truth], and discern that form by the intuition of the rational mind. But those things themselves we either touch if present by the bodily sense, or if absent remember their images as fixed in our memory, or picture, in the way of likeness to them, such things as we ourselves also, if we wished and were able, would laboriously build up: figuring in the mind after one fashion the images of bodies, or seeing bodies through the body; but after another grasping by simple intelligence what is about the eye of the mind, viz. the reasons and the unspeakably beautiful skill of such forms.

CHAPTER 7 *We conceive and beget the word within, from the things we have beheld in the eternal truth. The word, whether of the creature or of the Creator, is conceived by love.* 12. We behold, then, by the sight of the mind, in that eternal truth from which all things temporal are made, the form according to which we are, and according to which we do anything by true and right reason, either in ourselves, or in things corporeal; and we have the true knowledge of things, thence conceived, as it were as a word within us, and by speaking we beget it from within; nor by being born does it depart from us. And when we speak to others, we apply to the word, remaining within us, the ministry of the voice or of some bodily sign, that by some kind of sensible remembrance some similar thing may be wrought also in the mind of him that hears— similar, I say, to that which does not depart from the mind of him that speaks. We do nothing, therefore, through the members of the body in our words and actions by which the behavior of men is either approved or blamed, which we do not anticipate by a word uttered within ourselves. For no one willingly does anything, which he has not first said in his heart.

13. And this word is conceived by love, either of the creature or of the Creator, that is, either of changeable nature or of unchangeable truth.

NOTES (The Problem of Knowledge)

[1] *Enchiridion* 7, 20

[2] Observe that in the selection from the *Freedom of the Will* a similar point is made and that the fundamental truths of ethics are also given the qualifications of necessity, immutability, and eternality.

[3] Observe the similarity of this analysis to Plato's *Meno*.

[4] *Libri Tres contra Academicos*

[5] Translated by the Rev. Robert P. Russell, O.S.A., of Villanova University

✠ ✠ ✠

THE CREATED UNIVERSE

✠ ✠ ✠

Undoubtedly the best known and the most popular of Augustine's writings is the celebrated *Confessions* written about 400 A. D. some fourteen years after his conversion. Portalié observes that "they portray for us the history of his heart." [1] The term "Confessions" has a different connotation than the narrow one which we usually ascribe to it. For Augustine it meant not merely a confessions of his sins, but also and equally as important a confession of his faith and what Courcelle has termed a confession of praise [of God and His works]. The confession of praise appears throughout the entire work, the confession of faith appears primarily in the last three books in which he discusses time and creation. The first nine books are largely autobiographical. For a brief evaluation of the work, we can do no better than to quote the remarks of Portalié:

> None of the works of the holy doctor has been more universally praised and admired; none has caused more people to shed salutary tears. Whether for its penetrating analysis of the most complex experiences of the soul, or its communicative emotion, or its loftiness of feeling, or its depth of philosophical concepts, this book has no equal in literature. [2]

The first selection has been taken from Book XI of the *Confessions* in which Augustine proposes his famous theory of the nature of time.[3] The principal points to be noted in his discussion are: (1) The distinction that is drawn between the nature of time and eternity. (2) The paradox of the analysis of time, namely, that any attempt to divde time into past, present, and future will nullify the reality of past and future time and any measurement of present time. (3) That although we do measure time, our experience shows that we do not perceive or experience apparently any thing but a present time. (4) That there are three modes of present time: a present of things present, a present of things past, and a present of things future. (5) That although time is apparently subject to some form of spatial measurement, the present is but an indivisible instant, and hence has no space or extension. (6) That what is not measureable (the present) is the standard by which we measure that which is nonexistent (the past and the future). (7) That time cannot be considered merely as the measurement of the motion of the heavenly bodies or the motion of any body. (8) That time is measured in the mind and by the mental acts of expectation, consideration [attention], and memory. (9) That time is a distension of the soul into the future by expectation, into the past by memory, and in the present through duration and attention.

The selection from Books XI and XII of the *City of God* is concerned with the problem of time and eternity but primarily with the cyclical view of time which was held by many of the pagan writers of antiquity. Augustine is firm in his opposition to such a conception of time, for in his opinion it would destroy the true significance of history. He observes especially the impact of such a view upon the Christian faith and points out that this cyclical view would nullify the hope that is offered to man for his salvation and a life of eternal happiness. "Let us," he concludes, "keep to the straight path which is Christ."

The selection from Book XII of the *Confessions* is devoted entirely to a very close study and exegesis of the first two verses of Genesis. It is frequently repetitious and replete with metaphors, but it reveals the analytical genius of Augustine at its best. Expressing his thought in good part in Plotinian concepts, Augustine's principal concern is the meaning of creation and the interpretation of "heaven and earth." Creation *ex nihilo* is emphasized and it should be noted that this distinguishes the Augustinian and Christian view from the conceptions of antiquity which were always bound by the maxim *ex nihilo nihil fit*. Creation *ex nihilo* not only signalizes the omnipotence of the divine creativity but also enables

Augustine to avoid any possibility that God might have created the universe from His own substance or nature. However, that which commands most of Augustine's concern is *how* creation has taken place and this leads him to a lengthy and often minute analysis of the phrase "heaven and earth." Heaven and earth refer not to the physical heaven and earth but rather to that out of which all things have been created. Heaven is identified with a spiritual matter, that out of which the angels, who are closest to God, have been created. Earth is identified with matter which is wholly without form and at the greatest remove from God. That which is termed the "heaven of heavens" is identified as an intellectual heaven of which the angels alone of created beings have a direct knowledge. By far the greater part of Augustine's analysis is devoted to the notion of a formless matter, that which somehow exists but cannot be known. He calls it a "something nothing," invisible and without form, but not pure nothingness. His analysis continues with an account of the various interpretations that may be given to the first two verses of Genesis and eventually leads him to a view no longer accepted, that Scripture may yield more than one truth based on a single statement.

The several excerpts from *The Literal Meaning of Genesis* elaborate further upon the Augustinian view of creation and in particular upon his doctrine of the *rationes seminales.*

That all created being is good is a constant theme of Augustine and becomes a cardinal principle of all Christian philosophers. Given as an initial and irrevocable premise, it is incumbent upon Augustine to reconcile the apparent existence of that which is called evil with the goodness of God. The *Enchiridion* (from the Greek meaning handbook or manual) provides part of the answer to this problem.[4] The *Enchiridion* was written in 421 and is a simple but excellent outline of the basic truths of Christianity as requested by the monk Laurentius. The summary of such truths is organized under the three virtues of faith, hope, and charity, with by far the greater part of the work being given over to an exposition of the Apostles' Creed (faith). This is followed by a brief exposition of the Lord's Prayer and the last few sections touch even more briefly upon the commandment of charity. The *Enchiridion* is frequently singled out as the only systematic treatment by Augustine of Christian doctrine as a whole. The present selection (taken from chapters 9-14 and 96) covers the explanation of evil. Evil is defined as a privation of the good, a deficiency of being, and that which can have its source only in the good. The analysis is applied to both physical evil and moral evil, and it is emphasized that evil cannot have an independent existence, for it would be self-consuming.

This line of inquiry is further pursued in the selections from Books XI and XII of the *City of God,* but with more attention being given to the problem of moral evil or sin than to physical evil. The evil will is shown to be a consequent of man's fall from an original state of grace and spiritual communion with God. Man's original sin is described in terms of the sin of pride and man's disobedience to God, the punishment of which is man's disobedience to himself.

THE CONFESSIONS ✚ BOOK XI ✚ . . . I would hear and understand, how "In the Beginning Thou madest the heaven and earth." Moses wrote this, wrote and departed, passed hence from Thee to Thee; nor is he now before me. For if he were, I would hold him and ask him, and beseech him by Thee to open these things unto me, . . .

Lo, are they not full of their old leaven, who say to us, "What was God doing before He made heaven and earth? For if (say they) He were unemployed and wrought not, why does He not also henceforth, and for ever, as He did heretofore? For did any new motion arise in God, and a new will to make a creature, which He had never before made, how then would there be a true eternity, where there ariseth a will, which was not? For the will of God is not a creature, but before the creature; seeing nothing could be created, unless the will of the Creator had preceded. The will of God then belongeth to His very substance. And if aught have arisen in God's Substance, which before was not, that Substance cannot be truly called eternal. But if the will of God has been from eternity that the creature should be, why was not the creature also from eternity?"

Who speak thus, do not yet understand Thee, O Wisdom of God, Light of souls, understand not yet how the things be made, which by Thee, and in Thee are made: yet they strive to comprehend things eternal, whilst their heart fluttereth between the motions of things past and to come, and is still unstable. Who shall hold it, and fix it, that it be settled awhile, and awhile catch the glory of that ever-fixed Eternity, and compare it with the times which are never fixed, and see that it cannot be compared; and that a long time cannot become long, but out of many motions passing by, which cannot be prolonged altogether; but that in the Eternal nothing passeth, but the whole is present; whereas no time is all at once present: and that all time past, is driven on by time to come, and all to come followeth upon the past; and all past and to come, is created, and flows out of that which is ever present? Who shall hold the heart of man, that it may stand still, and see how eternity ever still-standing, neither past nor to come, uttereth the times past and to come? Can my hand do this, or the hand of my mouth by speech bring about a thing so great?

See, I answer him that asketh, "What did God before He made heaven and earth?" I answer not as one is said to have done merrily (eluding the pressure of the question), "He was preparing hell (saith he) for pryers into mysteries." It is one thing to answer enquiries, another to make sport of enquirers. So I answer not; for rather had I answer, "I know not," what I know not, than so as to raise a laugh at him who asketh deep things and gain praise for one who answereth false things. But I say that Thou, our God, art the Creator of every creature: and if by the name "heaven and earth," every creature be understood; I boldly say, "that before God made heaven and earth, He did not make any thing." For if He made, what did He make but a creature? And would I knew whatsoever I desire to know to my profit, as I know that no creature was made, before there was made any creature.

. . . For whence could innumerable ages pass by, which Thou madest not, Thou the Author and Creator of all ages? or what times should there be, which were not made by Thee? or how should they pass by, if they never were? Seeing then Thou art the Creator of all times, if any time was before Thou madest heaven and earth, why say they that Thou didst forego working? For that very time didst Thou make, nor could times pass by, before Thou madest those times. But if before heaven and earth there was no time, why is it demanded, what Thou then didst? For there was no "then," when there was no time.

Nor dost Thou by time, precede time: else shouldest Thou not precede all times. But Thou precedest all things past, by the sublimity of an ever-present eternity; and surpassest all future because they are future, and when they come, they shall be past; but Thou art the Same, and Thy years fail not. Thy years neither come nor go; whereas ours both come and go, that they all may come. Thy years stand together, because they do stand; nor are departing thrust out by coming years, for they pass not away; but ours shall all be, when they shall no more be. Thy years are one day; and Thy day is not daily, but To-day, seeing Thy To-day gives not place unto to-morrow, for neither doth it replace yesterday. Thy To-day, is Eternity: therefore didst Thou beget The Coeternal, to whom Thou saidst, This day have I begotten Thee. Thou hast made all things; and before all times Thou art: neither in any time was time not.

At no time then hadst Thou not made any thing, because time itself Thou madest. And no times are coeternal with Thee, because Thou abidest; but if they abode, they should not be times. For what is time? Who can readily and briefly explain this? Who can even in thought comprehend it, so as to utter a word about it? But what in discourse do we mention more familiarly and knowingly, than time? . . . What then is time? If no one asks me, I know: if I wish to explain it to one that asketh, I know not: yet I say boldly that I know, that if nothing passed away, time past were not; and if nothing were coming, a time to come were not; and if nothing were, time present were not. Those two times then, past and to come, how are they, seeing the past now is not, and that to come is not yet? But the present, should it always be present, and never pass into time past, verily it should not be time, but eternity. If time present (if it is to be time) only cometh into existence, because it passeth into time past, how can we say that either this is, whose cause of being is, that it shall not be; so, namely, that we cannot truly say that time is, but because it is tending not to be?

And yet we say, "a long time" and "a short time"; still, only of time past or to come. A long time past we call an hundred years since; and a long time to come, an hundred years hence. But a short time past, we call ten days since; and a short time to come, ten days hence. But in what sense is that long or short, which is not? For the past, is not now; and the future, is not yet. Let us not say then, "it is long"; but of the past, "it hath been long"; and of the future, "it will be long." O my Lord, my Light, shall not here also Thy Truth mock at man? For that past time which was long, was it long when it was now past, or when it was yet present? For then might it be long, when there was, what could be long; but when past, it was no longer; wherefore neither could that be long, which was not at all. Let us not then say, "time past hath been long": for we shall not find, what hath been long, seeing that since it was past, it is no more, but let us say "that present time was long"; because, when it was present, it was long. For it had not yet passed away, so as not to be; and therefore there was, what could be long; but after it was past, that ceased also to be long, which ceased to be.

Let us see then, thou soul of man, whether present time can be long: for to thee it is given to feel and to measure length of time. What wilt thou answer me? Are an hundred years, when present, a long time? See first, whether an hundred years can be present. For if the first of these years be now current, it is present, but the other ninety and nine are to come, and therefore are not yet, but if the second year be current, one is now past, another present, the rest to come. And so if we assume any middle year of this hundred to be present, all before it, are past; all after it, to come; wherefore an hundred years cannot be present. But see at least whether that one which is now current, itself is present; for if the current month be its first, the rest are to come; if the second, the first is already past, and the rest are not yet. Therefore, neither is the year now current present; and if not present as a whole, then is not the year present. For twelve months are a year; of which whatever be the current month is present, the rest past, or to come. Although neither is that current month present; but one day only; the rest being to come, if it be the first; past, if the last; if any of the middle, then amid past and to come.

See how the present time, which alone we found could be called long, is abridged to the length scarce of one day. But let us examine that also; because neither is one day present as a whole. For it is made up of four and twenty hours of night and day: of which, the first hath the rest to come; the last hath them past; and any of the middle hath those before it past, those behind it to come. Yea, that one hour passeth away in flying particles. Whatsoever of it hath flown away, is past; whatsoever remaineth, is to come. If an instant of time be conceived, which cannot be divided into the smallest particles of moments, that alone is it, which may be called present. Which yet flies with such speed from future to past, as not to be lengthened out with the least stay. For if it be, it is divided into past and future. The present hath no space. Where then is the time, which we may call long? Is it to come? Of it we do not say, "it is long"; because it is not yet, so as to be long; but we say, "it will be long." When therefore will it be? For if even then, when it is yet to come, it shall not be long (because what can be long, as yet is not), and so it shall then be long, when from future which as yet is not, it shall begin now to be, and have become present, that so there should exist what may be long; then does time present cry out in the words above, that it cannot be long.

And yet, Lord, we perceive intervals of times, and compare them, and say, some are shorter and others longer. We meas-

227

ure also, how much longer or shorter this time is than that; and we answer, "This is double, or treble; and that, but once, or only just so much as that." But we measure times as they are passing, by perceiving them; but past, which now are not, or the future, which are not yet, who can measure? unless a man shall presume to say, that can be measured, which is not. When then time is passing, it may be perceived and measured; but when it is past, it cannot, because it is not. . . .

Permit me, Lord, to seek further. O my hope, let not my purpose be confounded. For if times past and to come be, I would know where they be. Which yet if I cannot, yet I know, wherever they be, they are not there as future, or past, but present. For if there also they be future, they are not yet there; if there also they be past, they are no longer there. Wheresoever then is whatsoever is, it is only as present. Although when past facts are related, there are drawn out of the memory, not the things themselves which are past, but words which, conceived by the images of the things, they, in passing have through the senses left as traces in the mind. Thus my childhood, which now is not, is in time past, which now is not: but now when I recall its image, and tell of it, I behold it in the present, because it is still in my memory. Whether there be a like cause of foretelling things to come also; that of things which as yet are not, the images may be perceived before, already existing, I confess, O my God, I know not. This indeed I know, that we generally think before on our future actions, and that that forethinking is present, but the action whereof we forethink is not yet, because it is to come. Which, when we have set upon, and have begun to do what we were forethinking, then shall that action be; because then it is no longer future, but present.

Which way soever then this secret fore-perceiving of things to come be; that only can be seen, which is. But what now is, is not future, but present. When then things to come are said to be seen, it is not themselves which as yet are not (that is, which are to be), but their causes perchance or signs are seen, which already are. Therefore they are not future but present to those who now see that, from which the future, being foreconceived in the mind, is foretold. Which fore-conceptions again now are; and those who foretell those things, do behold the conceptions present before them. Let now the numerous variety of things furnish me some examples. I behold the daybreak, I foresee, that the sun is about to rise. What I behold is present; what I foresignify, to come; not the sun, which already is; but the sun-rising, which is not yet. And yet did I not in my mind imagine the sunrising itself (as now while I speak of it), I could not foretell it. But neither is that daybreak which I discern in the sky, the sun-rising, although it goes before it; nor that imagination of my mind; which two are seen now present, that the other which is to be may be foretold. Future things then are not yet: and if they be not yet, they are not: and if they are not, they cannot be seen; yet foretold they may be from this present, which are already, and are seen. . . .

What now is clear and plain is, that neither things to come nor past are. Nor is it properly said, "there be three times, past, present, and to come": yet perchance it might be properly said, "there be three times; a present of things past, a present of things present, a present of things future." For these three do exist in some sort, in the soul, but otherwhere do I not see them; present of things past, memory; present of things present, sight; present of things future, expectation. . . .

I said then even now, we measure times as they pass, in order to be able to say, this time is twice so much as that one; or, this is just so much as that; and so of any other parts of time, which be measurable. Wherefore, as I said, we measure times as they pass. And if any should ask me, "How knowest thou? I might answer, "I know, that we do measure, nor can we measure things that are not; and things past and to come, are not." But time present how do we measure, seeing it hath no space? It is measured while passing, but when it shall have passed, it is not measured; for there will be nothing to be measured. But whence, by what way, and whither passes it while it is a measuring? whence, but from the future? Which way, but through the present? whither, but into the past? From that therefore, which is not yet, through that, which hath no space, into that, which now is not. Yet what do we measure, if not time in some space? For we do not say, single, and double, and triple, and equal, or any other like way that we speak of time, except of spaces and times. In what space then do we measure time passing? In the future, whence it passeth through? But what is not yet, we measure not. Or in the present, by which it passes? but no space, we do not measure: or in the past, to which it passes? But neither do we measure that, which now is not.

My soul is on fire to know this most intricate enigma. Shut it not up, O Lord my God, good Father; through Christ I beseech Thee, do not shut up these usual yet hidden things, from my desire, that it be hindered from piercing into them; but let them dawn through Thy enlightening mercy, O Lord. . . . Behold, Thou hast made my days old, and they pass away, and how, I know not. And we talk of time, and time, and times, and times, "How long time is it since he said this"; "how long time since he did this"; and "how long time since I saw that"; and "this syllable hath double time to that single short syllable." These words we speak, and these we hear, and are understood, and understand. Most manifest and ordinary they are, and the self-same things again are but too deeply hidden, and the discovery of them were new.

I heard once from a learned man, that the motions of the sun, moon, and stars, constituted time, and I assented not. For why should not the motions of all bodies rather be times? Or, if the lights of heaven should cease, and a potter's wheel run round, should there be no time by which we might measure those whirlings, and say, that either it moved with equal pauses, or if it turned sometimes slower, otherwhiles quicker, that some rounds were longer, others shorter? Or, while we were saying this, should we not also be speaking in time? Or, should there in our words be some syllables short, others long, but because those sounded in a shorter time, these in a longer? God, grant to men to see in a small thing notices common to things great and small. The stars and lights of heaven, are also for signs, and for seasons, and for years, and for days; they are; yet neither should I say, that the going round of that wooden wheel was a day, nor yet he, that it was therefore no time.

I desire to know the force and nature of time, by which we measure the motions of bodies, and say this motion is twice as long as that. For I ask, Seeing "day" denotes not the stay only of the sun upon the earth (according to which day is one thing, night another); but also its whole circuit from east to east again; according to which we say, "there passed so many days," the night being included when we say, "so many days," and the nights not reckoned apart; seeing then a day is completed by the motion of the sun and by his circuit from east to east again, I ask, does the motion alone make the day, or the stay in which that motion is completed, or both? For if the first be the day; then should we have a day, although the sun should finish that course in so small a space of time, as one hour comes to. If the second, then should not that make a day, if between one sunrise and another there were but so short a stay, as one hour comes to; but the sun must go four and twenty times about, to complete one day. If both, then neither could that be called a day, if the sun should run his whole round in the space of one hour; nor that, if, while the sun stood still, so much time should over-pass, as the sun usually makes his whole course in, from morning to morning. I will not therefore now ask, what that is which is called day; but, what time is, whereby we, measuring the circuit of the sun, should say that it was finished in half the time it was wont, if so be it was finished in so small a space as twelve hours; and comparing both times, should call this a single time, that a double time; even supposing the sun to run his round from east to east, sometimes in that single, sometimes in that double time. Let no man then tell me, that the motions of the heavenly bodies constitutes times, because, when at the prayer of one, the sun had stood still, till he could achieve his victorious battle, the sun stood still, but time went on. For in its own allotted space of time was that battle waged and ended. I perceive time then to be a certain extension. But do I perceive it, or seem to perceive it? Thou, Light and Truth, wilt show me.

Dost Thou bid me assent, if any define time to be "motion of a body?" Thou dost not bid me. For that no body is moved, but in time, I hear; this Thou sayest; but that the motion of a body is time, I hear not; Thou sayest it not. For when a body is moved, I by time measure, how long it moveth, from the time it began to move until it left off. And if I did not see whence it began; and it continue to move so that I see not when it ends, I cannot meas-ure, save perchance from the time I began, until I cease to see. And if I took long, I can only pronounce it to be a long time, but not how long; because when we say "how long," we do it by comparison; as, "this is as long as that," or "twice so long as that," or the like. But when we can mark the distances of the places, whence and whither goeth the body moved, or his parts, if it moved as in a lathe, then can we say precisely, in how much time the motion of that body or his part, from this place unto that, was finished. Seeing therefore the motion of a body is one thing, that by which we measure how long it is, another; who sees not, which of the two is rather to be called time? For and if a body be sometimes moved, sometimes stands still, then we measure, not his motion only, but his standing still too by time; and we say, "it stood still, as much as it moved"; or "it stood still twice or thrice so long as it moved"; or any other space which our measuring hath either ascertained, or guessed; more or less, as we use to say. Time then is not the motion of a body.

And I confess to Thee, O Lord, that I yet know not what time is, and again I confess unto Thee, O Lord, that I know that

I speak this in time, and that having long spoken of time, that very "long" is not long, but by the pause of time. How then know I this, seeing I know not what time is? or is it perchance that I know not how to express what I know? Woe is me, that do not even know, what I know not. Behold, O my God, before Thee I lie not; but as I speak, so is my heart. Thou shalt light my candle; Thou, O Lord my God, wilt enlighten my darkness.

Does not my soul most truly confess unto Thee, that I do measure times? Do I then measure, O my God, and know not what I measure? I measure the motion of a body in time; and the time itself do I not measure? Or could I indeed measure the motion of a body how long it were, and in how long a space it could come from this place to that, without measuring the time in which it is moved? This same time then, how do I measure? Do we by a shorter time measure a longer, as by the space of a cubit, the space of a rood? for so indeed we seem by the space of a short syllable to measure the space of a long syllable, and to say that this is double the other. Thus measure we the spaces of stanzas, by the spaces of the verses, and the spaces of the verses, by the spaces of the feet, and the spaces of the feet, by the spaces of the syllables, and the spaces of the long, by the space of short syllables; . . . But neither do we this way obtain any certain measure of time; because it may be, that a shorter verse, pronounced more fully, may take up more time than a longer, pronounced hurriedly. And so for a verse, a foot, a syllable. Whence it seemed to me, that time is nothing else than protraction;[5] but of what, I know not; and I marvel, if it be not of the mind itself. For what, I beseech Thee, O my God, do I measure, when I say, either indefinitely "this is a longer time than that," or definitely "this is double that"? That I measure time, I know; and yet I measure not time to come, for it is not yet; nor present, because it is not protracted by any space; nor past, because it now is not. What then do I measure? Times passing, not past? for so I said.

Courage, my mind, and press on mightily. God is our helper, He made us, and not we ourselves. Press on where truth begins to dawn. Suppose, now, the voice of a body begins to sound, and does sound, and sounds on, and list, it ceases; it is silence now, and that voice is past, and is no more a voice. Before it sounded, it was to come, and could not be measured, because as yet it was not, and now it cannot, because it is no longer. Then therefore while it sounded, it might; because there then was what might be measured. But yet even then it was not at a stay; for it was passing on, and passing away. Could it be measured the rather for that? For while passing, it was being extended into some space of time, so that it might be measured, since the present hath no space. If therefore then it might, then, lo, suppose another voice hath begun to sound, and still soundeth in one continued tenor without any interruption; let us measure it while it sounds; seeing when it hath left sounding, it will then be past, and nothing left to be measured; let us measure it verily, and tell how much it is. But it sounds still, nor can it be measured but from the instant it began in, unto the end it left in. For the very space between is the thing we measure, namely, from some beginning unto some end. Wherefore, a voice that is not yet ended, cannot be measured, so that it may be said how long, or short it is, nor can it be called equal to another, or double to a single, or the like. But when ended, it no longer is. How may it then be measured? And yet we measure times; but yet neither those which are not yet, nor those which no longer are, nor those which are not lengthened out by some pause, nor those which have no bounds. We measure neither times to come, nor past, nor present, nor passing; and yet we do measure times.

"Deus Creator omnium," this verse of eight syllables alternates between short and long syllables. The four short then, the first, third, fifth, and seventh, are but single, in respect of the four long, the second, fourth, six, and eighth. Every one of these to every one of those, hath a double time: I pronounce them, report on them, and find it so, as one's plain sense perceives. By plain sense then, I measure a long syllable by a short, and I sensibly find it to have twice so much; but when one sounds after the other, if the former be short, the latter long, how shall I detain the short one, and how, measuring, shall I apply it to the long, that I may find this to have twice so much; seeing the long does not begin to sound, unless the short leaves sounding? And that very long one do I measure as present, seeing I measure it not till it be ended? Now his ending is his passing away. What then is it I measure: where is the short syllable by which I measure? where the long which I measure? Both have sounded, have flown, passed away, are no more; and yet I measure, and confidently answered that as to space of time this syllable is but single, that double. And yet I could not do this, unless they were already past and ended. It is not then themselves, which now are not, that I measure, but something in my memory, which there remains fixed.

It is in thee, my mind, that I measure times. Interrupt me not, that is interrupt not thyself with the tumults of thy impressions. In thee I measure times; the impression, which things

233

as they pass by cause in thee, remains even when they are gone; this it is which still present, I measure, not the things which pass by to make this impression. This I measure, when I measure times. Either then this is time, or I do not measure times. What when we measure silence, and say that this silence hath held as long as did that voice? do we not stretch out our thought to the measure of a voice, as if it sounded, that so we may be able to report of the intervals of silence in a given space of time? For though both voice and tongue be still, yet in thought we go over poems, and verses, and any other discourse, or dimensions of motions, and report as to the spaces of times, how much this is in respect of that, no otherwise than if vocally we did pronounce them. If a man would utter a lengthened sound, and had settled in thought how long it should be, he hath in silence already gone through a space of time, and committing it to memory, begins to utter that speech, which sounds on, until it be brought unto the end proposed. Yea it hath sounded, and will sound; for so much of it as is finished, hath sounded already, and the rest will sound. And thus passeth it on, until the present intent conveys over the future into the past; the past increasing by the diminution of the future, until by the consumption of the future, all is past.

But how is that future diminished or consumed, which as yet is not? or how that past increased, which is now no longer, save that in the mind which enacteth this, there be three things done? For it expects, it considers, it remembers; that so that which it expecteth, through that which it considereth, passeth into that which it remembereth. Who therefore denieth, that things to come are not as yet? and yet, there is in the mind an expectation of things to come. And who denies past things to be now no longer? and yet is there still in the mind a memory of things past. And who denieth the present time hath no space, because it passeth away in a moment? and yet our consideration continueth, through which that which shall be present proceedeth to become absent. It is not then future time, that is long, for as yet it is not: but a long future, is "a long expectation of the future," nor is it time past, which now is not, that is long; but a long past, is "a long memory of the past."

I am about to repeat a Psalm that I know. Before I begin, my expectation is extended over the whole; but when I have begun, how much soever of it I shall separate off into the past, is extended along my memory; thus the life of this action of mine is divided between my memory as to what I have repeated, and expectation as to what I am about to repeat; but "consideration" is present with me, that through it what was future, may be conveyed over, so as to become past. Which the more it is done again and again, so much the more the expectation being shortened, is the memory enlarged: till the whole expectation be at length exhausted, when that whole action being ended, shall have passed into memory. And this which takes place in the whole Psalm, the same takes place in each several portion of it, and each several syllable; the same holds in that longer action, whereof this Psalm may be a part; the same holds in the whole life of man, whereof all the actions of man are parts; the same holds through the whole age of the sons of men, whereof all the lives of men are parts.

But because Thy loving-kindness is better than all lives, behold, my life is but a distraction,[6] and Thy right hand upheld me, in my Lord the Son of man, the Mediator betwixt Thee, The One, and us many, many also through our manifold distractions amid many things, that by Him I may apprehend in Whom I have been apprehended, and may be recollected from my old conversation, to follow The One, forgetting what is behind, and not distended but extended, not to things which shall be and shall pass away, but to those things which are before, not distractedly but intently, I follow on for the prize of my heavenly calling, where I may hear the voice of Thy praise, and contemplate Thy delights, neither to come, nor to pass away. But now are my years spent in mourning. And Thou, O Lord, art my comfort, my Father everlasting, but I have been severed amid times, whose order I know not; and my thoughts, even the inmost bowels of my soul, are rent and mangled with tumultuous varieties, until I flow together into Thee, purified and molten by the fire of Thy love.

And now will I stand, and become firm in Thee, in my mould, Thy truth; nor will I endure the question of men, who by a penal disease thirst for more than they can contain, and say, "what did God before He made heaven and earth?" Or, "How came it into His mind to make anything, having never before made anything?" Give them, O Lord, well to bethink themselves what they say, and to find, that "never" cannot be predicated, when "time" is not. This then that He is said "never to have made"; what else is it to say, than "in no time to have made?" Let them see therefore, that time cannot be without created being, and cease to speak that vanity. May they also be extended towards those things which are before; and understand Thee before all times, the eternal Creator of all times, and that no times be coeternal with Thee, nor any creature, even if there be any creature before all times.

O Lord my God, what a depth is that recess of Thy mysteries, and how far from it have the consequences of my transgressions cast me! Heal mine eyes, that I may share the joy of Thy
light. Certainly, if there be a mind gifted with such vast knowledge and foreknowledge, as to know all things past and to come,
as I know one well-known Psalm, truly that mind is passing wonderful, and fearfully amazing; in that nothing past, nothing to
come in after-ages, is any more hidden from him than when I sung
that Psalm, was hidden from me what, and how much of it had
passed away from the beginning, what, and how much there remained unto the end. But far be it that Thou the Creator of the
Universe, the Creator of souls and bodies, far be it, that Thou
shouldest in such wise know all things past and to come. Far, far
more wonderfully, and far more mysteriously, dost Thou know
them. For not, as the feelings of one who singeth what he knoweth,
or heareth some well-known song, are through expectation of the
words to come, and the remembering of those that are past, varied,
and his senses divided—not so doth any thing happen unto Thee,
unchangeably eternal, that is, the eternal Creator of minds. Like
then as Thou in the Beginning knewest the heaven and the earth,
without any variety of Thy knowledge, so madest Thou in the Beginning heaven and earth, without any distraction of Thy action.
Whoso understandeth, let him confess unto Thee; and whoso understandeth not, let him confess unto Thee. Oh how high art Thou,
and yet the humble in heart are thy dwelling-place; for Thou raisest
up those that are bowed down, and they fall not, whose elevation
Thou art.

THE CITY OF GOD ✠ BOOK XI ✠ CHAPTER 4 Of all
visible things, the world is the greatest; of all invisible, the greatest
is God. But, that the world is, we see; that God is, we believe. That
God made the world, we can believe from no one more safely
than from God Himself. But where have we heard Him? Nowhere
more distinctly than in the Holy Scriptures, where His prophet
said, "In the beginning God created the heavens and the earth."
    But why did God choose then to create the heavens and
earth which up to that time He had not made? If they who put
this question wish to make out that the world is eternal and with-

out beginning, and that consequently it has not been made by God, they are strangely deceived, and rave in the incurable madness of impiety. For, though the voices of the prophets were silent, the world itself, by its well-ordered changes and movements, and by the fair appearance of all visible things, bears a testimony of its own, both that it has been created, and also that it could not have been created save by God, whose greatness and beauty are unutterable and invisible. As for those[7] who own, indeed, that it was made by God, and yet ascribe to it not a temporal but only a creational beginning, so that in some scarcely intelligible way the world should always have existed a created world, they make an assertion which seems to defend God from the charge of arbitrary hastiness, or of suddenly conceiving the idea of creating the world as a quite new idea, or of casually changing His will, though He be unchangeable. But I do not see how this supposition of theirs can stand in other respects, and chiefly in respect of the soul; for if they contend that it is co-eternal with God, they will be quite at a loss to explain whence there has accrued to it new misery, which through a previous eternity had not existed. For if they said that its happiness and misery ceaselessly alternate, they must say, further, that this alternation will continue for ever; whence will result this absurdity, that, though the soul is called blessed, it is not so in this, that it foresees its own misery and disgrace. And yet, if it does not foresee it, and supposes that it will be neither disgraced nor wretched but always blessed, then it is blessed because it is deceived; and a more foolish statement one cannot make. But if their idea is that the soul's misery has alternated with its bliss during the ages of the past eternity, but that now, when once the soul has been set free, it will return henceforth no more to misery, they are nevertheless of opinion that it has never been truly blessed before, but begins at last to enjoy a new and uncertain happiness; that is to say, they must acknowledge that some new thing, and that an important and signal thing, happens to the soul which never in a whole past eternity happened to it before. And if they deny that God's eternal purpose included this new experience of the soul, they deny that He is the Author of its blessedness, which is unspeakable impiety. If, on the other hand, they say that the future blessedness of the soul is the result of a new decree of God, how will they show that God is not chargeable with that mutability which displeases them? Further, if they acknowledge that it was created in time, but will never perish in time—that it has, like number, a beginning but no end—and that, therefore, having once made trial of misery and been delivered from it, it will never again return thereto, they will certainly admit that this takes place without any violation of the immutable counsel of God. Let them, then, in like manner believe regarding the world that it too could be made in time, and yet that God, in making it, did not alter His eternal design.

CHAPTER 5 Next, we must see what reply can be made to those who agree that God is the Creator of the world, but have difficulties about the time of its creation, and what reply, also, they can make to difficulties we might raise about the place of its creation. For, as they demand why the world was created then and no sooner, we may ask why it was created just here where it is and not elsewhere. For if they imagine infinite periods of time before the world, during which God could not have been idle, in like manner they may conceive outside the world infinite realms of space, in which, if any one says that the Omnipotent cannot hold His hand from working, will it not follow that they must adopt Epicurus' dream of innumerable worlds? with this difference only, that he asserts that they are formed and destroyed by the fortuitous movements of atoms, while they will hold that they are made by God's hand if they maintain that, throughout the boundless immensity of space, stretching interminably in every direction round the world, God cannot rest, and that the worlds which they suppose Him to make cannot be destroyed. For here the question is with those who, with ourselves, believe that God is spiritual, and the Creator of all existences but Himself. As for others, it is a condescension to dispute with them on a religious question, for they have acquired a reputation only among men who pay divine honors to a number of gods, and have become conspicuous among the other philosophers for no other reason than that, though they are still far from the truth, they are near it in comparison with the rest. While these, then, neither confine in any place, nor limit, nor distribute the divine substance, but, as is worthy of God, own it to be wholly though spiritually present everywhere, will they perchance say that this substance is absent from such immense spaces outside the world, and is occupied in one only (and that a very little one compared with the infinity beyond), the one, namely, in which is the world? I think they will not proceed to this absurdity. Since they maintain that there is but one world, of vast material bulk, indeed, yet finite, and in its own determinate position, and that this was made by the working of God, let them give the same account of God's resting in the infinite times before the world as they give of His resting in the infinite spaces outside of it. And as it does not follow that God set the world in the very spot it occupies and no other by accident rather than by divine reason, although no human reason can comprehend why it was so set, and though there was no merit in the spot chosen to give it the precedence of infinite others, so neither does it follow that we should suppose that God was guided by chance when He created the world in that and no earlier time, although previous times had been running by during an infinite past, and though there was no difference by which one time could be chosen in preference to another. But if they say that the thoughts of men are idle when they conceive infinite places, since there is no place beside the world, we reply that, by the same showing, it is vain to conceive of the past times of God's rest, since there is no time before the world.

CHAPTER 6 For if eternity and time are rightly distinguished by this, that time does not exist without some movement and transition, while in eternity there is no change, who does not see that there could have been no time had not some creature been made, by which some motion could give birth to change. . . . Since then, God, in whose eternity is no change at all, is the Creator and Ordainer of time, I do not see how He can be said to have created the world after spaces of time had elapsed, unless it be said that prior to the world there was some creature by whose movement time could pass. And if the sacred and infallible Scriptures say that in the beginning God created the heavens and the earth, in order that it may be understood that He had made nothing previously—for if He had made anything before the rest, this thing would rather be said to have been made "in the beginning"—then assuredly the world was made, not in time, but simultaneously with time. For that which is made in time is made both after and before some time—after that which is past, before that which is future. But none could then be past, for there was no creature by whose movements its duration could be measured. But simultaneously with time the world was made, if in the world's creation change and motion were created, as seems evident from the order of the first six or seven days. For in these days the morning and evening are counted, until, on the sixth day, all things which God then made were finished, and on the seventh the rest of God was mysteriously and sublimely signalized. What kind of days these were it is extremely difficult, or perhaps impossible, for us to conceive, and how much more to say!

BOOK XII ✢ CHAPTER 13 This controversy some philosophers have seen no other approved means of solving than by introducing cycles of time, in which there should be a constant renewal and repetition of the order of nature; and they have therefore asserted that these cycles will ceaselessly recur, one passing away and another coming, though they are not agreed as to whether one permanent world shall pass through all these cycles, or whether the world shall at fixed intervals die out and be renewed so as to exhibit a recurrence of the same phenomena—the things which have been and those which are to be coinciding. And from this fantastic vicissitude they exempt not even the immortal soul that has attained wisdom, consigning it to a ceaseless transmigration between delusive blessedness and real misery. For how can that be truly called blessed which has no assurance of being so eternally, and is either in ignorance of the truth, and blind to the misery that is approaching, or, knowing it, is in misery and fear? Or if it passes to bliss, and leaves miseries for ever, then there happens in time a new thing which time shall not end. Why not, then, the world also? Why may not man, too, be a similar thing? So that, by following the straight path of sound doctrine, we escape, I know not what circuitous paths, discovered by deceiving and deceived sages.

Some, too, in advocating these recurring cycles that restore all things to their original, cite in favor of their supposition what Solomon says in the book of Ecclesiastes: "What is that which hath been? It is that which shall be. And what is that which is done? It is that which shall be done: and there is no new thing under the sun. Who can speak and say, See, this is new? It hath been already of old time, which was before us." (Eccles. 1:9-10) This he said either of those things of which he had just been speaking—the succession of generations, the orbit of the sun, the course of rivers—or else of all kinds of creatures that are born and die. . . . However, some would understand these words as meaning that in the predestination of God all things have already existed, and that thus there is no new thing under the sun. At all events, far be it from any true believer to suppose that by these words of Solomon those cycles are meant, in which, according to those philosophers, the same periods and events of time are repeated; as if, for example, the philospher Plato, having taught in the school at Athens which is called the Academy, so, numberless ages before, at long but certain intervals, this same Plato, and the same school, and the same disciples existed, and so also are to be repeated during the countless cycles that are yet to be—far be it, I say, for us to believe this. For once Christ died for our sins; and, rising from the dead, He dieth no more. "Death hath no more dominion over Him"; (Rom. 6:9) and we ourselves after the resurrection shall be "ever with the Lord," (I Thess. 4:16) to whom we now say, as the sacred Psalmist dictates, "Thou shalt keep us, O Lord, Thou shalt preserve us from this generation." (Ps. 12:7) And that too which follows, is, I think, appropriate enough: "The wicked walk in a circle"; not because their life is to recur by means of these circles, which these philosophers imagine, but because the path in which their false doctrine now runs is circuitous.

CHAPTER 20 What pious ears could bear to hear that after a life spent in so many and severe distresses (if, indeed, that should be called a life at all which is rather a death, so utter that the love of this present death makes us fear that death which delivers us from it), that after evils so disastrous, and miseries of all kinds have at length been expiated and finished by the help of true religion and wisdom, and when we have thus attained to the vision of God and have entered into bliss by the contemplation of spiritual light and participation in His unchangeable immortality, which we burn to attain—that we must at some time lose all this, and that they who do lose it are cast down from that eternity, truth, and felicity to infernal mortality and shameful foolishness, and are involved in accursed woes, in which God is lost, truth held in detestation, and happiness sought in iniquitous impurities? and that this will happen endlessly again and again, recurring at fixed intervals, and in regularly returning periods? and that this everlasting and ceaseless revolution of definite cycles, which remove and restore true misery and deceitful bliss in turn, is contrived in order that God may be able to know His own works, since on the one hand He cannot rest from creating and, on the other, cannot know the infinite number of His creatures, if He always makes creatures? Who, I say, can listen to such things? Who can accept or suffer them to be spoken? Were they true, it were not only more prudent to keep silence regarding them, but even it were the part of wisdom not to know them. For if in the future world we shall not remember these things and by this oblivion be

241

blessed, why should we now increase our misery, already burdensome enough, by the knowledge of them? If, on the other hand, the knowledge of them will be forced upon us hereafter, now at least let us remain in ignorance, that in the present expectation we may enjoy a blessedness which the future reality is not to bestow; since in this life we are expecting to obtain life everlasting, but in the world to come are to discover it to be blessed, but not everlasting.

And if they maintain that no one can attain to the blessedness of the world to come, unless in this life he has been indoctrinated in those cycles in which bliss and misery relieve one another, how do they avow that the more a man loves God, the more readily he attains to blessedness—they who teach what paralyzes love itself? For who would not be more remiss and lukewarm in his love for a person whom he thinks he shall be forced to abandon, and whose truth and wisdom he shall come to hate; and this, too, after he has quite attained to the utmost and most blissful knowledge of Him that he is capable of? Can any one be faithful in his love, even to a human friend, if he knows that he is destined to become his enemy? God forbid that there be any truth in an opinion which threatens us with a real misery that is never to end, but is often and endlessly to be interrupted by intervals of fallacious happiness. For what happiness can be more fallacious and false than that in whose blaze of truth we yet remain ignorant that we shall be miserable, or in whose most secure citadel we yet fear that we shall be so? For if, on the one hand, we are to be ignorant of coming calamity, then our present misery is not so shortsighted, for it is assured of coming bliss. If, on the other hand, the disaster that threatens is not concealed from us in the world to come, then the time of misery which is to be at last exchanged for a state of blessedness is spent by the soul more happily than its time of happiness, which is to end in a return to misery. And thus our expectation of unhappiness is happy; but of happiness, unhappy. And therefore, as we here suffer present ills and hereafter fear ills that are imminent, it were truer to say that we shall always be miserable than that we can some time be happy.

But these things are declared to be false by the loud testimony of religion and truth; for religion truthfully promises a true blessedness, of which we shall be eternally assured, and which cannot be interrupted by any disaster. Let us therefore keep to the straight path, which is Christ, and, with Him as our Guide and Saviour, let us turn away in heart and mind from the unreal and futile cycles of the godless. . . .

THE CONFESSIONS ✠ BOOK XII ✠ . . . The lowliness of
my tongue confesseth unto Thy Highness, that Thou madest
heaven and earth; this heaven which I see, and this earth that
I tread upon it, whence is this earth that I bear about me; Thou
madest it. But where is that heaven of heavens, O Lord, which
we hear of in the words of the Psalm. The heaven of heavens is
the Lord's; but the earth hath He given to the children of men?
Where is that heaven which we see not, to which all this which
we see is earth? For this corporeal whole, not being wholly everywhere, hath in such wise received its portion of beauty in these
lower parts, whereof the lowest is this our earth; but to that heaven
of heavens, even the heaven of our earth, is but the earth: yea
both these great bodies, may not absurdly be called earth, to that
unknown heaven, which is the Lord's, not of the sons of men.

And now this earth was invisible and without form, and
there was I know not what depth of abyss, upon which there was
no light, because it had no shape. Therefore didst Thou command
it to be written, that darkness was upon the face of the deep;
what else than the absence of light? For had there been light,
where should it have been but by being over all, aloft, and enlightening? Where then light was not, what was the presence of
darkness but the absence of light? Darkness therefore was upon it,
because light was not upon it; as where sound is not, there is
silence. And what is to have silence there but to have no sound
there? Hast not Thou, O Lord, taught his soul, which confesseth
unto Thee? Hast not Thou taught me, Lord, that before Thou
formedst and diversifiedst this formless matter, there was nothing,
neither color, nor figure, nor body, nor spirit? and yet not altogether
nothing; for there was a certain formlessness, without any beauty.

How then should it [matter] be called, that it might be
in some measure conveyed to those of duller mind, but by some
ordinary word? And what, among all parts of the world can be
found nearer to an absolute formlessness, than earth and deep?
For, occupying the lowest stage, they are less beautiful than the
other higher parts are, transparent all and shining. Wherefore then
may I not conceive the formlessness of matter (which Thou hadst
created without beauty, whereof to make this beautiful world (to
be suitably intimated unto men by the name of earth invisible and
without form.

So that when thought seeketh what the sense may conceive
under this, and saith to itself, "It is no intellectual form, as life,

or justice; because it is the matter of bodies; nor object of sense, because being invisible, and without form, there was in it no object of sight or sense";—while man's thought thus saith to itself, it may endeavor either to know it, by being ignorant of it; or to be ignorant, by knowing it.

But I, Lord, if I would by my tongue and my pen, confess unto Thee the whole, whatever Thyself hath taught me of that matter,—the name whereof hearing before, and not understanding, when they who understood it not, told me of it, so I conceived of it as having innumerable forms and diverse, and therefore did not conceive it at all, my mind tossed up and down foul and horrible "forms" out of all order, but yet "forms" and I called it without form not that it wanted all form, but because it had such as my mind would, if presented to it, turn from, as unwonted and jarring, and human frailness would be troubled at. And still that which I conceived, was without form, not as being deprived of all form, but in comparison of more beautiful forms; and true reason did persuade me, that I must utterly uncase it of all remnants of form whatsoever, if I would conceive matter absolutely without form; and I could not; for sooner could I imagine that not to be at all, which should be deprived of all form, than conceive a thing betwixt form and nothing, neither formed, nor nothing, a formless almost nothing, So my mind gave over to question thereupon with my spirit, it being filled with the images of formed bodies, and changing and varying them, as it willed; and I bent myself to the bodies themselves and looked more deeply into their changeableness, by which they cease to be what they have been and begin to be what they were not; and this same shifting from form to form, I suspected to be through a certain formless state, not through a mere nothing; yet this I longed to know, not to suspect only. . . . For the changeableness of changeable things, is itself capable of all those forms, into which these changeable things are changed. And this changeableness, what is it? Is it soul? Is it body? Is it that which constitutes soul or body? Might one say, "a nothing something," an "is, is not," I would say, this were it: and yet in some way was it even then, as being capable of receiving these visible and compound figures.

But whence had it this degree of being but from Thee, from whom are all things, so far forth as they are? But so much the further from Thee, as the unliker Thee; for it is not farness of place. Thou therefore, Lord, who art not one in one place, and otherwise in another, but the Self-same, and the Self-same, and the Self-same, Holy, Holy, Holy, Lord God Almighty, didst in the Beginning, which is of Thee, in Thy Wisdom, which was born of Thine own Substance, create something, and that out of nothing. For Thou createdst heaven and earth; not out of Thyself; for so should they have been equal to Thine Only Begotten Son, and thereby to Thee also; whereas no way were it right that aught should be equal to Thee, which was not of Thee. And aught else besides Thee was there not, whereof Thou mightest create them, O God, One Trinity, and Trine Unity; and therefore out of nothing didst Thou create heaven and earth; a great thing, and a small thing; for Thou art Almighty and Good, to make all things good, even the great heaven, and the petty earth. Thou wert, and nothing was there besides, out of which Thou createdst heaven and earth; things of two sorts; one near Thee, the other near to nothing; one to which Thou alone shouldst be superior; the other, to which nothing should be inferior.

But that heaven of heavens was for Thyself, O Lord; but the earth which Thou gavest to the sons of men, to be seen and felt, was not such as we now see and feel. For it was invisible, without form, and there was a deep, upon which there was no light; or, darkness was above the deep, that is, more than in the deep. Because this deep of waters, visible now, hath even in his depths, a light proper for its nature; perceivable in whatever degree unto the fishes, and creeping things in the bottom of it. But that whole deep was almost nothing, because hitherto it was altogether without form; yet there was already that which could be formed. For Thou, Lord, madest the world of a matter without form, which out of nothing, Thou madest next to nothing, thereof to make those great things, which we sons of men wonder at. For very wonderful is this corporeal heaven; of which firmament between water and water, the second day, after the creation of light, Thou saidst, Let it be made, and it was made. Which firmament Thou calledst heaven; the heaven, that is, to this earth and sea, which Thou madest the third day, by giving a visible figure to the formless matter, which Thou madest before all days. For already hadst Thou made both an heaven, before all days; but that was the heaven of this heaven; because in the beginning Thou hadst made heaven and earth. But this same earth which Thou madest was formless matter, because it was invisible and without form, and darkness was upon the deep, of which invisible earth and without form, of which formlessness, of which almost nothing, mightest make all these things of which this changeable world consists, but subsists not; [8] whose very changeableness appears therein, that times can be observed and numbered in it. For times are made by the alterations of things, while the figures, the matter whereof is the invisible earth aforesaid, are varied and turned . . .

This then is what I conceive, O my God, when I hear Thy Scripture saying, In the beginning God made Heaven and Earth: and the Earth was invisible and without form, and darkness was upon the deep, and not mentioning what day Thou createdst them; this is what I conceive, that because of the Heaven of heavens,—that intellectual Heaven, whose Intelligences know all at once, not in part, not darkly, not through a glass, but as a whole, in manifestation, face to face; not, this thing now, that thing anon; but (as I said) know all at once, without any succession of times;—and because of the earth invisible and without form, without any succession of times, which succession presents "this thing now, that thing anon"; because where is no form, there is no distinction of things:—it is, then, on account of these two, a primitive formed, and a primitive formless; the one, heaven but the Heaven of heaven, the other earth but the earth invisible and without form; because of these two do I conceive, did Thy Scripture say without mention of days, In the Beginning God created Heaven and Earth. For forthwith it subjoined what earth it spake of; and also, in that the Firmament is recorded to be created the second day, and called Heaven, it conveys to us of which Heaven He before spake, without mention of days. . . .

For they say, "Though these things be true, yet did not Moses intend those two, when, by revelation of the Spirit, he said, In the beginning God created heaven and earth. He did not under the name of heaven signify that spiritual or intellectual creature which always beholds the face of God; nor under the name of earth, that formless matter." "What then?" "That man of God," say they, "meant as we say, this declared he by those words." "What?" "By the name of heaven and earth would he first signify," say they, "universally and compendiously, all this visible world; so as afterwards by the enumeration of the several days, to arrange in detail, and, as it were, piece by piece, all those things which it pleased the Holy Ghost thus to enounce. For such were that rude and carnal people to which he spake, that he thought them fit to be entrusted with the knowledge of such works of God only as were visible." They agree, however, that under the words earth invisible and without form, and that darksome deep (out of which it is subsequently shown, that all these visible things which we all know, were made and arranged during those "days") may, not incongruously, be understood of this formless first matter.

What now if another should say that "this same formlessness and confusedness of matter, was for this reason first conveyed under the name of heaven and earth, because out of it was this visible world with all those natures which most manifestly appear in it, which is ofttimes called by the name of heaven and earth, created and perfected?" What again if another say that "invisible and visible nature is not indeed inappropriately called heaven and earth; and so, that the universal creation, which God made in His Wisdom, that is, in the Beginning, was comprehended under those two words? Notwithstanding, since all things be made not of the substance of God, but out of nothing (because they are not the same that God is, and there is a mutable nature in them all, whether they abide, as doth the eternal house of God, or be changed, as the soul and body of man are) : therefore the common matter of all things visible and invisible (as yet unformed though capable of form) , out of which was to be created both heaven and earth (i.e. the invisible and visible creature when formed) , was entitled by the same names given to the earth invisible and without form, and the darkness upon the deep, but with this distinction, that by the earth invisible and without form is understood corporeal matter, antecedent to its being qualified by any form; and by the darkness upon the deep, spiritual matter, before it underwent any restraint of its unlimited fluidness, or received any light from Wisdom?"

It yet remains for a man to say, if he will, that "the already perfected and formed natures, visible and invisible, are not signified under the name of heaven and earth, when we read, In the beginning God made heaven and earth, but that the yet unformed commencement of things, the stuff apt to receive form and making, was called by these names, because therein were confusedly contained, not as yet distinguished by their qualities and forms, all those things which being now digested into order, are called Heaven and Earth, the one being the spiritual, the other the corporeal, creation."

All which things being heard and well considered, I will not strive about words: for that is profitable to nothing but the subversion of the hearers. But the law is good to edify, if a man use it lawfully: for that the end of it is charity, out of a pure heart and good conscience, and faith unfeigned. And well did our Master know, upon which two commandments He hung all the Law and the Prophets. And what doth it prejudice me, O my God, Thou light of my eyes in secret, zealously confessing these things, since divers things may be understood under these words which yet are all true,—what, I say, doth it prejudice me, if I think

247

otherwise than another thinketh the writer thought? All we readers verily strive to trace out and to understand his meaning whom we read; and seeing we believe him to speak truly, we dare not imagine him to have said anything, which ourselves either know or think to be false. While every man endeavors then to understand in the Holy Scriptures, the same as the writer understood, what hurt is it, if a man understand what Thou, the light of all true-speaking minds, dost show him to be true, although he whom he reads, understood not this, seeing he also understood a Truth, though not this truth?

For true it is, O Lord, that Thou madest heaven and earth; and it is true too, that the Beginning is Thy Wisdom, in Which Thou createdst all: and true again, that this visible world hath for its greater part the heaven and the earth, which briefly comprise all made and created natures. And true too, that whatsoever is mutable, gives us to understand a certain want of form, whereby it receiveth a form, or is changed, or turned. It is true, that that is subject to no times, which so cleaveth to the unchangeable Form, as though subject to change, never to be changed. It is true, that that formlessness which is almost nothing, cannot be subject to the alteration of times. It is true, that that whereof a thing is made, may by a certain mode of speech, be called by the name of the thing made of it; whence that formlessness, whereof heaven and earth were made, might be called heaven and earth. It is true, that of things having form, there is not any nearer to having no form, than the earth and the deep. It is true, that not only every created and formed thing, but whatsoever is capable of being created and formed, Thou madest, of Whom are all things. It is true, that whatsoever is formed out of that which had no form, was unformed before it was formed.

Out of these truths, of which they doubt not whose inward eye Thou hast enabled to see such things, and who unshakenly believe Thy servant Moses to have spoken in the Spirit of truth;—of all these then, he taketh one, who saith, In the Beginning God made the heaven and the earth; that is, "in His Word co-eternal with Himself, God made the intelligible and the sensible, or the spiritual and the corporeal creature." He another, that saith, In the Beginning God made heaven and earth; that is, "in His Word co-eternal with Himself, did God make the universal bulk of this corporeal world, together with all those apparent and known creatures, which it containeth." He another, that saith, In the Beginning God created heaven and earth; that is, "in His Word co-eternal with Himself, did God create the formless matter of the creature corporeal, wherein heaven and earth lay as yet confused, which, being now distinguished and formed, we at this day see in the bulk of this world." He another, who saith, In the Beginning God made heaven and earth; that is, "in the very beginning of creating and working, did God make that formless matter, confusedly containing in itself both heaven and earth; out of which, being formed, do they now stand out, and are apparent, with all that is in them."

And with regard to the understanding of the words following [Gen. 1:2], out of all those truths, he chooses one to himself, who saith, But the earth was invisible, and without form, and darkness was upon the deep; that is, "that corporeal thing that God made, was as yet a formless matter of corporeal things, without order, without light." Another, he who says, The earth was invisible and without form, and darkness was upon the deep; that is, "this all, which is called heaven and earth, was still a formless and darksome matter, of which the corporeal heaven and the corporeal earth were to be made, with all things in them, which are known to our corporeal senses." Another, he who says, The earth was invisible and without form, and darkness was upon the deep; that is, "this all, which is called heaven and earth, was still a formless and a darksome matter; out of which was to be made, both that intelligible heaven, otherwise called the Heaven of heavens, and the earth, that is, the whole corporeal nature, under which name is comprised this corporeal heaven also; in a word, out of which every visible and invisible creature was to be created." Another, he who says, The earth was invisible and without form, and darkness was upon the deep, "the Scripture did not call that formlessness by the name of heaven and earth; but that formlessness, saith he, already was, which he called the earth invisible and without form, and darkness upon the deep; of which he had before said, that God had made heaven and earth, namely, the spiritual and corporeal creature." Another, he who says, The earth was invisible and without form, and darkness was upon the deep; that is, "there already was a certain formless matter, of which the Scripture said before, that God made heaven and earth; namely, the whole corporeal bulk of the world, divided into two great parts, upper and lower, with all the common and known creatures in them."

For should any one attempt to dispute against these two last opinions, thus, "If you will not allow, that this formlessness of matter seems to be called by the name of heaven and earth; Ergo, there was something which God had not made, out of which to make heaven and earth; for neither hath Scripture told us, that God made this matter, unless we understand it to be signified by the name of heaven and earth, or of earth alone, when it is said, In the Beginning God made heaven and earth; that so in what follows, and the earth was invisible and without form, (although it pleased Him so to call the formless matter), we are to understand no other matter, but that which God made, whereof is written above, God made heaven and earth." The maintainers of either of those two latter opinions will, upon hearing this, return for answer, "we do not deny this formless matter to be indeed created by God, that God of Whom are all things very good; for as we affirm that to be a greater good, which is created and formed, so we confess that to be a lesser good which is made capable of creation and form, yet still good. We say, however, that Scripture hath not set down, that God made this formlessness, as also it hath not set down many others; as the Cherubim, and Seraphim, and those which the Apostle distinctly speaks of, Thrones, Dominions, Principalities, Powers. All which that God made, is most apparent. Or if in that which is said, He made heaven and earth, all things be comprehended, what shall we say of the waters, upon which the Spirit of God moved? For if they be comprised in this word earth; how then can formless matter be meant in that name of earth, when we see the waters so beautiful? Or if it be so taken; why then is it written, that out of the same formlessness, the firmament was made, and called heaven; and that the waters were made, is not written? For the waters remain not formless and invisible, seeing we behold them flowing in so comely a manner. But if they received that beauty, when God said, Let the waters under the firmament be gathered together, that so the gathering together be itself the forming of them; what will be said as to those waters above the firmament? Seeing neither if formless would they have been worthy of so honorable a seat, nor is it written, by what word they were formed. If then Genesis is silent as to God's making of any thing, which yet that God did make neither sound faith nor well-grounded understanding doubteth, nor again will any sober teaching dare to affirm these waters to be co-eternal with God, on the ground that we find them to be mentioned in the book of Genesis, but when they were created, we do not find; why (seeing truth teaches us) should we not understand that formless matter (which this Scripture calls the earth invisible and without form, and darksome deep) to have been created of God out of nothing, and therefore not to be co-eternal to Him; notwithstanding this history hath omitted to show when it was created?"

These things then being heard and perceived, according to the weakness of my capacity (which I confess unto Thee, O Lord, that knowest it), two sorts of disagreements I see may arise, when a thing is in words related by true reporters; one, concerning the truth of the things, the other, concerning the meaning of the relater. For we enquire one way about the making of the creature, what is true; another way, what Moses, that excellent minister of Thy Faith, would have his reader and hearer understand by those words. For the first sort, away with all those who imagine themselves to know as a truth, what is false; and for this other, away with all them too, which imagine Moses to have written things that be false. But let me be united in Thee, O Lord, with those and delight myself in Thee, with them that feed on Thy truth, in the largeness of charity, and let us approach together unto the words of Thy book, and seek in them for Thy meaning, through the meaning of Thy servant, by whose pen Thou hast dispensed them. . . .

For as a fountain within a narrow compass, is more plentiful, and supplies a tide for more streams over larger spaces, than any one of those streams, which, after a wide interval, is derived from the same fountain; so the relation of that dispenser of Thine, which was to benefit many who were to discourse thereon, does out of a narrow scantling of language, overflow into streams of clearest truth, whence every man may draw out for himself such truth as he can upon these subjects, one, one truth, another, another, by larger circumlocutions of discourse. For some, when they read, or hear these words, conceive that God like a man or some mass endued with unbounded power, by some new and sudden resolution, did, exterior to itself, as it were at a certain distance, create heaven and earth, two great bodies above and below, wherein all things were to be contained. And when they hear, God said, Let it be made, and it was made; they conceive of words begun and ended, sounding in time, and passing away; after whose departure, that came into being, which was commanded so to do; and whatever of the like sort, men's acquaintance with the material world would suggest. In whom, being yet little ones and carnal, while their weakness is by this humble kind of speech, carried on, as in a mother's bosom, their faith is wholesomely built up, whereby they hold assured, that God made all natures, which in admirable variety their eye beholdeth around. Which words, if any despising, as too simple, with a proud weakness, shall stretch himself beyond the guardian nest; he will, alas, fall miserably. Have pity, O Lord God, lest they who go by the way trample on the unfledged bird, and send Thine angel to replace it into the nest, that it may live, till it can fly.

But others, unto whom these words are no longer a nest, but deep shady fruit-bowers, see the fruits concealed therein, fly joyously around, and with cheerful notes seek out, and pluck them. For reading or hearing these words, they see that all times past and to come, are surpassed by Thy eternal and stable abiding; and yet that there is no creature formed in time, not of Thy making. Whose will, because it is the same that Thou art, Thou madest all things, not by any change of will, nor by a will, which before was not, and that these things were not out of Thyself, in Thine own likeness, which is the form of all things; but out of nothing, a formless unlikeness, which should be formed by Thy likeness (recurring to Thy Unity, according to their appointed capacity, so far as is given to each thing in his kind), and might all be made very good; whether they abide around Thee, or being in gradation removed in time and place, made or undergo the beautiful variations of the Universe. These things they see, and rejoice, in the little degree they here may, in the light of Thy truth.

Another bends his mind on that which is said, In the Beginning God made heaven and earth; and beholdeth therein Wisdom, the Beginning because it also speaketh unto us. Another likewise bends his mind on the same words, and by Beginning understands the commencement of things created; In the beginning He made, as if it were said, He at first made. And among them that understand In the Beginning to mean, "In Thy Wisdom Thou createdst heaven and earth," one believes the matter out of which the heaven and earth were to be created, to be there called heaven and earth; another, natures already formed and distinguished; another, one formed nature, and that a spiritual, under the name of Heaven, the other formless, a corporeal matter, under the name of Earth. They again who by the names heaven and earth, understand matter as yet formless, out of which heaven and earth were to be formed, neither do they understand it in one way; but the one, that matter out of which both the intelligible and the sensible creature were to be perfected; another, that only, out of which this sensible corporeal mass was to be made, containing in its vast bosom these visible and ordinary natures. Neither do they, who believe the creatures already ordered and arranged, to be in this place called heaven and earth, understand the same; but the one, both the invisible and visible, the other, the visible only, in which we behold this lightsome heaven, and darksome earth, with the things in them contained.

But he that no otherwise understands In the Beginning He made, than if it were said, At first He made, can only truly understand heaven and earth of the matter of heaven and earth, that is, of the universal intelligible corporeal creation. For if he would understand thereby the universe, as already formed, it may be rightly demanded of him, "If God made this first, what made He afterwards?" and after the universe, he will find nothing; whereupon must he against his will hear another question; "How did God make this first, if nothing after?" But when he says, God made matter first formless, then formed, there is no absurdity, if he but qualified to discern, what precedes by eternity, what by time, what by choice, and what in original. By eternity, as God is before all things; by time, as the flower before the fruit; by choice, as the fruit before the flower; by original, as the sound before the tune. Of these four, the first and last mentioned, are with extreme difficulty understood, the two middle easily. For a rare and too lofty a vision is it, to behold Thy Eternity, O Lord, unchangeably making things changeable; and thereby before them. And who, again, is of so sharpsighted understanding, as to be able without great pains to discern, how the sound is therefore before the tune; because a tune is a formed sound; and a thing not formed, may exist; whereas that which existeth not, cannot be formed. Thus is the matter before the thing made; not because it maketh it, seeing itself is rather made; nor is it before by interval of time; for we do not first in time utter formless sounds without singing, and subsequently adapt or fashion them into the form of a chant, as wood or silver, whereof a chest or vessel is fashioned. For such materials do by time also precede the forms of the things made of them, but in singing it is not so; for when it is sung, its sound is heard; for there is not first a formless sound, which is afterwards formed into a chant. For each sound, so soon as made, passeth away, nor canst thou find ought to recall and by art to compose. So then the chant is concentrated in its sound, which sound is its matter. And this indeed is formed, that it may be a tune; and therefore (as I said) the matter of the sound is before the form of the tune; not before, through any power it hath to make it a tune; for a sound is no way the work-master of the tune; but is something corporeal, subject to the soul which singeth, whereof to make a tune. Nor is it first in time; for it is given forth together with the tune; nor first in choice, for a sound is not better than a tune, a tune being not only a sound, but a beautiful sound. But it is first in original, because a tune receives not form to become a sound, but a sound receives a form to become a tune. By this example, let him that is able, understand how the matter of things was first made, and called heaven and earth, because heaven and earth were made out of it. Yet was it not made first in time; because the forms of things give rise to time; but that was without form; but now is, in time, an object of sense together with its form. And yet nothing can be related of that matter, but as though prior in time, whereas in value it is last (because things formed are superior to things without form) and is preceded by the Eternity of the Creator: that so there might be out of nothing, whereof somewhat might be created.

In this diversity of the true opinions, let Truth herself produce concord. And our God have mercy upon us, that we may use the law lawfully, the end of the commandment, pure charity. By this if a man demands of me, "which of these was the meaning of Thy servant Moses"; this were not the language of my Confessions, should I not confess unto Thee, "I know not"; and yet I know that those senses are true, those carnal ones excepted, of which I have spoken what seemed necessary. And even those hopeful little ones who so think, have this benefit, that the words of Thy Book affright them not, delivering high things lowlily, and with a few words a copious meaning. And all we who, I confess, see and express the truth delivered in those words, let us love one another, and jointly love Thee our God, the fountain of truth, if we are athirst for it, and not for vanities; yea, let us so honor this Thy servant, the dispenser of this Scripture, full of Thy Spirit, as to believe that, when by Thy Revelation he wrote these things, he intended that, which among them chiefly excels both for light of truth, and fruitfullness of profit.

So when one says, "Moses meant as I do"; and another, "Nay, but as I do," I suppose that I speak more reverently, "Why not rather as both, if both be true?" And if there be a third, or a fourth, yea if any other seeth any other truth in those words, why may not he be believed to have seen all these, through whom the One God hath tempered the holy Scriptures to the senses of many, who should see therein things true but divers? For I certainly (and fearlessly I speak it from my heart), that were I to indite any thing to have supreme authority, I should prefer so to write, that whatever truth any could apprehend on those matters, might be conveyed in my words, rather than set down my own meaning so clearly as to exclude the rest, which not being false, could not offend me. I will not therefore, O my God, be so rash, as not to believe, that Thou vouchsafedst as much to the great man. He without doubt, when he wrote those words, perceived and thought of what truth soever we have been able to find, yea and whatsoever we have not been able, nor yet are, but which may be found in them. . . .

Behold, O Lord my God, how much we have written upon a few words,[9] how much I beseech Thee! What strength of ours, yea what ages would suffice for all Thy books in this manner? Permit me then in these more briefly to confess unto Thee, and to choose some one true, certain, and good sense that Thou shalt inspire me, although many should occur, where many may occur; this being the law of my confession, that if I should say that which Thy minister intended, that is right and best; for this should I endeavor, which if I should not attain, yet I should say that, which Thy Truth willed by his words to tell me, which revealed also unto him what It willed.

THE LITERAL MEANING OF GENESIS ✠ BOOK V [10] ✠
13. Therefore it was not in a temporal order but in a logical order that this unformed matter was first made, yet capable of becoming the nature of bodies and spirits, from which was made what was to be made. This unformed matter could not itself be ordered before it came into being, and it was not ordered except by the sovereign Lord from whom all things are. This first matter, made by God before the creation of the first day, can perhaps be called heaven and earth, because the heaven and the earth were composed of it; or it has been called "the earth invisible, without order, and the shadowy depths," as we developed in the first book.

20. Moreover this follows: "But a spring rose out of the earth, watering all the surface of the earth." This suggests the moment when there was formed, according to the regular intervals of time, those beings issuing from the primitive state in which He had created all of them simultaneously. It was natural to begin with that element from which all the species of animals and plants took birth, in order that they might in time develop according to those properties which had been distributed to them. To be sure the seeds of which they were all formed, whether from flesh or from the products of vegetation, are formed in a kind of moisture. They include very active elements and draw an inex-

haustible power from those completed works of which God rested on the seventh day.

40. Let us then distinguish the works of God, which up to this moment are produced, from those works from which he rested on the seventh day. There are even those who are of the opinion that only the world itself was made by God, and that all that followed the creation of the world came about naturally and in accordance with the order that God has established, but that God has ceased from all creative activity. Against such an opinion may be offered these words of our Lord: "My father has never ceased working, and I too must be at work." (John 5:17) And so no one would suppose that the Father acted within Himself and not in the world, he added: "The Father loves the Son, and discloses to him all that he himself does . . . just as the Father bids the dead rise up and give them life, so the Son gives life to whomsoever he will." (John 5:20-21)[11] By such activity are produced great and miraculous events and even the lesser things of this earth, as the Apostle says: (I Cor. 15:36,38). Therefore, let us believe and understand, if we can, that God continues to act in the world and that if God failed to sustain creation it would perish.

BOOK VII. ✠ 42. All the testimony of Holy Scripture, the truth of which no one doubts, except the infidel or the impious, has led us to the opinion that God at the beginning of time created all beings simultaneously; some already in their natural state, others in potentiality and in their causes, just as through his omnipotence He has made beings that exist in the present and those that are to come. He rested from that which He had made, so that He might create and govern by His providence the temporal order and generation of things, which He had completed with respect to all the fixed species, but not completed with respect to their propagation in time. Thus because it [creation] was completed, he rested, and because it was incomplete his work continues even up to now. And if this can be more clearly explained, I will support such an opinion rather than resist it.

BOOK IX. ✠ 32. Everything in nature proceeds uniformly in accordance with natural laws, by which the tendencies of living beings are determined and which even an evil will cannot escape. The elements of the physical world have each their distinctive properties and character, which either enable it or leave it incapable of determining what it can or cannot do. Just as from the beginning of things, all things which are brought forth come forth and develop in their time, and die and disappear, each according to its kind. For this reason a bean is not produced from a grain of wheat, nor a grain of wheat from a bean, nor man from an animal, or an animal from a man. But above the whole movement and development of the things of nature is the power of the Creator which can do otherwise with all these things than their seminal reasons determine, not that He had not implanted in them the possibility of conforming to his purposes. For the omnipotence of God rests upon His wisdom and goodness and not upon blind power; and He caused to be produced at the proper time that which He has established as possible. Different, therefore, is the manner of things which causes this plant to grow in this way, another in that way; one bears fruit at one age, the other at another; similarly man has the gift of speech, the animal does not. These and similar rules of reason exist not only in God, but by Him they have been implanted in things and created with them. So that a stick dug out of the earth, polished, and without any roots, without earth and water might suddenly flower and be covered with fruit (Num. 17:8), or that a woman sterile in her youth should bear a child in her old age (Gen. 18:11; Gen. 21:2), or that an ass should talk (Num. 22:28), or anything else of this kind. He gave the creatures He made the power to accomplish these things (nor from them would He make anything which He had not ordained, since nothing exists in itself or is stronger than He): moreover by another means he provided that these have no powers in the natural order apart from those with which they had been created, so that their nature would remain subject to a stronger will.

THE ENCHIRIDION ✠ It is enough for the Christian to believe that the only cause of all created things, whether heavenly or earthly, whether visible or invisible, is the goodness of the Creator, the one true God and that nothing exists but Himself that does not derive its existence from Him; and that He is the Trinity—to wit, the Father, and the Son begotten of the Father, and the Holy Spirit proceeding from the same Father, but one and the same Spirit of Father and Son.

By the Trinity, thus supremely and equally and unchangeably good, all things were created; and these are not supremely and equally and unchangeably good, but yet they are good, even taken separately. Taken as a whole, however, they are very good, because their ensemble constitutes the universe in all its wonderful order and beauty.

And in the universe, even that which is called evil, when it is regulated and put in its own place, only enhances our admiration of the good; for we enjoy and value the good more when we compare it with the evil. For the Almighty God, who, as even the heathen acknowledge, has supreme power over all things, being Himself supremely good, would never permit the existence of anything evil among His works, if He were not so omnipotent and good that He can bring good even out of evil. For what is that which we call evil but the absence of good? In the bodies of animals, disease and wounds mean nothing but the absence of health; for when a cure is effected, that does not mean that the evils which were present—namely, the disease and wounds—go away from the body and dwell elsewhere: they altogether cease to exist; for the wound or disease is not a substance but a defect in the fleshly substance—the flesh itself being a substance, and therefore something good, of which those evils—that is, privations of the good which we call health—are accidents. Just in the same way, what are called vices in the soul are nothing but privations of natural good. And when they are cured, they are not transferred elsewhere: when they cease to exist in the healthy soul, they cannot exist anywhere else.

All things that exist, therefore, seeing that the Creator of them all is supremely good, are themselves good. But because they are not, like their Creator, supremely and unchangeably good, their good may be diminished and increased. But for good to be diminished is an evil, although, however much it may be diminished, it is necessary, if the being is to continue, that some good should remain to constitute the being. For however small or of whatever kind the being may be, the good which makes it a being cannot be destroyed without destroying the being itself. An uncorrupted nature is justly held in esteem. But if, still further, it be incorruptible, it is undoubtedly considered of still higher value. When it is corrupted, however, its corruption is an evil, because it is deprived of some sort of good. For if it be deprived of no good, it receives no injury; but it does receive injury, therefore it is deprived of good, Therefore so long as a being is in process of corruption, there is in it some good of which it is being deprived; and if a part of the being should remain which cannot be corrupted, this will certainly be an incorruptible being, and accordingly the process of corruption will result in the manifestation of this great good. But if it does not cease to be corrupted, neither can it cease to possess good of which corruption may deprive it. But if it should be thoroughly and completely consumed by corruption, there will then be no good left, because there will be no being. Wherefore corruption can consume the good only by consuming the being. Every being, therefore, is a good; a great good if it can not be corrupted; a little good, if it can; but in any case only the foolish or ignorant will deny that it is a good. And if it be wholly consumed by corruption, then the corruption itself must cease to exist, as there is no being left in which it can dwell.

Accordingly there is nothing of what we call evil, if there be nothing good. But a good which is wholly without evil is a perfect good. A good, on the other hand, which contains evil is a faulty or imperfect good; and there can be no evil where there is no good. From all this we arrive at the curious result: that since every being, so far as it is a being, is good, when we say that a faulty being is an evil being, we just seem to say that what is good is evil, and that nothing but what is good can be evil, seeing that every being is good, and that no evil can exist except in a being. Nothing, then, can be evil except something which is good. And although this, when stated, seems to be a contradiction, yet the strictness of reasoning leaves us no escape from the conclusion. We must, however, beware of incurring the prophetic condemnation: "Woe unto them that call evil good, and good evil; that put darkness for light, and light for darkness; that put bitter for sweet, and sweet for bitter." And yet our Lord says: "An evil man out of the evil treasure of his heart bringeth forth that which is evil." Now, what is an evil man but an evil being? for a man is a being. Now if a man is a good thing because he is a being, what is an evil man but an evil good? Yet, when we accurately distinguish these two things, we find that it is not because he is a man that he is an evil, or because he is wicked that he is a good; but that he is a good because he is a man, and an evil because he is wicked. Whoever, then, says, "To be a man is an evil," or, "To be wicked is a good," falls under the prophetic denunciation: "Woe unto them that call evil good, and good evil!" For he condemns the work of God, which is the man, and praises the defect of man, which is wickedness. Therefore

259

every being, even if it be a defective one, in so far as it is a being is good, and in so far as it is defective is evil.

Accordingly, in the case of these contraries which we call good and evil, the rule of the logicians, that two contraries cannot be predicated at the same time of the same thing, does not hold. No weather is at the same time dark and bright: no food or drink is at the same time sweet and bitter: no body is at the same time and in the same place black and white: none is at the same time and in the same place deformed and beautiful. And this rule is found to hold in regard to many, indeed nearly all, contraries, that they cannot exist at the same time in any one thing. But although no one can doubt that good and evil are contraries, not only can they exist at the same time, but evil cannot exist without good, or in anything that is not good. Good, however, can exist without evil. For a man or an angel can exist without being wicked; but nothing can be wicked except a man or an angel: and so far as he is a man or an angel, he is good; so far as he is wicked, he is an evil. And these two contraries are so far coexistent, that if good did not exist in what is evil, neither could evil exist; because corruption could not have either a place to dwell in or a source to spring from, if there were nothing that could be corrupted; and nothing can be corrupted except what is good, for corruption is nothing else but the destruction of good. From what is good, then, evils arose, and except in what is good they do not exist; nor was there any other source from which any evil nature could arise. For if there were, then, in so far as this was a being, it was certainly a good: and a being which was incorruptible would be a great good; and even one which was corruptible must be to some extent a good, for only by corrupting what was good in it could corruption do it harm.

Nor can we doubt that God does well even in the permission of what is evil. For He permits it only in the justice of His judgment. And surely all that is just is good. Although, therefore, evil, in so far as it is evil, is not a good; yet the fact that evil as well as good exists, is a good. For if it were not a good that evil should exist, its existence would not be permitted by the omnipotent God, who without doubt can as easily refuse to permit what He does not wish as bring about what He does wish. And if we do not believe this, the very first sentence of our creed is endangered, wherein we profess to believe in God the Father Almighty. For He is not truly called Almighty if He cannot do whatsoever He pleases, or if the power of His almighty will is hindered by the will of any creature whatsoever.

THE CITY OF GOD ✠ BOOK XI ✠ CHAPTER 21 For what else is to be understood by that invariable refrain, "And God saw that it was good," than the approval of the work in its design, which is the wisdom of God? For certainly God did not in the actual achievement of the work first learn that it was good, but, on the contrary, nothing would have been made had it not first been known by Him. While, therefore, He sees that that is good which, had He not seen it before it was made, would never have been made, it is plain that He is not discovering, but teaching that it is good. Plato, indeed, was bold enough to say that, when the universe was completed, God was, as it were, elated with joy.[12] And Plato was not so foolish as to mean by this that God was rendered more blessed by the novelty of His creation; but he wishes thus to indicate that the work now completed met with its Maker's approval, as it had while yet in design. It is not as if the knowledge of God were of various kinds, knowing in different ways things which as yet are not, things which are, and things which have been. For not in our fashion does He look forward to what is future, nor at what is present, nor back upon what is past; but in a manner quite different and far and profoundly remote from our way of thinking. For He does not pass from this to that by transition of thought, but beholds all things with absolute unchangeableness; so that of those things which emerge in time, the future, indeed, are not yet, and the present are now, and the past no longer are; but all of these are by Him comprehended in His stable and eternal presence. Neither does He see in one fashion by the eye, in another by the mind, for He is not composed of mind and body; nor does His present knowledge differ from that which it ever was or shall be, for those variations of time, past, present, and future, though they alter our knowledge, do not affect His "with whom is no variableness, neither shadow of turning." [13] Neither is there any growth from thought to thought in the conceptions of Him in whose spiritual vision all things which He knows are at once embraced. For as without any movement that time can measure, He Himself moves all temporal things, so He knows all times with a knowledge that time cannot measure. And therefore He saw that what He had made was good, when He saw that it was good to make it. And when He saw it made, He had not on that account a twofold nor any way increased knowledge of it; as if He had less knowledge before He made what He saw. For certainly He would not be the perfect worker He is, unless His knowledge were so perfect as to receive no addition from His finished works. Wherefore, if the only object had been to inform us who made the light, it had been enough to say, "God made the light;" and if further information regarding the means by which it was made had been intended, it would have sufficed to say, "And God said, Let there be light, and there was light," that we might know not only that God had made the world, but also that He had made it by the word. But because it was right that three leading truths regarding the creature be intimated to us, viz., who made it, by what means, and why, it is written, "God said, Let there be light, and there was light. And God saw the light that it was good." If, then, we ask who made it, it was "God." If, by what means, He said "Let it be," and it was. If we ask, why He made it, "it was good." Neither is there any author more excellent than God, nor any skill more efficacious than the word of God, nor any cause better than that good might be created by the good God. This also Plato has assigned as the most sufficient reason for the creation of the world, that good works might be made by a good God; [14] whether he read this passage, or perhaps, was informed of these things by those who had read them, or, by his quick-sighted genius, penetrated to things spiritual and invisible through the things that are created, or was instructed regarding them by those who had discerned them.

CHAPTER 22 This cause, however, of a good creation, namely, the goodness of God—this cause, I say, so just and fit, which, when piously and carefully weighed, terminates all the controversies of those who inquire into the origin of the world, has not been recognised by some heretics,[15] because there are, forsooth, many things, such as fire, frost, wild beasts, and so forth, which do not suit but injure this thin-blooded and frail mortality of our flesh, which is at present under just punishment. They do not consider how admirable these things are in their own places, how excellent in their own natures, how beautifully adjusted to the rest of creation, and how much grace they contribute to the universe by their own contributions as to a commonwealth; and how serviceable they are even to ourselves, if we use them with a knowledge of their fit adaptations—so that even poisons, which are destructive when used injudiciously, become wholesome and medicinal when used in conformity with their qualities and design; just as, on the other hand, those things which give us pleasure, such as food, drink, and the light of the sun, are found to be hurtful when immoderately or unseasonably used. And thus divine providence admonishes us not foolishly to vituperate things but to investigate their utility with care; and, where our mental capacity or infirmity is at fault, to believe that there is a utility, though hidden, as we have experienced that there were other things which we all but failed to discover. For this concealment of the use of things is itself either an exercise of our humility or a levelling of our pride; for no nature at all is evil, and this is a name for nothing but the want of good. But from things earthly to things heavenly, from the visible to the invisible, there are some things better than others; and for this purpose are they unequal, in order that they might all exist. Now God is in such sort a great worker in great things, that He is not less in little things—for these little things are to be measured not by their own greatness (which does not exist) but by the wisdom of their Designer; as, in the visible appearance of a man, if one eyebrow be shaved off, how nearly nothing is taken from the body, but how much from the beauty—for that is not constituted by bulk but by the proportion and arrangement of the members. But we do not greatly wonder that persons, who suppose that some evil nature has been generated and propagated by a kind of opposing principle proper to it, refuse to admit that the cause of the creation was this, that the good God produced a good creation. For they believe that He was driven to this enterprise of creation by the urgent necessity of repulsing the evil that warred against Him, and that He mixed His good nature with the evil for the sake of restraining and conquering it; and that this nature of His, being thus shamefully polluted and most cruelly oppressed and held captive, He labours to cleanse and deliver it, and with all His pains does not wholly succeed; but such part of it as could not be cleansed from that defilement is to serve as a prison and chain of the conquered and incarcerated enemy. The Manichaeans would not drivel, or rather, rave in such a style as this, if they believed the nature of God to be, as it is, unchangeable and absolutely incorruptible and subject to no injury; and if, moreover, they held in Christian sobriety, that the soul which has shown itself capable of being altered for the worse by its own will, and of being corrupted by sin, and so, of being deprived of the light of eternal truth—that this soul, I say, is not a part of God, nor of the same nature as God, but is created by Him, and is far different from its Creator.

CHAPTER 23 But it is much more surprising that some even of those who, with ourselves, believe that there is one only source of all things, and that no nature which is not divine can exist unless originated by that Creator, have yet refused to accept with a good and simple faith this so good and simple a reason of the world's creation, that a good God made it good; and that the things created, being different from God, were inferior to Him, and yet were good, being created by none other than Him. But they say that souls, though not, indeed, parts of God, but created by Him, sinned by abandoning God: that in proportion to their various sins, they merited different degrees of debasement from heaven to earth, and diverse bodies as prison-houses; and that his is the world, and this the cause of its creation, not the production of good things, but the restraining of evil. Origen is justly blamed for holding this opinion. For in the books which he entitles Περὶ ἀρχῶν, that is, *Of orgins*, this is his sentiment, this is his utterance. And I cannot sufficiently express my astonishment, that a man so erudite and well versed in ecclesiastical literature, should not have observed, in the first place, how opposed this is to the meaning of this authoritative Scripture, which, in recounting all the works of God, regularly adds, "And God saw that it was good;" and, when all were completed, inserts the words, "And God saw everything that he had made, and, behold, it was very good." [16] Was it not obviously meant to be understood that there was no other cause of the world's creation than that good creatures whould be made by a good God? In this creation, had no one sinned, the world would have been filled and beautified with nature's good without exception; and though there is sin, all things are not therefore full of sin, for the great majority of the heavenly inhabitants preserve their nature's integrity. And the sinful will, though it violated the order of its own nature, did not on that account escape the laws of God, who justly orders all things for good. For as the beauty of a picture is increased by well-managed shadows, so, to the eye that has skill to discern it, the universe is beautified even by sinners, though, considered by themselves, their deformity is a sad blemish.

BOOK XII ✛ CHAPTER 5 All natures, then, inasmuch as they are, and have therefore a rank and species of their own and a kind of internal harmony, are certainly good. And when they are in the places assigned to them by the order of their nature, they preserve such being as they have received. And those things which have not received everlasting being, are altered for better or for worse, so as to suit the wants and motions of those things to which the Creator's law has made them subservient; and thus they tend in the divine providence to that end which is embraced in the general scheme of the government of the universe. So that, though the corruption of transitory and perishable things brings them to utter destruction, it does not prevent their producing that which was designed to be their result. And this being so, God, who supremely is and who therefore created every being which has not supreme existence (for that which was made of nothing could not be equal to Him, and indeed could not be at all had He not made it), is not to be found fault with on account of the creature's faults, but is to be praised in view of the natures He had made.

BOOK XIV ✠ CHAPTER 10 But it is a fair question, whether our first parent or first parents (for there was a marriage of two), before they sinned, experienced in their animal body such emotions as we shall not experience in the spiritual body when sin has been purged and finally abolished. For if they did, then how were they blessed in that boasted place of bliss, Paradise? For who that is affected by fear or grief can be called absolutely blessed? And what could those persons fear or suffer in such affluence of blessings, where neither death nor ill-health was feared, and where nothing was wanting which a good will could desire, and nothing present which could interrupt man's mental or bodily enjoyment? Their love to God was unclouded, and their mutual affection was that of faithful and sincere marriage; and from this love flowed a wonderful delight, because they always enjoyed what was loved. Their avoidance of sin was tranquil; and, so long as it was maintained, no other ill at all could invade them and bring sorrow. Or did they perhaps desire to touch and eat the forbidden fruit, yet feared to die; and thus both fear and desire already, even in that blissful place, preyed upon those first of mankind? Away with the thought that such could be the case where there was no sin! And, indeed, this is already sin, to desire those things which the law of God forbids and to abstain from them through fear of punishment, not through love of righteousness. Away, I say, with the thought, that before there was any sin, there should already have been committed regarding that fruit the very sin which our Lord warns us against regarding a women: "Whosoever looketh on a woman to lust after her hath committed adultery with her already in his heart." [17] As happy, then, as were these our first parents, who were agitated by no mental perturbations and annoyed by no bodily discomforts, so happy should the whole human race have been, had they not introduced that evil which they have transmitted to their posterity, and had none of their descendants committed iniquity worthy of damnation; but this original blessedness continuing until, in virtue of that benediction which said, "Increase and multiply," [18] the number of the predestined saints should have been completed, there would then have been bestowed that higher felicity which is enjoyed by the most blessed angels—a blessedness in which there should have been a secure assurance that no one would sin, and no one die; and so should the saints have lived, after no taste of labour, pain, or death, as now they live in the resurrection, after they have endured all these things.

CHAPTER 11 But because God foresaw all things and was therefore not ignorant that man also would fall, we ought to consider this holy city in connection with what God foresaw and ordained and not according to our own ideas, which do not embrace God's ordination. For man, by his sin, could not disturb the divine counsel nor compel God to change what He had decreed; for God's foreknowledge had anticipated both—that is to say, both how evil the man whom he had created good should become and what good He Himself should even then derive from him. For though God is said to change His determinations (so that in a tropical sense the Holy Scripture says even that God repented), [19] this is said with reference to man's expectation, or the order of natural causes, and not with reference to that which the Almighty had foreknown that He would do. Accordingly God, as it is written, made man upright, [20] and consequently with a good will. For if he had not had a good will, he could not have been upright. The good will, then is the work of God; for God created him with it. But the first evil will, which preceded all man's evil acts, was rather a kind of falling away from the work of God to its own works than any positive work. And therefore the acts resulting were evil, not having God, but the will itself for their end; so that the will or the man himself, so far as his will is bad, was as it were the evil tree bringing forth evil fruit. Moreover, the bad will, though it be not in harmony with, but opposed to, nature, inasmuch as it is a vice or blemish, yet it is true of it as of all vice, that it cannot exist except in a nature, and only in a nature created out of nothing, and not in that which the Creator has begotten of Himself, as He begot the Word, by whom all things were made. For though God formed man of the dust of the earth, yet the

266

earth itself, and every earthly material, is absolutely created out of nothing; and man's soul, too, God created out of nothing, and joined to the body, when He made a man. But evils are so thoroughly overcome by good, that though they are permitted to exist, for the sake of demonstrating how the most righteous foresight of God can make a good use even of them, yet good can exist without evil, as in the true and supreme God Himself and as in every invisible and visible celestial creature that exists above this murky atmosphere; but evil cannot exist without good, because the natures in which evil exists, in so far as they are natures, are good. And evil is removed, not by removing any nature or part of a nature, which had been introduced by the evil, but by healing and correcting that which had been vitiated and depraved. The will, therefore, is then truly free, when it is not the slave of vices and sins. Such was it given us by God; and this being lost by its own fault, can only be restored by Him who was able at first to give it. And therefore the truth says, "If the Son shall make you free, ye shall be free indeed"; [21] which is equivalent to saying, If the Son shall save you, ye shall be saved indeed. For He is our Liberator, inasmuch as He is our Saviour.

Man then lived with God for his rule in a paradise at once physical and spiritual. For neither was it a paradise only physical for the advantage of the body, and not also spiritual for the advantage of the mind; nor was it only spiritual to afford enjoyment to man by his internal sensations, and not also physical to afford him enjoyment through his external senses. But obviously it was both for both ends. But after that proud and therefore envious angel (of whose fall I have said as much as I was able in the eleventh and twelfth books of this work, as well as that of his fellows, who, from being God's angels, became his angels), preferring to rule with a kind of pomp of empire rather than to be another's subject, fell from the spiritual Paradise, and essaying to insinuate his persuasive guile into the mind of man, whose unfallen condition provoked him to envy now that himself was fallen, he chose the serpent as his mouthpiece in that bodily Paradise in which it and all other earthly animals were living with those two human beings, the man and his wife, subject to them, and harmless; and he chose the serpent because, being slippery and moving in tortuous windings, it was suitable for his purpose. And this animal being subdued to his wicked ends by the presence and superior force of his angelic nature, he abused as his intrument, and first tried his deceit upon the woman, making his assault upon the weaker part of that human alliance, that he might gradually gain the whole, and not supposing that the man would readily give ear to him, or be deceived, but that he might yield to the error of the woman. For as Aaron was not induced to agree with the people when they blindly wished him to make an idol, and yet yielded to constraint; and as it is not credible that Solomon was so blind as to suppose that idols should be worshipped, but was drawn over to such sacrilege by the blandishments of women; so we cannot believe that Adam was deceived, and supposed the devil's word to be truth, and therefore transgressed God's law, but that he by the drawings of kindred yielded to the woman, the husband to the wife, the one human being to the only other human being. For not without significance did the apostle say "And Adam was not deceived, but the woman being deceived was in the transgression"; [22] but he speaks thus, because the woman accepted as true what the serpent told her, but the man could not bear to be severed from his only companion, even though this involved a partnership in sin. He was not on this account less culpable, but sinned with his eyes open. And so the apostle does not say, "He did not sin," but "He was not deceived." For he shows that he sinned when he says, "By one man sin entered into the world," [23] and immediately after more distinctly, "In the likeness of Adam's transgression." But he meant that those are deceived who do not judge that which they do to be sin; but he knew. Otherwise how were it true "Adam was not deceived?" But having as yet no experience of the divine severity, he was possibly deceived in so far as he thought his sin venial. And consequently he was not deceived as the woman was deceived, but he was deceived as to the judgment which would be passed on his apology: "The woman whom thou gavest to be with me, she gave me of the tree, and I did eat." [24] What need of saying more? Although they were not both deceived by credulity, yet both were entangled in the snares of the devil and taken by sin.

CHAPTER 12 If any one finds a difficulty in understanding why other sins do not alter human nature as it was altered by the transgression of those first human beings, so that on account of it this nature is subject to the great corruption we feel and see, and to death, and is distracted and tossed with so many furious and contending emotions, and is certainly far different from what it was before sin, even though it were then lodged in an animal body—if, I say, any one is moved by this, he ought not to think that that sin was a small and light one because it was committed about food, and that not bad nor noxious, except because it was forbidden; for in that spot of singular felicity God could not have created and planted any evil thing. But by the precept He gave, God commended obedience, which is, in a sort, the mother and guardian of all the virtues in the reasonable creature, which was so created that submission is advantageous to it, while the fulfilment of its own will in preference to the Creator's is destruction. And as this commandment enjoining abstinence from one kind of food in the midst of great abundance of other kinds was so easy to keep—so light a burden to the memory—and, above all, found no resistance to its observance in lust, which only afterwards sprung up as the penal consequence of sin, the iniquity of violating it was all the greater in proportion to the ease with which it might have been kept.

CHAPTER 13 Our first parents fell into open disobedience because already they were secretly corrupted; for the evil act had never been done had not an evil will preceded it. And what is the origin of our evil will but pride? "For pride is the beginning of sin." [25] And what is pride but the craving for undue exaltation? And this is undue exaltation, when the soul abandons Him to whom it ought to cleave as its end and becomes a kind of end to itself. This happens when it becomes its own satisfaction. And it does so when it falls away from that unchangeable good which ought to satisfy it more than itself. This falling away is spontaneous; for if the will had remained stedfast in the love of that higher and changeless good by which it was illumined to intelligence and kindled into love, it would not have turned away to find satisfaction in itself and so become frigid and benighted; the woman would not have believed the serpent spoke the truth, nor would the man have preferred the request of his wife to the command of God, nor have supposed that it was a venial transgression to cleave to the partner of his life even in a partnership of sin. The wicked deed, then—that is to say, the transgression of eating the forbidden fruit—was committed by persons who were already wicked. That "evil fruit" [26] could be brought forth only by "a corrupt tree." But that the tree was evil was not the result of nature; for certainly it could become so only by the vice of the will, and vice is contrary to nature. Now nature could not have been depraved by vice had it not been made out of nothing. Consequently, that it is a nature, this is because it is made by God; but that it falls away from Him, this is because it is made out of nothing. But man did not so fall away (*defecit*) as to become absolutely nothing; but being turned towards himself, his being became more contracted than it was when he clave to Him who supremely is. Accordingly, to exist in himself, that is, to be his own satisfaction after abandoning God, is not quite to become a nonentity but to approximate to that. And therefore the holy Scriptures designate the proud by another name, "Self-pleasers." For it is good to have the heart lifted up, yet not to one's self, for this is proud, but to the Lord, for this is obedience, and can be the act only of the humble. There is, therefore, something in humility which, strangely enough exalts the heart, and something in pride which debases it. This seems, indeed, to be contradictory, that loftiness should debase and lowliness exalt. But pious humility enables us to submit to what is above us; and nothing is more exalted above us than God; and therefore humility, by making us subject to God, exalts us. But pride, being a defect of nature, by the very act of refusing subjection and revolting from Him who is supreme, falls to a low condition; and then comes to pass what is written: "Thou castedst them down when they lifted up themselves." [27] For he does not say, "When they had been lifted up," as if first they were exalted, and then afterwards cast down; but "when they lifted up themselves" even then they were cast down; that is to say, the very lifting up was already a fall. And therefore it is that humility is specially recommended to the City of God as it sojourns in this world, and is specially exhibited in the City of God, and in the person of Christ its King; while the contrary vice of pride, according to the testimony of the sacred writings, specially rules his adversary the devil. And certainly this is the great difference which distinguishes the two cities of which we speak, the one being the society of the godly men, the other of the ungodly, each associated with the angels that adhere to their party, and the one guided and fashioned by love of self, the other by love of God.

The devil, then, would not have ensnared man in the open and manifest sin of doing what God had forbidden, had man not already begun to live for himself. It was this that made him listen with pleasure to the words, "Ye shall be as gods," [28] which they would much more readily have accomplished by obediently adhering to their supreme and true end than by proudly living to themselves. For created gods are gods not by virtue of what is in themselves but by a participation of the true God. By craving to be more, man becomes less; and by aspiring to be self-sufficing, he fell away from Him who truly suffices him. Accordingly, this wicked desire which prompts man to please himself as if he were himself light, and which thus turns him away from that light by which, had he followed it, he would himself have become light—this wicked desire, I say, already secretly existed in him, and the open sin was but its consequence. For that is true which is written, "Pride goeth before destruction, and before honour is humility:" [29] that is to say, secret ruin precedes open ruin, while the former is not counted ruin. For who counts exaltation ruin, though no sooner is the Highest forsaken than a fall is begun? But who does not recognise it as ruin, when there occurs an evident and indubitable transgression of the commandment? And consequently, God's prohibition had reference to such an act as, when committed, could not be defended on any pretense of doing what was righteous. And I make bold to say that it is useful for the proud to fall into an open and indisputable transgression and so displease themselves, as already, by pleasing themselves, they had fallen. For Peter was in a healthier condition when he wept and was dissatisfied with himself, than when he boldly presumed and satisfied himself. And this is averred by the sacred Psalmist when he says, "Fill their faces with shame, that they may seek Thy name, O Lord";[30] that is, that they who have pleased themselves in seeking their own glory may be pleased and satisfied with Thee in seeking Thy glory.

CHAPTER 14 But it is a worse and more damnable pride which casts about for the shelter of an excuse even in manifest sins, as these our first parents did, of whom the woman said, "The serpent beguiled me, and I did eat;" and the man said, "The woman whom Thou gavest to be with me, she gave me of the tree, and I did eat." [31] Here there is no word of begging pardon, no word of entreaty for healing. For though they do not, like Cain, deny that they have perpetrated the deed, yet their pride seeks to refer its wickedness to another—the woman's pride to the serpent, the man's to the woman. But where there is a plain transgression of a divine commandment, this is rather to accuse than to excuse oneself. For the fact that the woman sinned on the serpent's persuasion and the man at the woman's offer, did not make the transgression less, as if there were any one whom we ought rather to believe or yield to than God.

CHAPTER 15 Therefore, because the sin was a despising of the authority of God—who had created man; who had made him in His own image; who had set him above the other animals; who had placed him in Paradise; who had enriched him with abundance of every kind and of safety; who had laid upon him neither many, nor great, nor difficult commandments, but, in order to make a wholesome obedience easy to him, had given him a single very brief and very light precept by which He reminded that creature whose service was to be free that He was Lord—it was just that condemnation followed, and condemnation such that man, who by keeping the commandments should have been spiritual even in his flesh, became fleshly even in his spirit; and as in his pride he had sought to be his own satisfaction, God in His justice abandoned him to himself, not to live in the absolute independence he affected, but instead of the liberty he desired, to live dissatisfied with himself in a hard and miserable bondage to him to whom by sinning he had yielded himself, doomed in spite of himself to die in body as he had willingly become dead in spirit, condemned even to eternal death (had not the grace of God delivered him) because he had forsaken eternal life. Whoever thinks such punishment either excessive or unjust shows his inability to measure the great iniquity of sinning where sin might so easily have been avoided. For as Abraham's obedience is with justice pronounced to be great, because the thing commanded, to kill his son, was very difficult, so in Paradise the disobedience was the greater, because the difficulty of that which was commanded was imperceptible. And as the obedience of the second Man was the more laudable because He became obedient even "unto death," [32] so the disobedience of the first man was the more detestable because he became disobedient even unto death. For where the penalty annexed to disobedience is great, and the thing commanded by the Creator is easy, who can sufficiently estimate how great a wickedness it is, in a matter so easy, not to obey the authority of so great a power, even when that power deters with so terrible a penalty?

In short, to say all in a word, what but disobedience was the punishment of disobedience in that sin? For what else is man's misery but his own disobedience to himself, so that in consequence of his not being willing to do what he could do, he now wills to do what he cannot? For though he could do all things in Paradise before he sinned, yet he wished to do only what he could do, and therefore he could do all things he wished. But now, as we recognize in his offspring, and as divine Scripture testifies, "Man is like to vanity." [33] For who can count how many things he wishes which he cannot do, so long as he is disobedient to himself, that is, so long as his mind and his flesh do not obey his will? For in spite of himself his mind is both frequently disturbed, and his flesh suffers, and grows old, and dies; and in spite of ourselves we suffer whatever else we suffer, and which we would not suffer if our nature absolutely and in all its parts obeyed our will. But is it not the infirmities of the flesh which hamper it in its service? Yet what does it matter *how* its service is hampered, so long as the fact remains, that by the just retribution of the sovereign God whom we refused to be subject to and serve, our flesh, which was subjected to us, now torments us by insubordination although our disobedience brought trouble on ourselves, not upon God?

NOTES (The Created Universe)

[1] For the most comprehensive and authoritative analysis of the *Confessions*, see the recently published work of Pierre Courcelle *Les "Confessions" de Saint Augustin*, Etudes Augustiniennes, Paris, 1963.

[2] E. Portalié, S. J., *A Guide to the Thought of Saint Augustine*, Chicago, 1960, p. 40.

[3] An excellent and appreciative study of the problem will be found in Robert Jordan's "Time and Contingency in St. Augustine," *Review of Metaphysics*, March 1955.
For a critical evaluation of the Augustinian arguments on time see the article by J. N. Findlay in *Logic and Language* (First Series) ed. by Anthony Flew. Oxford: Basil Blackwell, 1955, pp. 41 ff.

[4] The full title of the work is *Enchiridion ad Laurentium sive de fide, spe et charitate* and it is sometimes rendered simply *Faith, Hope and Charity*.

[5] *distentionem* (extended, a spreading out)

[6] *distentio* (a thinning out of reality)

[7] Neo-Platonists

[8] meaning that at every instant it requires the support of God.

[9] Gen. 1:1-2.

[10] The translations that follow have been made from the text of Migne.

[11] The Scriptural quotations in this section are from the R. A. Knox translation of the *New Testament*, Sheed and Ward, New York, 1952.)

[12] The reference is to the *Timaeus*, 37 C., where he says, "When the parent Creator perceived this created image of the eternal gods in life and motion, He was delighted, and in His joy considered how He might make it still liker its model."

[13] Jas. 1:17.

[14] The passage referred to is in the *Timaeus*, 29 D.: "Let us say what was the cause of the Creator's forming this universe. He was good; and in the good

no envy is ever generated about anything whatever. Therefore, being free from envy, He desired that all things should, as much as possible, resemble Himself."

[15] The Manichaeans, to wit.

[16] Gen. 1:31.

[17] Matt. 5:28.

[18] Gen. 1:28.

[19] Gen. 6:6; I Sam. 15:11.

[20] Eccles. 7:29.

[21] John 8:36.

[22] I Tim. 2:14.

[23] Rom. 5:12

[24] Gen. 3:12.

[25] Ecclus. 10:13.

[26] Matt. 7:18.

[27] Ps. 72:18.

[28] Gen. 3:5.

[29] Prov. 18:12.

[30] Ps. 83:16.

[31] Gen. 3:12-13.

[32] Phil. 2:8.

[33] Ps. 144:4.

✠ ✠ ✠

MORAL PHILOSOPHY

✠ ✠ ✠

The first three selections in this section are concerned principally with the nature of virtue and more especially with the place
and the significance of the virtue of charity.

   *The Morals of the Catholic Church and the Morals of the
Manicheans* was written at Rome in 388. It is composed of two
books, the second of which is directed against both the morals of the
Manicheans and their account of the origin of evil. Book I, from
which this selection is taken, is restricted to certain features of the
morals of the Catholic Church. It is pointed out that man's chief
good and highest happiness is God. Virtue is then shown to be that
excellence of the soul by means of which man can follow after God
and attain Him as the Supreme Good. To follow after God means
to love God and to be united with Him. From this identification of
virtue with love or charity follows the fourfold division of virtue:
the cardinal virtues of temperance, fortitude, justice, and prudence.
The difference between the Greek conception of virtue and that
taught by Augustine should be noted. For the Greeks virtue was
'excellence' (arete) and a sufficient means for man to achieve goodness and the happy life. For Augustine virtue must be reinterpreted
in the light of charity or the love of God. Consequently, the

275

hierarchy of virtues which Aristotle developed to serve as a guide for the attainment of happiness must be supplemented by a hierarchy of the forms of love or what we spoke of previously as the order of love.

Letter 167, written in the spring of 415 to St. Jerome, is a further development and exposition of the virtue of charity, which will now be seen more clearly to be the very essence of the Augustinian ethics. In this letter Augustine is also concerned with ethical views of the Stoics. He rejects their doctrine of the equality of all sins and insists on the distinction of sins. He then proceeds to show that virtue or charity may be defined as "the love with which that which ought to be loved is loved."

The selection from *Christian Doctrine* develops the important distinction for the Augustinian ethics between use and enjoyment. The conclusion is drawn that God alone can be enjoyed and that all other things should only be used. From this distinction there follows an account of the order of love as the law of the moral life. God is to be loved above all else and to attain such a love and the perfection of the moral life, we require the theological virtues of faith, hope, and charity, the greatest of which is charity.

The brief excerpt from Book V of the *City of God* presents a defense of man's free will especially in its relation to the foreknowledge of God.

The next three selections bring out much more markedly the theological requirements for ethics. Each points up the necessity of grace in the moral life of man. *Grace and Free Will* was written in 426 and directed to the monks of Hadrumetum, now the city of Sousse in Tunisia. The treatise was written to allay the fears of the monks that the divine grace is incompatible with the freedom of man and to give a complete and comprehensive account of the nature of grace and its role in man's salvation. With the *The Predestination of the Saints* and *The Gift of Perseverance* it forms the principal refutation of the Semipelagian doctrine that Augustine combatted in his later years.* It contains one of the most vigorous defenses of the freedom of the will, and this takes on

---

*Semipelagianism is much less extreme than the Pelagian heresy which attacked the doctrine of original sin, held that man's freedom was absolute, and declared that man could acquire perfection and salvation without grace. The Semipelagian doctrine arose out of reaction to Augustine's teaching on grace, perseverance, and predestination. The Semipelagians accepted the need for grace but apparently believed that it could be obtained naturally through the good use of the will. Predestination they identified with God's foreknowledge that some men would persevere and others would not. They denied that God gave

added significance when we recall that the treatise was written during the Pelagian controversies and at a time therefore in which Augustine was most anxious to defend the necessity of grace. Both grace and free will are necessary then for the good life. Augustine proceeds to a denial that grace is ever given for our merits. Grace is essentially a gift of God and faith is that grace of God by which we are saved. Justification, then, is not by our good works but only through grace. From this it follows that salvation is dependent upon grace rather than upon merit or good works, and that grace fulfills the law and frees man's nature from sin. Augustine concludes his analysis by returning again to his favorite theme of charity. Especially in chapter 38 he observes the need we have for God's love and the relation of this love to grace and the law.

The selection from *The Predestination of the Saints* sets forth very briefly the distinction between grace and predestination and explains why grace (faith in this case) is not given to all.

The third selection in this group is taken from *The Gift of Perseverance.* This treatise like, *The Predestination of the Saints,* was directed against the Semipelagians of France and was written at approximately the same time (428-429). It is an extended analysis of the grace of perseverance, noting why it is given to some and not to others, its relation to the doctrine of predestination, and a further exposition of the nature of predestination.

The final selection is taken from the *City of God.* In brief excerpts from Books XIV and XV the origins of the two cities are described. The religious or philosophical origin is traced to man's two loves: love of God and love of self. The mystical origin is traced to Cain and Abel. To the former is ascribed the origin of the earthly city, to the latter the origin of the heavenly city. The end of the two cities is the theme of Book XIX. The evils of the earthly city are noted vividly and in some detail. The earthly city is contrasted in this respect with what Augustine describes as peace or the tranquillity of order which man can hope to attain in the life to come. After a discussion of the virtue of justice and the definition of a republic (*res publica*) in terms of love, the book reverts

---

man the power, i.e. the grace to persevere, nor did they consider perseverance itself to be a gift of God. The Semipelagians were treated with respect by Augustine who addressed them as brethren, and they in turn apparently had no intention of rejecting the teachings of the Church but only in correcting what they considered to be errors of interpretation by Augustine. Perhaps an oversimplified way of distinguishing between Pelagians and Semipelagians would be to say that the former were almost wholly naturalistic in their religious attitude, whereas the latter were only seminaturalistic.

again to the theme of peace. Man's sojourn in the earthly city is viewed as a pilgrimage which, for those who belong to the heavenly city through faith, will lead man to a life of true peace and eternal happiness. Those who belong wholly to the earthly city will inherit the second death of an eternal misery.

THE MORALS OF THE CATHOLIC CHURCH ✚ CHAPTER 3 *Happiness is in the enjoyment of man's chief good. Two conditions of the chief good: first, nothing is better than it; second, it cannot be lost against the will.* How then, according to reason, ought man to live? We all certainly desire to live happily; and there is no human being but assents to this statement almost before it is made. But the title 'happy' cannot, in my opinion, belong either to him who has not what he loves, whatever it may be, or to him who has what he loves if it is hurtful, or to him who does not love what he has, although it is good in perfection. For one who seeks what he cannot obtain suffers torture, and one who has got what is not desirable is cheated, and one who does not seek for what is worth seeking for is diseased. Now in all these cases the mind cannot but be unhappy, and happiness and unhappiness cannot reside at the same time in one man; so in none of these cases can the man be happy. I find, then, a fourth case, where the happy life exists—when that which is man's chief good is both loved and possessed. For what do we call enjoyment but having at hand the objects of love? And no one can be happy who does not enjoy what is man's chief good, nor is there any one who enjoys this who is not happy. We must then have at hand our chief good, if we think of living happily.

We must now inquire what is man's chief good, which of course cannot be anything inferior to man himself. For whoever follows after what is inferior to himself, becomes himself inferior. But every man is bound to follow what is best. Wherefore man's chief good is not inferior to man. Is it then something similar to man himself? It must be so, if there is nothing above man which he is capable of enjoying. But if we find something which is both superior to man and can be possessed by the man who loves it, who can doubt that in seeking for happiness man should endeavor to reach that which is more excellent than the being who makes the endeavor? For if happiness consists in the enjoyment of a good than which there is nothing better, which we call the chief good, how can a man be properly called happy who has not yet attained to his chief good? Or how can that be the chief good beyond which something better remains for us to arrive at? Such, then, being the chief good, it must be something which cannot be lost against the will. For no one can feel confident regarding a good which he knows can be taken from him, although he wishes to keep and cherish it. But if a man feels no confidence regarding the good which he enjoys how can he be happy while in such fear of losing it?

CHAPTER 4 *Man—What?* Let us then see what is better than man. This must necessarily be hard to find, unless we first ask and examine what man is. I am not now called upon to give a definition of man. The question here seems to me to be—since almost all agree, . . . that we are made up of soul and body—what is man? Is he both of these? or is he the body only, or the soul only? For although the things are two, soul and body, and although neither without the other could be called man, . . . still it is possible that one of these may be held to be man and may be called so. What then do we call man? Is he soul and body, as in a double harness, or like a centaur? Or do we mean the body only, as being in the service of the soul which rules it, as the word lamp denotes not the light and the case together, but only the case, yet it is on account of the light that it is so called? Or do we mean only the mind, and that on account of the body which it rules, as horseman means not the man and the horse, but the man only, and that as employed in ruling the horse? This dispute is not easy to settle; or, if the proof is plain, the statement requires time. This is an expenditure of time and strength which we need not incur. For whether the name man belongs to both or only to the soul, the chief good of man is not the chief good of the body; but what is the chief good either of both soul and body or of the soul only, that is man's chief good.

CHAPTER 5 *Man's chief good is not the chief good of the body only, but the chief good of the soul.* Now if we ask what is the chief good of the body, reason obliges us to admit that it is that by means of which the body comes to be in its best state. But of all the things which invigorate the body, there is nothing better or greater than the soul. The chief good of the body, then, is not bodily pleasure, not absence of pain, not strength, not beauty, not swiftness, or whatever else is usually reckoned among the goods of the body, but simply the soul. For all the things mentioned the soul supplies to the body by its presence, and, what is above them all, life. Hence I conclude that the soul is not the chief good of man, whether we give the name of man to soul and body together or to the soul alone. For as, according to reason, the chief good of the body is that which is better than the body and from which the body receives vigor and life, so whether the soul itself is man or soul and body both, we must discover whether there is anything which goes before the soul itself, in following which the soul comes to the perfection of good of which it is capable in its own kind. If such a thing can be found, all uncertainty must be at an end, and we must pronounce this to be really and truly the chief good of man.

If, again, the body is man, it must be admitted that the soul is the chief good of man. But clearly, when we treat of morals—when we inquire what manner of life must be held in order to obtain happiness—it is not the body to which the precepts are addressed, it is not bodily discipline which we discuss. In short, the observance of good *customs* belongs to that part of us which inquires and learns which are the prerogatives of the soul: so, when we speak of attaining to virtue, the question does not regard the body. But if it follows, as it does, that the body which is ruled over by a soul possessed of virtue is ruled both better and more honorably and is in its greatest perfection in consequence of the perfection of the soul which rightfully governs it, that which gives perfection to the soul will be man's chief good, though we call the body man. For if my coachman, in obedience to me, feeds and drives the horses he has charge of in the most satisfactory manner, himself enjoying the more of my bounty in proportion to his good conduct, can any one deny that the good condition of the horses, as well as that of the coachman, is due to me? So the question seems to me to be not, whether soul and body is man, or the soul only, or the body only, but what gives perfection to the soul; for when this is obtained, a man cannot but be either perfect or at least much better than in the absence of this one thing.

CHAPTER 6 *Virtue gives perfection to the soul; the soul obtains virtue by following God; following God is the happy life.* No one will question that virtue gives perfection to the soul. But it is a very proper subject of inquiry whether this virtue can exist by itself or only in the soul. Here again arises a profound discussion, needing lengthy treatment; but perhaps my summary will serve the purpose. God will, I trust, assist me, so that, notwithstanding our feebleness, we may give instruction on these great matters briefly as well as intelligibly. In either case, whether virtue can exist by itself without the soul or can exist only in the soul, undoubtedly in the pursuit of virtue the soul follows after something, and this must be either the soul itself or virtue or something else. But if the soul follows after itself in the pursuit of virtue, it follows after a foolish thing; for before obtaining virtue it is foolish. Now the height of a follower's desire is to reach that which he follows after. So the soul must either not wish to reach what it follows after, which is utterly absurd and unreasonable, or, in following after itself while foolish, it reaches the folly which it flees from. But if it follows after virtue in the desire to reach it, how can it follow what does not exist? or how can it desire to reach what it already possesses? Either, therefore, virtue exists beyond the soul, or if we are not allowed to give the name of virtue except to the habit and disposition of the wise soul, which can exist only in the soul, we must allow that the soul follows after something else in order that virtue may be produced in itself; for neither by following after nothing nor by following after folly, can the soul, according to my reasoning, attain to wisdom.

This something else then, by following after which the soul becomes possessed of virtue and wisdom, is either a wise man or God. But we have said already that it must be something that we cannot lose against our will. No one can think it necessary to ask whether a wise man, supposing we are content to follow after him, can be taken from us in spite of our unwillingness or our persistence. God then remains, in following after whom we live well, and in reaching whom we live both well and happily. If any deny God's existence, why should I consider the method of dealing with them, when it is doubtful whether they ought to be dealt with at all? At any rate, it would require a different starting-point, a different plan, a different investigation from what we are now engaged in. I am now addressing those who do not deny the existence of God, and who, moreover, allow that human affairs are not disregarded by Him. For there is no one, I suppose, who makes any profession of religion but will hold that divine Providence cares at least for our souls.

CHAPTER 15 *The Christian definition of the four virtues.* As to virtue leading us to a happy life, I hold virtue to be nothing else than perfect love of God. For the fourfold division of virtue I regard as taken from four forms of love. For these four virtues . . . I should have no hesitation in defining them: that temperance is love giving itself entirely to that which is loved; fortitude is love readily bearing all things for the sake of the loved object; justice is love serving only the loved object, and therefore ruling rightly; prudence is love distinguishing with sagacity between what hinders it and what helps it. The object of this love is not anything, but only God, the chief good, the highest wisdom, the perfect harmony. So we may express the definition thus: that temperance is love keeping itself entire and incorrupt for God; fortitude is love bearing everything readily for the sake of God; justice is love serving God only, and therefore ruling well all else, as subject to man; prudence is love making a right distinction between what helps it towards God and what might hinder it.

CHAPTER 19 *Description of the duties of temperance, according to the Sacred Scriptures.* It is now time to return to the four virtues, and to draw out and prescribe a way of life in conformity with them, taking each separately. First, then, let us consider temperance, which promises us a kind of integrity and incorruption in the love by which we are united to God. The office of temperance is in restraining and quieting the passions which make us pant for those things which turn us away from the laws of God and from the enjoyment of His goodness, that is, in a word, from the happy life. For there is the abode of truth; and in enjoying its contemplation and in cleaving closely to it, we are assuredly happy; but departing from this, men become entangled in great errors and sorrows. For, as the apostle says, "The root of all evils is covetousness; which some having followed, have made shipwreck of the faith, and have pierced themselves through with many sorrows." (I Tim. 6:10) . . .

Paul then says that covetousness is the root of all evils; and by covetousness the old law also intimates that the first man fell. Paul tells us to put off the old man and put on the new. By the old man he means Adam who sinned; and by the new man, him whom the Son of God took to Himself in consecration for our redemption. For he says in another place, "The first man is of the earth, earthy; the second man is from heaven, heavenly. As is the earthy, such are they also that are earthy; and as is the heavenly, such are they also that are heavenly. And as we have borne the image of the earthy, let us also bear the image of the heavenly" (I Cor. 15:47-49)—that is, put off the old man and put on the new. The whole duty of temperance, then, is to put off the old man and to be renewed in God—that is, to scorn all bodily delights and the popular applause, and to turn the whole love to things divine and unseen. Hence that following passage which is so admirable: "Though our outward man perish, our inward man is renewed day by day." (II Cor. 4:16) Hear, too, the prophet singing, "Create in me a clean heart, O God, and renew a right spirit within me." (Ps. 51:10) What can be said against such harmony except by blind barkers? . . .

CHAPTER 22 *Fortitude comes from the love of God.* On fortitude we must be brief. The love, then of which we speak, which ought with all sanctity to burn in desire for God, is called temperance, in not seeking for earthly things, and fortitude, in bearing the loss of them. But among all things which are possessed in this life, the body is, by God's most righteous laws, for the sin of old, man's heaviest bond, which is well known as a fact but most incomprehensible in its mystery. Lest this bond should be shaken and disturbed, the soul is shaken with the fear of toil and pain; lest it should be lost and destroyed, the soul is shaken with the fear of death. For the soul loves it from the force of habit, not knowing that by using it well and wisely its resurrection and reformation will, by the divine help and decree, be without any trouble made subject to its authority. But when the soul turns to God wholly in this love, it knows these things, and so will not only disregard death, but will even desire it.

Then there is the great struggle with pain. But there is nothing, though of iron hardness, which the fire of love cannot subdue. And when the mind is carried up to God in this love, it will soar above all torture free and glorious, with wings beauteous and unhurt, on which chaste love rises to the embrace of God. Otherwise God must allow the lovers of gold, the lovers of praise, the lovers of women to have more fortitude than the lovers of Himself, though love in those cases is rather to be called passion or lust. And yet even here we may see with what force the mind presses on with unflagging energy, in spite of all alarms, towards that it loves; and we learn that we should bear all things rather than forsake God, since those men bear so much in order to forsake Him.

CHAPTER 24 *Of justice and prudence.* What of justice that pertains to God? As the Lord says, "Ye cannot serve two masters," (Matt. 6:24) and the apostle denounces those who serve the creature rather than the Creator, was it not said before in the Old Testament, "Thou shalt worship the Lord thy God, and Him only shalt thou serve?" (Deut. 6:13) I need say no more on this, for these books are full of such passages. The lover, then, whom we are describing, will get from justice this rule of life, that he must with perfect readiness serve the God whom he loves, the highest good, the highest wisdom, the highest peace; and as regards all other things, must either rule them as subject to himself or treat them with a view to their subjection. This rule of life is, as we have shown, confirmed by the authority of both Testaments.

With equal brevity we must treat of prudence, to which it belongs to discern between what is to be desired and what to be shunned. Without this, nothing can be done of what we have already spoken of. It is the part of prudence to keep watch with most anxious vigilance, lest any evil influence should stealthily creep in upon us. Thus the Lord often exclaims, "Watch"; (Matt. 24:42) and He says, "Walk while ye have the light, lest darkness come upon you." (John 12:35) And then it is said, "Know ye not that a little leaven leaventh the whole lump?" (I Cor. 5:6) And no passage can be quoted from the Old Testament more expressly condemning this mental somnolence, which makes us insensible to destruction advancing on us step by step, than those words of the prophet, "He who despiseth small things shall fall by degrees." (Ecclus. 19:1) On this topic I might discourse at length did our haste allow of it. And did our present task demand it, we might perhaps prove the depth of these mysteries, by making a mock of which profane men in their perfect ignorance fall, not certainly by degrees, but with a headlong overthrow.

CHAPTER 25 *Four moral duties regarding the love of God, of which love the reward is eternal life and the knowledge of the truth.* I need say no more about right conduct. For if God is man's chief good, which you cannot deny, it clearly follows, since to seek the chief good is to live well, that to live well is nothing else but to love God with all the heart, with all the soul, with all the mind; and, as arising from this, that this love must be preserved entire and incorrupt, which is the part of temperance; that it give way before no troubles, which is the part of fortitude; that it serve no other, which is the part of justice; that it be watchful in its inspection of things lest craft or fraud steal in, which is the part of prudence. This is the one perfection of man, by which alone he can succeed in attaining to the purity of truth. This both Testaments enjoin in concert; this is commended on both sides alike. . . .

Let us then, as many as have in view to reach eternal life, love God with all the heart, with all the soul, with all the mind. For eternal life contains the whole reward in the promise of which we rejoice; nor can the reward precede desert, nor be given to a man before he is worthy of it. What can be more unjust that this, and what is more just than God? We should not then demand the reward before we deserve to get it. Here, perhaps, it is not out of place to ask what is eternal life; or rather let us hear the Bestower of it: "This," He says, "is life eternal, that they should know Thee, the true God, and Jesus Christ whom Thou hast sent." So eternal life is the knowledge of the truth. See, then, how perverse and preposterous is the character of those who think that their teaching of the knowledge of God will make us perfect, when this is the reward of those already perfect! What else, then, have we to do but first to love with full affection Him whom we desire to know? Hence arises that principle on which we have all along insisted, that there is nothing more wholesome in the Catholic Church than using authority before argument.

CHAPTER 26 *Love of ourselves and of our neighbor.* To proceed to what remains. It may be thought that there is nothing here about man himself, the lover. But to think this, shows a want of clear perception. For it is impossible for one who loves God not to love himself. For he alone has a proper love for himself who aims diligently at the attainment of the chief and true good; and if this is nothing else but God, as has been shown, what is to prevent one who loves God from loving himself? And then, among men should there be no bond of mutual love? Yea, verily; so that we can think of no surer step towards the love of God than the love of man to man.

Let the Lord then supply us with the other precept in answer to the question about the precepts of life; for He was not satisfied with one as knowing that God is one thing and man another, and that the difference is nothing less than that between the Creator and the thing created in the likeness of its Creator. He says then that the second precept is, "Thou shalt love they neighbor as thyself." (Matt. 22:39) Now you love yourself suitably when you love God better than yourself. What, then, you aim at in yourself you must aim at in your neighbor, namely, that he may love God with a perfect affection. For you do not love him as yourself, unless you try to draw him to that good which you yourself are pursuing. For this is the one good which has room for all to pursue it along with thee. From this precept proceed the duties of human society, in which it is hard to keep from error. But the first thing to aim at is, that we should be benevolent, that is, that we cherish no malice and no evil design against another. For man is the nearest neighbor of man. . . .

LETTER 167 ✠ From Augustine to Jerome, on James 2:10 ✠ CHAPTER 1:1. My brother Jerome, . . . I ask you, and in God's name beseech you, to do something which will, I believe, be of great service to many, namely, to explain to me . . . the sense in which we are to understand these words in the Epistle of James, "Whosoever shall keep the whole law, and yet offend in one point, he is guilty of all." . . .

3. . . . Does this affirm that the person who shall have committed theft, nay, who even shall have said to the rich man, "Sit thou here," and to the poor man, "Stand thou there," is guilty of homicide, and adultery, and sacrilege? And if he is not so, how can it be said that a person who has offended in one point has become guilty of all? Or are the things which the apostle said concerning the rich man and the poor man not to be reckoned among those things in one of which if any man offend he becomes guilty of all? But we must remember whence that sentence is taken, and what goes before it, and in what connection it occurs. "My brethren," he says, "have not the faith of our Lord Jesus Christ, the Lord of glory, with respect of persons. For if there come into your assembly a man with a gold ring, in goodly apparel, and there come in also a poor man in vile raiment; and ye have respect to him that weareth the gay clothing, and say unto him, Sit thou here in a good place; and say to the poor, Stand thou there, or sit here under my footstool: are ye not then partial in yourselves, and are become judges of evil thoughts? Hearken, my beloved brethren, hath not God chosen the poor of this world, rich in faith, and heirs of the kingdom which He hath promised to them that love Him? But ye have despised the poor." (Jas. 2:1-6) —inasmuch as you have said to the poor man, "Stand thou there," when you would have said to a man with a gold ring, "Sit thou here in a good place." And then there follows a passage explaining and enlarging upon that same conclusion: "Do not rich men oppress you by their power, and draw you before the judgment seats? Do not they blaspheme that worthy name by the which ye are called? If ye fulfil the royal law according to the Scripture, Thou shalt love thy neighbor as thyself, ye do well: but if ye have respect to persons, ye commit sin, and are

convinced of the law as transgressors." (Jas. 2:6-9) See how the apostle calls those transgressors of the law who say to the rich man, "Sit here," and to the poor, "Stand there." See how, lest they should think it a trifling sin to transgress the law in this one thing, he goes on to add: "Whosoever shall keep the whole law, and yet offend in one point, he is guilty of all. For He that said, Do not commit adultery, said also, Do not kill. Now if thou do not kill, yet, if thou commit adultery, thou art become a transgressor of the law," according to that which he had said: "Ye are convinced of the law as transgressors." Since these things are so, it seems to follow, unless it can be shown that we are to understand it in some other way, that he who says to the rich man, "Sit here," and to the poor, "Stand there," not treating the one with the same respect as the other, is to be judged guilty as an idolater, and a blasphemer, and an adulterer, and a murderer—in short,—not to enumerate all, which would be tedious,—as guilty of all crimes, since, "offending in one, he is guilty of all."

CHAPTER 2:4. But has he who has one virtue all virtues? and has he no virtues who lacks one? If this be true, the sentence of the apostle is thereby confirmed. But what I desire is to have the sentence explained, not confirmed, since of itself it stands more sure in our esteem than all the authority of philosophers could make it. And even if what has just been said concerning virtues and vices were true, it would not follow that therefore all sins are equal. For as to the inseparable coexistence of the virtues, this is a doctrine in regard to which, if I remember rightly, what, indeed, I have almost forgotten (though perhaps I am mistaken), all philosophers who affirm that virtues are essential to the right conduct of life are agreed. The doctrine of the equality of sins, however, the Stoics alone dared to maintain in opposition to the unanimous sentiments of mankind: an absurd tenet, which in writing against Jovinianus (a Stoic in this opinion, but an Epicurean in following after and defending pleasure) you have most clearly refuted from the Holy Scriptures. In that most delightful and noble dissertation you have made it abundantly plain that it has not been the doctrine of our authors, or rather of the Truth Himself, who has spoken through them, that all sins are equal. I shall now do my utmost in endeavoring, with the help of God, to show how it can be that, although the doctrine of philosophers concerning virtues is true, we are nevertheless not compelled to admit the Stoics' doctrine that all sins are equal. If I succeed, I will look for your approbation, and in whatever respect I come short, I beg you to supply my deficiencies.

5. Those who maintain that he who has one virtue has all and that he who lacks one lacks all, reason correctly from the fact that prudence cannot be cowardly, nor unjust, nor intemperate; for if it were any of these it would no longer be prudence. Moreover, if it be prudence only when it is brave, and just, and temperate, assuredly wherever it exists it must have the other virtues along with it. In like manner, also, courage cannot be imprudent, or intemperate, or unjust; temperance must of necessity be prudent, brave, and just; and justice does not exist unless it be prudent, brave, and temperate. Thus, wherever any one of these virtues truly exists, the others likewise exist; and where some are absent, that which may appear in some measure to resemble virtue is not really present.

6. There are, as you know, some vices opposed to virtues by a palpable contrast, as imprudence is the opposite of prudence. But there are some vices opposed to virtues simply because they are vices which, nevertheless, by a deceitful appearance resemble virtues; as, for example, in the relation, not of imprudence, but of craftiness to the said virtue of prudence. I speak here of that craftiness which is wont to be understood and spoken of in connection with the evilly disposed, not in the sense in which the word is usually employed in our Scriptures, where it is often used in a good sense, as "Be crafty as serpents," (Matt. 10:16) and again, "to give craftiness to the simple." (Prov. 1:4) It is true that among heathen writers one of the most accomplished of Latin authors, speaking of Catiline, has said: "Nor was there lacking on his part craftiness to guard against danger," using "craftiness" (astutia) in a good sense; but the use of the word in this sense is among them very rare, among us very common. So also in regard to the virtues classed under temperance. Extravagance is most manifestly opposite to the virtue of frugality; but that which the common people are wont to call niggardliness is indeed a vice, yet one which, not in its nature but by a very deceitful similarity of appearance, usurps the name of frugality. In the same manner injustice is by a palpable contrast opposed to justice; but the desire of avenging oneself is wont often to be a counterfeit of justice, but it is a vice. There is an obvious contrariety between courage and cowardice; but hardihood, though differing from courage in nature, deceives us by its resemblance to that virtue. Firmness is a part of virtue; fickleness is a vice far removed from and undoubtedly opposed to it; but obstinacy lays

claim to the name of firmness, yet is wholly different, because firmness is a virtue, and obstinacy is a vice.

7. To avoid the necessity of again going over the same ground, let us take one case as an example, from which all others may be understood. Catiline, as those who have written concerning him had means of knowing, was capable of enduring cold, thirst, hunger, and patience in fastings, cold, and watchings beyond what any one could believe, and thus he appeared, both to himself and to his followers, a man endowed with great courage. But this courage was not prudent, for he chose the evil instead of the good; was not temperate, for his life was disgraced by the lowest dissipation; was not just, for he conspired against his country; and therefore it was not courage, but hardihood usurping the name of courage to deceive fools; for if it had been courage, it would not have been a vice but a virtue, and if it had been a virtue, it would never have been abandoned by the other virtues, its inseparable companions.

8. On this account, when it is asked also concerning vices, whether where one exists all in like manner exist, or where one does not exist none exist, it would be a difficult matter to show this, because two vices are wont to be opposed to one virtue, one that is evidently opposed and another that bears an apparent likeness. Hence the hardihood of Catiline is the more easily seen not to have been courage, since it had not along with it other virtues; but it may be difficult to convince men that his hardihood was cowardice, since he was in the habit of enduring and patiently submitting to the severest hardships to a degree almost incredible. But perhaps on examining the matter more closely, this hardihood itself is seen to be cowardice, because he shrunk from the toil of those liberal studies by which true courage is acquired. Nevertheless, as there are rash men who are not guilty of cowardice, and there are cowardly men who are not guilty of rashness, and since in both there is vice, for the truly brave man neither ventures rashly nor fears without reason, we are forced to admit that vices are more numerous than virtues.

9. Accordingly, it happens sometimes that one vice is supplanted by another, as the love of money by the love of praise. Occasionally, one vice quits the field that more may take its place, as in the case of the drunkard, who, after becoming temperate in the use of drink, may come under the power of niggardliness and ambition. It is possible, therefore, that vices may give place to vices, not to virtues, as their successors, and thus they are more numerous. When one virtue, however, has entered, there will infallibly be

(since it brings all the other virtues along with it) a retreat of all vices whatsoever that were in the man; for all vices were not in him, but at one time so many, at another a greater or smaller number might occupy their place.

CHAPTER 3:10 We must inquire more carefully whether these things are so; for the statement that "he who has one virtue has all, and that all virtues are awanting to him who lacks one," is not given by inspiration, but is the view held by many men, ingenious, indeed, and studious, but still men. But I must avow that, in the case—I shall not say of one of those from whose name the word virtue is said to be derived but even of a woman who is faithful to her husband and who is so from a regard to the commandments and promises of God and, first of all, is faithful to Him—I do not know how I could say of her that she is unchaste or that chastity is no virtue or a trifling one. I should feel the same in regard to a husband who is faithful to his wife; and yet there are many such, none of whom I could affirm to be without any sins, and doubtless the sin which is in them, whatever it be, proceeds from some vice. Whence it follows that though conjugal fidelity in religious men and women is undoubtedly a virtue, for it is neither a nonentity nor a vice, yet it does not bring along with it all virtues, for if all virtues were there, there would be no vice; and if there were no vice, there would be no sin; but where is the man who is altogether without sin? Where, therefore, is the man who is without any vice, that is, fuel or root, as it were of sin, when he who reclined on the breast of the Lord says, "If we say that we have no sin, we deceive ourselves, and the truth is not in us"? . . . (I John 1:8)

11. Far be it, however, from any believer to think that so many thousands of the servants of Christ, who, lest they should deceive themselves, and the truth should not be in them, sincerely confess themselves to have sin, are altogether without virtue! For wisdom is a great virtue, and wisdom herself has said to man, "Behold the fear of the Lord, that is wisdom." (Job xxviii. 28.) Far be it from us, then, to say that so many and so great believing and pious men have not the fear of the Lord, which the Greeks call εὐσέβεια, or more literally and fully, θεοσέβεια. And what is the fear of the Lord but His worship? and whence is He truly worshipped except from love? Love, then, out of a pure heart, and a good conscience, and faith unfeigned, is the great and true virtue, because it is "the end of the commandment." (I Tim. 1:5) Deservedly is love said to be "strong as death," (Song of Sol. 8:6) be-

cause, like death, it is vanquished by none; or because the measure of love in this life is even unto death, as the Lord says, "Greater love hath no man than this, that a man lay down his life for his friends"; (John 15:13) or, rather, because, as death forcibly separates the soul from the senses of the body, so love separates it from fleshly lusts. Knowledge, when it is of the right kind, is the handmaid to love, for without love "knowledge puffeth up," (I Cor. 8:1) but where love, by edifying, has filled the heart, there knowledge will find nothing empty which it can puff up. Moreover, Job has shown what is that useful knowledge by defining it where, after saying, "The fear of the Lord, that is wisdom," he adds, "and to depart from evil is understanding." (Job 28:28) Why do we not say then that the man who has this virtue has all virtues, since "love is the fulfilling of the law?" (Rom. 13:10) Is it not true that the more love exists in a man, the more he is endowed with virtue; and the less love he has, the less virtue is in him, for love is itself virtue; and the less virtue there is in a man, so much the more vice will there be in him? Therefore, where love is full and perfect, no vice will remain.

12. The Stoics, therefore appear to me to be mistaken in refusing to admit that a man who is advancing in wisdom has any wisdom at all and in affirming that he only has it who has become altogether perfect in wisdom. They do not, indeed, deny that he has made progress, but they say that he is in no degree entitled to be called wise, unless, by emerging, so to speak, from the depths, he suddenly springs forth into the free air of wisdom. For, as it matters not when a man is drowning whether the depth of water above him be many stadia or only the breadth of a hand or finger, so they say, in regard to the progress of those who are advancing towards wisdom, that they are like men rising from the bottom of a whirlpool towards the air, but that unless they, by their progress, so escape as to emerge wholly from folly as from an overwhelming flood, they have not virtue and are not wise; but that, when they have so escaped, they immediately have wisdom in perfection, and not a vestige of folly whence any sin could be originated remains.

13. This simile, in which folly is compared to water and wisdom to air, so that the mind emerging, as it were, from the stifling influence of folly, breathes suddenly the free air of wisdom, does not appear to me to harmonize sufficiently with the authoritative statement of our Scriptures; a better simile, so far, at least, as illustration of spiritual things can be borrowed from material things, is that which compares vice or folly to darkness and virtue or wisdom to light. The way to wisdom is therefore not like that of a

man rising from the water into the air, in which, in the moment of rising above the surface of the water, he suddenly breathes freely but, like that of a man proceeding from darkness into light, on whom more light gradually shines as he advances. So long, therefore, as this is not fully accomplished, we speak of the man as of one going from the dark recesses of a vast cavern towards its entrance, who is more and more influenced by the proximity of the light as he comes nearer to the entrance of the cavern; so that whatever light he has proceeds from the light to which he is advancing, and whatever darkness still remains in him proceeds from the darkness out of which he is emerging. Therefore it is true that in the sight of God "shall no man living be justified," (Ps. 143:2) and yet that "the just shall live by his faith." (Hab. 2:4) On the one hand, "the saints are clothed with righteousness," (Job 29:14) one more, another less; on the other hand, no one lives here wholly without sin—one sins more, another less, and the best is the man who sins least.

CHAPTER 4:14. . . . Even though it were true that he who has one virtue has all virtues and that he who lacks one virtue has none, this would not involve the consequence that all sins are equal; for although it is true that where there is no virtue there is nothing right, it by no means follows that among bad actions one cannot be worse than another, or that divergence from that which is right does not admit of degrees. I think, however, that it is more agreeable to truth and consistent with the Holy Scriptures to say that what is true of the members of the body is true of the different dispositions of the soul . . . namely, that as in the same body one member is more fully shone upon by the light, another is less shone upon, and a third is altogether without light and remains in the dark under some impervious covering, something similar takes place in regard to the various dispositions of the soul. If this be so, then according to the manner in which every man is shone upon by the light of holy love, he may be said to have one virtue and to lack another virtue or to have one virtue in larger and another in smaller measure. For in reference to that love which is the fear of God, we may correctly say both that it is greater in one man than in another and that there is some of it in one man and none of it in another; we may also correctly say as to an individual that he has greater chastity than patience and that he has either virtue in a higher degree than he had yesterday, if he is making progress, or that he still lacks self-control but possesses, at the same time, a large measure of compassion.

15. To sum up generally and briefly the view which, so far as relates to holy living, I entertain concerning virtue—virtue is the love with which that which ought to be loved is loved. This is in some greater, in others less, and there are men in whom it does not exist at all; but in the absolute fulness which admits of no increase, it exists in no man while living on this earth; so long, however, as it admits of being increased there can be no doubt that, in so far as it is less than it ought to be, the shortcoming proceeds from vice. Because of this vice "there is not a just man upon earth that doeth good and sinneth not"; (Eccles. 7:20) . . . He, then, who sees aright, sees whence and when and where he must hope for that perfection to which nothing can be added. Moreover, if there had been no commandments, there would have been no means whereby a man might certainly examine himself and see from what things he ought to turn aside, whither he should aspire, and in what things he should find occasion for thanksgiving or for prayer. Great, therefore, is the benefit of commandments, if to free will so much liberty be granted that the grace of God may be more abundantly honored.

CHAPTER 5:16. If these things be so, how shall a man who shall keep the whole law, and yet offend in one point, be guilty of all? May it not be, that since the fulfilling of the law is that love wherewith we love God and our neighbor, on which commandments of love "hang all the law and the prophets," (Matt. 22:40) he is justly held to be guilty of all who violates that on which all hang? Now, no one sins without violating this love; "for this, thou shalt not commit adultery; thou shalt do no murder; thou shalt not steal; thou shalt not covet; and if there be any other commandment, it is briefly comprehended in this saying, Thou shalt love thy neighbor as thyself. Love worketh no ill to his neighbor: therefore love is the fulfilling of the law." (Rom. 13:9-10) No one, however, loves his neighbor who does not out of his love to God do all in his power to bring his neighbor also, whom he loves as himself, to love God, whom if he does not love, he neither loves himself nor his neighbor. Hence it is true that if a man shall keep the whole law, and yet offend in one point, he becomes guilty of all, because he does what is contrary to that love on which hangs the whole law. A man, therefore, becomes guilty of all by doing what is contrary to that on which all hang.

17. Why, then, may not all sins be said to be equal? May not the reason be that the transgression of the law of love is greater

in him who commits a more grievous sin and is less in him who commits a less grievous sin? And in the mere fact of his committing any sin whatever, he becomes guilty of all; but in committing a more grievous sin, or in sinning in more respects than one, he becomes more guilty; committing a less grievous sin, or sinning in fewer respects, he becomes less guilty—his guilt being thus so much the greater, the more he has sinned; the less, the less he has sinned. Nevertheless, even though it be only in one point that he offend, he is guilty of all, because he violates that love on which all hang. If these things be true, an explanation is by this means found, clearing up that saying of the man of apostolic grace, "In many things we offend all." (Jas. 3:2) For we all offend, but one more grievously, another more slightly, according as each may have committed a more grievous or a less grievous sin; every one being great in the practice of sin in proportion as he is deficient in loving God and his neighbor and, on the other hand, decreasing in the practice of sin in proportion as he increases in the love of God and of his neighbor. The more, therefore, that a man is deficient in love, the more is he full of sin. And perfection in love is reached when nothing of sinful infirmity remains in us. . . .

21. I have written at great length, which perhaps may have been tedious to you, as you, although approving of the statements now made, do not expect to be addressed as if you were but learning truths which you have been accustomed to teach to others. If, however, there be anything in these statements . . . which your erudite judgment condemns, I beseech you to point this out to me in your reply, and do not hesitate to correct my error. For I pity the man who, in view of the unwearied labor and sacred character of your studies, does not on account of them both render to you the honor which you deserve and give thanks unto our Lord God by whose grace you are what you are. Wherefore, since I ought to be more willing to learn from any teacher the things of which to my disadvantage I am ignorant than prompt to teach any others what I know, with how much greater reason do I claim the payment of this debt of love from you, by whose learning ecclesiastical literature in the Latin tongue has been, in the Lord's name, and by His help, advanced to an extent which had been previously unattainable. Especially, however, I ask attention to the sentence: "Whosoever shall keep the whole law, and offend in one point is guilty of all." If you know any better way, my beloved brother, in which it can be explained, I beseech you by the Lord to favor us by communicating to us your exposition.

C HRISTIAN DOCTRINE ✤ BOOK I ✤ CHAPTER 2
What a thing is, and what a sign. 2. All instruction is either about things or about signs; but things are learnt by means of signs. I now use the word "thing" in a strict sense to signify that which is never employed as a sign of anything else: for example, wood, stone, cattle, and other things of that kind. . . . There are signs of another kind, those which are never employed except as signs: for example, words. No one uses words except as signs of something else; and hence may be understood what I call signs: those things, to wit, which are used to indicate something else. Accordingly, every sign is also a thing; for what is not a thing is nothing at all. Every thing, however, is not also a sign. . . .

CHAPTER 3 *Some things are for use, some for enjoyment.* 3. There are some things, then, which are to be enjoyed, others which are to be used, others still which enjoy and use. Those things which are objects of enjoyment make us happy. Those things which are objects of use assist, and (so to speak) support us in our efforts after happiness, so that we can attain the things that make us happy and rest in them. We ourselves, again, who enjoy and use these things, being placed among both kinds of objects, if we set ourselves to enjoy those which we ought to use, are hindered in our course and sometimes even led away from it; so that, getting entangled in the love of lower gratifications, we lag behind in, or even altogether turn back from, the pursuit of the real and proper objects of enjoyment.

CHAPTER 4 *Difference of use and enjoyment.* 4. For to enjoy a thing is to rest with satisfaction in it for its own sake. To use, on the other hand, is to employ whatever means are at one's disposal to obtain what one desires, if it is a proper object of desire; for an un-lawful use ought rather to be called an abuse. Suppose, then, we were wanderers in a strange country, and could not live happily away from our fatherland, and that we felt wretched in our wander-ing, and wishing to put an end to our misery, determined to return home. We find, however, that we must make use of some mode of conveyance, either by land or water, in order to reach that father-land where our enjoyment is to commence. But the beauty of the country through which we pass and the very pleasure of the motion charm our hearts, and turning these things which we ought to use into objects of enjoyment, we become unwilling to hasten the end of our journey; and becoming engrossed in a factitious delight, our thoughts are diverted from that home whose delights would make us truly happy. Such is a picture of our condition in this life of mortality. We have wandered far from God; and if we wish to return to our Father's home, this world must be used, not enjoyed, that so the invisible things of God may be clearly seen, being understood by the things that are made—that is, that by means of what is material and temporary we may lay hold upon that which is spiritual and eternal.

CHAPTER 5 *The Trinity the true object of enjoyment*. 5. The true objects of enjoyment, then, are the Father and the Son and the Holy Spirit, who are at the same time the Trinity, one Being, supreme above all, and common to all who enjoy Him, if He is an object, and not rather the cause of all objects, or indeed even if He is the cause of all. For it is not easy to find a name that will suitably express so great excellence, unless it is better to speak in this way: The Trinity, one God, of whom are all things, through whom are all things, in whom are all things. . . .

CHAPTER 6 *In what sense God is ineffable*. 6. Have I spoken of God, or uttered His praise, in any worthy way? Nay, I feel that I have done nothing more than desire to speak; and if I have said anything, it is not what I desired to say. How do I know this, except from the fact that God is unspeakable? But what I have said, if it had been unspeakable, could not have been spoken. And so God is not even to be called "unspeakable," because to say even this is to speak of Him. Thus there arises a curious contradiction of words, because if the unspeakable is what cannot be spoken of, it is not unspeakable if it can be called unspeakable. And this opposition of words is rather to be avoided by silence than to be explained away by speech. And yet God, although nothing worthy of His greatness can be said of Him, has condescended to accept the worship of men's mouths, and has desired us through the medium of our own words to rejoice in His praise. For on this principle it is that He is called *Deus* (God). For the sound of those two syllables in itself conveys no true knowledge of His nature; but yet all who know the Latin tongue are led, when that sound reaches their ears, to think of a nature supreme in excellence and eternal in existence.

CHAPTER 7 *What all men understand by the term God.* 7. For when the one supreme God of gods is thought of, even by those who believe that there are other gods, and who call them by that name, and worship them as gods, their thought takes the form of an endeavor to reach the conception of a nature, than which nothing more excellent or more exalted exists. And since men are moved by different kinds of pleasures, partly by those which pertain to the bodily senses, partly by those which pertain to the intellect and soul, those of them who are in bondage to sense think that either the heavens, or what appears to be most brilliant in the heavens, or the universe itself, is God of gods: or if they try to get beyond the universe, they picture to themselves something of dazzling brightness, and think of it vaguely as infinite, or of the most beautiful form conceivable; or they represent it in the form of the human body, if they think that superior to all others. Or if they think that there is no one God supreme above all the rest, but that there are many or even innumerable gods of equal rank, still these too they conceive as possessed of shape and form, according to what each man thinks the pattern of excellence. Those, on the other hand, who endeavor by an effort of the intelligence to reach a conception of God, place Him above all visible and bodily natures and even above all intelligent and spiritual natures that are subject to change. All, however, strive emulously to exalt the excellence of God: nor could any one be found to believe that any being to whom there exists a superior is God. And so all concur in believing that God is that which excels in dignity all other objects.

CHAPTER 8 *God to be esteemed above all else, because He is unchangeable wisdom.* 8. And since all who think about God think of Him as living, they only can form any conception of Him that is not absurd and unworthy who think of Him as life itself; and, whatever may be the bodily form that has suggested itself to them, recognize that it is by life it lives or does not live, and prefer what is living to what is dead; who understand that the living bodily form itself, however it may outshine all others in splendor, overtop them in size, and excel them in beauty, is quite a distinct thing from the life by which it is quickened; and who look upon the life as incomparably superior in dignity and worth to the mass which is quickened and animated by it. Then, when they go on to look into the nature of the life itself, if they find it mere nutritive life, without sensibility, such as that of plants, they consider it inferior to sentient life, such as that of cattle; and above this, again, they place intelligent life, such as that of men. And, perceiving that even this is subject to change, they are compelled to place above it again, that unchangeable life, which is not at one time foolish, at another time wise, but on the contrary is wisdom itself. For a wise intelligence, that is, one that has attained to wisdom, was previous to its attaining wisdom, unwise. But wisdom itself never was unwise, and never can become so. And if men never caught sight of this wisdom, they could never with entire confidence prefer a life which is unchangeably wise to one that is subject to change. This will be evident, if we consider that the very rule of truth by which they affirm the unchangeable life to be the more excellent, is itself unchangeable: and they cannot find such a rule, except by going beyond their own nature; for they find nothing in themselves that is not subject to change.

CHAPTER 9 *All acknowledge the superiority of unchangeable wisdom to that which is variable.* 9. Now, no one is so egregiously silly as to ask, "How do you know that a life of unchangeable wisdom is preferable to one of change?" For that very truth about which he asks, how I know it? is unchangeably fixed in the minds of all men and presented to their common contemplation. And the man who does not see it is like a blind man in the sun, whom it profits nothing that the splendor of its light, so clear and so near, is poured into his very eyeballs. The man, on the other hand, who sees, but shrinks from this truth, is weak in his mental vision from dwelling long among the shadows of the flesh. And thus men are driven back from their native land by the contrary blasts of evil habits, and pursue lower and less valuable objects in preference to that which they own to be more excellent and more worthy.

CHAPTER 10 *To see God, the soul must be purified.* 10. Wherefore, since it is our duty fully to enjoy the truth which lives unchangeably and since the triune God takes counsel in this truth for the things which He has made, the soul must be purified that it may have power to perceive that light and to rest in it when it is perceived. And let us look upon this purification as a kind of journey or voyage to our native land. For it is not by change of place that we can come nearer to Him who is in every place but by the cultivation of pure desires and virtuous habits.

CHAPTER 11 *Wisdom becoming incarnate, a pattern to us of purification.* 11. But of this we should have been wholly incapable, had not Wisdom condescended to adapt Himself to our weakness and to show us a pattern of holy life in the form of our own humanity. Yet, since we, when we come to Him, do wisely, He, when He came to us, was considered by proud men to have done very foolishly. And since we, when we come to Him, become strong, He, when He came to us, was looked upon as weak. But "the foolishness of God is wiser than men; and the weakness of God is stronger than men." (I Cor. 1:25) And thus, though Wisdom was Himself our home, He made Himself also the way by which we should reach our home.

CHAPTER 22 *God alone to be enjoyed.* 20. Among all these things, then, those only are the true objects of enjoyment which we have spoken of as eternal and unchangeable. The rest are for use, that we may be able to arrive at the full enjoyment of the former. We, however, who enjoy and use other things are things ourselves. For a great thing truly is man, made after the image and similitude of God, not as respects the mortal body in which he is clothed but as respects the rational soul by which he is exalted in honor above the beasts. And so it becomes an important question whether men ought to enjoy, or to use, themselves, or to do both. For we are commanded to love one another: but it is a question whether man is to be loved by man for his own sake or for the sake of something else. If it is for his own sake, we enjoy him; if it is for the sake of something else, we use him. It seems to me, then, that he is to be loved for the sake of something else. For if a thing is to be loved for its own sake, then in the enjoyment of it consists a happy life, the hope of which at least, if not yet the reality, is our comfort in the present time. But a curse is pronounced on him who places his hope in man. (Jer. 17:5)

21. Neither ought any one to have joy in himself, if you look at the matter clearly, because no one ought to love even himself for his own sake but for the sake of Him who is the true object of enjoyment. For a man is never in so good a state as when his whole life is a journey towards the unchangeable life and his affections are entirely fixed upon that. If, however, he loves himself for his own sake, he does not look at himself in relation to God but turns his mind in upon himself, and so is not occupied with anything that is unchangeable. And thus he does not enjoy himself at his best, because he is better when his mind is fully fixed upon, and his affections wrapped up in, the unchangeable good than when he turns from that to enjoy even himself. Wherefore if you ought not

to love even yourself for your own sake, but for His in whom your love finds its most worthy object, no other man has a right to be angry if you love him too for God's sake. For this is the law of love that has been laid down by Divine authority: "Thou shalt love thy neighbor as thyself;" but, "Thou shalt love God with all thy heart, and with all thy soul, and with all thy mind": (Matt. 22:37-39) so that you are to concentrate all your thoughts, your whole life, and your whole intelligence upon Him from whom you derive all that you bring. For when He says, "With all thy heart, and with all thy soul, and with all thy mind," He means that no part of our life is to be unoccupied and to afford room, as it were, for the wish to enjoy some other object, but that whatever else may suggest itself to us as an object worthy of love is to be borne into the same channel in which the whole current of our affections flows. Whoever, then, loves his neighbor aright, ought to urge upon him that he too should love God with his whole heart, and soul, and mind. For in this way, loving his neighbor as himself, a man turns the whole current of his love both for himself and his neighbor into the channel of the love of God, which suffers no stream to be drawn off from itself by whose diversion its own volume would be diminished.

CHAPTER 23 *Man needs no injunction to love himself and his own body.* 22. Those things which are objects of use are not all, however, to be loved, but those only [are to be loved] which are either united with us in a common relation to God, such as a man or an angel, or are so related to us as to need the goodness of God through our instrumentality, such as the body. For assuredly the martyrs did not love the wickedness of their persecutors, although they used it to attain the favor of God. As, then, there are four kinds of things that are to be loved,—first, that which is above us; second, ourselves; third, that which is on a level with us; fourth, that which is beneath us,—no precepts need be given about the second and fourth of these. For, however far a man may fall away from the truth, he still continues to love himself and to love his own body. The soul which flies away from the unchangeable Light, the Ruler of all things, does so that it may rule over itself and over its own body; and so it cannot but love both itself and its own body.

CHAPTER 26 *The command to love God and our neighbor includes a command to love ourselves.* 27. Seeing, then, that there is

300

no need of a command that every man should love himself and his own body, seeing, that is, that we love ourselves and what is beneath us but connected with us, through a law of nature which has never been violated, and which is common to us with the beasts (for even the beasts love themselves and their own bodies), it only remained necessary to lay injunctions upon us in regard to God above us and our neighbor beside us. "Thou shalt love," He says, "the Lord thy God with all thy heart, and with all thy soul, and with all thy mind. . . . Thou shalt love thy neighbor as thyself. On these two commandments hang the law of the prophets." (Matt. 22:37-40) Thus the end of the commandment is love, and that twofold: the love of God and the love of our neighbor. Now, if you take yourself in your entirety—that is, soul and body together—and your neighbor in his entirety, soul and body together (for man is made up of soul and body), you will find that none of the classes of things that are to be loved is overlooked in these two commandments. For though, when the love of God comes first and the measure of our love for Him is prescribed in such terms that it is evident all other things are to find their centre in Him, nothing seems to be said about our love for ourselves; yet when it is said, "Thou shalt love thy neighbor as thyself," it at once becomes evident that our love for ourselves has not been overlooked.

CHAPTER 27 *The order of love.* 28. Now he is a man of just and holy life who forms an unprejudiced estimate of things and keeps his affections also under strict control, so that he neither loves what he ought not to love, nor fails to love what he ought to love, nor loves that more which ought to be loved less, nor loves that equally which ought to be loved either less or more, nor loves that less or more which ought to be loved equally. No sinner is to be loved as a sinner; and every man is to be loved as a man for God's sake; but God is to be loved for His own sake. And if God is to be loved more than any man, each man ought to love God more than himself. Likewise we ought to love another man better than our own body, because all things are to be loved in reference to God, and another man can have fellowship with us in the enjoyment of God, whereas our body cannot; for the body only lives through the soul, and it is by the soul that we enjoy God.

CHAPTER 35 *The fulfilment and end of Scripture is the love of God and our neighbor.* 39. Of all, then, that has been said since we entered upon the discussion about things, this is the sum: that we should clearly understand that the fulfilment and the end of the Law and of all Holy Scripture, is the love of an object which is to be enjoyed and the love of an object which can enjoy that other in fellowship with ourselves. For there is no need of a command that each man should love himself. The whole temporal dispensation for our salvation, therefore, was framed by the providence of God that we might know this truth and be able to act upon it; and we ought to use that dispensation, not with such love and delight as if it were a good to rest in but with a transient feeling rather, such as we have towards the road, or carriages, or other things that are merely means. . . .

CHAPTER 36 *That interpretation of Scripture which builds us up in love is not perniciously deceptive.* . . . 40. Whoever, then, thinks that he understands the Holy Scriptures, or any part of them, but puts such an interpretation upon them as does not tend to build up this twofold love of God and our neighbor, does not yet understand them as he ought. If, on the other hand, a man draws a meaning from them that may be used for the building up of love, even though he does not happen upon the precise meaning which the author whom he reads intended to express in that place, his error is not pernicious, and he is wholly clear from the charge of deception. For there is involved in deception the intention to say what is false; and we find plenty of people who intend to deceive but nobody who wishes to be deceived. . . .

CHAPTER 37 *Dangers of mistaken interpretation.* For if he takes up rashly a meaning which the author whom he is reading did not intend, he often falls in with other statements which he cannot harmonize with this meaning. And if he admits that these statements are true and certain, then it follows that the meaning he had put upon the former passage cannot be the true one: and so it comes to pass, one can hardly tell how, that out of love for his own opinion, he begins to feel more angry with Scripture than he is with himself. And if he should once permit that evil to creep in, it will utterly destroy him. "For we walk by faith, not by sight." (II Cor. 5:7) Now faith will totter if the authority of Scripture begin to shake. And then, if faith totter, love itself will grow cold. For if a man has fallen from faith, he must necessarily also fall from love; for he cannot love what he does not believe to exist. But if he both believes and loves, then through good works and through diligent attention to the precepts of morality, he comes to hope also that he shall attain the object of his love. And so these are the three things to which all knowledge and all prophecy are subservient: faith, hope, love.

CHAPTER 38 *Love never faileth.* 42. But sight shall displace faith, and hope shall be swallowed up in that perfect bliss to which we shall come; love, on the other hand, shall wax greater when these others fail. For if we love by faith that which as yet we see not, how much more shall we love it when we begin to see! And if we love by hope that which as yet we have not reached, how much more shall we love it when we reach it! For there is this great difference between things temporal and things eternal, that a temporal object is valued more before we possess it and begins to prove worthless the moment we attain it, because it does not satisfy the soul, which has its only true and sure resting place in eternity: an eternal object, on the other hand, is loved with greater ardor when it is in possession than while it is still an object of desire, for no one in his longing for it can set a higher value on it than really belongs to it, so as to think it comparatively worthless when he finds it of less value than he thought; on the contrary, however high the value any man may set upon it when he is on his way to possess it, he will find it, when it comes into his possession, of higher value still.

CHAPTER 39 *He who is mature in faith, hope, and love, needs Scripture no longer.* 43. And thus a man who is resting upon faith, hope, and love and who keeps a firm hold upon these does not need the Scriptures except for the purpose of instructing others. Accordingly, many live without copies of the Scriptures, even in solitude, on the strength of these three graces. So that in their case, I think, the saying is already fulfilled: "Whether there be prophecies, they shall fail; whether there be tongues, they shall cease; whether there be knowledge, it shall vanish away." (I Cor. 13:8) Yet by means of these instruments (as they may be called), so great an edifice of faith and love has been built up in them, that, holding to what is perfect, they do not seek for what is only in part perfect—of course, I mean, so far as is possible in this life; for, in comparison with the future life, the life of no just and holy man is perfect here. Therefore the apostle says: "Now abideth, faith, hope, charity, these three; but the greatest of these is charity." (I Cor. 13:13) Because, when a man shall have reached the eternal world, while the other two graces will fail, love will remain greater and more assured.

THE CITY OF GOD ✣ BOOK V ✣ CHAPTER 9 The manner in which Cicero addresses himself to the task of refuting the Stoics, shows that he did not think he could effect anything aginst them in argument unless he had first demolished divination. And this he attempts to accomplish by denying that there is any knowledge of future things and maintaining with all his might that there is no prediction of events. Thus he both denies the foreknowledge of God and attempts by vain arguments and by opposing to himself certain oracles very easy to be refuted to overthrow all prophecy, even such as is clearer than the light (though even these oracles are not refuted by him).

. . . we, in order that we may confess the most high and true God Himself, do confess His will, supreme power, and prescience. Neither let us be afraid lest, after all, we do not do by will that which we do by will, because He, whose foreknowledge is infallible, foreknew that we would do it. It was this which Cicero was afraid of, and therefore opposed foreknowledge. The Stoics also maintained that all things do not come to pass by necessity, although they contended that all things happen according to destiny. What is it, then, that Cicero feared in the prescience of future things? Doubtless it was this, that if all future things have been foreknown, they will happen in the order in which they have been foreknown; and if they come to pass in this order, there is a certain order of things foreknown by God; and if a certain order of things, then a certain order of causes, for nothing can happen which is not preceded by some efficient causes. But if there is a certain order of causes according to which everything happens which does happen, then by fate, says he, all things happen which do happen. But if this be so, then is there nothing in our own power, and there is no such thing as freedom of will; and if we grant that, says he, the whole economy of human life is subverted. In vain are laws enacted. In vain are reproaches, praises, chidings, exhortations had recourse to; and there is no justice whatever in the appointment of rewards for the good, and punishments for the wicked. And that consequences so disgraceful, and absurd, and pernicious to humanity may not follow, Cicero chooses to reject the foreknowledge of future things, and shuts up the religious mind to this alternative, to make choice between two things, either that something is in our own power, or that there is foreknowledge—both of which cannot be true; but if the one is affirmed, the other is thereby denied. . . . But the religious mind chooses both, confesses both, and maintains both by the faith of piety. But how so? says Cicero; for the knowledge of future things being granted, there follows a chain of consequences which ends in this, that there can be nothing depending on our own free wills. And further, if there is anything depending on our wills, we must go backwards by the same steps of reasoning till we arrive at the conclusion that there is no foreknowledge of future things. For we go backwards through all the steps in the following order: If there is free will, all things do not happen according to fate; if all things do not happen according to fate, there is not a certain order of causes; and if there is not a certain order of causes, neither is there a certain order of things foreknown by God—for things cannot come to pass except they are preceded by efficient causes—but, if there is no fixed and certain order of causes foreknown by God, all things cannot be said to happen according as He foreknew that they would happen. And further, if it is not true that all things happen just as they have been foreknown by Him, there is not, says he, in God any foreknowledge of future events.

Now, against the sacrilegious and impious darings of reason, we assert both that God knows all things before they come to pass, and that we do by our free will whatsoever we know and feel to be done by us only because we will it. . . . But it does not follow that, though there is for God a certain order of all causes, there must therefore be nothing depending on the free exercise of our own wills, for our wills themselves are included in that order of causes which is certain to God, and is embraced by His foreknowledge, for human wills are also causes of human actions; and He who foreknew all the causes of things would certainly among those causes not have been ignorant of our wills. For even that very concession which Cicero himself makes is enough to refute him in this argument. For what does it help him to say that nothing takes place without a cause, but that every cause is not fatal, there being a fortuitous cause, a natural cause, and a voluntary cause? It is sufficient that he confesses that whatever happens must be preceded by a cause. For we say that those causes which are called fortuitous are not a mere name for the absence of causes, but are only latent, and we attribute them either to the will of the true God, or to that of spirits of some kind or other. And as to natural causes, we by no means separate them from the will of Him who is the author and framer of all nature. But now as to voluntary cause, they are referable either to God, or to angels, or to men . . . The cause of things, therefore, which makes but is not made, is God; but all other causes both make and are made. Such are all created spirits, and especially the rational. Material causes, therefore, which may rather be said to be made than to make, are not to be reckoned among efficient causes, because they can only do what the will of spirits do by them. How, then, does an order of causes which is certain to the foreknowledge of God necessitate that there should be nothing which is dependent on our wills, when our wills themselves have a very important place in the order of causes? . . .

CHAPTER 10 Wherefore, neither is that necessity to be feared, for dread of which the Stoics labored to make such distinctions among the causes of things as should enable them to rescue certain things from the dominion of necessity and to subject others to it. Among those things which they wished not to be subject to necessity they placed our wills, knowing that they would not be free if subject to necessity. For if that is to be called *our necessity* which is not in our power, but even though we be unwilling effects what it can effect—as, for instance, the necessity of death—it is manifest that our wills by which we live uprightly or wickedly are not under such a necessity; for we do many things which, if we were not willing, we should certainly not do. This is primarily true of the act of willing itself—for if we will, it *is*; if we will not, it *is* not—for we should not will if we were unwilling. But if we define necessity to be that according to which we say that it is necessary that anything be of such or such a nature, or be done in such and such a manner, I know not why we should have any dread of that necessity taking away the freedom of our will. For we do not put the life of God or the foreknowledge of God under necessity if we should say that it is necessary that God should live for ever and foreknow all things; as neither is His power diminished when we say that He cannot die or fall into error—for this is in such a way impossible to Him, that if it were possible for Him, He would be of less power. But assuredly

He is rightly called omnipotent, though He can neither die nor fall into error. For He is called omnipotent on account of His doing what He wills, not on account of His suffering what He wills not; for if that should befall Him, He would by no means be omnipotent. Wherefore, He cannot do some things, for the very reason that He is omnipotent. So also, when we say that it is necssary that when we will, we will by free choice, in so saying we both affirm what is true beyond doubt, and do not still subject our wills thereby to a necessity which destroys liberty. Our wills, therefore, *exist* as *wills*, and do themselves whatever we do by willing, and which would not be done if we were unwilling. But when anyone suffers anything, being unwilling, by the will of another, even in that case will retains its essentail validity—we do not mean the will of the party who inflicts the suffering, for we resolve it into the power of God. For if a will should simply exist, but not be able to do what it wills, it would be overborne by a more powerful will. Nor would this be the case unless there had existed will, and that not the will of the other party, but the will of him who willed, but was not able to accomplish what he willed. Therefore, whatsoever a man suffers contrary to his own will, he ought not to attribute to the will of men, or of angels, or of any created spirit, but rather to His will who gives power to wills. It is not the case, therefore, that because God foreknew what would be in the power of our wills, there is for that reason nothing in the power of our wills. For he who foreknew this did not foreknow nothing. Moreover, if He who foreknew what would be in the power of our wills did not foreknow nothing, but something, assuredly, even though He did foreknow, there is something in the power of our wills. Therefore we are by no means compelled, either, retaining the prescience of God, to take away the freedom of the will, or, retaining the freedom of the will, to deny that He is prescient of future things, which is impious. But we embrace both. We faithfully and sincerely confess both. The former, that we may believe well; the latter, that we may live well. For he lives ill who does not believe well concerning God. Wherefore, be it far from us, in order to maintain our freedom, to deny the prescience of Him by whose help we are or shall be free. Consequently, it is not in vain that laws are enacted and that reproaches, exhortations, praises, and vituperations are had recourse to; for these also He foreknew, and they are of great avail, even as great as He foreknew that they would be of. Prayers, also, are of avail to procure those things which He foreknew that He would grant to those who offered them; and with justice have rewards been appointed for good deeds and punishments for sins. For a man does not therefore sin because God foreknew that he would sin. Nay, it cannot be doubted but that it is the man himself who sins when he does sin, because He, whose foreknowledge is infallible, foreknew not that fate, or fortune, or something else would sin, but that the man himself would sin, who, if he wills not, sins not. But if he shall not will to sin, even this God did foreknow.

G RACE AND FREE WILL ✛ BOOK I ✛ CHAPTER 1 *The occasion and argument of this work.* With reference to those persons who preach up the liberty of the human will and maintain it with such pertinacity as boldly to deny, and endeavor to do away with, that grace of God which calls us to Him and delivers us from the evils we have deserved, whereby also we obtain the meritorious qualities which lead to everlasting life, we have already said a good deal in discussion and committed it to writing, so far as the Lord has vouchsafed to enable us. But since there are some persons who [take the opposite course, and] so defend God's grace as to deny man's free will, or else suppose that free will is denied when grace is defended, I have determined to write some thoughts on this point to your love, my brother Valentinus, and the rest of you, who are serving God together under the impulse of a mutual charity. . . .

BOOK II ✛ CHAPTER 2 *He proves the existence of free will in man from the precepts addressed to him by God; these precepts are given that there may be no excuse from ignorance.* Now He has revealed to us, through His Holy Scriptures, that there is in man's will a liberty of choice. But how He has revealed this I do not attempt to explain by human testimony but by divine. There is, to begin with, the fact that God's precepts themselves would be of no use to a man unless his will were at full liberty to choose, so that by its assent he might obtain the promised reward as he obeys the precepts. For these are given that no one might be able to plead the excuse of ignorance, as the Lord says concerning the Jews in the gospel: "If I had not come and spoken unto them, they would not have sin; but now they have no cloak [or excuse] for their sin." (John 15:22) Of what sin does He speak but of that great one which He foreknew, while speaking thus, that they would make their own—that is, the death they were going to inflict upon Him? For they had no sin before Christ came to them in the flesh. The apostle also says: "The wrath of God is revealed from heaven against all ungodliness and unrighteousness of men, who hold the truth in unrighteousness; because that which may be known of God is manifest in them; for God hath shown them. For the invisible things of Him are from the creation of the world clearly seen—being understood by the things that are made—even his Eternal power and Godhead, so that they are without excuse." (Rom. 1:18-20) In what sense does he pronounce them to be "without excuse," except of such excuse as human pride is apt to allege in such words as, "If I had only known, I would have done it; I did not do it because I was ignorant of it"; or, "I would do it if I knew how; but I do not know, therefore I don't do it"? All such excuse is removed from them when the precept is given them, or the knowledge is made manifest to them how to avoid sin.

CHAPTER 3 *Sinners are convicted when attempting to excuse themselves by blaming God, because they have free will.* There are, however, persons who attempt to find excuse for themselves even from God. The Apostle James says to such: "Let no man say when he is tempted, I am tempted of God; for God cannot be tempted with evil, neither tempteth He any man. But every man is tempted when he is drawn away of his own lust, and enticed. Then, when lust hath conceived, it bringeth forth sin; and sin, when it is finished, bringeth forth death." (Jas. 1:13-15 . . . And in the book of Ecclesiasticus we read: "Say not thou, It is through the Lord that I fell away; for thou oughtest not to do the things that He hateth: nor do thou say, He hath caused me to err; for He hath no need of the sinful man. The Lord hateth all abomination, and they that fear God love it not. He himself made man from the beginning, and left him in the hand of His counsel. If thou be willing, thou shalt keep His commandments, and perform true fidelity. He hath set fire and water before thee: stretch forth thine hand to which thou wilt. Before man is life and death, and whichsoever pleaseth him shall be given to him." (Ecclus. 15: 11-17) Observe how very plainly is set before our view the liberty of the human will.

CHAPTER 4 *The divine commands which are most suited to the will itself illustrate its freedom.* What is the import of the fact that in so many passages God requests His commandments to be kept and fulfilled and of the way in which He makes this request, if the will is not free? What means "the happy man," of whom the Psalmist says that "his pleasure [or will] has been in the law of the Lord?" (Ps. 1:2) Does he not clearly enough show that a man, by his own will and choice, takes his stand in the law of God? Then, again, there are so many commandments which in a certain way expressly adapt themselves to the human will; for instance, there is, "Be not overcome of evil," (Rom. 12:1) and others of similar import, such as, "Be not like a horse or a mule, which have no understanding"; (Ps. 32:9) and "Reject not the counsels of thy mother"; (Prov. 1:8) and "Be not wise in thine own conceit"; (Prov. 3:11) and "Forget not my law"; (Prov. 3:1) and "Forbear not to do good to the poor"; (Prov. 3:27). . . . with numberless other passages of the inspired Scriptures. And what do they all show us but the liberty of man's will in its preferences and choice? . . .

BOOK IV ✠ CHAPTER 6 *God's grace to be maintained against the Pelagians; the Pelagian heresy not an old one.* There is, however, a fear of all these and similar testimonies of Holy Scripture being understood, in the maintenance of free will, in such a way as to leave no room for God's assistance and grace in leading a godly life and a good conversation, to which the eternal reward is due; and a fear, moreover, of a poor wretched man so misunderstanding his own case, when he leads a good life and performs good works (or rather thinks that he leads a good life and performs good works) , as to dare to glory in himself, and not in the Lord, and to put his entire hope of righteous living in himself alone; so that the prophet Jeremiah's malediction follows him when he says, "Cursed is the man who trusteth in man, and maketh flesh his arm, and whose heart departeth from the Lord." (Jer. 17:5) Understand, my brethren, I pray you, this passage of the prophet. For the prophet did not say, "Cursed is the man who puts his hope in his own self." It might seem to some that the passage "Cursed is the man who trusteth in man" was spoken in the sense that no man should have any confidence in any other person, but in himself. In order, therefore, to show that his advice to a man was not to have any confidence in himself, even after saying, "Cursed is the man who trusteth in man" he immediately

310

added, "And maketh flesh his arm" [or strengthened the flesh of his arm"]. He used the word *"arm"* to designate *power in operation.* By the term "flesh," however, must be understood *human frailty.* And therefore he strengthens the flesh of his arm who supposes that a power which is frail and weak (in a word, human) is sufficient for him to perform good works, and therefore puts not his trust in God for help. This is the reason why he subjoined the further clause "And whose heart departeth from the Lord." Of this character is the Pelagian heresy, which is not an ancient one, but has only lately come into existence. Against this system of error there was first a good deal of discussion; then, as the ultimate resource, it was referred to sundry episcopal councils, the proceedings of which, not, indeed, in every instance, but in some, I have despatched to you for your perusal. In order, then, to our performance of good works, let us not put our trust in man, strengthening the flesh of our own arm; nor let our heart ever depart from the Lord, but let it say to him, "Be Thou my helper; forsake me not, nor despise me, O God of my salvation." (Ps. 27:9)

CHAPTER 7 *Grace is necessary along with free will to lead a good life. Continence the result of God's gift and free will. They to whom it is given order their will so as to accomplish its desire.* Therefore, my dearly beloved, as we have now proved by our former quotations of Holy Scripture that there is in man's will a freedom of choice and determination in order to lead a good life and perform right actions, so now let us see what inspired passages there also are concerning the grace of God, without which we are not able to do any good thing. And first of all, I will say something about the very profession which you make in your brotherhood. Now your society, in which you are leading lives of continence, could not hold together unless you forbore the pleasure of matrimony. Well, the Lord was one day conversing on this very topic, when His disciples remarked to Him, "If such be the case of a man with his wife, it is not good to marry." He then answered them, "All men cannot receive this saying, save they to whom it is given." (Matt. 19:10) And was it not to Timothy's free will that the apostle appealed, when he exhorted him in these words: "Keep thyself pure" [*Contine te ipsum,* Exercise continence]? (I Tim. 5:22) He also explained the power of the will in this matter when He said, "He standeth stedfast in heart—having no necessity, but possessing power over his own will—to keep his virgin." (I Cor. 7:37) And yet all men do not receive this say-

311

ing, except those to whom the power is given. Now they to whom this is not given either are unwilling or do not fulfil their will; whereas they to whom it is given so order their will as to accomplish what they wish. In order, therefore, that this saying, which is not received by all men, may yet be received by some, God's grace and free will combine in securing to them the gift. . . .

BOOK V ✠ CHAPTER 10 *Free will and God's grace are simultaneously commended. The error of the Pelagians that grace is given according to men's merits.* When God says, "Turn ye unto me, and I will turn unto you," (Zech. 1:3) one of these clauses—that which invites our return to God—is evidently addressed to our free will; while the other, which promises His return to us, appertains to His grace. Here, possibly, the Pelagians think they have a justification for their opinion which they so prominently advance, that God's grace is given in proportion to our merits. In the East, indeed, that is to say in the province of Palestine, in which is the city of Jerusalem, Pelagius, when examined in person by the bishop, did not venture to affirm this. For it happened that among the objections which were brought up against him, this in particular was alleged, that he maintained that the grace of God was bestowed according to our merits—an opinion which was so diverse from Catholic doctrine and so hostile to the grace of Christ, that unless he had anathematized it, as laid to his charge, he himself must have left the council under anathema. He pronounced, indeed, the required condemnation of the dogma but how insincerely, his later books show; for in them he maintains absolutely no other opinion than that the grace of God is bestowed in proportion to our own deserts. Such deductions do they make out of the Scriptures—like the one which I just now quoted, "Turn ye unto me, and I will turn unto you"—as if it were owing to the merit of our conversion to God that His grace were given us, wherein He Himself even turns unto us. Now the persons who hold this opinion fail to observe that unless our conversion to God were itself God's gift, it would not be said to Him in prayer, "Turn us again, O God of hosts"; (Ps. 80:7) and, "Thou, O God, wilt turn and quicken us"; (Ps. 85:6) and again, "Convert us, O God of our salvation," (Ps. 85:4) —with other passages of similar import, too numerous to mention here. For, with respect to our coming unto Christ, what else does it mean than our being turned and converted to Him upon our believing? And yet He says: "No man can come unto me, except it were given unto him of my Father." . . . (John 6:65)

CHAPTER 12 *He proves out of St. Paul that grace is not given according to men's merits.* Now there was, no doubt, a decided merit in the Apostle Paul, but it was an *evil* one, while he persecuted the Church, and he says of it: "I am not meet to be called an apostle, because I persecuted the Church of God" (I Cor. 15:9) And it was while he was in possession of this evil merit that a good one was rendered to him instead of the evil; and therefore, he went on at once to say, "But by the grace of God I am what I am." (I Cor. 15:10) Then, in order to exhibit the action of his free will besides, he added in the next clause, "And His grace within me was not in vain, but I labored more abundantly than they all." This freedom of will in man he consistently appeals to in the case of others also, as when he says to them, "We beseech you that ye receive not the grace of God in vain" [so as to be idle]. (II Cor. 6:1) Now, how could he enjoin any effort on them, if they received God's grace in such a manner as to merge in it, and lose their own will? However [there was the other extreme to guard against], the will itself must not be deemed capable of doing any good thing without the grace of God; therefore, after saying, "His grace within me was not in vain," or idle, "but I labored more abundantly than they all," he immediately added the qualifying clause, "Yet not I, but the grace of God which was with me." In other words, Not I alone, but only the grace of God. Nor was he himself solitary in action, but God's grace operated along with him. For the accomplishment, however, of the radical change within him—his call from heaven and his conversion by that great and most effectual call—God's grace operated alone, because his merits, though great were yet evil. . . .

BOOK VI ✛ CHAPTER 13 From these and similar passages of Scripture, we gather the proof that God's grace is not given according to our merits. The truth is, we see that it is bestowed not only when there are no good deserts, but when even evil ones precede; and we still observe the same unmerited gifts conferred day after day. But it is plain that when grace has been given, even our merits begin to be good—only it is by grace; for, were that only to withdraw itself, man falls, not raised up but only precipitated by his free will. Wherefore no man ought, even when he begins to possess good merits, to attribute them to himself, but to God, who is thus addressed by the Psalmist: "Be Thou my helper, forsake me not." (Ps. 27:9) By saying, "Forsake me not," he shows that if he were to be forsaken, he is unable of himself to do any good thing. . . . So necessary is it for a man that he should be not only justified when unrighteous by the grace of God —that is, to be changed from unholiness to righteousness—when he is requited with good for his evil; but that, even after he has become justified by faith, grace should accompany him on his way afterwards, and he should lean upon it, lest he stumble and fall. On this account it is written concerning the Church herself in the book of Canticles: "Who is this that cometh up in white raiment, leaning upon the arm of her beloved kinsman?" (Cant. 8:5) She, who could by no possibility have been so pure in vesture by herself alone, has become clad in white. And by whom has she been thus whitened, except by Him who says by the prophet, "Though your sins be as purple, I will make them white as snow"? (Isa. 1:18) At the time she was made white, she deserved nothing good; but now that she is white, she walketh rightly; but it is only by her continuing ever to lean upon Him by whom she was whitened. Wherefore, Jesus Himself, on whom the Church leans in her raiment of white, said to His disciples, "Without me ye can do nothing." (John 15:5)

CHAPTER 14 Let us return now to the Apostle Paul, who, as we have observed, obtained God's grace, who recompenses good for evil, when, so far from having any good deserts of his own, he was really involved in many evil ones. Let us see what he says when his sufferings at the end of his life were approaching. These are his words, writing to Timothy: "I am now ready to be offered, and the time of my departure is at hand. I have fought a good fight; I have finished my course, I have kept the faith." (II Tim. 4:6-7) He enumerates these as being now his good merits; that, as after his ill deserts he obtained grace, so now, after his good merits, he might receive the crown. Observe, therefore what follows: "There is henceforth laid up for me," he says, "a crown of righteousness, which the Lord, the righteous Judge, shall give me at that day." (II Tim. 4:8) Now, to whom could the righteous Judge award the crown, except to him on whom the merciful Father had bestowed grace? And how could the crown be one "of righteousness," unless the grace had preceded which "justifieth the ungodly?" How, moreover, could the one now be awarded as a debt, unless the other had been before bestowed as a free gift?

CHAPTER 15 *The Pelagians profess that the only grace which is given according to our merits is that of the forgiveness of sins;*

God crowns in us His own gifts, not our merits. When, however, the Pelagians say that the only grace which is not awarded according to our merits is that whereby a man has his sins forgiven him, that the final grace which is bestowed upon us, even eternal life, is given in return for preceding merits, they must not be allowed to go without an answer. If, indeed, they understand our merits in such a sense as to acknowledge even them to be the gifts of God, then their opinion would not deserve reprobation. But inasmuch as they preach up human merits to such an extent as to declare that a man has them of his own very self, then the apostle's reply becomes an absolutely correct one: "Who maketh thee to differ from another? And what hast thou, that thou didst not receive? Now, if thou didst receive it, why dost thou glory as if thou hadst not received it? (I Cor. 4:7) To a man who holds such views, it is perfect truth to say: It is His own gifts that God crowns, not your merits, although you hold these as done by your own self, not by Him. If, indeed, they are of such a character, they are evil, and God does not crown them; but if they are good, they are God's gifts, because, as the Apostle James says,"Every good gift and every perfect gift is from above, and cometh down from the Father of lights." (Jas. 1:17) In accordance with which John also, the Lord's forerunner, declares: "A man can receive nothing, except it be given him from heaven" (John 3:27) —from heaven, of course, for from thence came also the Holy Ghost, when Jesus ascended up on high, led captivity captive, and give gifts to men. Inasmuch, then, as your merits are God's gifts, God does not crown your merits *as such,* but only as His own gifts. . . .

CHAPTER 17 *Faith the free gift of God.* . . . . "I have kept the faith." But he who says this is the same who declares in another passage, "I have obtained mercy of the Lord to be faithful." (I Cor. 7:25) He does not say, I obtained mercy because I was faithful, but "in order that I might be faithful," thus showing that even faith itself cannot be had without God's exercise of mercy, and that consequently it is the gift of God. This he very expressly teaches us when he says, "For by grace are ye saved through faith, and that not of yourselves; it is the gift of God." (Eph. 2:8) They might say, We received grace because we believed; as if they would attribute the faith to themselves, and the grace to God. Therefore, to prevent such an error, the apostle having said, "Ye are saved through faith," added the correcting clause, "And that not of yourselves, but it is the gift of God."

And then, lest they should claim to have deserved so great a gift by any works of their own, he immediately added, "Not of works, lest any man should boast." (Eph. 2:9) Not that he meant to deny good works, or to empty them of their value, because he says that God renders to every man according to his works; but he would have works proceed from faith, and not faith from works. Therefore it is from Him that we have works of righteousness, from whom also comes faith itself, concerning which it is written, "The just shall live by faith." (Hab. 2:4)

CHAPTER 18 *Faith without good works is not sufficient for salvation.* Unintelligent persons, indeed, with regard to the apostle's statement: "We conclude that a man is justified by faith without the deeds of the law," (Rom. 3:28) have thought him to mean that faith is sufficient for a man, even if he lead a bad life and has no good deeds to allege. Impossible is it that such a character should be deemed a "vessel of election" by the apostle, who, after declaring that "in Christ Jesus neither circumcision availeth anything, nor uncircumcision," (Gal. 5:6) adds the important statement, "but faith which worketh by love." It is such faith which severs the faithful children of God from unclean devils— for even these "believe and tremble," (Jas. 2:19) as the Apostle James says, but they do no good works. Therefore they possess not the faith by which the just man lives—the faith which operates through love in such wise that God recompense it according to its works with eternal life. But inasmuch as we have even our good works from God, from whom likewise comes our faith and our love, therefore the selfsame great teacher of the Gentiles has designated "eternal life" itself as His gracious "gift."

BOOK VIII ✚ CHAPTER 19 *How is eternal life both a reward for service and a free gift of grace?* And hence there arises no small question, which must be solved with the Lord's permission. If eternal life is bestowed as a recompense for good works, as the Scripture most openly declares: "Then He shall reward every man according to his works," (Matt. 16:27) how can eternal life be a matter of grace, seeing that grace is not given in return for works, but is a gratuitous award, as the apostle himself tells us: "To him that worketh is the reward not reckoned of grace, but of debt"; (Rom. 4:4) and again: "There is a remnant saved according to the election of grace"; with these words immediately subjoined:

"And if of grace, then is it no more of works; otherwise grace is no more grace"? (Rom. 11:5-6) How, I ask again, is eternal life a matter of grace, when it is received after works? Does the apostle happen not to have given the designation of *grace* to eternal life? Nay, he has so called it, with a clearness which none could gainsay. It requires no acute intellect, but only an attentive reader to discover this. For after saying, "The wages of sin is death," he at once added, "The gift of God [*gratia Dei*] is eternal life through Jesus Christ our Lord." (Rom. 6:23)

CHAPTER 20 *The question answered. In what sense the apostle says that we are not saved by works. Justification is grace simply and entirely. Eternal life is reward and grace.* Now this question seems to me to be by no means capable of solution, unless we understand that even those good works of ours, which are recompensed with eternal life, are occasioned by the grace of God, because of what is said by the Lord Jesus: "Without me ye can do nothing." (John 15:5) The apostle himself undoubtedly [felt the difficulty of the subject] after saying, "By grace are ye saved through faith; and that not of yourselves, it is the gift of God: not of works, lest any man should boast"; (Eph. 2:8-9) he evidently saw the possibility of men's concluding from such a statement that good works are not necessary to those who believe, but that faith alone is sufficient for them. Then, again, there was the possibility, as he perceived, of men's boasting of their good works, as if they were of themselves capable of performing them. To meet, therefore, these erroneous opinions on both sides, he immediately added, "We are His workmanship, created in Christ Jesus unto good works, which God hath before ordained that we should walk in them." (Eph. 2:10) [And here question after question arises.] What is the purport of his saying, "Not of works, lest any man should boast," while commending the grace of God? And then why does he afterwards, when giving a reason for using such works, say, "For we are his workmanship, created in Christ Jesus unto good works"? Why, therefore, does it run, "Not of works, lest any man should boast"? Now, hear, and understand the point. The excluding phrase, "Not of works," is spoken of the works which you suppose have their origin in yourself alone; but you have to think of works to which God has moulded (that is, has formed and created) you. For of these he says, "We are his workmanship, created in Christ Jesus unto good works." Now he does not here speak of that creation which made us human

317

beings, but of that in reference to which one said who was already in full manhood, "Create in me a clean heart, O God"; (Ps. 1:12) concerning which also the apostle says, "Therefore, if any man be in Christ, he is a new creature: old things are passed away; behold, all things are become new. And all things are of God." (II Cor. 5:17-18) We are moulded, therefore, that is, formed and created, "unto the good works, which" we have not ourselves prepared, but "God hath before ordained that we should walk in them." It follows, then, dearly beloved, beyond all doubt, that as your good life is nothing else than God's gift and grace, so also the eternal life which is the recompense of a good life is the gift and grace of God; moreover it is a free and gratuitous gift, even as that was a free and gratuitous gift of which it is the recompense. But the *good* life, thus rewarded, is solely and simply grace; therefore the *eternal* life, which is its reward—and because it is its reward—is grace *for* grace, as if it were the remuneration of righteousness; in order that that may be realized, because it is true, that God "shall reward every man according to his works." . . . (Matt. 16:27)

BOOK XIV ✢ CHAPTER 27 *Grace effects the fulfilment of the law, the deliverance of nature, and the suppression of sin's dominion. Subterfuge of the Pelagians.* It has, however, been shown to demonstration that instead of really maintaining the freedom of will, they have only inflated a theory of it, which, having no stability, has fallen to the ground. Neither the knowledge of God's law, nor nature, nor the remission of sins represents [as they pretend] that grace which is given to us through our Lord Jesus Christ; but it is this very grace which accomplishes the fulfilment of the law, and the liberation of nature, and the removal of the dominion of sin. Being, therefore, frustrated on these points, they resort to another expedient and endeavor to show in the best way they can that the grace of God is given us according to our merits. For they say: "Granted that it [grace] is not given to us in proportion to the merits of our good works, inasmuch as it is through it that we do any good thing, still it is bestowed upon us in proportion to our merits of a good will; for," say they, "the good will of him who prays precedes his prayer, even as the good will of the believer preceded his faith, so that in proportion to these deserts the grace of God follows, as He hears [and answers the prayer]."

CHAPTER 28 *Faith is the gift of God.* I have already discussed the point concerning the faith, that is, the disposition and will of the man who believes; and I went so far as to show that it appertains to grace—so that the apostle did not tell us that he obtained mercy because he was faithful; but he said, "I have obtained the mercy of the Lord in order to be faithful." (I Cor. 7:25) And there are many other passages of similar import—among them that in which he bids us "think soberly, according as God hath dealt to every man the proportion of faith"; (Rom. 12:3) and that which I have already quoted; "By grace are ye saved through faith; and that not of yourselves; it is the gift of God"; (Eph. 2:8) . . . Then, again, there is the passage, especially noticeable, in which he says, "We, having the same spirit of faith," (II Cor. 4:13) for his phrase is not *the knowledge of faith,* but *"the spirit of faith";* and he expressed himself thus in order that we might understand how that faith is given to us, even when it is not sought, so that other blessings may be granted to it at its request. For "how," says he, "shall they call upon Him in whom they have not believed?" (Rom. 10:14) The spirit of grace, therefore, causes us to have faith, in order that through faith we may, on praying for it, obtain the ability to do what we are commanded. On this account the apostle himself constantly puts faith before the law; since we are not able to do what the law commands unless we obtain the strength to do it by the prayer of faith.

CHAPTER 29 *God is able to convert opposing wills, and to take away from the heart its hardness.* Now if faith is simply the property of man's free will, and is not the gift of God, why do we pray for those who will not believe that they may have faith? This it would be absolutely useless to do, unless we believe with perfect propriety that Almighty God can turn to the practice of belief men's wills, however perverse and opposed to faith they may be. Man's free will is addressed when it is said, "Today, if ye will hear His voice, harden not your hearts." (Ps. 95:7-8) But if God were not able to remove from the human heart even its obstinacy and hardness, He would not commission the prophet to say, "I will take from them their heart of stone, and will give them a heart of flesh." (Ezek. 11:19) That all this was foretold in reference to the New Testament is shown clearly enough by the apostle when he says, "Ye are our epistle, . . . written not with ink, but with the Spirit of the living God; not in tables of stone, but in fleshly 'tables of the heart". (II Cor. 3:2-3) We

319

must not, of course, suppose that such a pharse as this is used as if those might live fleshly who ought to lead spiritual lives; but inasmuch as a stone has no feeling, with which man's hard heart is compared, what was there left Him to compare man's intelligent heart with but the flesh, which possesses feeling? God, speaking by the mouth of the prophet Ezekiel, says, "I will you then another heart, and I will put a new spirit within you; and I will take the stony heart out of their flesh, and will give them a heart of flesh; that they may walk in my statutes, and keep mine ordinances, and do them: and they shall be my people, and I will be their God, saith the Lord." (Ezek. 11:19-20) Now can we possibly, without extreme absurdity, maintain that there has previously existed in any man the meritorious recommendation of a good will, to entitle him to the removal of his stony heart, when all the while this very heart of stone signifies nothing else than the harshest will, such as is absolutely inflexible against God? For wherever a good will precedes, there is, of course, no longer existing a heart of stone. . . .

BOOK XV ✝ CHAPTER 31 *Free will does something in the heart's conversion; God gives what He commands. In what sense it is said, "If thou wilt, thou shalt keep the commandments."* Lest, however, it should be thought that men themselves in this matter do nothing by their free will, it is said in the Psalm, "Harden not your hearts;" (Ps. 95:8) and in Ezekiel himself "Cast away from you all your transgressions, which ye have impiously committed against me; and make you a new heart and a new spirit; and keep all my commandments. For why will ye die, O house of Israel, saith the Lord? for I have no pleasure in the death of him that dieth, saith the Lord God: wherefore turn yourselves, and live ye." We should remember that it is He who says, "Turn yourselves and live," to whom it is said in prayer, "Turn us again, O God." (Ps. 79:4) We should not forget that He says, "Cast away from you all your transgressions," when it is even He who justifies the ungodly. We should bear in mind that He says, "Make you a new heart and a new spirit," who also promises, "I will give you a new heart, and a new spirit will I put within you." How is it then, that He who says, "Make you," also says, "I will give you"? Why does He command, if He means Himself to give? Why does He give if man is to make, except it be that He gives what He commands when He helps him to obey upon whom He lays His command? There is, however, always within us a free will—but it is not always good; for it is either free from righteousness when it serves sin—and then it is evil—or else it is free from sin when it is the servant of righteousness—and then it is good. But the grace of God is evermore good; and by its means it comes to pass that a man is under the influence of a good will, though he was previously possessed by an evil one. By the same grace it also comes to pass that the very will, which has now begun to be good, is enlarged and grows so great as to be able to fulfil whatever divine commandments it may wish, when it has once firmly and completely formed its desire. This is the purport of what the Scripture says: "If thou wilt, thou shalt keep the commandments"; so that the man who has the will but not the power discovers that he does not yet possess a perfect will, and prays that he may have it so perfected that it may be sufficient for keeping the commandments; and then, indeed, he receives assistance enough to perform what he is commanded. The will is then of use when we have the power; just as the power is also then of use when we have the will. For what does it profit us if we possess will without power, or else lack the will when we possess the power? . . .

BOOK XVII ✛ CHAPTER 33 *A good will, when small and weak; an ample will, great love. Operating and cooperating grace. The burden of human sufferings a heavy weight for an infirm will; a light one for charity.* He who wishes to keep God's commandment, but is unable to do so, already possesses a good will, but as yet a small and weak one; he will, however, become able when he shall have acquired a great and robust will. When the martyrs kept the great commandments which they obeyed, they acted under a mighty will—that is, with a great love. Of this intense charity the Lord Himself thus speaks: "Greater love hath no man than this, that a man lay down his life for his friends." (John 15:13) In accordance with this, the apostle also says, "He that loveth his neighbor hath fulfilled the law. For this: Thou shalt not commit adultery, Thou shalt not kill, Thou shalt not steal, Thou shalt not covet; and if there be any other commandment, it is briefly comprehended in this saying, namely, Thou shalt love thy neighbor as thyself. Love worketh no ill to his neighbor: therefore love is the fulfilling of the law." (Rom. 13:8-10) This perfection of love the Apostle Peter did not yet possess, when he for fear thrice denied the Lord. "There is no fear in love," says the Evangelist

John in his first Epistle, "but perfect love casteth out fear." (I John 4:18) But yet, however, small and imperfect his love was, it was not wholly wanting when he said to the Lord, "I will lay down my life for Thy sake"; (John 13:37) for he supposed himself able to effect what he felt himself willing to do. And who was it that had begun to give him his love, however small, but He who prepares the human will and perfects by His cooperation what He initiates by His operation? Forasmuch as He begins His influence by working in us that we may have the will and completes it by working with us when we have the will. . . . He operates, therefore, without us, in order that we may become willing; but when we once possess the will and so use it as to act, He cooperates with us. We can, however, ourselves do nothing to effect good works of piety without Him either working that we may will or cooperating when we will. Now, concerning the former point—His operation to produce will in us—it is said: "It is God which worketh in you, even to will." (Phil. 2:13) While of His cooperation with us, when we possess the will and proceed to put it into action, the apostle says, "We know that all things work together for good [or, He cooperates in all things for good] to them that love God." (Rom. 8:28)

CHAPTER 36 *Love commended by our Lord Himself.* Moreover, the Lord Jesus Himself teaches us that the whole law and the prophets depend upon the two precepts which enjoin love to God and love to our neighbor. Concerning these two commandments the following is written in the Gospel according to St. Mark: "And one of the scribes came, and having heard them reasoning together, and perceiving that He had answered them well, asked Him: Which is the first commandment of all? And Jesus answered him: The first of all the commandments is, Hear, O Israel! the Lord our God is one Lord; and thou shalt love the Lord thy God with all thine heart, and with all thy soul, and with all thy mind, and with all thy strength. (Deut. 6:4-5) And the second is like unto it: Thou shalt love they neighbor as thyself. (Lev. 19:18) There is none other commandment greater than these." (Mark 12:28-31) Also, in the Gospel according to St. John, He says, "A new commandment I give unto you that ye love one another; as I have loved you, that ye also love one another. By this shall all men know that ye are my disciples, if ye have love to one another." (John 13:34-35)

BOOK XVIII ✠ CHAPTER 37 *The love which fulfils the commandments is not of ourselves, but of God. The law without grace is the letter that killeth.* All these commandments, however, respecting love or charity (which are so great, and such that whatever action a man may think he does well is by no means well done if done without charity) would be given to men in vain if they possess not a will to choose freely. But forasmuch as these precepts are given in the law, both old and new (although in the new came the grace which was promised in the old, the law, moreover, being without grace the letter which killeth, but under grace the Spirit which giveth life), from what source is there in men the love of God and of one's neighbor but from God Himself? For indeed, if it be not of God but of men, the Pelagians have gained the victory; but if it come from God, then we have vanquished the Pelagians. Let, then, the Apostle John sit in judgment between us; and let him say to us, "Beloved, let us love one another." (I John 4:7) Now, when they begin to extol themselves on these words of John and to ask why this precept is addressed to us at all if we have no ability of our own selves to love one another, the same apostle proceeds at once, to their confusion, to add, "For love is of God." (I John 4:7) It comes not of ourselves, therefore, but it is of God. Wherefore, then, is it said, "Let us love one another, for love is of God," unless it be as a precept to our free will, admonishing it to seek the gift of God? Now, this would be indeed a thoroughly fruitless admonition if the will did not previously receive some donation of love, which might seek to be enlarged with such completeness as might fulfil whatever injunction was laid upon it. When it is said, "Let us love one another," it is law; when it is said, "For love is of God," it is grace. For God's "wisdom carries law and mercy upon her tongue." (Prov. 3:16) Accordingly, it is written in the Psalm, "For He who gave the law will give blessings." (Ps. 84:6)

CHAPTER 38 *We should not love God unless He first loved us. The apostles chose Christ because they were chosen; they were not chosen because they chose Christ.* Let no one, then, deceive you, my brethren, because we should not love God unless he first loved us. John again gives us the plainest proof of this when he says, "We love Him because He first loved us." (I John 4:19) Grace makes us lovers of the law; but the law itself, without grace, makes us breakers of the law. And nothing else than this is shown us by the words of our Lord when He says to His disciples, "Ye have not chosen me, but I have chosen you." (John 15:16) For if we first loved Him, in order that by this merit He might love us, then we first chose Him that we might deserve to be chosen by Him. He, however, who is the Truth says another thing, and flatly contradicts this vain conceit of men. "You have not chosen me," He says. If, therefore, you have not chosen me, undoubtedly you have not loved me (for how could they choose one whom they did not love?) "But I," says He, "have chosen you." And then could they possibly help choosing Him themselves afterwards, and preferring Him to all the blessings of this world? But having been themselves chosen, they chose Him; yet it was not because they chose Him that they were themselves chosen. There could be no merit in men's choice of Christ, if it were not that God's grace was prevenient in His choosing them. Whence the Apostle Paul pronounces in the Thessalonians this benediction: "The Lord make you to increase and abound in love one toward another, and toward all men." (I Thes. 3:12) . . .

BOOK XIX ✠ CHAPTER 40 *The dark ignorance of the Pelagians in maintaining that the knowledge of the law comes from God, but that love comes from ourselves.* It is no wonder that light shineth in darkness, and the darkness comprehendeth it not. In John's Epistle the Light declares, "Behold what manner of love the Father hath bestowed upon us, that we should be called the sons of God." (I John 3:1) And in the Pelagian writings the darkness says, "Love comes to us of our own selves." Now, if they only possessed the true love, that is, Christian charity, they would also know whence they obtained possession of it; even as the apostle knew when he said, "But we have received not the spirit of the world, but the Spirit which is of God, that we might know the things that are freely given to us of God." (I Cor. 2:12) John says, "God is love." (I John 4:16) And thus the Pelagains affirm that they actually have, not God Himself from God, but from their own selves; and although they allow that we have the knowledge of the law from God, they will yet have it that love springs out of our very selves. Nor do they listen to the apostle when he says, "Knowledge puffeth up, but charity edifieth." (I Cor. 8:1) Now what can be more absurd, nay, what more insane and more alien from the very sacredness of love itself, than to maintain that from God proceeds the knowledge which, apart from love, puffs us up, while love which prevents the possibility of this inflation of knowledge springs from ourselves? And again, when the apostle speaks of "the love of Christ as surpassing knowledge," (Eph. 3:19) what can be more insane than to suppose that the knowledge which must be subordinated to love comes from God, while the love which surpasses knowledge comes from man? The true faith, however, and sound doctrine declare that both graces are from God; the Scripture says, "From the presence [of the Lord] cometh knowledge and understanding." (Prov. 2:6) And another Scripture says, "Love is of God." (I John 4:7) We read of "the Spirit of wisdom and understanding." (Isa. 11:2) Also of "the Spirit of power, and of love, and of a sound mind." (II Tim. 1:7) But love is a greater gift than knowledge; for whenever a man has the gift of knowledge, love is necessary by the side of it, that he be not puffed up. For "charity envieth not, vaunteth not itself, is not puffed up." (I Cor. 13:4) . . .

BOOK XXIV ✠ CHAPTER 46 *Understanding and wisdom must be sought from God.* Peruse attentively this treatise, and if you understand it give God the praise; but where you fail to understand it, pray for understanding, for God will give you this faculty. Remember what the Scriptures say: "If any of you lack wisdom, let him ask of God, who giveth to all men liberally, and upbraideth not; and it shall be given to him." (Jas. 1:5) Wisdom itself cometh down from above, as the Apostle James himself tells us. There is, however, another wisdom, which you must repel from you, and pray against its remaining in you; this the same apostle expressed his detestation of when he said, "But if ye have bitter envying and strife in your hearts, . . . this is not the wisdom which descendeth from above, but is earthly, sensual, devilish. For wherever there is envying and strife, there is also confusion, and every evil work. But the wisdom which is from above is first pure, then peaceable, gentle, and easy to be entreated, full of mercy and good works, without partiality, and without hypocrisy." (Jas. 3:13-17) What blessing, then, will that man not have who has prayed for this wisdom and obtained it of the Lord? And from this you may understand what grace is; because if this wisdom were of ourselves, it would not be from above; nor would it be an object to be asked for of the God who created us. Brethren, pray he also for us, that we may live "soberly, righteously, and godly in this present world; looking for that blessed hope, and the glorious appearing of our Lord and Saviour Jesus Christ," (Titus 2:12) to whom belong the honor, and the glory, and the kingdom, with the Father and the Holy Ghost, for ever and ever. Amen.

THE PREDESTINATION OF THE SAINTS ✠ BOOK VIII ✠ CHAPTER 16 *Why the gift of faith is not given to all.* Faith, then, as well in its beginning as in its completion, is God's gift; and let no one have any doubt whatever, unless he desires to resist the plainest sacred writings, that this gift is given to some, while to some it is not given. And why it is not given to all ought not to disturb the believer, who believes that all have gone from one into a condemnation, which undoubtedly is most righteous; so that even if none were delivered therefrom, there would be no just cause for finding fault with God. Whence it is plain that it is a great grace for many to be delivered, and to acknowledge in those that are not delivered what would be due to themselves; so that he that glorieth may glory not in his own merits, which he sees to be equalled in those that are condemned, but in the Lord. And why He delivers one rather than another, "His judgments are unsearchable, and His ways past finding out." (Rom. 11:33) For it is better in this case for us to hear or to say, "O man, who art thou that repliest against God?" (Rom. 9:20) than to dare to say, as if we could know what He has chosen to be kept secret. Since, moreover, He could not will anything unrighteous. . . .

BOOK X ✠ CHAPTER 19 *In what respects predestination and grace differ.* Moreover, that which I said, "That the salvation offered by this religion has never failed him who was worthy of it, and that he whom it failed was not worthy." If it be discussed and asked whence any man can be worthy, there are not wanting those who say by human will. But we say, by divine grace or predestination. Further, between grace and predestination there is only this difference, that predestination is a preparation for grace, while grace is actually the endowment itself. When, therefore, the apostle says, "Not of works, lest any man should boast. For we are His workmanship, created in Christ Jesus in good works," (Eph. 2:9-10) it is grace; but what follows—"which God hath prepared that we should walk in them"—is predestination, which cannot exist without foreknowledge, although foreknowledge may exist without predestination; because God foreknew by predestination those things which He was about to do, whence it was said, "He made those things that shall be." (Isa. 45:11) Moreover, He is able to foreknow even those things which He does not Himself do—as all sins whatever; because, although there are some which are in such wise sins as they are also the penalties of sins, whence it is said, "God gave them over to a reprobate mind, to do those things which are not convenient," (Rom. 1:28) it is not in such a case the sin that is God's, but the judgment. Therefore God's predestination in respect of good is, as I have said, the preparation of grace; which grace is the effect of that very predestination. Therefore when God promised to Abraham in his seed the faith of the nations, saying, "I have established thee a father of many nations," (Gen. 17:5) whence the apostle says, "Therefore it is of faith, that the promise, according to grace, might be established to all the seed," (Rom. 4:16) He promised not concerning the power of our will, but concerning His own predestination. For He promised what He Himself would do, not what men would do. Because, although men do those good things which pertain to God's worship. He Himself makes them to do what He has commanded; it is not they that cause Him to do what He has promised. Otherwise the fulfilment of God's promises would not be in the power of God, but in that of men; and thus what was promised by God to Abraham would be given to Abraham by men themselves. Abraham, however, did not believe thus, but "he believed, giving glory to God, that what He promised He is able also to perform." (Rom. 4:21) He does not say, "to foretell." He does not say, "to foreknow"; for He can foretell and foreknow the doings of strangers also; but He says, "He is able also to do"; and thus He is speaking not of the doings of others, but of His own.

THE GIFT OF PERSEVERANCE ✠ BOOK I ✠ CHAPTER 1 *Of the nature of the perseverance here discoursed of.* I have now to consider the subject of perseverance with greater care . . . I assert, therefore, that the perseverance by which we persevere in Christ even to the end is the gift of God; and I call that the end by which is finished that life wherein alone there is a risk of falling. Therefore it is uncertain whether any one has received this gift so long as he is still alive. For if he fall before he dies, he assuredly is said not to have persevered; and most truly is it said. . . . But how should he who has not persevered have ever been persevering, since it is only by persevering that any one shows himself persevering—and this he has not done? But lest any one should struggle against this, and say, If from the date at which any one became a believer he has lived—for the sake of argument—ten years, and in the midst of them has fallen from the faith, has he not persevered for five years? I am not contending about words. If it be thought that this also should be called perseverance, as it were for so long as it lasts, assuredly he is not to be said to have had in any degree that perseverance of which we are now discoursing, by which one perseveres in Christ even to the end. . . .

CHAPTER 9 *When perseverance is granted to a person, he cannot but persevere.* Now, moreover, when the saints say, "Lead us not into temptation, but deliver us from evil," (Matt. 6:13) whatever do they pray for but that they may persevere in holiness? For, assuredly, when that gift of God is granted to them—which is sufficiently plainly shown to be God's gift, since it is asked of Him—that gift of God, then, being granted to them that they may not be led into temptation, none of the saints fails to keep his perseverance in holiness even to the end. For there is not any one who ceases to persevere in the Christian purpose unless he is first of all led into temptation. If, therefore, it be granted to him according to his prayer that he may not be led [into temptation], certainly by the gift of God he persists in that sanctification which by the gift of God he has received. . . .

BOOK VII ✠ CHAPTER 13 *Temptation the condition of man.* If, then, there were no other proofs, this Lord's prayer alone would be sufficient for us on behalf of the grace which I am defending; because it leaves us nothing wherein we may, as it were glory as in our own, since it shows that our not departing from God is not given except by God, when it shows that it must be asked for from God. For he who is not led into temptation does not depart from God. This is absolutely not in the strength of free will, such as it now is; but it had been in man before he fell. . . . But, after the fall of man, God willed it to pertain only to His grace that man should approach to Him; nor did He will it to pertain to aught but His grace that man should not depart from Him. . . .

CHAPTER 15 *Why God willed that He should be asked for that which He might give without prayer.* On which account also He willed that He should be asked that we may not be led into temptation, because if we are not so led, we by no means depart from Him. And this might have been given to us even without our praying for it, but by our prayer He willed us to be admonished from whom we receive these benefits. For from whom but from Him do we receive from whom it is right for us to ask? Truly in this matter let not the Church look for laborious disputations, but consider its own daily prayers. It prays that the unbelieving may believe; therefore God converts to the faith. It prays that believers may persevere; therefore God gives perseverance to the end. God foreknew that He would do this. THIS IS THE VERY PREDESTINATION OF THE SAINTS, "whom He has chosen in Christ before the foundation of the world, that they should be holy and unspotted before Him in love; predestinating them unto the adoption of children by Jesus Christ to Himself, according to the good pleasure of His will, to the praise of the glory of His grace, in which He hath shown them favor in His beloved Son, in whom they have redemption through His blood, the forgiveness of sins according to the riches of His grace, which has abounded towards them in all wisdom and prudence; that He might show them the mystery of His will according to His good pleasure which He hath purposed in Him, in the dispensation of the fulness of times to restore all things in Christ which are in heaven and which are in earth; in Him, in whom also we have obtained a share, being predestinated according to His purpose who worketh all things," (Eph. 1:4-11) Against a trumpet of truth so clear as this, what man of sober and watchful faith can receive any human arguments?

BOOK VIII ✠ CHAPTER 16 *Why is not grace given according to merit?* But why, says one, is not the grace of God given according to men's merits? I answer, Because God is merciful. Why, then, it is asked is it not given to all? And here I reply, Because God is a Judge. And thus grace is given by Him freely; and by His righteous judgment it is shown in some what grace confers on those to whom it is given. Let us not then be ungrateful, that according to the good pleasure of His will a merciful God delivers so many to the praise of the glory of His grace from such deserved perdition; as, if He should deliver no one therefrom, He would not be unrighteous. Let him, therefore, who is delivered love His grace. Let him who is not delivered acknowledge his due. If, in remitting a debt, goodness is perceived, in requiring it, justice—unrighteousness is never found to be with God.

CHAPTER 17 *The difficulty of the distinction made in the choice of one and the rejection of another.* "But why," it is said, "in one and the same case, not only of infants, but even of twin children, is the judgment so diverse?" Is it not a similar question, Why in a different case is the judgment the same? Let us recall, then, those laborers in the vineyard who worked the whole day, and those who toiled one hour. Certainly it is a differing case of labor expended, and yet there was the same judgment in paying the wages. Did the murmurers in this case hear anything from the householder except, Such is my Will? Certainly such was his liberality towards some, that there could be no injustice towards others. And both these classes, indeed, are among the good. Nevertheless, in what refers to justice and grace, it may be truly said to the guilty who is condemned, even concerning the guilty who is delivered, "Take what is thine, and go thy way"; (Matt. 20:14) "I will give unto this one that which is not due"; "is it not lawful for me to do what I will? is thine eye evil because I am good?" And how if he should say, why not to me also? he will hear, and with reason, "Who art thou, O man, that repliest against God?" (Rom. 9:20) And although assuredly in the one case you see a most benignant benefactor and in your own case a most righteous exactor, in neither case do you behold an unjust God. For although He would be righteous even if He were to punish both, he who is delivered has good ground for thankfulness, he who is condemned has not any ground for finding fault.

CHAPTER 18 *But why should one be punished more than another?* "But if," it is said, "it was necessary that, although all were not condemned, He should still show what was due to all, and so that He should commend His grace more freely to the vessels of mercy; why in the same case will He punish me rather than another, or deliver him rather than me?" I say not this. If you ask wherefore, [I say] that I confess that I can find no answer

330

to make. And if you further ask why is this, it is because in this matter even as His anger is righteous and as His mercy is great, so His judgments are unsearchable. . . .

BOOK XIV ✠ CHAPTER 34 *The doctrine of predestination not opposed to the advantage of preaching.* But they say that the explanation of predestination is opposed to the advantage of preaching—as if, indeed, it were opposed to the preaching of the apostle! Did not that teacher of the heathen so often, in faith and truth, as well commend predestination, as without ceasing preach the word of God? Because he said, "It is God that worketh in you both to will and to do for His good pleasure," (Phil. 2:13) Did he not also exhort that we should both will and do what is pleasing to God? or because he said, "He who hath begun a good work in you shall carry it on even unto the day of Christ Jesus," (Phil. 1:6) did he on that account cease to persuade men to begin and to persevere unto the end? Doubtless, our Lord Himself commanded men to believe, and said, "Believe in God, believe also in me": (John 14:1) and yet His judgment is not therefore false, nor is His explanation idle when He says, "No man cometh unto me"— that is, no man believeth in me—"except it were given him of my Father." (John 6:66) Nor, again, because this explanation is true, is the former precept vain. Why, therefore, do we think the explanation of predestination useless to preaching, to precept, to exhortation, to rebuke,—all which things the divine Scripture repeats frequently—seeing that the same Scripture commends this doctrine? . . .

CHAPTER 35 *What predestination is.* Will any man dare to say that God did not foreknow those to whom He would give to believe, or whom He would give to His Son, that of them He should lose none? And, certainly, if He foreknew these things, He as certainly foreknew His own kindness, wherewith He condescends to deliver us. This is THE PREDESTINATION OF THE SAINTS—nothing else; to wit, the foreknowledge and the preparation of God's kindnesses, whereby they are most certainly delivered, whoever they are that are delivered. But where are the rest left by the righteous divine judgment except in the mass of ruin, where the Tyrians and the Sidonians were left? who, moreover, might have believed if they had seen Christ's wonderful miracles. But since it was not given to them to believe, the means of believing also was denied them. From which fact it appears that some have in their understanding itself a naturally divine gift of intelligence, by which they may be moved to the faith, if they either hear the words or behold the signs fitted for their minds; and yet if, in the more lofty judgment of God, they are not by the predestination of grace separated from the mass of perdition, neither those very divine words nor deeds are applied to them by which they might believe if they only heard or saw such things. Moreover, in the same mass of ruin the Jews were left, because they could not believe such great and eminent mighty works as were done in their sight. For the gospel has not been silent about the reason why they could not believe, since it says: "But though He had done such great miracles before them, yet they believed not on Him; that the saying of Esaias the prophet might be fulfilled which he spake, Lord, who hath believed our report, and to whom hath the arm of the Lord been revealed? And, therefore, they could not believe, because that Esaias said again, He hath blinded their eyes and hardened their heart, that they should not see with their eyes nor understand with their heart, and be converted, and I should heal them." (John 12:37-40) Therefore the eyes of the Tyrians and Sidonians were not so blinded nor was their heart so hardened, since they would have believed if they had seen such mighty works as the Jews saw. But it did not do them any good that they were able to believe, because they were not predestinated by Him whose judgments are inscrutable and His ways past finding out. Neither would it have been a hindrance to them that they could not believe, if they had been so predestinated as that God should illuminate those blind eyes and should will to take away the stony heart from those hardened ones. But what the Lord said of the Tyrians and Sidonians may perchance be understood in another way: yet that no one comes to Christ unless it were given him, and that it is given to those who are chosen in Him before the foundation of the world, he confesses beyond a doubt who hears the divine utterance, not with the deaf ears of the flesh but with the ears of the heart; and yet this predestination, which is plainly enough unfolded even by the words of the gospels, did not prevent the Lord's saying as well in respect of the commencement, what I have a little before mentioned, "Believe in God: believe also in me," as in respect of perseverance, "A man ought always to pray, and not to faint." (Luke 18:1) For they hear these things and do them to whom it is given; but they do them not, whether they hear or do not hear, to whom it is not given. Because, "To you," said He, "it is given to know the mystery of the kingdom of heaven, but to them it is not given." (Matt. 13:11) Of these, the one refers to the mercy, the other to the judgment, of Him to whom our soul cries, "I will sing of mercy and judgment unto Thee, O Lord." . . . (Ps. 101:1)

CHAPTER 41 *He proves that what is alleged against the preaching of predestination may be said against God's grace.* For either predestination must be in such wise preached, in the way and degree in which the Holy Scripture plainly declares it, that in the predestinated the gifts and calling of God are without repentance; or it must be avowed that God's grace is given in respect of our merits—which is the opinion of the Pelagians; although that opinion of theirs, as I have often said already, may be read in the doings of the Eastern bishops to have been condemned by the lips of Pelagius himself. Further, from the heretical perversity of the Pelagians, those on whose account I am discoursing, are only removed, inasmuch as, although they will not confess that they who by God's grace become obedient and so abide are predestinated, they still confess, nevertheless, that this grace prevents their will to whom it is given; in such a way certainly as that grace may not be thought to be given freely, as the truth declares, but rather according to the merits of a preceding will, as the Pelagian error says in contradiction to the truth. Therefore, also, grace precedes faith; otherwise, if faith precedes grace, beyond a doubt will also precedes it, because there cannot be faith without will. But if grace precedes faith because it precedes will, certainly it precedes all obedience; it also precedes charity, by which alone God is truly and pleasantly obeyed. And all these things grace works in him to whom it is given, and in whom it precedes all these things. Among these benefits there remains perseverance unto the end, which is daily asked for in vain from the Lord, if the Lord by His grace does not effect it in him whose prayers He hears. See now how foreign it is from the truth to deny that perseverance even to the end of this life is the gift of God; since He Himself puts an end to this life when He wills, and if He puts an end before a fall that is threatening, He makes the man to persevere even unto the end. But more marvellous and more manifest to believers is the liberality of God's goodness, that even to infants, although there is no possibility of giving obedience to that age, this grace is given. To whomsoever, therefore, God gives those gift of His, beyond a doubt He has foreknown that He will bestow

333

them on him, and in His foreknowledge He has prepared them for him. Therefore, those whom he predestinated, them He also called with that calling which I am not reluctant often to make mention of, of which it is said, "The gifts and calling of God are without repentance." (Rom. 11:29) For in His foreknowledge, which cannot be deceived and changed, the ordering of His future doings is absolutely, and is nothing but, predestination. But, as he whom God has foreknown as being chaste, although he may regard it as uncertain, so acts as that he may be chaste, although he may regard that as uncertainty, does not, therefore not act in such a manner as to be chaste because he hears that he will be what he will be by the gift of God. Nay, rather, his love rejoices, and he is not puffed up as if he had not received it. Not only, therefore, is he not hindered from this work by the preaching of predestination, but he is even assisted to it. So that although he glories he may glory in the Lord. . . .

CHAPTER 68 *Conclusion.* Let those who read this, if they understand, give God thanks, and let those who do not understand, pray that they may have the inward teacher from whose presence comes knowledge and understanding. But let those who think that I am in error consider again and again carefully what is here said, lest perchance they themselves may be mistaken. And when, by means of those who read my writings, I become not only wiser, but even more perfect, I acknowledge God's favor to me; and this I especially look for at the hands of the teachers of the Church, if what I write comes into their hands, and they condescend to acknowledge it.

THE CITY OF GOD ✠ BOOK XIV ✠ CHAPTER 28 Accordingly, two cities have been formed by two loves: the earthly by the love of self, even to the contempt of God; the heavenly by the love of God, even to the contempt of self. The former, in a word, glories in itself, the latter in the Lord. For the one seeks glory from men; but the greatest glory of the other is God, the witness of conscience. . . . In the one, the princes and the nations it subdues are ruled by the love of ruling; in the other, the princes and the subjects serve one another in love, the latter obeying, while the former take thought for all. The one delights in its own strength, represented in the persons of its rulers; the other says to its God, "I will love Thee, O Lord my strength." (Ps. 18:1) And therefore the wise men of the one city, living according to man, have sought for profit to their own bodies or souls, or both, and those who have known God "glorified Him not as God, neither were thankful, but became vain in their imaginations, and their foolish heart was darkened; professing themselves to be wise"—that is, glorying in their own wisdom, and being possessed by pride—"they became fools, and changed the glory of the incorruptible God into an image made like to corruptible man, and to birds, and four-footed beasts, and creeping things." For they were either leaders or followers of the people in adoring images "and worshipped and served the creature more than the Creator, who is blessed for ever." (Rom. 1:21-25) But in the other city there is no human wisdom, but only godliness, which offers due worship to the true God, and looks for its reward in the society of the saints, of holy angels as well as holy men, "that God may be all in all." (I Cor. 15:28)

BOOK XV ✠ CHAPTER 1 . . . I trust we have already done justice to these great and difficult questions regarding the beginning of the world, or of the soul, or of the human race itself. This race we have distributed into two parts, the one consisting of those who live according to man, the other of those who live according to God. And these we also call mystically the two cities, or the two communities of men, of which the one is predestined to reign eternally with God and the other to suffer eternal punishment with the devil. This, however, is their end, and of it we are to speak afterwards. At present . . . it seems suitable to attempt an account of their career, from the time when our two first parents began to propagate the race until all human generation shall cease. For this whole time or world-age, in which the dying give place and those who are born succeed, is the career of these two cities concerning which we treat.

Of these two first parents of the human race, then, Cain was the first-born and belonged to the city of men; after him was born Abel, who belonged to the city of God. For as in the individual the truth of the apostle's statement is discerned, "that is not first which is spiritual, but that which is natural, and afterward that which is spiritual," (I Cor. 15:46) whence it comes to pass that each man, being derived from a condemned stock, is first of all born of Adam evil and carnal and becomes good and spiritual only afterwards by regeneration through Christ: so was it in the human race as a whole. When these two cities began to run their course by a series of deaths and births, the citizen of this world was the first-born, and after him the stranger in this world, the citizen of the city of God, predestinated by grace, elected by grace, by grace a stranger below, and by grace a citizen above. By grace—for so far as regards himself he is sprung from the same mass, all of which is condemned in its origin; but God like a potter . . . of the same lump made one vessel to honor, another to dishonor. But first the vessel to dishonor was made, and after it another to honor. For in each individual, as I have already said, there is first of all that which is reprobate, that from which we must begin, but in which we need not necessarily remain; afterwards is that which is well approved, to which we may by advancing attain, and in which, when we have reached it, we may abide. Not, indeed, that every wicked man shall be good, but that no one will be good who was not first of all wicked; but the sooner any one becomes a good man, the more speedily does he receive this title and abolish the old name in the new. Accordingly, it is recorded of Cain that he built a city, but Abel, being a sojourner, built none. For the city of the saints is above, although here below it begets citizens, in whom it sojourns till the time of its reign arrives, when it shall gather together all in the day of the resurrection; and then shall the promised kingdom be given to them, in which they shall reign with their Prince, the King of the ages, time without end. . . .

BOOK XIX ✠ CHAPTER 4 If, then, we be asked what the city of God has to say . . . regarding the supreme good and evil, it will reply that life eternal is the supreme good, death eternal the supreme evil, and that to obtain the one and escape the other we must live rightly. And thus it is written, "The just lives by faith," for we do not as yet see our good and must therefore live by faith; neither have we in ourselves power to live rightly; we can do so only if He who has given us faith to believe in His help do help us when we believe and pray. As for those who have supposed that the sovereign good and evil are to be found in this life and have placed it either in the soul or the body, or in both, or, to speak more explicitly, either in pleasure or in virtue, or in both; in repose or in virtue, or in both; in pleasure and repose, or in virtue, or in all combined—all these have, with a marvellous shallowness, sought to find their blessedness in this life and in themselves. . . .

For what flood of eloquence can suffice to detail the miseries of this life? Cicero, in the *Consolation* on the death of his daughter, has spent all his ability in lamentation; but how inadequate was even his ability here? For when, where, how in this life can these primary objects of nature be possessed so that they may not be assailed by unforeseen accident? Is the body of the wise man exempt from any pain which may dispel pleasure, from any disquietude which may banish repose? The amputation or decay of the members of the body puts an end to its integrity, deformity blights its beauty; weakness, its health; lassitude, its vigor; sleepiness or sluggishness, its activity—and which of these is it that may not assail the flesh of the wise man? Comely and fitting attitudes and movements of the body are numbered among the prime natural blessings; but what if some sickness makes the members tremble? what if a man suffers from curvature of the spine to such an extent that his hands reach the ground, and he goes upon all fours like a quadruped? Does not this destroy all beauty and grace in the body, whether at rest or in motion? What shall I say of the fundamental blessings of the soul, sense and intellect, of which the one is given for the perception, and the other for the comprehension of truth? But what kind of sense is it that remains when a man becomes deaf and blind? Where are reason and intellect when disease makes a man delirious? We can scarcely, or not at all, refrain from tears, when we think of or see the actions and words of such frantic persons and consider how different from, and even opposed to, their own sober judgment and ordinary conduct their present demeanor is. And what shall I say of those who suffer from demoniacal possession? Where is their own intelligence hidden and buried while the malignant spirit is using their body and soul according to his own will? And who is quite sure that no such thing can happen to the wise man in this life? . . .

In fine, virtue itself . . . though it holds the highest place among human good things, what is its occupation save to wage perpetual war with vices—not those that are outside of us, but within; not other men's, but our own—a war which is waged especially by that virtue which the Greeks call σωφροσύνη, and we temperance, and which bridles carnal lusts, and prevents them from winning the consent of the spirit to wicked deeds? For we must not fancy that there is no vice in us, when, as the apostle says, "The flesh lusteth against the spirit"; (Gal. 5:17) for to this vice there is a contrary virtue, when, as the same writer says,

"The spirit lusteth against the flesh." "For these two," he says, "are contrary one to the other, so that you cannot do the things which you would." But what is it we wish to do when we seek to attain the supreme good, unless that the flesh should cease to lust against the spirit, and that there be no vice in us against which the spirit may lust? . . . Far be it from us, then, to fancy that while we are still engaged in this intestine war, we have already found the happiness which we seek to reach by victory. And who is there so wise that he has no conflict at all to maintain against his vices?

What shall I say of that virtue which is called prudence? Is not all its vigilance spent in the discernment of good from evil things, so that no mistake may be admitted about what we should desire and what avoid? And thus it is itself a proof that we are in the midst of evils, or that evils are in us; for it teaches us that it is an evil to consent to sin and a good to refuse this consent. And yet this evil, to which prudence teaches and temperance enables us not to consent, is removed from this life neither by prudence nor by temperance. And justice, whose office it is to render to every man his due . . . does not this virtue demonstrate that it is as yet rather laboring towards its end than resting in its finished work? . . . Then that virtue which goes by the name of fortitude is the plainest proof of the ills of life, for it is these ills which it is compelled to bear patiently. And this holds good, no matter though the ripest wisdom coexists with it. And I am at a loss to understand how the Stoic philosophers can presume to say that these are no ills, though at the same time they allow the wise man to commit suicide and pass out of this life if they become so grievous that he cannot or ought not to endure them. But such is the stupid pride of these men who fancy that they can become happy by their own resources, that their wise man, or at least the man whom they fancifully depict as such, is always happy, even though he become blind, deaf, dumb, multi-lated, racked with pains, or suffer any conceivable calamity such as may compel him to make away with himself; and they are not ashamed to call the life that is beset with these evils happy. O happy life, which seeks the aid of death to end it! If it is happy, let the wise man remain in it; but if these ills drive him out of it, in what sense is it happy? Or how can they say that these are not evils which conquer the virtue of fortitude and force it not only to yield but so to rave that it in one breath calls life happy and recommends it to be given up? For who is so blind as not to see that if it were happy it would not be fled from? And if they say we should flee from it on account of the infirmities that beset it, why then do they not lower their pride and acknowledge that it is miserable? . . .

CHAPTER 5 We give a much more unlimited approval to their idea that the life of the wise man must be social. For how could the city of God . . . either take a beginning or be developed, or attain its proper destiny, if the life of the saints were not a social life? But who can enumerate all the great grievances with which human society abounds in the misery of this mortal state? Who can weigh them? Hear how one of their comic writers makes one of his characters express the common feelings of all men in this matters: "I am married; this is one misery. Children are born to me; they are additional cares." (Terence, *Adelphi,* V, 4) What shall I say of the miseries of love which Terence also recounts—"slights, suspicions, quarrels, war today, peace tomorrow?" *(Eunuchus,* I, 1) Is not human life full of such things? On all hands we experience these slights, suspicions, quarrels, war, all of which are undoubted evils; while, on the other hand, peace is a doubtful good, because we do not know the heart of our friend, and though we did know it today, we should be as ignorant of what it might be tomorrow. Who ought to be, or who are more friendly than those who live in the same family? And yet who can rely even upon this friendship, seeing that secret treachery has often broken it up and produced enmity as bitter as the amity was sweet, or seemed sweet by the most perfect dissimulation? . . . If, then, home, the natural refuge from the ills of life, is itself not safe, what shall we say of the city, which, as it is larger, is so much the more filled with lawsuits, civil and criminal, and is never free from the fear, if sometimes from the actual outbreak, of disturbing and bloody insurrections and civil wars?

CHAPTER 6 What shall I say of these judgments which men pronounce on men and which are necessary in communities, whatever outward peace they enjoy? Melancholy and lamentable judgments they are, since the judges are men who cannot discern the consciences of those at their bar and are therefore frequently compelled to put innocent witnesses to the torture to ascertain the truth regarding the crimes of other men. What shall I say of torture applied to the accused himself? He is tortured to discover whether he is guilty, so that, though innocent, he suffers most undoubted punishment for crime that is still doubtful, not because it is proved that he committed it, but because it is not ascertained that he did not commit it. Thus the ignorance of the judge frequently involves an innocent person in suffering. And what is still more unendurable . . . is this, that when the judge puts the accused to the question, that he may not unwittingly put an innocent man to death, the result of this lamentable ignorance is that this very person, whom he tortured that he might not condemn him if innocent, is condemned to death both tortured and innocent. . . . If such darkness shrouds social life, will a wise judge take his seat on the bench or no? Beyond question he will. For human society, which he thinks it a wickedness to abandon, constrains him and compels him to this duty. And he thinks it no wickedness that innocent witnesses are tortured regarding the crimes of which other men are accused; or that the accused are put to the torture, and though innocent make false confessions regarding themselves and are punished; or that, though they be not condemned to die, they often die during, or in consequence of, the torture . . . These numerous and important evils he does not consider sins; for the wise judge does these things, not with any intention of doing harm, but because his ignorance compels him, and because human society claims him as a judge. But though we therefore acquit the judge of malice, we must none the less condemn human life as miserable. . . .

CHAPTER 7 After the state or city comes the world, the third circle of human society—the first being the house and the second the city. And the world, as it is larger, so it is fuller of dangers, as the greater sea is the more dangerous. And here, in the first place, man is separated from man by the difference of languages. For if two men, each ignorant of the other's language, meet and are not compelled to pass but, on the contrary, to remain in company, dumb animals, though of different species, would more easily hold intercourse than they, human beings though they be. For their common nature is no help to friendliness when they are prevented by diversity of language from conveying their sentiments to one another; so that a man would more readily hold intercourse with his dog than with a foreigner. But the imperial city has endeavored to impose on subject nations not only her yoke but her language, as a bond of peace, so that interpreters, far from being scarce, are numberless. This is true; but how many great wars, how much slaughter and bloodshed, have provided this unity!

And though these are past, the end of these miseries has not yet come. For though there have never been wanting, nor are yet wanting, hostile nations beyond the empire, against whom wars have been and are waged, yet, supposing there were no such nations, the very extent of the empire itself has produced wars of a more obnoxious description—social and civil wars—and with these the whole race has been agitated, either by the actual conflict or the fear of a renewed outbreak. If I attempted to give an adequate description of these manifold disasters, these stern and lasting necessities, though I am quite unequal to the task, what limit could I set? But, say they, the wise man will wage just wars. As if he would not at all the rather lament the necessity of just wars, if he remembers that he is a man; for if they were not just he would not wage them and would therefore be delivered from all wars. For it is the wrong-doing of the opposing party which compels the wise man to wage just wars; and this wrong-doing, even though it gave rise to no war, would still be a matter of grief to man because it is man's wrong-doing. Let every one, then, who thinks with pain on all these great evils, so horrible, so ruthless, acknowledge that this is misery. And if any one either endures or thinks of them without mental pain, this is a more miserable plight still, for he thinks himself happy because he has lost human feeling. . . .

CHAPTER 10 But not even the saints and faithful worshippers of the one true and most high God are safe from the manifold temptations and deceits of the demons. For in this abode of weakness and in these wicked days, this state of anxiety has also its use, stimulating us to seek with keener longing for that security where peace is complete and unassailable. There we shall enjoy the gifts of nature, that is to say, all that God the Creator of all natures has bestowed upon ours—gifts not only good but eternal—not only of the spirit, healed now by wisdom, but also of the body renewed by the resurrection. There the virtues shall no longer be struggling against any vice or evil but shall enjoy the reward of victory, the eternal peace which no adversary shall disturb. This is the final blessedness, this the ultimate consummation, the unending end. Here, indeed, we are said to be blessed when we have such peace as can be enjoyed in a good life; but such blessedness is mere misery compared to that final felicity. When we mortals possess such peace as this mortal life can afford, virtue, if we are living rightly, makes a right use of the advantages of this peaceful condition; and when we have it not, virtue makes a good use even of the evils a man suffers. But this is true virtue, when it refers all the advantages it makes a good use of, and all that it does in making good use of good and evil things, and itself also, to that end in which we shall enjoy the best and greatest peace possible.

CHAPTER 11 And thus we may say of peace, as we have said of eternal life, that it is the end of our good; and the rather because the Psalmist says of the city of God, the subject of this laborious work, "Praise the Lord, O Jerusalem; praise they God, O Zion: for He hath strengthened the bars of thy gates; He hath blessed thy children within thee; who hath made thy borders peace." (Ps. 147:12-14) For when the bars of her gates shall be strengthened, none shall go in or come out from her; consequently we ought to understand the peace of her borders as that final peace we are wishing to declare. For even the mystical name of the city itself, that is, *Jerusalem,* means, as I have already said, "Vision of Peace." But as the word peace is employed in connection with things in this world in which certainly life eternal has no place, we have preferred to call the end or supreme good of this city life eternal rather than peace. . . . But, on the other hand, as those who are not familiar with Scripture may suppose that the life of the wicked is eternal life, either because of the immortality of the soul, which some of the philosophers even have recognized, or because of the needless punishment of the wicked, which forms a part of our faith, and which seems impossible unless the wicked live for ever, it may therefore be advisable, in order that every one may readily understand what we mean, to say that the end or supreme good of this city is either peace in eternal life, or eternal life in peace. For peace is a good so great that even in this earthly and mortal life there is no word we hear with such pleasure, nothing we desire with such zest, or find to be more thoroughly gratifying. So that if we dwell for a little longer on this subject, we shall not, in my opinion, be wearisome to our readers, who will attend both for the sake of understanding what is the end of this city of which we speak and for the sake of the sweetness of peace which is dear to all.

CHAPTER 12 Whoever gives even moderate attention to human affairs and to our common nature, will recognize that if there is no man who does not wish to be joyful, neither is there any one who does not wish to have peace. For even they who make war desire nothing but victory—desire, that is to say, to attain to peace with glory. For what else is victory than the conquest of those who resist us? and when this is done there is peace. It is, therefore, with the desire for peace that wars are waged, even by those who take pleasure in exercising their warlike nature in command and battle. And hence it is obvious that peace is the end sought for by war. For every man seeks peace by waging war, but no man seeks war by making peace. For even they who intentionally interrupt the peace in which they are living have no hatred of peace but only wish it changed into a peace that suits them better. They do not, therefore, wish to have no peace but only one more to their mind. And in the case of sedition, when men have separated themselves from the community, they yet do not effect what they wish, unless they maintain some kind of peace with their fellow conspirators. And therefore even robbers take care to maintain peace with their comrades, that they may with greater effect and safety invade the peace of other men. And if an individual happen to be of such unrivalled strength and to be so jealous of partnership that he trusts himself with no comrades, but makes his own plots and commits depredations and murders on his own account, yet he maintains some shadow of peace with such persons as he is unable to kill, and from whom he wishes to conceal his deeds. In his own home, too, he makes it his aim to be at peace with his wife and children and any other members of his household. . . . For he sees that peace cannot be maintained unless all the members of the same domestic circle be subject to one head, such as he himself is in his own house. . . . And thus all men desire to have peace with their own circle whom they wish to govern as suits themselves. For even those whom they make war against they wish to make their own and impose on them the laws of their own peace. . . .

. . . the most savage animals encompass their own species with a ring of protecting peace. . . . For what tigress does not gently purr over her cubs and lay aside her ferocity to fondle them? What kite, solitary as he is when circling over his prey, does not seek a mate, build a nest, hatch the eggs, bring up the young birds, and maintain with the mother of his family as peaceful a domestic alliance as he can? How much more powerfully do the laws of man's nature move him to hold fellowship and maintain peace with all men so far as in him lies, since even wicked men wage war to maintain the peace of their own circle and wish that, if possible, all men belonged to them, that all men and things might serve but one head, and might, either through love or fear, yield themselves to peace with him! It is thus that pride in its perversity apes God. It abhors equality with other men under Him; but, instead of His rule, it seeks to impose a rule of its own upon its equals. It abhors, that is to say, the just peace of God and loves its own unjust peace; but it cannot help loving peace of one kind or other. For there is no vice so clean contrary to nature that it obliterates even the faintest traces of nature.

He, then, who prefers what is right to what is wrong and what is well-ordered to what is perverted, sees that the peace of unjust men is not worthy to be called peace in comparison with the peace of the just. And yet even what is perverted must of necessity be in harmony with, and in dependence on, and in some part of the order of things, for otherwise it would have no existence at all. Suppose a man hangs with his head downwards, this is certainly a perverted attitude of body and arrangement of its members; for that which nature requires to be above is beneath, and *vice versa*. This perversity disturbs the peace of the body, and is therefore painful. Nevertheless the spirit is at peace with its body and labors for its preservation and hence the suffering; but if it is banished from the body by its pains, then, as long as the bodily framework holds together, there is in the remains a kind of peace among the members, and hence the body remains suspended. And inasmuch as the earthly body tends towards the earth, and rests on the bond by which it is suspended, it tends thus to its natural peace, and the voice of its own weight demands a place for it to rest; and though now lifeless and without feeling, it does not fall from the peace that is natural to its place in creation, whether it already has it, or is tending towards it. . . .

CHAPTER 13 The peace of the body then consists in the duly proportioned arrangement of its parts. The peace of the irrational soul is the harmonious repose of the appetites; and that of the rational soul, the harmony of knowledge and action. The peace of body and soul is the well-ordered and harmonious life and health of the living creature. Peace between man and God is the well-ordered obedience of faith to eternal law. Peace between man and man is well-ordered concord. Domestic peace is the well-ordered concord between those of the family who rule and those who obey. Civil peace is a similar concord among the citizens. The peace of the celestial city is the perfectly ordered and harmonious enjoyment of God and of one another in God. The peace of all things is the tranquillity of order. Order is the distribution which allots things equal and unequal, each to its own place. And hence, though the miserable, in so far as they are such, do certainly not enjoy peace but are severed from the tranquillity of order in which there is no disturbance. Nevertheless, inasmuch as they are deservedly and unjustly miserable, they are by their very misery connected with order. Thy are not, indeed, conjoined with the blessed, but they are disjoined from them by the law of order. And though they are disquieted, their circumstances are notwithstanding adjusted to them, and consequently they have some tranquillity of order and therefore some peace. But they are wretched because, although not wholly miserable, they are not in that place where any mixture of misery is impossible. They would, however, be more wretched if they had not that peace which arises from being in harmony with the natural order of things. When they suffer, their peace is in so far disturbed; but their peace continues in so far as they do not suffer and in so far as their nature continues to exist. As, then, there may be life without pain, while there cannot be pain without some kind of life, so there may be peace without war, but there cannot be war without some kind of peace, because war supposes the existence of some natures to wage it, and these natures cannot exist without peace of one kind or other.

And therefore there is a nature in which evil does not or even cannot exist; but there cannot be a nature in which there is no good. Hence not even the nature of the devil himself is evil, in so far as it is nature, but it was made evil by being perverted. . . .

God, then, . . . imparted to men some good things adapted to this life, to wit, temporal peace, such as we can enjoy in this life from health and safety and human fellowship, and all things needful for the preservation and recovery of this peace, such as the objects which are accommodated to our outward senses, light, night, the air, and waters suitable for us, and everything the body requires to sustain, shelter, heal, or beautify it: and all under this most equitable condition, that every man who made a good use of these advantages suited to the peace of his mortal condition, should receive ampler and better blessings, namely, the peace of immortality, accompanied by glory and honor in an endless life made fit for the enjoyment of God and of one another in God; but that he who used the present blessings badly should both lose them and should not receive the others.

CHAPTER 14 The whole use, then, of things temporal has a reference to this result of earthly peace in the earthly community, while in the city of God it is connected with eternal peace. And therefore, if we were irrational animals, we should desire nothing beyond the proper arrangement of the parts of the body and the satisfaction of the appetites—nothing, therefore, but bodily comfort and abundance of pleasures, that the peace of the body might contribute to the peace of the soul. . . . But, as man has a rational soul, he subordinates all this which he has in common with the beasts to the peace of his rational soul, that his intellect may have free play and may regulate his actions, and that he may thus enjoy the well-ordered harmony of knowledge and action which constitutes, as we have said, the peace of the rational soul. . . . But, owing to the liability of the human mind to fall into mistakes, this very pursuit of knowledge may be a snare to him unless he has a divine Master, whom he may obey without misgiving, and who may at the same time give him such help as to preserve his own freedom. And because, so long as he is in this mortal body, he is a stranger to God, he walks by faith, not by sight; and he therefore refers all peace, bodily or spiritual or both, to that peace which mortal man has with the immortal God, so that he exhibits the well-ordered obedience of faith to eternal law. But as this divine Master inculcates two precepts—the love of God and the love of our neighbor—and as in these precepts a man finds three things he has to love—God, himself, and his neighbor— and that he who loves God loves himself thereby, it follows that he must endeavor to get his neighbor to love God, since he is ordered to love his neighbor as himself. He ought to make this endeavor in behalf of his wife, his children, his household, all within his reach, even as he would wish his neighbor to do the same for him if he needed it; and consequently he will be at peace, or in well-ordered concord, with all men, as far as in him lies and this is the order of this concord, that a man, in the first place, injure no one, and in the second, do good to every one he can reach. . . . This is the origin of domestic peace, or the well-ordered concord of those in the family who rule and those who obey. But in the family of the just man who lives by faith and is as yet a pilgrim journeying on to the celestial city, even those who rule serve those whom they seem to command; for they rule not from a love of power but from a sense of duty they owe others—not because they are proud of authority, but because they love mercy.

CHAPTER 15 This is prescribed by the order of nature: it is thus that God created man. For "let them," He says, "have dominion over the fish of the sea, and over the fowl of the air, and over every creeping thing which creepeth on the earth." (Gen. 1:26) He did not intend that His rational creature, who was made in His image, should have dominion over anything but the irrational creation—not man over man but man over the beasts. And hence the righteous men in primitive times were made shepherds of cattle rather than kings of men, God intending thus to teach us what the relative position of the creatures is and what the desert of sin; for it is with justice, we believe, that the condition of slavery is the result of sin. And this is why we do not find the word "slave" in any part of Scripture until righteous Noah branded the sin of his son with this name. It is a name, therefore, introduced by sin and not by nature. The origin of the Latin word for slave is supposed to be found in the circumstance that those who by the law of war were liable to be killed were sometimes preserved by their victors, and were hence called servants. (*Servus,* a slave, from *servare,* to preserve.) And these circumstances could never have arisen save through sin. For even when we wage a just war, our adversaries must be sinning; and every victory, even though gained by wicked men, is a result of the first judgment of God, who humbles the vanquished either for the sake of removing or of punishing their sins. . . . The prime cause, then, of slavery is sin, which brings man under the dominion of his fellow—that which does not happen save by the judgment of God, with whom there is no unrighteousness, who knows how to award fit punishments to every variety of offence. But our Master in heaven says, "Every one who doeth sin is the servant of sin." (John 8:34) And thus there are many wicked masters who have religious men as their slaves, and who are yet themselves in bondage; "for of whom a man is overcome, of the same is he brought in bondage." (II Pet. 2:19) And beyond question it is a happier thing to be the slave of a man than of a lust; for even this very lust of ruling, to mention no others, lays waste men's hearts with the most ruthless dominion. Moreover, when men are subjected to one another in a peaceful order, the lowly position does as much good to the servant as the proud position does harm to the master. But by nature, as God first created us, no one is the slave either of man or of sin. This servitude is, however, penal, and is appointed by that law which enjoins the preservation

347

of the natural order and forbids its disturbance; for if nothing had been done in violation of that law, there would have been nothing to restrain by penal servitude. And therefore the apostle admonishes slaves to be subject to their masters and to serve them heartily and with good will, so that if they cannot be freed by their masters, they may themselves make their slavery in some sort free, by serving not in crafty fear but in faithful love, until all unrighteousness pass away, and all principality and every human power be brought to nothing, and God be all in all. . . .

CHAPTER 17 . . . The earthly city, which does not live by faith, seeks an earthly peace, and the end it proposes, in the well-ordered concord of civil obedience and rule, is the combination of men's wills to attain the things which are helpful to this life. The heavenly city, or rather the part of it which sojourns on earth and lives by faith, makes use of this peace only because it must, until this mortal condition which necessitates it shall pass away. Consequently, so long as it lives like a captive and a stranger in the earthly city, though it has already received the promise of redemption and the gift of the Spirit as the earnest of it, it makes no scruple to obey the laws of the earthly city, whereby the things necessary for the maintenance of this mortal life are administered; and thus, as this life is common to both cities, so there is a harmony between them in regard to what belongs to it. . . . This heavenly city, then, while it sojourns on earth, calls citizens out of all nations and gathers together a society of pilgrims of all languages, not scrupling about diversities in the manners, laws, and institutions whereby earthly peace is secured and maintained but recognizing that, however various these are, they all tend to one and the same end of earthly peace. It, therefore, is so far from rescinding and abolishing these diversities that it even preserves and adapts them, so long only as no hindrance to the worship of the one supreme and true God is thus introduced. Even the heavenly city, therefore, while in its state of pilgrimage, avails itself of the peace of earth, and, so far as it can without injuring faith and godliness, desires and maintains a common agreement among men regarding the acquisition of the necessaries of life and makes this earthly peace bear upon the peace of heaven; for this alone can truly be called and esteemed the peace of the reasonable creatures, consisting as it does in the perfectly ordered and harmonious enjoyment of God and of one another

in God. When we shall have reached that peace, this mortal life shall give place to one that is eternal, and our body shall be no more this animal body which by its corruption weighs down the soul but a spiritual body feeling no want and in all its members subjected to the will. In its pilgrim state the heavenly city possesses this peace by faith; and by this faith it lives righteously when it refers to the attainment of that peace every good action towards God and man; for the life of the city is a social life. . . .

CHAPTER 21 This, then, is the place where I should fulfil the promise I gave in the second book of this work and explain, as briefly and clearly as possible, that if we are to accept the definitions laid down by Scipio in Cicero's *De Republica,* there never was a Roman republic; for he briefly defines a republic as the weal of the people. And if this definition be true, there never was a Roman republic, for the people's weal was never attained among the Romans. For the people, according to his definition, is an assemblage associated by a common acknowledgment of right and by a community of interests. And what he means by a common acknowledgment of right he explains at large, showing that a republic cannot be administered without justice. Where, therefore, there is no true justice there can be no right. For that which is done by right is justly done, and what is unjustly done cannot be done by right. For the unjust inventions of men are neither to be considered nor spoken of as rights; for even they themselves say that right is that which flows from the fountain of justice and deny the definition which is commonly given by those who misconceive the matter, that right is that which is useful to the stronger party. Thus, where there is not true justice there can be no assemblage of men associated by common acknowledgment of right, and therefore there can be no people, as defined by Scipio or Cicero; and if no people, then no weal of the people but only of some promiscuous multitude unworthy of the name of people. Consequently, if the republic is the weal of the people, and there is no people if it be not associated by a common acknowledgment of right, and if there is no right where there is no justice, then most certainly it follows that there is no republic where there is no justice. . . .

. . . And it is when the soul serves God that it exercises a right control over the body; and in the soul itself the reason must be subject to God, if it is to govern as it ought the passions

349

and other vices. Hence, when a man does not serve God, what justice can we ascribe to him, since in this case his soul cannot exercise a just control over the body, nor his reason over his vices? And if there is no justice in such an individual, certainly there can be none in a community composed of such persons. Here, therefore, there is not that common acknowledgment of right which makes an assemblage of men a people whose affairs we call a republic. . . .

CHAPTER 23 . . . And therefore, where there is not this righteousness whereby the one supreme God rules the obedient city according to His grace, so that it sacrifices to none but Him, and whereby, in all the citizens of this obedient city, the soul consequently rules the body and reason the vices in the rightful order, so that, as the individual just man, so also the community and people of the just, live by faith, which works by love, that love whereby man loves God as He ought to be loved and his neighbor as himself—there, I say, there is not an assemblage associated by a common acknowledgment of right and by a community of interests. But if there is not this, there is not a people, if our definition be true, and therefore there is no republic; for where there is no people, there can be no republic.

CHAPTER 24 But if we discard this definition of a people, and, assuming another, say that a people is an assemblage of reasonable beings bound together by a common agreement as to the objects of their love, then, in order to discover the character of any people, we have only to observe what they love. Yet whatever it loves, if only it is an assemblage of reasonable beings and not of beasts and is bound together by an agreement as to the objects of love, it is reasonably called a people; and it will be a superior people in proportion as it is bound together by higher interests, inferior in proportion as it is bound together by lower. According to this definition of ours, the Roman people is a people, and its weal is without doubt a commonwealth or republic. But what its tastes were in its early and subsequent days, and how it declined into sanguinary seditions and then to social and civil wars, and so burst asunder or rotted off the bond of concord in which the health of a people consists, history shows, and in the preceding books I have related at large. And yet I would not on this account say either that it was not a people, or that its administration was not a republic, so long as there remains an assemblage of reasonable beings bound together by a common agreement as to the objects of love. But what I say of this people and of this republic I must be understood to think and say of the Athenians or any Greek state, of the Egyptians, of the early Assyrian Babylon, and of every other nation, great or small, which had a public government. For, in general, the city of the ungodly, which did not obey the command of God that it should offer no sacrifice save to Him alone, and which, therefore, could not give to the soul its proper command over the body, nor to the reason its just authority over the vices, is void of true justice. . . .

CHAPTER 25 For though the soul may seem to rule the body admirably and the reason the vices, if the soul and reason do not themselves obey God, as God has commanded them to serve Him, they have no proper authority over the body and the vices. For what kind of mistress of the body and the vices can that mind be which is ignorant of the true God and which, instead of being subject to His authority, is prostituted to the corrupting influences of the most vicious demons? It is for this reason that the virtues which it seems to itself to possess, and by which it restrains the body and the vices that it may obtain and keep what it desires, are rather vices than virtues, so long as there is no reference to God in the matter. For although some suppose that virtues which have a reference only to themselves and are desired only on their own account are yet true and genuine virtues, the fact is that even then they are inflated with pride and are therefore to be reckoned vices rather than virtues. For as that which gives life to the flesh is not derived from flesh but is above it, so that which gives blessed life to man is not derived from man but is something above him; and what I say of man is true of every celestial power and virtue whatsoever. . . .

CHAPTER 27 But the peace which is peculiar to ourselves we enjoy now with God by faith and shall hereafter enjoy eternally with Him by sight. But the peace which we enjoy in this life, whether common to all or peculiar to ourselves, is rather the solace of our misery than the positive enjoyment of felicity. Our very righteousness, too, though true in so far as it has respect to the true good, is yet in this life of such a kind that it consists rather

351

in the remission of sins than in the perfecting of virtues. . . . In this, then, consists the righteousness of a man, that he submit himself to God, his body to his soul, and his vices, even when they rebel, to his reason, which either defeats or at least resists them; and also that he beg from God grace to do his duty and the pardon of his sins, and that he render to God thanks for all the blessings he receives. But, in that final peace to which all our righteousness has reverence, and for the sake of which it is maintained, as our nature shall enjoy a sound immortality and incorruption, and shall have no more vices, and as we shall experience no resistance either from ourselves or from others, it will not be necessary that reason should rule vices which no longer exist, but God shall rule the man, and the soul shall rule the body, with a sweetness and facility suitable to the felicity of a life which is done with bondage. And this condition shall there be eternal, and we shall be assured of its eternity; and thus the peace of this blessedness and the blessedness of this peace shall be the supreme good.

CHAPTER 28 But, on the other hand, they who do not belong to this city of God shall inherit eternal misery, which is also called the second death, because the soul shall then be separated from God its life and therefore cannot be said to live, and the body shall be subjected to eternal pains. And consequently this second death shall be the more severe, because no death shall terminate it. But war being contrary to peace, as misery to happiness and life to death, it is not without reason asked what kind of war can be found in the end of the wicked answering to the peace which is declared to be the end of the righteous? The person who puts this question has only to observe what it is in war that is hurtful and destructive, and he shall see that it is nothing else than the mutual opposition and conflict of things. And can he conceive a more grievous and bitter war than that in which the will is so opposed to passion and passion to the will that their hostility can never be terminated by the victory of either and in which the violence of pain so conflicts with the nature of the body that neither yields to the other? For in this life, when this conflict has arisen, either pain conquers and death expels the feeling of it, or nature conquers and health expels the pain. But in the world to come the pain continues that it may torment, and the nature endures that it may be sensible of it; and neither ceases to exist, lest punishment also should cease. . . .

✛ ✛ ✛

APPENDIX

✛ ✛ ✛

✝ ✝ ✝

WRITINGS OF ST. AUGUSTINE

✝ ✝ ✝

The following classification of the works of St. Augustine is taken with many omissions and some modifications from the *Oeuvres de Saint Augustin,* Vol. 1 of the *Bibliothèque Augustinienne,* in the Introduction by F. Cayré and F. Van Steenberghen, Desclée de Brouwer, Belgium, 1949, pp. 101-103.

I. First Period (386-396 A. D.)

A. *Philosophical Dialogues.*

Contra academicos (386); *De beata vita* (386); *De ordine* (386); *Soliloquia* (387); *De immortalitate animae* (387; *De grammatica* (387); *De quantitate animae* (387–88); *De Musica* (389–391); *De magistro* (389); *De libero arbitrio* (388–395).

B. *Anti-Manichean Writings.*

De moribus Ecclesiae cath. et de moribus manichaeorum (388); *De Genesi contra manichaeos* (388–390); *De duabus animabus* (391); *Disputatio contra Fortunatum* (392).

C. *Theological and Exegetical Writings.*

De vera religione (389–391); *De 83 diversis quaestionibus* (389–396); *De utilitate credendi* (391); *De fide et symbolo* (393). *Letters and Sermons.*

II. Second Period (396–411)

A. *Last Anti-Manichean Writings.*

Contra Epistolam Fundamenti (397); *Contra Faustum* (397–398); *De natura boni* (399).

B. *Writings against the Donatists.*

Contra Epistolam Parmeniani (400) ; *De baptismo* (400) ; *Contra litteras Petiliani* (401; 402; 405) ; *De unitate Ecclesiae* (405).

C. *Theological and Exegetical Writings.*

Confessiones (398–99) ; *De Trinitate* (400–416) ; *De Genesi ad litteram* (400–415) ; *De diversis quaestionibus ad Simplicianum* (396–97) ; *De doctrina christiana* (397, 426) ; *De consensu evangelistarum* (400). *Letters, Sermons,* and *Discourses on the Psalms.*

III. Third Period (411–430).

A. *Anti-Pelagian Writings*

De peccatorum meritis et remissione (411; 412) ; *De spiritu et littera* (412) ; *De fide et operibus* (413) ; *De natura et gratia* (415) ; *De gratia Christi et peccato originali* (418) ; *De anima et ejus origine* (419–420) ; *Contra Julianum, haer. pel. defensorem* (421) ; *Contra Julianum opus imperfectum* (429–430).

B. *Writings against the Semi-Pelagians.*

De gratia et libero arbitrio (426) ; *De correptione et gratia* (426) ; *De praedestinatione sanctorum* (428–429) ; *De dono perseverantiae* (428-429).

C. *Theological and Exegetical Writings.*

De Civitate Dei (413–426) ; *Tractatus in Joannem* (416) ; *Enchiridion* (421) ; *De doctrina christiana,* Bk. IV. (426) ; *Retractiones* (426–427). *Letters, Sermons,* and *Discourses on the Psalms.*

AN OUTLINE OF
THE LIFE OF ST. AUGUSTINE

✛ ✛ ✛

I. Early Life to Conversion (354–386)

354. Born at Tagaste, Africa (Souk Arrhas, Algeria), November 13. His father, Patricius, was a Roman administrator and a pagan. His mother Monica (or Monnica) was a Christian.

370. Returns home from studying rhetoric and literature at Madaura, after an idle childhood. Falls into dissipation and sin. At end of year departs for Carthage.

371. Patricius dies. Augustine supported at Carthage by his mother and his friend Romanianus. Takes a mistress.

372. Birth of his son Adeodatus.

372-373. Cicero's *Hortensius* awakens in him a strong desire for true wisdom. Converted to Manicheism.

373. Teaches at Tagaste.

374. Returns to Carthage after the death of a close friend. Teaches at Carthage. Wins a prize in a poetry contest.

379. Abandons astrology.

382. Meeting with Faustus. Break with Manicheism imminent.

383. Moves to Rome and establishes a school of rhetoric. Embraces Scepticism. Visits Ambrose at Milan.

384. Accepts a post at Milan. Attends the sermons of Bishop Ambrose. Develops considerable interest in and enthusiasm for the philosophies of Plato and Plotinus.

385. Doubts about Christianity removed through the teaching of Ambrose, but he is held back by the flesh. He becomes again a Catechumen.

386. Talks with Simplicianus, reads of conversion of famous Neo-Platonic rhetorician Victorinus. Studies St. Paul and is converted through a voice from heaven. Gives up his profession of rhetorician.

II. Conversion to the Episcopate (386–396)

386. Retires to Cassiciacum (Sept. to March). Writes the dialogues *Against the Academics, The Happy Life, Divine Providence*.

387. Returns to Milan. With Adeodatus and Alypius is baptized by Ambrose (April 24).

387. Leaves Milan. Death of Monica at Rome (autumn). Augustine remains in Rome.

388. Returns to Africa. Establishes monastery at Tagaste.

389. Death of Adeodatus. Writes the dialogues *The True Religion The Teacher,* and *Music*.

391. Ordained priest at Hippo by Bishop Valerius.

392. Controversies with the Manicheans. Refutation of Fortunatus.

393. Attends Council of Hippo. Gives a discourse on *Faith and the Creed*.

395. Consecrated Bishop of Hippo.

III. The Episcopate (396–430)

397. Refutation of Manes. Begins the *Confessions*.

399. Attends First Council of Carthage. Completes the *Confessions*. Controversies with the Donatists. Writes *The Nature of the Good*. Begins *The Trinity*.

401. Refutation of the *Epistle of Petilianus,* a Donatist.

403–410. Rigorous repression of the Donatists.

411. Plays a prominent role in the conference between the Catholic Bishops and the Donatists. Waning influence of Donatism.

412. Beginning of the controversies with the Pelagians.

413. Begins his famous work the *City of God*.

415. Writes *Nature and Grace* in refutation of Pelagius.

416. Completes *The Trinity*.

421. Writes six books in refutation of Bishop Julian.

425. Writes *Grace and Free Will*.

426. Completes the *City of God*. Appoints Heraclius as his successor.

428. Writes the *Retractions*.

429. Writes *The Predestination of the Saints* and *The Gift of Perseverance*.

430. Dies August 28 in the third month of the siege of Hippo by the Vandals.

✢ ✢ ✢

SELECTED BIBLIOGRAPHY

✢ ✢ ✢

Works of a General and Introductory Nature

Battenhouse, R. W., and others. *A Companion to the Study of St. Augustine.* New York: Oxford, 1955.

Bourke, Vernon J. *Augustine's Quest of Wisdom.* Milwaukee: Bruce Publishing Company, 1945.

Cayré, Fulbert. *Initiation à la philosophie de s. Augustin.* Paris: Desclée de Brouwer, 1947.

Gilson, E. *The Christian Philosophy of St. Augustine.* New York: Random House, 1960.

Marrou, Henri. *St. Augustine and His Influence Through the Ages.* London: Longmans, 1957.

Portalié, E. *A Guide to the Thought of Saint Augustine.* Chicago: Henry Regnery Company, 1960.

Biography and Intellectual Development

Bardy, G. *Saint Augustin, l'homme et l'oeuvre.* Paris: Desclée de Brouwer, 1940.

Possidius. *Life of St. Augustine* (in Early Christian Biographies). New York: Fathers of the Church, Inc., 1952, pp. 69-125.

Van Der Meer, F. *Augustine the Bishop.* New York: Sheed and Ward, 1961.

Alfaric, Prosper. *L'évolution intéllectuelle de saint Augustin.* Paris: Nourry, 1918.

Courcelle, Pierre. *Les "Confessions" de Saint Augustin.* Paris: Etudes Augustiniennes, 1963.

Marrou, H. I. *Saint Augustin et la fin de la culture antique.* Paris: De Boccard, 1938.

O'Meara, J. *The Young Augustine.* New York: Longmans, 1954.

Sciacca, M.F. *Saint Augustin et le Néoplatonisme.* Louvain: Nauwelaerts, 1956.

Faith and Understanding

Boyer, C. *L'idée de vérité dans la philosophie de s. Augustin.* Paris: Beauchesne et ses Fils, 1951.

Cayré, Fulbert. "Contemplation et Raison d'après s. Augustin." Paris: *Mélanges Augustiniens,* 1–51.

Cushman, R. E. "Faith and Reason in the Thought of St. Augustine." New York: *Church History* 19 (1950) 171–194.

Gilson, E. "L'idée de philosophie chez saint Augustin et chez saint Thomas d'Aquin," *Acta hebdomadae Augustinianae-Thomisticae.* Rome: Marietti 1931, 75–87.

Existence of God

Cayré, Fulbert. *Dieu présent dans la vie de l'esprit.* Paris: Desclée de Brouwer, 1951.

Boyer, C. *Essais sur la doctrine de Saint Augustin.* 2nd ed. Paris: Beauchesne et ses Fils, 1932.

Grabowski, Stanislaus J. *All-present God. A Study in St. Augustine.* St. Louis:, Herder 1953.

Psychology of St. Augustine

Ferraz, M. *De la psychologie de s. Augustine.* 2 ed. Paris, 1869.

Fortin, E. L. *Christianisme et Culture Philosophique au Cinquième Siécle.* Paris: Etudes Augustiniennes, 1959.

Gardeil, Ambroise. *La structure de l'âme et l'expérience mystique.* Paris: Lecoffre, 1927.

Schmaus, Michael. *Die psychologische Trinitätslehre des hl. Augustinus.* Münster: Aschendorff, 1927.

The Problem of Knowledge

Cayré, Fulbert. *La contemplation augustinienne*. Paris: Desclée de Brouwer, 1954.

Hessen, Johannes. *Augustins Metaphysik der Erkenntnis*. Leiden: E. J. Brill, 1960.

Jolivet, Regis. *Dieu soleil des esprits*. Paris: Desclée de Brouwer, 1934.

Keeler, L. W. *Sancti Augustini doctrina de cognitione*. Rome: Univ. Gregoriana, 1933.

Allers, R. "St. Augustine's Doctrine on Illumination." *Franciscan Studies* 12 (1952), 27–46.

The Created Universe

Guitton, J. *Le temps et l'éternité chez Plotin et saint Augustin*. Paris: Aubier, 1956.

Jolivet, R. *Le problème du mal d'après saint Augustin*. Paris: Beauchesne et ses Fils, 1936.

Martin, Jules. *Saint Augustin*. 2 ed. Paris: Alcan, 1907.

McKeough, Michael J. *The Meaning of the rationes seminales in Saint Augustine*. Washington: Catholic U., 1926.

Moral Philosophy

Clark, M. T. *Augustine, Philosopher of Freedom*. New York, 1958.

Combes, G. *La charité d'après s. Augustin*. Paris: Desclée de Brouwer, 1934.

Holte, Ragnar. *Béatitude et Sagesse*. Paris: Etudes Augustiniennes, 1962.

Mausbach, J. *Die Ethik des hl. Augustinus*. 2 vols. Freiburg: Herder, 1909.

INDEX

✠ ✠ ✠

DATE DUE